MW01226937

Local Governance in Transition

Local GOVERNANCE in Transition

Toward Sustainable Canadian Communities

Mary Louise McAllister

UBCPress · Vancouver

Printed in Canada on FSC-certified ancient-forest-free paper (100% post-consumer recycled) that is processed chlorine- and acid-free, with vegetable-based inks.

UBC Press is a Benetech Global Certified Accessible™ publisher. The epub version of this book meets stringent accessibility standards, ensuring it is available to people with diverse needs.

Library and Archives Canada Cataloguing in Publication

Title: Local governance in transition : toward sustainable Canadian communities / Mary Louise McAllister.

Names: McAllister, Mary Louise, author.

Description: Includes bibliographical references and index.

Identifiers: Canadiana (print) 20240304861 | Canadiana (ebook) 20240304918 | ISBN 9780774870320 (softcover) | ISBN 9780774870344 (EPUB) | ISBN 9780774870337 (PDF)

Subjects: LCSH: Municipal government—Canada. | LCSH: Local government—Canada. | LCSH: Sustainable development—Canada. | LCSH: Social problems—Canada.

Classification: LCC JS1710 .M33 2024 | DDC 352.160971—dc23

UBC Press gratefully acknowledges the financial support for our publishing program of the Government of Canada, the Canada Council for the Arts, and the British Columbia Arts Council.

This book has been published with the help of a grant from the Canadian Federation for the Humanities and Social Sciences, through the Awards to Scholarly Publications Program, using funds provided by the Social Sciences and Humanities Research Council of Canada.

UBC Press is situated on the traditional, ancestral, and unceded territory of the xʷməθkʷəy̓əm (Musqueam) people. This land has always been a place of learning for the xʷməθkʷəy̓əm, who have passed on their culture, history, and traditions for millennia, from one generation to the next.

UBC Press
The University of British Columbia
www.ubcpress.ca

Contents

Maps, Figures, and Boxes

BOXES

Preface

Acknowledgments

Local governments are on the front lines when it comes to sustaining the well-being of their communities and the vital social and ecological systems on which they depend. Global climate change, collapsing valued ecosystems, epidemics, and growing societal inequalities pose serious – and even existential – threats. Addressing these complex issues, therefore, requires new approaches to governance. This book considers the barriers and opportunities confronting municipalities when tackling the challenge of fostering long-term sustainability in Canadian cities. It is directed at students, academics, and practitioners interested in local government and in how Canadian municipalities are addressing contemporary sustainability challenges. The book has three main objectives. The first is to present an overview of local political history, structures, and public administration. This exploration provides a foundation for the second objective: to present an understanding of the theories and approaches offered by various interdisciplinary fields that might be used to foster more sustainable communities. Third, this book examines efforts under-taken by Canadian municipalities to address the accumulating social and ecological challenges that confront local governments across the country. Communities throughout Canada are collaborating on the development of new initiatives and policy innovations with the goal of achieving more sustainable cities. These varied efforts offer important lessons to students of local politics and environmental studies and to practitioners.

This book offers an introduction to local government, systems thinking, and sustainability studies, an account of the historical legacy of local government, and considerations of local democracy, the machinery of government and public administration, collaborative and multi-level governance, place-based governance, municipalities as global actors, information and communications technologies (ICTs), nature-based solutions to environmental degradation, sustainable infrastructure, public health and well-being, diverse economies, institutional learning, and transitions toward sustainability.

Acknowledgments

It takes a village to raise a child. This interdisciplinary work required more than a village to see it to completion. I reached across Canada, and elsewhere, to draw on the insights and expertise of local government officials and colleagues from many disciplines. Friends and family also played important roles – not only as supporters but also by sharing their time, considerable knowledge, and professional expertise on topics discussed in this book. And as one always counts on with friends and family, they provided their own rigorous critiques.

I am very grateful to the anonymous peer reviewers. Their intelligent, knowledgeable, and perspicacious comments helped to strengthen this exploratory text about local governments struggling to address "wicked" problems and to sustain their communities. The external readers took a significant amount of time out of their own lives and academic work to improve this contribution. I have done my best to address each of their comments. The complexity of the subject matter inevitably raises more questions to be addressed than the allotted space permits. I thank them for their generosity of time and dedication to the profession.

In addition to the peer reviewers, several people from various disciplines and professions, including family members, set aside their valuable time to read the entire manuscript or chapters. I am indebted to Joel Arthurs, Alberto Fonseca, William Kennedy, Christie Arthurs, Kate McAllister, Simron Jit Singh, Donna Appavoo, and Akshaya Neil Arya. Others who contributed textboxes, photos, or insights or who participated in interviews over the years include Paivi Abernethy, MJ Dooher, Catherine Evans, Paul Habsch, Amanda Hooykaas, Brian and Valerie Jarus, Yousaf Khan, Dorothy Larkman, Stuart MacKinnon, Sylvia McMechan, Tanya Markvart, Sylvia McMechan, Greg Michalenko, Merv Mulligan, Anthony Perl, Kennedy Stewart, Jen Vasic, Joseph Wasylycia-Leis, and Peter Woolstencroft. Many thoughtful individuals willingly shared their ideas about sustainability and local government – too many to list here. Among them are my colleagues and students in the Faculty of Environment at the University of Waterloo and in our Food for Thought and Thinking Out Loud discussion groups. Most certainly, any mistakes of omission or commission are mine alone.

Randy Schmidt, senior acquisitions editor at UBC Press, has a remarkable talent for keeping the peer-assessment process pleasant and manageable while ensuring that a manuscript benefits from a rigorous review. He has a broad knowledge of many fields of inquiry discussed in these pages and so was able to give me intelligent, insightful advice about how to navigate such an interdisciplinary task – all while keeping the text within reasonable bounds. Life circumstances necessitated a lengthy pause in the project. When I was able to pick it up again, Randy was ready. Equipped with allusions to Milton, he helped me to see my way through to the end – figuratively, if not literally! I enjoyed working with Katrina Petrik, the remarkably efficient and congenial production editor at UBC Press who provided ready answers to all my questions. She ensured a smooth and pleasant production process. I would also like to thank Carmen Tiampo, Robert Lewis, Eric Leinberger, John van der Woude, Irma Rodriguez, Judith Earnshaw, and Cheryl Lemmens for all their helpful and important contributions to this book.

Many decades ago, my father and mother (Edwin and Anne Black) planted the seeds of this work. Both of them passed away in 2023. My father, initially a journalist and news editor, was later a professor of Canadian politics, federalism, and political communication. He was my mentor – his teaching style Socratic. Perhaps that is why you will find no easy answers or panaceas in this text. My mother's early emphasis on the value of reading and academia, and her love of the outdoors, contributed to my lifelong appreciation of nature and books. My partner-in-life, Evangelos Kattides, has made this book possible in so many ways. Not only has he cheerfully supported this very time-consuming project, but he also took care of many other responsibilities, freeing me to research and write for concentrated periods of time. (Ευχαριστώ Άγγελε μου. Σιγά-σιγά.) This book came together with the kindness and support of family, friends, colleagues, and many others who care about the health and sustainability of our communities. Thank you all.

Map 1 Canada, showing provincial and territorial boundaries and capitals

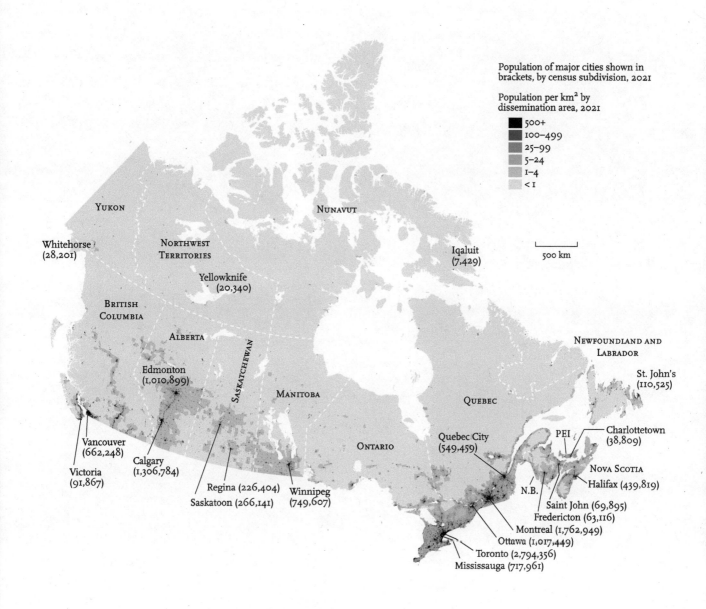

Population of major cities shown in brackets, by census subdivision, 2021

Population per km² by dissemination area, 2021

- 500+
- 100–499
- 25–99
- 5–24
- 1–4
- < 1

500 km

YUKON

NORTHWEST TERRITORIES

NUNAVUT

Whitehorse (28,201)

Iqaluit (7,429)

Yellowknife (20,340)

BRITISH COLUMBIA

ALBERTA

SASKATCHEWAN

NEWFOUNDLAND AND LABRADOR

Edmonton (1,010,899)

MANITOBA

St. John's (110,525)

QUEBEC

Quebec City (549,459)

ONTARIO

PEI

Charlottetown (38,809)

Vancouver (662,248)

Calgary (1,306,784)

NOVA SCOTIA

Halifax (439,819)

Victoria (91,867)

Regina (226,404)

Winnipeg (749,607)

N.B.

Saskatoon (266,141)

Saint John (69,895)

Fredericton (63,116)

Montreal (1,762,949)

Ottawa (1,017,449)

Toronto (2,794,356)

Mississauga (717,961)

Map 2 Canada, showing population of major cities and population density

Local Governance in Transition

Introduction

Complexity, climate change, collapsing valued ecosystems, political strife, social inequality, and the proliferation of new information and communications technologies (ICTs) are all defining characteristics of the twenty-first century. Local decision makers are confronted with a bewildering and growing number of unpredictable tasks heaped onto their already overflowing pile of responsibilities. However, the monumental scale of the challenges confronting municipal governments is surpassed by the catastrophic consequences if they are not adequately addressed. These possibilities have been thoroughly delineated in numerous studies, including works published by the 2005 Millennium Ecosystem Assessment Program and by the Intergovernmental Panel on Climate Change, and they are further discussed in two reports published by the Government of Canada: *Canada's Changing Climate Report* (Bush and Lemmen 2019) and its supplement (Bush et al. 2022). Municipalities cannot simply add a suite of sustainability goals to their already teetering stack of responsibilities – particularly when they are expected to pursue these goals using institutional mechanisms that were created for a different and less complex era.

The times require a reconsideration of priorities; trade-offs are inevitable. The goals of municipalities of a hundred years ago and the institutional bodies designed to support them are not well suited to contemporary needs. The reconceptualization of local decision-making structures and systems is necessary to address and respond effectively to a vastly different set of imperatives. These days, municipalities need to be like earthquake-proof buildings that require a network of trusses and base isolators to withstand unexpected shocks. Local governments should be structured in ways that allow them to adapt and be resilient when confronted with unforeseen events. The ability of municipalities to respond to rapid and often unanticipated social-ecological disruptions varies considerably depending on the context in which they are operating. Local governments might best fulfill their contemporary mandates guided by a framework designed to sustain valued social-ecological systems. Such an approach recognizes that humans are rooted in natural systems rather than separate from or in a position of dominion over them; the latter is a perspective that has dominated modern, industrialized societies. Governing systems are part of complex, interconnected, and dynamic social-ecological systems. These systems of human-environmental interactions operate at different temporal and spatial scales (see Chapter 1). Communities that can respond and adapt most readily to forecasted or unexpected disruptive events are those that have decision-making systems in place designed with flexibility in mind. These open systems have built-in redundancies and rely on a degree of modularity. Moreover, they are somewhat organic – capable of adaptive learning and adopting alternative strategies.

Many rapidly growing urban areas are bumping up against their political boundaries; they need planning approaches that can accommodate urban density while maintaining livable cities. The latter goal entails governing systems that foster social equity and well-being, biophysical conservation, protection of valued ecological systems, and vibrant local economies. Proactive responses to these requirements may be desirable but are difficult to implement. Defenders of the status quo frequently throw up political and social barricades. Moreover, the best-laid plans are often overwhelmed by cumulative, adverse, and unanticipated environmental effects. This is an era of "wicked," complex problems. Their resolution requires inclusive, interdisciplinary, and interjurisdictional collaboration.

Local institutions and political behaviours have been constructed on a scaffold of past governing practices and traditions created in quite different temporal and spatial contexts from those that exist today. Ingrained institutional practices have brought a measure of stability and order to municipal governments, enabling them to provide local services to many of their citizens. Sometimes, municipalities have successfully adapted and responded to contemporary needs. At other times, long-held conventions have undermined effective governance. Knowing how these institutions are structured can help to identify limitations, strengths, problems, and opportunities. This book offers an introduction to Canadian local government and policy for students of political science, sustainability sciences, and urban studies. It is also written for city staff or elected officials who would like a primer in local government that is illustrated by contemporary examples. For the international reader, this work provides an understanding of local governance in the context of Canada's unique geography, history, and politics. Many of the issues are similar to those encountered in local communities throughout the world. Nevertheless, how they present themselves and how local governments attempt to address them vary according to local political culture, geography, and the social-ecological environment.

In addition to an introduction to local government, this book presents emerging local responses to accumulating social-ecological challenges – imperatives that are confronting city halls across the country. It offers an institutional and policy understanding of local governance for readers interested in addressing environmental issues at the local level. The text draws on sustainability-science literature and on concepts related to systems approaches that are used to analyze complex, interconnected problems. In sum, it explores and presents the knowledge gap in the literature between local government, urban studies, and sustainability science. As the author, I am acutely aware that for many of the topics mentioned, entire books can (and have) been written. I have not attempted to offer a single, integrated theory from one perspective. This is an exploratory, explanatory effort that offers an overview of the diverse approaches and theories that inform local government, sustainability sciences, and other fields.

Creative administrative and policy strategies to address various governance and environmental challenges are included in order to illustrate different approaches employed by various municipalities. Contributions by local officials, community leaders, and key informants in Canadian urban governance highlight local initiatives related to social, economic, political, and ecological sustainability. These responses might not be viewed as the best solutions by everyone because sustainability is a contested concept. What works and is sustainable in one context may not work in another place or time. There are always trade-offs when making decisions for a local community. However, for municipalities and for those interested in sustainable local governance, these innovations do suggest some possible ways forward that might offer valuable ideas, practical solutions, and concepts.

The following chapters consider how some contemporary Canadian local governments have framed, negotiated, and responded to questions of urban sustainability. Specific attention is paid to innovative strategies – social, political, economic, and biophysical. Emphasis is placed primarily on city governance, although much of the text is also relevant to smaller towns and rural areas. Particularly pertinent are examples where municipalities introduce new approaches with respect to questions of local democracy, public administration, collaborative and multi-level governance, the politics of place, the impact of ICTs, infrastructure, ecosystem planning and management, blue-green infrastructure, public health and well-being, local economies and quality-of-life indicators, and institutional learning.

This investigation of transitions to sustainable local governance is interdisciplinary, drawing on literature from the fields of political science, sustainability science, geography, planning, ecology, communications, public health, sociology, and ecological economics. Much like resilient systems that have built-in redundancies, some ideas are repeated or reframed in the chapters where they have contextual relevance. This work is organized into three parts based on three themes that are also woven throughout the book: the politics of time and space, networks and partnerships, and the reimagining of local governance.

Part 1, "Through Time and Space: Canadian Local Government," discusses the evolution of Canadian local government framed by an exploration of evolving societal perceptions of time and space. As economic historian Harold A. Innis (1951) once observed, the political biases associated with notions of time and space have shaped physical and social landscapes, favouring certain dominant interests over others in the process.

The main themes of the book are introduced by exploring the evolving role of local government through an investigation of contemporary assumptions of time and space (see Chapter 1). Conventional conceptions of time and space adopted throughout Western liberal political society have frequently privileged monoculture and homogenization over diversity and modularity, centralization and globalization over decentralization and localism, reductionism over redundancy, and silos over systems. Some of these trends may well have stimulated desirable results for sustainability in certain contexts. In addition, a centralized system of governance may provide for more robust regulatory environmental and social protections. Conversely, decentralization of authority could contribute to the fragmentation of desired social or biophysical systems and weaken state protections of vulnerable systems and people. By and large, however, dominant globalizing and centralizing forces are serving to undermine the health of communities and the social-ecological systems on which they depend. Transformative processes are needed to reconceptualize the role of local governments in fostering sustainable, resilient communities.

Throughout its history, changing and often competing notions of time and space have influenced the evolution of Canadian local governance (see Chapter 2). Differing political and geographic considerations of scale have affected the distribution of resources, services, and political power. A focus on the politics of scale also helps to explain the opportunities and constraints facing communities and their residents when confronted with complex contemporary challenges. Local governments are expected to develop a plethora of local public policies, often ones that were inconceivable a couple of generations ago. At the same time, they continue to provide services related to their traditional responsibilities, including housing, parks and recreation, infrastructure, public health and safety, and local economic development. The nature of these responsibilities, however, has changed in terms of scale, complexity, and even context. Policy planning for horse and buggy travel a century and more ago, for example, has now been replaced by planning for a complex mixture of modes of transportation: e-scooters, autonomous cars, air travel, public transit, active (or human-powered) transportation, and still in some places, the horse and buggy. Moreover, new technological, environmental, and political developments have introduced the need to consider policies related to automated surveillance systems, the impacts of climate change, public health threats, or the introduction of disruptive technologies and the sharing economy.

The ability of municipalities to achieve their own agendas depends a great deal on how well they can successfully navigate intergovernmental partnerships, federalism, and multi-level governance (see Chapter 3). Recent trends are reinforcing political centralization. For example, unprecedented, hasty, and authoritarian decisions taken by some provincial governments are damaging to democracy, the environment, and the ability of municipalities to deliver services. Local governments have often been called "creatures of the province" with good reason. They have no formal constitutional authority, they fall under provincial legislation, and they possess limited fiscal resources. Yet, cities – where more than 80 percent of the Canadian population resides – are active players in global, national, and regional arenas, particularly when it comes to environmental issues. Municipalities take many decisions that have a much larger impact both on the health and well-being of their cities and beyond their boundaries than might be assumed from an initial reading of their formal jurisdictional authority. The complex social and environmental problems that they face require innovative, integrated processes functioning at multiple scales. Local governing capacity to implement decisions is constrained by political, economic, social, geographic, or ecological variables operating at many scales, from global to local.

Through their formal democratic institutions, local governments do have some capacity to take decisions that can help to foster a healthy civil society (see Chapter 4). The fundamental question of who gets to make decisions for the common good is of keen interest to anyone who cares about questions of power, democracy, a just society, and a healthy environment. The interplay between city residents, municipal governments, and other political players (in both formal and informal settings) highlights the contested nature of contemporary local democracy and the formal institutions with the mandate to pursue it.

Local governments are pressured to find new ways to accommodate some form of participatory democracy (see Chapter 5). Moreover, they have been doing so using governing structures originally designed to be formal decisional bodies based on hierarchical notions of representative liberal democracy. In recent decades, members of the interested public are much less content to be passive political observers by just casting their ballot at a municipal election. A governing system that accommodates and effectively represents a diversity of perspectives is an important element of a healthy civil society; it is also an essential component of a sustainable community.

Agency, capacity, political will, transparency, and public accountability are requisite characteristics of good governance in the administration of the public interest (see Chapter 6). These are not new concepts and have long been regarded as desirable attributes in a liberal-democratic system of government. They are also important values in the quest to foster healthy, sustainable communities. The other foundational pillars of public administration – effectiveness and efficiency – are not used as rallying cries by concerned

social activists. Yet, without these guiding principles, little could be achieved in the way of sustainable governance. The application of these principles enables local governments to pass and implement policies. Despite the dramatic changes occurring in cities, many of the traditional public administration rules, norms, procedures, principles, and practices prevail to this day. The strengths and limitations of these and other local institutions are considered in the context of the long-term sustainability of local communities. This discussion concludes the first part of the book, with its focus on the formal roles and mechanisms of municipal governments as they have been conventionally understood and portrayed, setting the stage for a discussion of new emerging forms of governance.

Part 2, "Networks and Partnerships: Connected Cities and Overlapping Responsibilities," considers the movement toward multi-level governance – an approach that embraces multi-scale collaborations. Horizontal collaborations are at work within city hall, breaking down decision-making silos to tackle interrelated policy challenges. Municipalities are also forming partnerships with members of civil society, the private sector, nongovernmental organizations (NGOs), and other levels of government (see Chapter 7). Beyond municipal boundaries, local governments are networking with other municipalities and other government bodies on collaborative, multi-scale efforts (see Chapter 8).

Dominating all of these challenges is arguably the foremost policy issue of the twenty-first century: global climate change (see Chapter 9). Municipalities have taken a prominent international stand on this front, and a number of Canadian mayors, local governments, and associations have taken a leadership role. Other existential issues include global pandemics, food and water insecurity, the degradation of vital ecological systems, social inequity, and political and economic instability. These issues directly affect Canadian residents, who look to their governments to provide a safe and healthy living environment. Municipalities are banding together globally to tackle major issues caused by climate change, poverty, hunger, housing, war, natural disasters, and many other circumstances. City governments are now becoming major international players.

The exponential growth of information and communications technologies has also had an impact on cities in myriad ways – some visible and others hidden or unanticipated (see Chapter 10). Networked cities are reconfiguring the ways that people conceptualize communities and their boundaries; spatial and temporal considerations take on a whole new meaning in this digital age. The promise of so-called smart technologies to encourage the conservation of resources or to provide access to open data while fostering a digital democracy tells only part of the story. The application of ICTs can reinforce the digital divide and social inequality; the choice to promote their application over other policies may not lead to a result that equitably distributes the benefits. Smart cities may also give the impression that they prioritize intended design and the placement of information technology tools firmly in the hands of the local decision makers and citizens. Many outcomes, however, are unanticipated and can have very undesirable rebound effects. Communications technologies – personal handheld devices, public webcams, intelligent streets – are laying down digital pathways that shape cities in surprising ways. The question that remains to be answered is whether there may be a way forward that can incorporate technological knowledge in a manner that is socially equitable and ecologically sustainable.

Part 3, "Reimagining Local Governance: Transitioning toward Sustainability," explores some of the emerging socio-political, ecological, technological, and economic trends affecting municipalities. It also offers some normative ideas proffered by aspirational communities of interest, sustainability scholars, and emerging alternative governance discourses. A focus on sustainable landscapes addresses the biophysical, built, and social infrastructure of a municipality.

Canada's communities are situated in tremendously diverse physical environments with ecosystems that include deserts, wetlands, subtropical rainforests, prairies, mixed-wood plains, maritime coasts, taiga forests, and arctic tundra. However, what all these diverse geographies have in common are ecological threats to their air, soil, water, flora, and fauna (see Chapter 11). The scale of environmental challenges, from global climate change to degraded local bioregions, requires local governments to network with

many partners in order to sustain valued ecosystems at all scales. The important roles that biodiversity and the ecological function of specific natural ecosystems play in sustaining daily living are now recognized by governments all over the world. As a result, biophysical considerations are being factored into local asset management plans, each with its unique set of governing challenges.

The places and the ways in which people produce, prepare, and consume food also shape the biophysical, built, and social fabric of communities. Some geographers refer to this food environment as a foodscape, which can be characterized spatially by various factors. An inner city without many services or a suburban area dominated by large supermarkets or box stores can be considered a foodscape. Alternatively, neighbourhood markets, food forests for foraging, and urban farms might be the exemplary elements. Questions of social equity might be framed in terms of food justice and access to nutritional, affordable, and culturally appropriate food. Other considerations might involve the relationship between food systems and social-ecological sustainability. Here, concepts such as the circular food economy, regenerative agriculture, and permaculture might come into play. Temporal considerations include aspects of food production and consumption when addressing the implications of highly processed fast food versus slow, locally produced food. The decisions that local governments take to foster or to undermine sustainable food systems can have a profound effect on community health.

The extensive and expensive grey infrastructural systems that characterize the built city landscapes constitute a primary policy consideration of municipalities (see Chapter 12). These built systems are groaning under the weight of intensive population growth and consumer demand. Circular, regenerative management innovations are emerging alternatives to the linear, end-of-pipe approaches that have dominated for over a century. Increasingly, governments are both diversifying and integrating the infrastructure of their energy, transportation, waste, water, and digital systems. ICTs are important tools when measuring, regulating, and monitoring the material stocks that flow through an urban system – or urban metabolism. This book offers some examples of integrated systems approaches to infrastructure in diverse Canadian municipalities.

In addition to shaping the natural and built environment, local governments (deliberately or otherwise) play a large part in crafting the social landscape (see Chapter 13). Questions of place and space heavily influence urban planning, policy, and implementation. For example, the impact of a city designed to facilitate the easy movement of the automobile will differ from that of one considered to be pedestrian-friendly. An individual's familiar route to work, school, or social activity will evoke a different sense of place depending on the distance, navigability, and physical surroundings. A downtown area that provides inclusive public spaces will generate a set of human interactions that is distinct from one designed primarily with commercial interests in mind. Who benefits and who loses due to the way that space is planned? Support for the idea that citizens[1] have a "right to the city," with all that this term entails, is far from universal, but this proposition is garnering increasing attention in community governance. Attention to place in the design of socio-political territory and physical spaces affects civics, a sense of belonging, and the health of communities.

One example of efforts to design convivial, welcoming, and safe spaces is that offered by the Healthy Cities and Communities movement, which was first introduced in Ontario in the 1980s and quickly spread to thousands of communities around the world. Forty years later, Healthy Cities and Communities networks in one form or another are well established across Canada. This holistic concept takes into account the major determinants of public or community health – the social, ecological, and economic factors. Pathways to healthy communities require inclusive public engagement, capacity building, diverse forms of collaboration at all scales, political support, effective public policy, enhanced protective measures for vulnerable populations, acknowledgment and redress of systemic biases and racism, widespread public trust in protective agencies, and community development. The abrupt arrival of the COVID-19 pandemic threw into sharp relief that public health is a fundamental prerequisite for human survival and long-term sustainability.

Vibrant local economies are also a key element of a healthy city (see Chapter 14). This has always been the case. Nevertheless, how these economies are defined, measured, and promoted is a subject of lively debate. Alternative economic models are often presented as the key to a sustainable community. The value of sustainable livelihoods and community well-being cannot be captured by classical liberal economic models, which employ inadequate assessment tools determined solely by financial, consumer, or economic-prosperity indicators. Assessment tools such as the Canadian Index of Wellbeing (n.d.) offer alternative, more nuanced models for achieving healthier communities. Measurement systems that incorporate human assets and capabilities can be employed to assess the value of human work that is not captured in classical economic models. Ecological economic models can be used to factor social and biophysical ecosystem services into calculations when evaluating policies and projects.

As we collectively stumble through the twenty-first century at breakneck speed, the need to govern under conditions of rapid social-ecological change is perhaps a defining challenge for municipalities. Municipalities have begun to explore governing approaches characterized by social and institutional learning, adaptation, and knowledge production in order to foster the sustainable systems on which all communities depend (see Chapter 15). Ultimately, if cities are to transition toward sustainability,[2] they will need to become co-producers of knowledge by engaging the public and networking with other governments and organizations. Going forward, effective institutions and approaches will be those that encourage continuous learning and improvement and that can adjust and respond to unanticipated events – social, economic, or biophysical. Openness, flexibility, and resilience will be required to allow them to adapt to shocks delivered in the form of natural or human-made catastrophes.

Canadian local governments are confronted by unprecedented global technological, ecological, and societal forces that can have cascading effects. Municipalities are constrained institutionally and financially in their ability to act. Nevertheless, communities throughout the country are collaborating on the development of new initiatives and policy innovations with the goal of achieving healthier cities. Some are leading the way, whereas others are lagging behind. These varied efforts can offer important lessons for other municipalities in this complex era. For over half a century, the clarion call for action has been sounding. In this third decade of the new millennium, we are reminded daily of existential threats to our social and ecological systems. There is little question about the need for serious transformative change in our institutions and actions if we are to create a more sustainable future. Local governments, if they have the political will and capacity, are in a position to partner with other actors in order to make it happen.

NOTES

1 Unless otherwise specified, the term "citizen" is used in this book to denote a local inhabitant, including immigrants and residents, rather than to invoke the more circumscribed legal definition of a person who has certain rights associated with being a Canadian citizen.

2 Striving for sustainability is a process that involves working with dynamic, evolving, and interacting social-ecological systems. Sustainability is not a static end state. Rather, the goal is to nudge desired systems in a more sustainable direction. This is why we speak of transitions *toward* sustainability, rather than *to* sustainability.

PART ONE

P.1 St. Jacob's, Ontario, 2018

Through Time and Space
Canadian Local Government

A pedestrian walks along the sidewalk at 5 kilometres an hour. A horse pulls a buggy down the street at 16 kilometres an hour. A light-rail train glides through the city at 27 kilometres an hour. A car traverses a region at 50 kilometres an hour. An electronic message shoots instantaneously across the country and beyond. The ways that people move through their communities, spend their time, and experience their environment are shaped by a complex mix of factors operating at different temporal and spatial scales (see Giddens 1984 and Gregory 1984). Those seeking to influence political and social structures and outcomes will prioritize (intentionally or otherwise) certain time and space considerations over others. Their biases shape the forces and systems that create the physical and social fabric of communities. Questions of power and privilege factor into the mix, affecting the ability of citizens to have intentional agency over their own time and mobility. Understanding these biases sheds light on the operations of local governments, as well as on the processes and outcomes of political decisions. Other interrelated factors such as location, environment, resources, and political history also influence the evolution of communities and their governments.

All municipalities have distinct local historical provenances and legacies. Early European explorers and settlers of North America perceived a vast geographic space to be conquered and dominated. In marked contrast, the First Peoples interacted with this environment using temporal and spatial perspectives that differed completely from those held by the European

usurpers. The first few hundred post-contact years witnessed the rise of rapidly industrializing areas in eastern Canada, the farm-based communities of the prairie provinces, the rough-and-tumble frontier towns that popped up on the West Coast, and the remote settler communities in the northern territories. The resource-exporting country oriented itself toward external markets while politically operating at a scale that suited Western liberal statist goals (e.g., see Magnusson 2009). Throughout the twentieth century, local governments continued to evolve; advances in transportation and communications linked territories, and public- and private-sector interests capitalized on both time and space efficiencies. Technological developments, urbanization, the centralization of political authority, and the development of the welfare state had a homogenizing effect on communities. It would be misleading, however, to underplay the diversity of Canadian localities in terms of their requirements and challenges, as well as their governing ideologies and approaches. For example, one need only look at Canada's northern territories to appreciate that local governance takes on a whole new meaning given the distinct geographic and cultural imperatives of a land that has supported Indigenous peoples for thousands of years.

The geographic and cultural diversity of Canadian communities notwithstanding, the rapid industrialization and urbanization in Western liberal democracies were accompanied by the growth of governing institutions that possessed hierarchical, specialized systems of public administration. These developments, in turn, generated questions about the power and control wielded by so-called technocratic elites. As early as 1911, sociologist Robert Michels warned of the "iron law of oligarchy," arguing that it was inevitable for democratic organizations to tend toward oligarchy – the control of an organization by the few or by a governing elite (cited in Diefenbach 2019, 545). This thesis has held considerable sway with political observers for over 100 years. Government decision makers have access to and control over key financial, human, legal, administrative, and information resources. Given the plethora of daily decisions, it is inevitable that modern policy processes appear to lack public transparency and accountability. It has been argued, however, that oligarchy in democratic institutions is not necessarily inevitable. Checks can be put in place to limit the power of elites, including formal, democratic mechanisms (e.g., regularly held elections); legislation, regulations, rules, and procedures to foster accountable and transparent processes (e.g., access to municipal information); open managerial cultures that encourage "open and transparent" democratic discussions within organizations (557); as well as codes of conduct, shared forms of governance, results-based accountability, meaningful political communications, and an effective participatory democracy.

The unique provenances of communities throughout Canada have contributed to the formation of different sets of public expectations and responses from their governments. The institutional frameworks and the public organizational structures that comprise the machinery of local governments are based on certain liberal-democratic principles of accountability to elected representatives and are intended to provide efficient, effective local services. The names and functions of various organizational structures have evolved over time. The arrangement of departments has often been shifted around, but the basic scaffolding remains the same. What have seen dramatic changes are the political, social, and ecological environments in which local governments must operate.

Diversity, time, and space are among the thematic concepts that run throughout this book. They are relevant factors when contemplating local institutions and the ideas and forces that drive them. The ideological, cultural, and institutional foundations of local governments, their organizational structures, and how they have evolved are of specific interest in the six chapters of Part 1. Do local governments meet the diverse needs of all their citizens and residents in a democratic manner, and in the process, do they foster a healthy civic culture? These questions also inevitably lead one to consider what constitutes a legitimate decision on the part of government. Canada's diverse communities of interest frequently vie for political influence at any given time, and their notions of a legitimate political decision can vary enormously. And then there are the unvoiced perspectives of various groups that are largely excluded from public decision making and shunted to the margins politically, geographically, and socially. This consideration also applies to the constituencies yet to come – the future generations that will be affected by current behaviours and by decisions taken today.

1 Sustainable Communities
Governance in a Complex Era

INTRODUCTION: THE IMPORTANCE OF BEING LOCAL

The Internet of Things, resilient cities, sustainable social-ecological systems, adaptation to climate change, sharing economies, disruptive technology, the Anthropocene, inclusive cities, and knowledge co-production are all issues now registering on the public radar. Many have been around for decades but were confined to the more theoretical realm of the academic or specialist. Along with other developments, however, they are rapidly redesigning the local political landscape. This swiftly shifting environment requires a whole suite of responses from local decision makers – people who are attempting to learn and respond to the very real and immediate emergencies presenting themselves on any number of fronts. Nevertheless, local governments are still constrained by an institutional legacy bestowed on them long ago and by provincial overseers who frequently appear committed to maintaining the constitutional status quo.

What is this legacy, why do we have local governments, and what purpose do they serve? A review of the early origins of Canadian municipalities suggests that, in large part, they were initially the result of a British decision to achieve some peace and stability in the unruly colonies. Subsequently, as cities and suburbs sprung up across the country, local governments were viewed as useful institutions for delivering services efficiently and effectively. These priorities remain today. We are now motoring our way through the third decade of the twenty-first century. Local governments continue to attempt to fulfill the func-

tions traditionally ascribed to them, but additional governing imperatives and public expectations are being piled on at a bewildering speed. Perhaps it is time to reconceptualize, or at the very least to expand, our functional notion of local governments as efficient providers of local services, political stability, and modest exercises in political participation. Cities have a central part to play in a global, existential project to sustain the vital social and ecological systems on which we collectively depend. This book focuses on the role that local government could play or – in some illuminating cases – is already playing to foster sustainability in an era of unprecedented technological, social, and environmental change.

TRADITIONAL ROLES OF LOCAL GOVERNMENT

In the eighteenth century, prior to Confederation, local governments were introduced to instill a measure of political stability and order to British North America. The new Canadian federation was formed in 1867 with a centralist national government in place to subdue provincial political discord while facilitating continental commercial expansion. Local governments were placed under provincial jurisdiction. As political scientist Peter J. Smith (1987, 28) has noted, "The localist attachments in Canadian political culture ... would have to be satisfied with the greatly inferior provincial governments they were given." In the unsettled West, municipal-style government did not arrive until the late 1880s. The Hudson's Bay Company and the Canadian Pacific Railway were dominant corporate forces that shaped early settlement and development patterns. The northern territories were assigned a different type of administrative structure due to their unique political, demographic, cultural, and geographic characteristics.

In the growing cities of North America during the late nineteenth and early twentieth centuries, local decision makers, planners, and engineers were influenced by science-based forms of utilitarianism to advance what was considered the public good – a conception that frequently coincided with the interests of those who owned property and businesses. Also present during these years were some more radical city planning approaches that promoted public health and welfare, social assistance, housing, and improved health conditions. For the most part, however, planning reflected the "progressive" business mood of the day and was spurred on by an urban reform movement ostensibly directed at eliminating the corrupt politics that were perceived to interfere with efficient city management. The "city beautiful" approach was based on notions of aesthetic, efficient, scientific planning and zoning.[1] Establishing parks, boulevards, civic centres, and good transportation routes was expected to result in an orderly, beautiful, and prosperous city while enhancing the value of land.

Such ideals continued to prevail in the ensuing century; local governments have been considered important because they provide public services at a scale that cannot be managed efficiently by a central government. They have also been valued for the opportunities that they offer in terms of public participation and pluralism by creating "alternative sources of political power rooted in elected territorial governments" (Sancton 2011, 25). Local governments have long been viewed as important institutions for fostering local democracy and civics – a position argued by two well-known nineteenth-century theorists, Alexis de Tocqueville and John Stuart Mill. Liberal-democratic principles associated with individual and property rights and with the public interest could be achieved through representative government and regularly held universal elections. These ideas are popular today, although in the 1800s, "universal" and "rights" generally referred to male, property-owning citizens. The majority of inhabitants were thereby excluded: the First Peoples, women, many racialized and religious groups, and others (see Chapter 2).

Pragmatism and political expediency underlay much of the early impetus for local government. Its importance was downplayed in comparison to that of the provincial and national governments. Over time, this perspective began to shift, resulting in an evolution away from mid-twentieth-century arguments about the limited importance of local government (Crawford 1954; Dahl 1961) and toward a twenty-first-century public awareness that many of the most crucial social and ecological issues of our times arise in cities. Local governments are now tasked with addressing many of them. Unfortunately, municipalities lack many of the tools and resources and much of the political authority required to do so.

Provincial governments very often (although not always) treat local governments primarily as effective vehicles for the delivery of services. One notable example is the Ontario Progressive Conservative government's introduction of the Efficient Local Government Act in 2018. The government unilaterally introduced this legislation and cut the size of the City of Toronto's council from forty-four to twenty-five councillors, citing efficiency and cost savings. Both in Toronto and elsewhere across Canada, the action generated outrage among numerous communities of interest, whose members viewed the province's conduct as both undemocratic and counterproductive in terms of effective governance (Kalvapalle 2018). Nevertheless, the provincial government prevailed in this matter and others, claiming its legal right to overrule the city government. It even went so far as to threaten to invoke the notwithstanding clause, Section 33 of the Canadian Charter of Rights and Freedoms. This clause (which enables provinces to opt out of the Charter) has rarely been used. Such a move might be seen by the public as a way to quash their rights and freedoms. Soon thereafter, further unprecedented pieces of legislation followed in rapid succession, undermining the efforts of local governments to sustain their cities' environments, services, and democracy. The ways that different provincial governments perceive and value municipal governments have varied over time and between jurisdictions (see Chapter 2).

REDEFINING LOCAL GOVERNMENT

Progress in cities is frequently equated with material economic development. City decision makers rely on property development (and its accompanying revenue) to provide public goods and services and to encourage investment and employment. Economic growth draws people and capital into the city, thereby generating more property development and associated infrastructure. Technological developments have hastened the speed of production and the growth of material wealth, leading to the ever-increasing consumption of resources. As Enzo Tiezzi wrote in *The End of Time* (1984),

> "Time is money." Progress is measured by speed of production ... The faster we transform nature, the more time we save ... Nature obeys different laws to economics, it works in "entropic time":[2] the faster we consume natural resources and the energy available in the world, the less time is left for our survival. "Technological time" is inversely proportional to "entropic time"; "economic time" is inversely proportional to "biologic time."
>
> Our limited resources and the limited resistance of our planet and its atmosphere clearly indicate that the more we accelerate the energy and matter flow through our Earth system, the shorter is the life span of our species. (Cited in Pulselli and Tiezzi 2009, 25)

In response to emerging societal and environmental demands, local decision makers are now being pressured to reconsider some of their fundamental assumptions, structures, and processes. Analysts and local governments are beginning to acknowledge that the conventional approach of measuring prosperity solely through economic indicators such as gross domestic product (GDP) is of limited utility in determining a population's well-being. A holistic group of indicators, such as the Canadian Index of Wellbeing (n.d.) (see Chapter 13), would provide a more accurate assessment. These more comprehensive assessment tools suggest that equating prosperity solely with the speedy, efficient production and consumption of material goods is counterproductive. It works against the social, ecological, and economic well-being of cities

and their residents both now and in the long run. In this context, local governments require a much more nuanced approach when defining their roles and functions than has historically been the case.

Notions of local democracy have also shifted with the times (see Chapter 5). In the latter half of the twentieth century, assisted by the proliferation of communications media, members of the public became politically active beyond traditional means. Different constituencies began to participate in local governance outside of representative democracy's formal mechanisms of voting, presenting petitions to city council, and running for local councils, agencies, or boards. Expectations of meaningful public consultation became the political norm. Political scientist B. Guy Peters (1996, 47) stated, "This is clearly an age in which government finds it difficult to legitimate its actions without active public involvement." Local democracy is now often equated with some form of participatory democracy, along with a healthy measure of self-governance. These developments have not been without consequences. Change can be difficult to effect, for example, if one group or another protests local decisions and pursues avenues of appeal through provincial or federal governing bodies. Competing voices seek to be heard in a multiplicity of forums, and new types of social media are facilitating this trend. Governance can best be conceptualized as a contested, contradictory process "constituted out of political struggle" (Laforest 2011, 14).

Despite these difficulties, civic engagement is a vital tool in the pursuit of sustainable cities. As noted by Niki Frantzeskaki and colleagues (2018, 281–82), civil society has long performed an essential role in advocating for more sustainable practices. They argue that a heterogeneity of interests – including NGOs, community groups, and various associations and networks – can play an important part in fostering innovative transitions toward sustainability. Moreover, such transitions require "deep radical change ... in ways of thinking, doing, and organizing ... as well as in ways of knowing and relating" (282), which is difficult to achieve within formal institutions. No doubt, members of civil society can just as readily hamper progress toward sustainability. They might, for instance, react against multi-density zoning changes in their neighbourhoods, local efforts at socially inclusive policies, or the introduction of bicycle lanes that inhibit on-street parking. Nevertheless, without the concerted efforts of community groups to lobby governments, speak to media, and conduct campaigns, much of the progress toward healthier communities would not have taken place.

GOVERNMENT OR INTERACTIVE GOVERNANCE?

A widespread normative assumption in academic and popular literature is that local decision making for sustainability requires the active and meaningful participation of members of civil society, nongovernmental actors, and private-sector interests. Urban analysts of the changing political environment suggest that local governments constitute only one set of many influential actors that shape cities. In fact, although many people think of local government primarily in terms of city hall, it encompasses a much wider field of actors and entities, such as school boards, library boards, and health boards – entities that are active players in local governance yet legally independent or at arm's length from the local government in many jurisdictions. But the notion of governance goes beyond the more limiting notions of local *government*. As political scientist Zack Taylor (2019, 8) elaborates,

> I understand urban governance to involve governments and nongovernmental actors at all levels – federal, provincial or state, and local – as they shape the development of cities. Instead of viewing national or provincial governments as forces external to the city, my approach views local government as but one type of actor in a broader field of urban governance.

The concept of governance also recognizes the political influence of nonstate actors, including the private sector and civil society, but it does so in a context that can accommodate the recognition of variables like diversity, complexity, dynamics, and scale. Jan Kooiman and Maarten Bavinck (2013, 9) point out that these major variables influence "the governability of societal systems and their three components: a system-to-be-governed, a governing system and a system of governing interactions mediating between the two." Considerations include social concerns, such as poverty, health, and social justice, as well as physical concerns, such as climate change and other environmental issues. The term "interactive governance" acknowledges the important role that formal institutions play in governance and emphasizes the interactions between political actors that create opportunity and "contribute to the tackling of societal problems" (11). Network or interactive governance, a trend seen in governance literature as a way to address complex problems, contains its own set of problems, including questions of transparency, co-optation of agendas and interest groups, and accountability (see Chapter 8).

SUSTAINABLE LOCAL GOVERNANCE

Emerging environmental imperatives are driving Canadian local governments to find creative, integrative solutions to address sustainability challenges. What is it that local governments seek to sustain? Sustainability is an elusive idea that requires the protection and enhancement of desirable social-ecological systems – the systems that connect humans and the environment (Berkes 2017). In other words, as Alastair W. Moore and colleagues (2018) suggest, social-ecological systems are "substantially concerned with space and place, providing concepts regarding interactions between spaces, e.g., ecosystems, environments, economic zones, the urban, etc., each with its own socially constructed meaning." But which systems specifically are to be sustained, and how is that to be achieved? Donella H. Meadows and Diana Wright (2008) explain that systems, at their most basic level, are comprised of elements, interconnections, and a purpose or function. These systems are interconnected both temporally (i.e., past, present, and future) and spatially (i.e., scaling outward and upward from the local to the global). Desirable sustainable social-ecological systems are frequently associated with notions of biophysical vitality, social justice, and economic sufficiency. The pursuit and definition of these concepts are debated and negotiated in international, domestic, and local political arenas. The sustainability of cities and the ecosystems on which they depend rests a great deal on the ability of decision makers (from the local to the global) to take meaningful steps to address serious environmental issues.[3]

THE SOCIAL METABOLISM OF CITIES

One way to understand the systemic relationship between social systems and the biophysical systems that support them is through the concept of social metabolism. Social systems require a continuous flow of energy and materials from the biophysical environment to sustain themselves. Cities, for example, require the "colonization of nature," which has been defined as "purposive intervention into natural systems aimed at improving their utility for societal purposes" (Haberl et al. 2016a, 1). Both social and biophysical systems are continually co-evolving. A quantitative analysis of how materials like energy, biomass, and water flow through a city can give decision makers crucial information about how to sustainably design urban systems. Material flows accounting, as it has come to be known, is now used throughout the world to provide information on resource extraction and use (Mayer et al. 2016, 218). Some of these material flows, such as food and packaging, quickly become waste, whereas the remainder – including the built infrastructure, machines, and other durable products – stay in the system longer, adding to the material stocks. When the "circulation integrity and availability of critical resources" are at risk (referred to as a metabolic risk), a desired social-ecological system might reach a tipping point where the system collapses (Singh et al. 2022, 4).

In the context of local governance, trade-offs are inevitably made between and within different systems and scales. Policy makers must determine which systems should be sustained and how. When it comes to urban transportation, for example, should the focus be on building a transit system, such as light rail, along the spine of a city to facilitate human mobility while minimizing environmental impact? Or should the focus be on human behaviours and interactions with environments as whole systems, where mobility is only one consideration among many? Other possibilities include encouraging less public mobility through a more decentralized city form or through the use of information and communications technologies (ICTs), developing flexible, adaptive systems that can accommodate changes in human-environmental interactions, and planning cities using the model of a circular economy to reduce material flows. What are the temporal and spatial boundaries of the system to be sustained, and which political actors should or can have a determining role?

The concept of sustainability (or sustainable development) first garnered notable international political action in the late 1980s with the release of the watershed report *Our Common Future* by the World Commission on Environment and Development (1987), known as the Brundtland Commission. This report established the importance of creating governing strategies that recognize biophysical limits to industrial economic growth, and it connected social equity and justice to any successful strategies. Equity within and between generations and limits to growth have since become hallmarks of many sustainability initiatives. Canadian public servant and environmentalist Jim MacNeill was secretary-general of the World Commission on Environment and Development and lead author of *Our Common Future*. As the organization ICLEI – Local Governments for Sustainability (2015, 10) posits, "Sustainable cities work towards an environmentally, socially, and economically healthy and resilient habitat for existing populations, without compromising the ability of future generations to experience the same."

RESILIENT CITIES

A concept that has achieved a measure of political salience is the resilient community or city. Resiliency concerns the question of how well a city can deal with a disruptive social or environmental event. Like "sustainability," the term "resiliency" is contested. Scientifically, "resilience" has been defined as "the capacity of a system to absorb disturbance and still retain its basic function and structure" (B.H. Walker and Salt 2006, xiii). One conceptualization of resiliency suggests that complex self-organizing social-ecological systems move through four phases or adaptive cycles: rapid growth, conservation, release, and reorganization. If a system changes a great deal, it can cross a threshold and start behaving in different and sometimes unanticipated ways (Gunderson and Holling

2002; B.H. Walker and Salt 2006, 11, 31). It can lose its basic function and structure. The achievement or maintenance of desirable local social-ecological systems requires that effective governing institutions foster resilient systems that are sustainable into the future.

The resiliency of systems is determined by factors related to diversity, modularity, and tightness of feedbacks. Diversity refers to institutions, economies, responses to challenges, land use, and interactions between systems. Modularity, as opposed to highly connected systems, allows for parts of a system to self-organize in the event of a shock. For example, the global agri-food industry is a tightly coupled, unsustainable system and therefore vulnerable to collapse. It poses risks related to global public health (Waltner-Toews 2004), the global food supply (Clapp 2012), ecological biodiversity, and socio-economic stability. Alternatively, locally connected food systems based on a circular economy help to reduce these vulnerabilities (see Chapter 11). This consideration applies to other policy areas as well, including energy, transportation, and communications systems. They are also interrelated. For example, on July 8, 2022, one of Canada's three major telecommunications companies, Rogers Communications, experienced a widespread outage over the course of twenty-four hours, affecting more than 12 million subscribers. Significant disruptions were experienced across the country, including in banking and business services and in emergency, social, and health services. Modularity ensures tighter feedback signals so that system disruptions or threats can be more readily detected, regionally contained, and mitigated (Hopkins 2009, 57).

In the context of a community, George Francis (2016, 155) suggests that "resiliency refers to the ongoing ability of a community to work together, to identify its strengths and challenges, to mobilize its assets, and to work collectively to meet its needs. Municipalities are in the front line as first responders." ICLEI – Local Governments for Sustainability (2019) states, "A 'Resilient City' is prepared to absorb and recover from any shock or stress while maintaining its essential functions, structures, and identity as well as adapting and thriving in the face of continual change. Building resilience requires identifying and assessing hazard risks, reducing vulnerability and exposure, and lastly, increasing resistance, adaptive capacity, and emergency preparedness."

If a municipality is to be resilient and to have the capacity to act effectively, normative factors need to be considered. For example, Patricia Romero-Lankao, Olga Wilhelmi, and Mikhail Chester (2018, 98) suggest that "urban resilience is related to normative and ethical principles such as the unequally distributed resources that individuals and organizations have (or potentially have) to effectively mitigate and adapt to the hazards and stresses they encounter." Social inequality, then, will affect the resiliency of a community if certain populations or areas of a system are left vulnerable and do not have the capacity to absorb or adapt to disturbances beyond a certain threshold.

There may be some general agreement on many goals, principles, practices, and strategies for fostering healthy communities. However, Canadian municipal approaches to sustainability are by no means uniform given their tremendous diversity and dispersion throughout a huge geographic territory. The densely populated city of Toronto has rivalled Chicago as the fourth largest in North America and one of the world's most culturally diverse cities. In contrast, the town of Trinity Bay in Newfoundland and Labrador has fewer than 100 people (Statistics Canada 2022a) and is located on the northern tip of a bay jutting out into the Atlantic Ocean. In addition to their population disparities, Canadian communities vary enormously in their forms of government, culture, economic base, and physical characteristics. Whether large or small, each one has a unique set of sustainability challenges determined by its context. Rural and remote municipalities, such as Trinity Bay, although not pressured by the social-environmental impacts of large populations, have their own sets of challenges (see Figure 1.1).

For example, large urban centres have access to many more resources and tools – human, fiscal, educational, and technological. Smaller local governments are severely constrained in their ability to address social-ecological problems, such as those caused by climate change, social inequity, high costs of living, sewerage, and limited economic opportunities. Transit systems, social and educational programs, housing, and conservation initiatives all require resources and a fiscal base that small rural and remote communities do not possess. Remoteness from urban centres equipped with health and social programs deepens and extends sustainability challenges and social polarization (Walmsley and Kading 2018a). One study of environmental injustice has examined how Ontario rural communities have been called upon to play "host" to urban environmental agendas for renewable power, such as wind generation and the processing of waste from large urban centres (C. Walker, Mason, and Bednar 2018, 118). The risks and costs to the rural areas are perceived to far outweigh the benefits (120). Examples of this kind underline the need for a place-based governance approach that recognizes the specific needs of each community (see Chapter 8). Unique policy outcomes are generated by the interplay of factors such as climate change, geography, history, demographics, planning, economics, design, and political culture. Unlike their counterparts in Prince George, British Columbia, for example, waste management officials in Windsor, Ontario, need not consider how to deal with black bears that have acquired a taste for urban cuisine. Rather, they have a whole different set of context-related factors to consider.

Global issues like climate change also call into play diverse strategies as municipalities cope with extreme weather events that can lead to record levels of flooding, forest fires, hurricanes, drought, or ice melt. Given this reality, it is worthwhile emphasizing that place matters and that there are inevitable trade-offs involved in each community when considering which valued system components should be sustained, who should participate in making decisions, what kinds of decisions are needed, and how decisions will be reached. That is why it is imperative to learn about the governing institutions and processes that determine these decisions.

Historically, local governments have been organized along formal, institutional, and hierarchical bureaucratic lines. Today, however, much of the sustainability literature as well as many local political strategies call for more networked, collaborative, horizontal approaches to decision making – ones that reach beyond the auspices of local government institutions. A local governance approach recognizes that although municipal governments play a key role in

1.1 Trinity Bay, Newfoundland and Labrador, 2022 | Courtesy of Tanya Markvart, tanyamarkvart.com

shaping local communities, they constitute only one set of politically influential actors. Ann Dale, William T. Dushenko, and Pamela Robinson (2012, 4) suggest that the pursuit of sustainability is a process of reconciliation among three imperatives: "the ecological imperative to ensure global biophysical carrying capacity for the future, the social imperative to ensure the development of culturally sustainable systems of governance, and the economic imperative to ensure a viable standard of living for all." For such a reconciliation to occur, these scholars call for nothing less than an institutional transformation. They are not alone. Commonly shared views about the actions needed for the pursuit of sustainability have emerged from a diversity of fields. Box 1.1 outlines these

---

BOX 1.1   Key elements of local governing strategies for sustainability

Requisite characteristics of, and approaches by, municipal governments when transitioning toward sustainability include:

- embracing a sustainability ethic based on criteria that will guide decision making (R.B. Gibson 2013, 2017) and possessing the agency, capacity, and political will to apply this ethic to governance and community decision making (Evans et al. 2006; Bulkeley et al. 2018; Romero-Lankao, Wilhelmi, and Chester 2018)
- adopting the seven main characteristics of good governance identified by the United Nations Global Campaign on Urban Good Governance, launched in 2002: sustainability, subsidiarity, equity, efficiency, transparency and accountability, civic

engagement and citizenship, and security (UN-Habitat 2002; see also Tindal et al. 2017 and Z. Taylor 2016)

- employing place-based strategies that recognize the inextricable relationship between the social and physical environment (Dale, Dushenko, and P. Robinson 2012; R.B. Gibson 2013; Singh et al. 2013; Armitage, Charles, and Berkes 2017; A.W. Moore et al. 2018; N.J. Bennett et al. 2019)
- creating and collaborating in governing processes that have a good fit with the spatial and temporal scales of valued ecosystems, accounting for the dynamics and functioning of these ecosystems' processes (Daly 1996; Ekstrom and Young 2009; Leman Stefanovic and Scharper 2012; Wittmer and Gundimeda 2012; Loucks et al. 2017)

- implementing more comprehensive measures to identify and assess the community's well-being and to value its natural and social assets, as well as its economy (Canadian Index of Wellbeing n.d.; Sen 1985; Robeyns and Byskov 2020)
- possessing a capability to learn, collaborate, innovate, adapt, and engage in transitional and long-term thinking (Kelly and Adger 2000; R.B. Gibson and Hassan 2005; Smit and Wandel 2006; Armitage, Berkes, and Doubleday 2007; Blackmore 2010; Abernethy 2014; Francis 2016; Bai et al. 2018; Castán Broto et al. 2019).

Note: The accompanying names of analysts who discuss these considerations constitute only a small subset of a large group of sustainability scholars in Canada and elsewhere.

---

themes. They arise throughout this text in the discussion of local efforts toward sustainability.

As noted above, governing trade-offs must be made between competing priorities, and sustainability efforts will vary in response to local circumstances. Although there are commonly shared themes, one can envision municipalities taking many different approaches to sustainable cities, depending on the emphasis. As a result, an ethic comprised of a set of sustainability criteria is needed in order to guide local decision makers if they are to avoid substantive trade-offs that will lead to serious adverse impacts. One well-known approach, pioneered in Canada and tested in a number of communities, has been developed by Robert Gibson (2013, 3), whose "overlapping and interacting" core criteria include "long-term social-ecological system integrity; livelihood sufficiency and

opportunity for everyone; intragenerational equity; intergenerational equity; resource maintenance and efficiency; social-ecological civility and democratic governance; precaution and adaptation; and immediate and long-term integration." Trade-offs between these principles are inevitable and context-dependent. For governing decisions to be considered legitimate by the public, the trade-offs made by governments require informed, publicly inclusive discussions to ensure transparency and an awareness of their implications for the community's long-term sustainability.

Converting agendas into action requires political will, agency, and capacity as well as biophysical, human, and financial resources. Moreover, the complex, interconnected mix of factors and actors that characterize contemporary decision-making arenas call for inclusive political processes to facilitate social and institutional learning, a critical reflexivity, self-organization, adaptation, and anticipatory action when needed.

ADAPTATION, TRANSFORMATION, AND LEARNING

Incremental change is built into liberal-democratic governance systems. Typical examples of tools frequently wielded in the name of environmental protection include a variety of technological solutions, environmental legislation and taxation, ecological land-use planning, social and community health, and public education programs. Many, if not most, students of sustainability believe that the incremental steps taken within the current liberal-capitalist growth paradigm are insufficient in terms of reversing or halting the unsustainable trajectory in this era of the Anthropocene. A transformation of existing societal and institutional values, assumptions, and approaches is required to reverse the current adverse trends. Some observers go further in their prognostications, arguing that it is necessary to explore how societies might deal with what they view as an inevitable degree of collapse in valued social and ecological systems (Jacobs 2005; Tainter 2011; Quilley 2017; Bendell 2018). As James Howard Kunstler (2009, 15) notes, "We face a dire and unprecedented period of difficulty." This future scenario is characterized by a severe drop in health and wellness and in human civility, as well as by a great degree of strife. A casual perusal of recent headlines in mainstream journals confirms such prognoses. So where do we go from here?

One possible future scenario has been presented by the well-known Transition Towns movement, which envisions a post-carbon future based on re-localization and community initiatives. In Canada, this movement seems to have evolved into complementary local efforts under other banners promoting local food production, renewable energy, or circular economy initiatives. The literature is replete with analyses and prescriptions for avoiding or mitigating adverse environmental impacts of anthropogenic (or human-caused) activities and for developing strategies to tackle climate change adaptation and post-carbon futures. These analyses have generated a substantial body of literature on transitions toward sustainability (Romero-Lankao, Frantzeskaki, and Griffith 2018). According to Sarah Burch and colleagues

(2018, 307), "Explorations of governance in the transitions literature seek to overcome the failures that have emerged from rigid, hierarchical, fragmented, conventional, top-down, government-centric approaches by moving towards systems-based, flexible, and participatory strategies that foster social learning through governance."

Daunting barriers stand in the way of cities attempting to pursue sustainability initiatives. One of the most persistent is that known as path-dependent institutional behaviour, whereby the practices of the past are systemically ingrained into the present and frequently left unquestioned. How very common it is to hear "But that is not the way it is done" in meetings at city hall when decision makers are confronted with a recommended change to existing processes, plans, or policies. As John S. Dryzek (2014, 941) observes,

> Path dependency means that early decisions constrain later ones; as the costs of changing course become high, actors develop material stakes in stable institutions, and institutions arrange feedback that reinforces their own necessity (consider, for example, how market institutions punish policy deviations from market orthodoxy). The ideas and norms generated by an institution's operation can further solidify the path. What all this means is that an established institution may constrain possibilities for future choice across institutions by its mere presence.

It follows that if existing processes are not working, governments need to question their very foundations (Dryzek and Pickering 2017). Reflexivity is required, which sociologist Anthony Giddens (1984, 3) has asserted is "grounded in the continuous monitoring of action which human beings display and expect others to display" (see also Meuleman 2018). Reflexivity has been defined as "the ability of a structure, process or set of ideas to reconfigure its response to reflection on its performance" (Dryzek and Pickering 2017, 353). An important tool in the reflective process is deliberative democracy, where "collective reasoning" takes place and an appreciation for long-term sustainability can be fostered (354). Discussions facilitate a process of collective and ongoing social learning. The notion of "reflection-in-action" is seen as a new response to a situation, often in conditions of uncertainty that can lead to "on-the-spot" experimentation (Schön 1995, 247). Institutional learning and reflection are considered by many analysts to be an essential component in transitions toward sustainability (see Chapter 15).

CONSTRAINTS AND POSSIBILITIES

It is important to emphasize here that some of the local initiatives mentioned in this book may be limited in scope and impact. One of the goals here, however, is to share ideas about what has been tried in various Canadian municipalities so that they can learn from each other and possibly adopt similar initiatives while adapting them to their own specific needs. Local governments require the capacity and the opportunities to experiment and to act as incubators for innovation (Hancock 2016; Torfing 2019). There is no question that the ability to pursue innovative sustainability strategies might be (and frequently is) constrained by a number of factors, many of which interact with and reinforce each other in positive feedback loops, from the global level right down to local institutions.

Throughout the world, including Canada, dominant political and economic forces, facilitated by global capitalism and associated ideologies and structures, encourage the concentration of wealth, resources, and power in the hands of ever fewer individuals and corporations. Western political institutional structures are informed by notions of economic liberalism that are based on the tenets of individualism and private property. One outcome has been unsustainable material growth powered by a fossil-fuelled economy. Tightly coupled economic and biophysical systems, operating at different temporal and spatial scales, are undermining diversity, modularity, redundancy, and resiliency in social-ecological systems. These trends are spurred on by highly integrated information and communications systems. Powerful private communications conglomerates wield immense power over both medium and message (see Chapter 10). Growing social polarization and inequality have further aggravated ecological degradation, which is concentrated in geographic areas where people have the fewest

resources and limited political influence. The world is now experiencing mass human migrations as a result of anthropogenic activities, whether they be a result of war, climate change, or extreme poverty (see Chapter 9). Recent years have also seen a growing global movement of reactionary populism against the perceived privileges of liberal elites (and their progressive agendas, such as environmentalism). This movement provides fertile ground for the formation and institution of populist, authoritarian, leader-dominated governments that threaten liberal-democratic representative institutions. Reactionary (or right-wing) populism is both a factor in and a manifestation of growing societal polarization, ethnic discrimination, and inequality.

In Canada, the national government shares political authority with the provincial and territorial governments. Local governments fall under the constitutional jurisdiction of the provinces and territories, although some aspects of local government are also considered a federal responsibility (see Chapter 3). As a result, local governments are subject to the will of senior governments, most notably the provinces and territories. Because of actions taken by senior governments, local governments have frequently been restrained in their ability to represent their communities. Numerous examples can be offered from across the country, including municipal amalgamations that reduce council sizes, limiting democratic representation; provincial planning laws that override municipal decision-making processes; legislation that changes electoral processes or the role of elected representatives; and infrastructural development that bulldozes local environmental initiatives. Provincial and local political agendas are also influenced by electoral cycles that favour more immediate and tangible displays of public spending (e.g., the construction of new infrastructure and buildings) over complex, less visible, and longer-term initiatives aimed at sustaining valued ecosystems.

Within local governments themselves, initiatives toward sustainability are often resisted by the path-dependent behaviours of elected incumbents or municipal staff. Path-dependent behaviour refers to the predisposition to maintain the rules, norms, conduct, and procedures of the past. Incentives to change existing practices toward sustainability may be outweighed by the perceived benefit of maintaining the status quo, which has served decision makers well in the past. This resistance to change is also present in the wider community. Single-home ratepayers often push back against neighbourhood changes like the densification of residential areas and the introduction of multi-family dwellings. This phenomenon is known as NIMBY (not-in-my-backyard) syndrome. Although Canada has a multicultural society, the composition of its elected local government bodies does not represent its cultural and social diversity. Such diversity can promote social innovation and problem solving, as well as representative and participatory forms of democracy. In addition, there is still a privileging of solutions that are driven primarily by scientific, expert, and technological knowledge, to the exclusion of other types of knowledge and learning in decision making. Technology and science have an important role to play in fostering sustainability but only as part of a policy-making toolkit. Governments also often resort to path-dependent behaviours when they are called upon to immediately respond to social and physical crises.

Social and environmental crises are on the rise as a result of "wicked" challenges such as climate change, the growth of homelessness, epidemics and pandemics, mass human migrations as a result of war, and environmental disasters. Crisis decision making generates reactive, rather than proactive, governing practices that, in turn, limit the ability of governments to engage in long-term planning. In addition, municipalities rely on sources of revenue that depend heavily on property development and its associated uses. This dependency presents a notable dilemma when trying to sustain valued ecosystems. The problem is worsened by the ongoing privatization of land and the loss of public commons, as well as by the associated loss of social and biophysical diversity. Local decisions are typically based on conventional forms of valuation, such as GDP, rather than on more nuanced forms of assessments using indicators of societal and biophysical well-being. The above list is not complete, but it does illustrate the enormity of the sustainability challenges ahead. These limitations are acknowledged here and referred to throughout this book in

order to ground the discussion in the current realities of governing in this complex era.

Despite these significant barriers to change, local governments are taking tangible steps toward sustainability across Canada. These efforts are well worth exploring for the lessons and opportunities that they offer. But which ones are likely to take hold as opposed to those that fall by the wayside? For an observer of municipal government, attempts to determine which ones will succeed in becoming long-term sustainable efforts and which ones will not are often exercises in clairvoyance. It is not easy to discern what program will have traction over the long term as opposed to being a short-lived ephemeral experiment. However, as discussed below, certain characteristics might indicate which initiatives are most likely to be successful. And here, the term "successful" is used only to denote widespread salience on public and private agendas that can lead to their implementation and staying power. It is not intended to imply that they are necessarily the ideal or preferred answer to any sustainability problems.

THE CHARACTERISTICS OF "SUCCESSFUL" SUSTAINABILITY INITIATIVES

Legal and Institutional Support
Initiatives that have legal support through legislation and regulations will tend to see initiatives take root, grow, and possibly be disseminated. The banning of the use of cosmetic pesticides on lawns is one well-known example that had its roots in a court case pitting a municipality against a pesticide company, and over time the ban spread throughout Canada (see Chapter 3). Other examples include environmental-protection legislation, public consultation on municipal-planning legislation, and various pieces of human rights legislation that affect the shape of cities.

Political Will, Leadership, and Commitment
Across the country, in Canadian cities large and small, one can find numerous examples of environmental innovations that came about as a result of the dedication and leadership of elected representatives and city staff who had a vision to foster a more sustainable municipality. Over the past couple of decades, some

mayors in Canada's three largest cities and provinces – notably David Miller of Toronto, Gregor Robertson of Vancouver, and Valérie Plante of Montreal – have championed the cause of a sustainable city and have also played related leadership roles in the international arena (see Chapter 9).

Multi-level Government Support

Programs that have traction and engender the commitment of financial and human resources by senior governments are those that have a widespread impact on people and become a major issue of concern to voters. Initiatives that align with goals agreed to by political leaders in international forums, such as the United Nations Sustainable Development Goals (SDGs) (United Nations General Assembly 2015) (see Figure 9.2), will also garner support from receptive governments. At the time of writing, some major issues of concern include housing, health care, climate change, cost of living, and education. One municipal partnership scheme that has received federal funding is the Circular Cities and Regions Initiative, whose participants include twenty-five communities across Canada. This scheme was created through a partnership between the National Zero Waste Council, the Federation of Canadian Municipalities, RECYC-QUÉBEC, and the Recycling Council of Alberta (see Chapter 12). Another initiative is the Low Carbon Cities Canada (LC3) network, a federally endowed partnership of seven of Canada's largest cities and the Federation of Canadian Municipalities (see Chapter 7). However, given the provincial authority over municipalities, supportive provincial legislative and regulatory frameworks are important ingredients in successful multi-level, polycentric arrangements. In Canada, the work of senior-level governments in support of polycentric arrangements is often uneven and inconsistent. Much depends on the political agendas of the day.

Extensive Political and Administrative Collaboration

The partnerships that local governments forge with regional governments and with other political communities of interest are often the result of collabora-tive, polycentric governance efforts. Through formal and informal partnerships and communications, networking can lead to the long-term viability of an initiative. Well-established, decentralized, networked organizations also have some built-in redundancies that allow them to remain viable. If one member of the network falters or if one funding source dries up, there are other possibilities still available. Long-term sustainable outcomes are maximized when participants from many communities of interest pool human and financial resources and engage in knowledge sharing (see Chapters 6 and 7).

Media Attention and Promotion by Influential Interest Groups

The ability of citizen activists to capture media attention and to gain the financial support of well-established interest groups can help citizens to successfully pressure governments into making policy changes and can shift the public discourse toward a focus on specific areas of concern. Examples include movements protesting climate change, environmental contamination, or racial discrimination and other forms of social injustice (see Chapters 2 and 13). It is important to remember that public protests are not necessarily organized to advance causes related to social or ecological sustainability. Throughout history, protest movements and the media have also been used to prevent changes to the status quo, as vividly highlighted by the surge in recent years of reactionary populism around the world, including in Canada.

A Successful Urban Experiment That Is Then Diffused to Other Communities

One of the advantages of decentralized government and other forms of distributed decision making is that it is possible to innovate and experiment with new ideas and policies from which others can learn. If an initiative is instigated by a municipality and does not lead to a desired result, the impact is contained. Alternatively, an innovation tried in one place can be adapted and emulated elsewhere. Numerous cases abound, including the banning of pesticides (mentioned above), active transportation initiatives, community gardens, universal-planning design, public consultation, the use of information and communications technologies to foster e-democracy, and energy and water conservation. Some of these experiments are inevitably going to be short-lived and deemed unsuccessful, but lessons can be learned from these efforts. It should also be noted that even these initiatives, instead of necessarily failing, may have evolved over time, leading to new projects, or they may have been merged with others under a new name to better suit the needs of local participants (see Part 3).

A Crisis or Major Disruption in the Status Quo

A serious disruption to a community may lead to significant changes in politics and the shape of a city. Major disasters that disrupt the status quo can allow for a reconsideration of past practices and can make room for new approaches and designs. Such is the case with natural disasters, which can lead to new emergency management policies, as well as result in the adoption of leading-edge approaches to the physical rebuilding of a community. The COVID-19 pandemic also generated some innovations. For example, throughout the world, including in Canada, when normal traffic patterns were disrupted by the policies implemented to manage the outbreak, active transportation became a policy focus (Nikitas et al. 2021). Conversely, these major disruptions also allow for the possibility that more centralist, authoritarian, or reactionary forces may step in and take over in times of emergency, posing threats to local democracy.

Social-Technical Innovations for Efficiency and Conservation

Environmental or social innovations that do not disrupt existing ideological belief systems or threaten dominant political or private interests are more likely to gain traction. Examples are companies certified as B Corporations or those operating within the context of liberal-capitalist norms while reducing their environmental footprint (see Chapter 14). Social-technical approaches also fit this classification. These efforts apply technological solutions and pricing incentives to encourage energy or water conservation. They are becoming widespread and are often delivered through private-public partnerships or through green-economy approaches that can benefit business and governments that are attempting to conserve valued environmental goods and services (see Chapter 12). Another example is the development of more efficient forms of public transit with the purported benefits of reducing travel time for commuters and alleviating traffic congestion (see Chapter 12).

In sum, the most readily adopted and implemented changes directed toward sustainability are those that have some combination of certain characteristics: they are easily introduced, readily understood, and have widespread benefits; they are promoted by political champions; they have extensive networks or partners; they garner significant support from senior governments in terms of policy, resources, and funding; and/or they are implemented without major disturbances to existing dominant socio-economic and political systems and practices. However, given the state of serious global threats to sustainability, it may very well be that nothing less than holistic transformations in ideology, culture, practices, and institutions will suffice. Yet changes of such disruptive magnitude could lead to unanticipated, cascading, or undesirable outcomes for other systems. In short, this is an era of wicked problems.

WICKED PROBLEMS AND INSTITUTIONAL PRESCRIPTIONS

For those tutored in formal institutional analysis, it is tempting to search for legal and formal structural solutions, such as bestowing more legal authority and resources on local governments so that they can get on with the job of fostering healthier, more sustainable cities. To be sure, one can readily find numerous examples of how local authorities have been severely hampered by senior governments in delivering much-needed action that would advance these objectives. If municipalities had more capacity to self-govern, it would be easier to facilitate change at this level of governance. But the devolution of authority (accompanied by additional resources) is insufficient to effect the transformative changes needed. Complex, wicked social-ecological challenges are not resolvable through mere institutional tinkering or by local governments acting alone.

The concept of a wicked problem was first framed in the late 1960s by Horst W.J. Rittel and Melvin M. Webber (1972), and it was further developed in social planning by C. West Churchman (1967). Recently, the term has been widely used in the context of complex issues such as climate change, natural disasters, and pandemics. Brian W. Head and John Alford (2015, 712) suggest that wicked problems are those considered to be "complex, unpredictable, open ended, or intractable" since they are resistant to solutions. Furthermore, a wicked problem is "associated with social pluralism (multiple interests and values of stakeholders), institutional complexity (the context of interorganizational cooperation and multilevel governance), and scientific uncertainty (fragmentation and gaps in reliable knowledge)" (716). In a governing context, wicked problems tend to cross institutional and ecological boundaries. New collaborative governing models operating at different temporal and spatial scales are emerging to respond to the challenges posed by wicked problems.

Dryzek (2014, 952), like others, acknowledges that although dominant governments can be "highly problematic ... haste to institutional prescription is also problematic, threatening to short-circuit the kind of learning process necessary in the novel and complex conditions accompanying the challenge of the Anthropocene." Moreover, one cannot assume that institutional prescription will be effective without factoring in temporal and spatial considerations. Scale is important. As noted above, the transformation toward sustainability is not achievable at one level of governance. It is not possible without supportive action on a larger scale that includes polycentric, multilevel, and place-based governance (see Chapters 6, 7, and 8). As Fikret Berkes (2017, 1) explains, "Social (human) and ecological (biophysical) systems are linked by mutual feedbacks, and are interdependent and co-evolutionary." The mechanistic institutional-structural constructs that are typically associated with public administration and city government do not align with conceptual lenses that require complex, adaptive social-ecological systems thinking.

Transformative sustainability is not something that local governments were originally structured to achieve given their provenance in principles of order, stability, service delivery, and economic development.

Nevertheless, forms of urban autonomy can be achieved in a variety of ways, as noted by Harriet Bulkeley and colleagues (2018, 706): "Critically, autonomy is neither a one-dimensional property of the organisation of the state (in political, administrative or financial terms) nor an attribute that can be readily conferred on a particular territory or form of society; rather, autonomy is a multifaceted political project, achieved relationally and as such subject to political change." Going beyond the formal powers of city authorities, urban autonomy might be most helpfully conceptualized in terms of operating within a system of collaborative governance where other actors and factors figure into the mix. Bulkeley and colleagues suggest that this collaboration should include non-governmental actors, take into account social processes, and involve city decision makers working together to create new political spaces. They note that "inevitably autonomy, as a political project, must involve significant challenges of addressing social and environmental justice, both internally and in relation to wider global concerns" (717).

CONCLUSION: LOCAL GOVERNMENT IN TRANSITION

> *New forms of civic leadership are emerging in cities across the country – leadership that emphasizes longer-term holistic community visions, multi-sectoral collaboration, and civic engagement. Under this evolving reality, urban and community change is reframed as an iterative process of learning-by-doing through experimentation, reflection, and innovation.*
>
> – Bradford and Baldwin 2018, 19

A transformation toward sustainability and the low-carbon future that is needed to avoid serious climate change impacts can be instigated at many scales and levels of governance and in various forums. Some analysts refer to transition experiments. Daniel

Rosenbloom and colleagues (2018, 370) define such experiments as "deliberate interventions that explicitly test a novel configuration of social and technical elements (e.g., new partnerships of actors, emerging practices and technologies, and novel applications) that could lead to substantial low-carbon change in energy systems." They argue that these types of experiments foster social learning about change among actors to "improve and scale up possible responses to climate change" and to build capacity among innovators while reducing risk during the process and promoting citizen engagement and education (371).

Although these experiments can take place at different scales, the temporal and spatial context in which they occur will affect outcome – a fact that underlines the important role of local governance. In contrast to the higher orders of governance, the local scale is where public participation appears to be most robust and where there is a history of local civic engagement in areas such as urban planning and renewal (Guay and Hamel 2014, 167). Neighbourhoods are where the costs and benefits of a policy decision might be most immediately visible (167). Fires, floods, environmental contamination, poverty, and social injustice are most directly felt where people live their daily lives.

It is also at this scale that initiatives can be more readily introduced and attempted. Along with transition experiments, another emerging practice is the "urban living lab," which is frequently included in the toolbox of the people working toward sustainability transitions. An urban living lab has been defined as "a local place for innovative solutions that aims to solve urban challenges and contribute to long-term sustainability by actively and openly co-constructing solutions with citizens and other stakeholders" (Chronéer, Ståhlbröst, and Habibipour 2019, 60). The broader term "living labs" often refers to initiatives that foster innovation through the collaborative development and application of new ICTs in order to create smart cities. For the purposes of this book, the term "urban living labs" refers to initiatives built on a sustainable model of governance and focused on social-technical, long-term sustainable solutions that are "bounded to

a place where local issues in the urban area can be experimented with while contributing to global challenges" (60). These urban living labs are springing up in cities around the world, including in Canada.

Local politics is an integral component in these urban sustainability experiments or labs. Capacity and political will constitute key ingredients in any transitional efforts. It is in this context that the importance of a place-focused politics comes to the fore, nurturing social and civic learning and democracy. Patsy Healey (2018, 65) argues that place matters to people and that civic discussions about valued places can create "a public value" within a community of citizens. In the process of considering how a place should be perceived and interacted with, people enter into discussions, seek common ground, and learn what it is to be part of a political community. As Healey concludes,

> Whether a place-focused politics develops around a neighbourhood or a city or a region or a wider territory which gets called up through political processes of recognition, it thus needs to be continually challenged to pay attention to its wider relations as well as its internal dynamics. The civil sphere of a place-focused political community thus interacts with and needs to be infused by membership of other political communities and civil spheres, including at the scale of a national political community. As many now argue, vigorous debate within multiple, overlapping civil spheres can make a difference by mobilising knowledge about these relations and dynamics, rights and responsibilities, in all kinds of dimensions, opening possibilities and honing political programmes and specific actions by energetic critique. (76)

The possibilities are there. It is important to be cognizant of the immensity of the social-ecological problems that we are collectively facing. At the same time, however, we must consider the ways that it is possible to move forward. And in this critical task, local governments have an important part to play, notwithstanding the many barriers along the way. Local governments were founded on notions of order and stability, service delivery, efficiency, public well-being, prosperity, and democracy. These goals still form the bases of their mandates, but today the ongoing subject of keen debate is how best to define and operationalize these goals in a way that helps to sustain communities and the systems on which they depend into the future.

NOTES

1 Zoning is a planning tool used to partition land in order to separate incompatible land uses.
2 Entropy refers to the dissipated, irreversible flow of energy – the second law of thermodynamics.
3 In this book, "environment" is used to refer to interconnected social and biophysical systems.

2 The Historical Legacy
The Evolution of Canadian Local Government

INTRODUCTION: THROUGH TIME AND SPACE

Canadian local governments' social and environmental legacies emerged from a unique set of circumstances related to the country's colonial past, frontier-resource economy, diverse social and physical geographies, and settlement patterns. The evolving human and physical landscapes of Canadian communities rode on waves of shifting ideological perspectives and public notions of time and space. In the early centuries of colonization and settlement, Indigenous peoples were pushed to the margins, abused, and exploited – a story largely untold in history books until very recently. The insatiable search for resources powered the westward journeys of European explorers through rivers, trails, and ultimately, railways. Colonists followed, with trading posts and small settlements becoming towns arranged along convenient transportation routes. Uneven patterns of development and diverse social-ecological settings contributed to disparate municipal governing approaches. Investigations into the historical formation of local political institutions and cities help to explain the opportunities and constraints facing municipalities today.

The art of living sustainably has been inextricably tied to our spatial and temporal perspectives. The use of a "time-space" (Harvey 1989) lens to frame this chapter serves to illustrate how the unconscious adoption of the dominant assumptions of the liberal nation-state can influence the pursuit of sustainable cities.[1] Unless we consciously choose otherwise, our lives will beat in time to the rhythms of an industrial, global economy. On a daily basis, we move through and interact with physical, imagined, and virtual spaces that have been shaped by complex socio-political, economic, and ecological forces at various scales. Perceptions of time and space are social constructs embedded within public ideologies about how we can best govern ourselves. This chapter's historical exploration of local governing institutions is situated within a broader acknowledgment of evolving societal notions of time and space.

It has been suggested that in Canada's early history, liberal notions of time, or "industrial, linear, 'clock' time," facilitated the efficient capitalization of the country's natural resources (McEachern 2005, 274). The adoption of new transportation and communications innovations supported a national plan aimed at stitching together vast expanses of territory. Geographic historian Cole Harris (2008, 314) speaks of these innovations as "years of rapid time-space compression associated with turnpike roads, canals, and by the 1830s, railways." Harris's use of this concept of "time-space compression," a term attributed to British geographer David Harvey (1989), aptly captures Canadian political history. Increased speed and the reduced cost of overland transportation facilitated the development of national, provincial, and territorial economies and bureaucracies. In the process, Harris (2008, 315) notes, "The state was moving from a system of indirect rule (through local intermediaries) to direct rule (through state officials) and, increasingly, to national standards."

Canada was formed as a federal state under what was known as the British North America Act (later renamed the Constitution Act 1867), which was passed by the British Parliament. This legislation assigned equal but different powers to a national government and to subnational provincial governments. Local governments were not given legislative authority. Mutually reinforcing national and provincial objectives and Canada's open, resource-based economy set the stage for centralizing political and economic forces – a process that has continued apace to this day. These state policy objectives frequently superseded many ambitions that local governments might have had regarding the determination of their own goals and their own temporal and spatial boundaries.

What is the appropriate scale of a political organization? Much depends on the ultimate objectives of people and their governments. As political theorist Warren Magnusson (2009, 109) has observed, if the dominant political approach is to set the scale in alignment with the goals of the modern liberal-capitalist state, those operating outside "the metric of the state" could be at a decided disadvantage when it comes to policy decisions, programs, and the distribution of state resources. The most striking examples might include small, rural, and First Nations communities. Despite such challenges, local initiatives can – and do – take place outside the dominant trends established by the nation-state or global economy. History has frequently demonstrated that temporal and spatial assumptions related to the consideration of both physical and political scales have generated dynamic and unpredictable outcomes. As Magnusson suggests,

> To speak of politics is to invoke the domain of human possibility: a world of judgment, choice and action. The premise of politics is uncertainty: an uncertainty that provokes differing judgments and leads to courses of action that have indeterminate outcomes. Although there are always efforts to impose a fixed scale on politics, the scale of the political can never be fully determined in advance. (116)

SEVEN-GENERATIONS DECISION MAKING

> We the Original Peoples of this land know the Creator put us here.
> The Creator gave us laws that govern all our relationships to live in harmony with nature and mankind.
> The Laws of the Creator defined our rights and responsibilities.
> The Creator gave us our spiritual beliefs, our languages, our culture, and a place on Mother Earth, which provides us with all our needs.
> We have maintained our Freedom, our Languages, and our Traditions from time immemorial.
>
> – Assembly of First Nations n.d.

Long before Europeans colonized North America, First Nations, Inuit, and Dene peoples populated the land and set up well-established forms of government founded on concepts of kinship or territorially based groups (Cassidy and Bish 1989). Several million Indigenous people formed social and trading networks throughout the continent. Many of the Indigenous peoples were nomadic, although some, such as the Haudenosaunee (or Iroquois), were farmers. The Haudenosaunee Confederacy (n.d.) espoused a philosophy that was founded on principles of long-term sustainability and the protection of future generations:

> An essential value which forms the foundation for much of the Haudenosaunee ways is the duty of preparing for the *seventh generation*. The nations of the Haudenosaunee believe that we borrow the earth from our children's children and it is our duty to protect it and the culture for future generations. All decisions made now are made with the future generations, who will inherit the earth, in mind. (Emphasis added)

Cam McEachern (2005, 276) points out that First Nations "openness to relate to time in the context of many conditions, not just sequential events, fits into a different metaphysical and epistemological world view, one which entertains a more unified view of people, animals, and the rest of nature than the Western European tradition has nurtured." The governing traditions of First Nations have rested on an ethic of noninterference, which has a very specific meaning to Indigenous peoples. This ethic respects a person's independence and personal freedom and discourages coercion. It helps to ensure a group's survival and is important in maintaining community harmony (Aboriginal Justice Implementation Commission 1999).

Dorothy Larkman, an elder of the Matachewan First Nation, explains this holistic belief system, noting that the ethic of noninterference extends to human interactions with the biophysical world. This ethic is based on traditions of respect for the natural environment and stewardship of all the creatures that exist within it (see Box 2.1).

In contrast to the First Peoples' belief system, the colonizing governments brought with them a notion of noninterference that meant establishing a system of government that privileged land ownership and private property. Given the differences between these world views and associated governing systems, the treaties introduced by the Europeans had no meaning to Indigenous peoples, who held the understanding that land could be neither owned nor given away. Historically, Indigenous patterns of living and governing were adapted to the surrounding natural environment. Human beings were seen as only one element of an integrated biophysical world where other species were to be respected and accommodated in harmony with the natural environment (MacDowell 2012, 17, 19–20). As anthropologist Wade Davis (2009, 217–18) notes with respect to the subjects of climate change and unsustainable economic systems,

These voices matter because they can still be heard to remind us that there are indeed alternatives, other ways of orienting human beings and social, spiritual, and ecological space. This is not to suggest naively that we abandon everything and attempt to mimic the way of non-industrial societies, or that any culture be asked to forfeit its right to draw from the genius of technology ... By their very existence, the diverse cultures of the world bear witness to the folly of those who say that we cannot change, as we all know we must, the fundamental manner in which we inhabit this planet.

Today, in recognition of their unique status, Indigenous governments possess distinct sets of political arrangements and powers within the Canadian state. Many governing arrangements require types of legislation and agreements that are different from the more limiting forms of municipal government. First Nations, Inuit, and Métis are three distinct Indigenous groups with collective rights who hold Aboriginal title to certain lands and resources, guaranteed under Section 35 of the 1982 Constitution Act. Indigenous governance has its own challenges that are different from those of non-Indigenous communities. Several

---

BOX 2.1   The ethic of noninterference

As shared by Dorothy Larkman (pers. comm., October 30, 2019), an elder of the Matachewan First Nation,

The Indigenous worldview that creation in its entirety has life and should therefore be given the high degree of respect afforded any individual. The "undesirable behavior" of interfering in life's individual freedom can have serious consequences. An example of this could be seen as global warming. Following the Indigenous ethic of non-interference can be seen in requesting life in order for one to acquire what one needs to survive, i.e., offering tobacco prior to hunting, identifying need and requesting an animal come to give its life for survival of another's life. If the person making the request is unsuccessful in acquiring food, the individual must self-reflect on any incursions it may have made that has upset the balance of life and make right any identified wrongs. This relates to the need to ensure that one is taking into account seven generations to come.

legal, cultural, and socio-economic characteristics distinguish the governance of an Indigenous community from that of municipalities. They are not local governments, but as Davis notes, the traditional knowledge that they have shared, and continue to share, provides relevant lessons for those engaged with charting a more sustainable path forward.

Despite constitutional acknowledgment of Aboriginal rights, royal commissions, and many notable contributions by Indigenous people themselves,[2] they continue to suffer from serious, harmful forms of overt and systemic discrimination. As a result, the individual and collective health and well-being of Indigenous peoples have been undermined, resulting in much higher rates of morbidity and mortality than the national average. They are also experiencing the adverse intergenerational impacts of egregious policies directed at the extirpation of Indigenous cultures. One such policy was the introduction of an abusive residential school system, aided by the Sixties Scoop, which removed children from their parents and communities (Truth and Reconciliation Commission of Canada 2015). Thousands of these children were abused and neglected in the schools, and many of them died and were buried in unmarked graves (Truth and Reconciliation Commission of Canada 2016). These facts have only recently been recognized by Canadian institutions, which are shaped by Western liberal ideologies.

SPACE AND FRONTIER ECONOMICS

European settlement efforts in Canada stretch back approximately 1,000 years to the Norse settlement at L'Anse aux Meadows in Newfoundland. In 1492, explorer John Cabot arrived on the province of Newfoundland and Labrador's east coast in what is now one of North America's oldest cities: St. John's. In claiming the land for King Henry VII of England, Cabot ignored the prior claims and rights of the First Peoples, who had inhabited the continent for thousands of years. In the 1500s, French and British authorities governed early local colonial settlements. Their imperialist ambition for North America was to exploit abundant natural resources for their economic benefit. Soon after arrival, Europeans benefited from Indigenous

people's extensive knowledge of the environment, hunting and fishing grounds, trading routes, and wilderness survival skills. Nevertheless, Indigenous peoples and their traditions, for the most part, were swept aside or violently quashed in the quest of the colonial powers to conquer and settle the territory. The once thriving Indigenous populations, decimated by old world diseases, were forcibly separated from their traditional territories and restricted to small tracts of land known as reserves (MacDowell 2012, 29). They were pushed to the peripheries and spatially segregated as European settlements spread farther west (76).

After the British took control of the Canadas from the French in 1763, the Court of the Quarter Sessions governed British North American settlements until the mid-1800s. Local property owners provided advice on matters of local concern. Classical liberal notions of property ownership and political entitlement were firmly cemented into the foundations of local government from its very inception. These notions of property ownership extended to the practice of slavery, which was not abolished in British North America until 1834, leaving a legacy that continues to inhibit progress toward a just and equitable society. Other brutal and dehumanizing practices persisted, with the result that targeted groups of people were banned from fully participating in local political life.

The political and economic elites of the eighteenth and nineteenth centuries tended to interpret democracy as a form of undesirable mob rule that would lead to economically unsound choices. British authorities rejected several attempts to achieve some local autonomy. Many ordinary citizens, in what was a predominantly rural society, also viewed the notion of local government with considerable suspicion. Farmers, in particular, often regarded local government as a vehicle for the economic elites to raise taxes for their own projects – an assumption that was not far off the mark.

Pockets of people attempted "home rule." Some of the 80,000 New England Loyalists – people loyal to the British Crown who fled north to Canada during the American Revolution (1775–83) – were able to inject some democratic spirit (within narrowly defined, specific groups) by bringing with them the idea of the New England town hall meeting. For the most part, however, progress toward municipal reform was slow. Where it did occur, the so-called local democracy of that era excluded many, including women (unless they were unmarried property owners), those without substantial property, First Nations, African Canadians, and various other racialized groups.

Over time, certain male property-owning settlers gained a measure of independence. In 1785, Canada saw the establishment of its first municipality: Saint John, New Brunswick. The *Report on the Affairs of British North America* (1839), presented by John George Lambton, 1st Earl of Durham, promoted the formation of municipalities. The Durham Report has been regarded by a number of historians as "the charter of Canadian democracy and self-government" (McCready 1929, 168). The ensuing political stability also maintained the existing dominant economic order by providing the British with raw resources (Isin 1992, 156).

The 1840 Act of Union formed the Province of Canada. In Ontario, the Municipal Corporations Act of 1849, also known as the Baldwin Act, provided for a comprehensive institutional system of local government. Named after political reformer Robert Baldwin, who agitated for democratic responsible government, the Baldwin Act established a two-tier system of municipal government. The upper tiers of local government were known as counties, and the lower tiers were comprised of cities, towns, villages, and townships. Local councils had authority to pass bylaws and to raise taxes. This piece of legislation provided a legal framework that continues to shape municipalities today (see Z. Taylor 2019). In 1867, Canada became a federation, with Ottawa as the national capital.

In the unsettled western provinces, municipal-style government did not arrive until the late 1880s because the scattered population inhabited only remote pockets of land. The Hudson's Bay Company and the Canadian Pacific Railway were dominant corporate forces that shaped early settlement and development patterns. The northern territories, located in a remote geographical setting, were given a different type of administrative structure to accommodate their unique political, economic, and social needs.

Like Clockwork

> *The city was like a watch; wheels within wheels. The factories were the great wheel; industry the mainspring: the Council, the balance heel; and the Board of Trade, the hair-spring.*
>
> – Description of Berlin, Ontario (early Kitchener), in W.V. Uttley, *A History of Kitchener, Ontario* (1937), cited in Bloomfield 1987, 24

By the turn of the twentieth century, eastern North American cities had industrialized, and their rapid development was frequently praised by the elites, who drew on analogies to machines and clockworks. Workers, citizens, and managers were cogs in a giant wheel that powered the engine of prosperity. In the United States, Henry Ford first set up his automobile company in 1903 and within ten years was cranking out automobiles using a new efficient system: the assembly line. Years later, social reformers adopted the term "Fordism" to represent the dark side of the alienating industrial working environment that occupied the lives of so many urban residents. Industrial-efficiency expert Frederick W. Taylor (1915) applied "scientific" methods to factory workers in order to improve productivity, giving birth to the term "scientific management." The social problems associated with the machine age were effectively captured in Charlie Chaplin's satiric 1936 silent film *Modern Times*.

Despite this social commentary, mechanization had become a metaphor for progress – industrial, social, economic, and political. In his article "Time, Work-Discipline, and Industrial Capitalism," Edward Palmer Thompson (1967, 90) observed how industrial capitalism had reshaped values associated with time, such that "in mature capitalist society, all time must be consumed, marketed, put to use." These imperatives overpowered the societal values and ways of being in rural and traditional societies, whose time might have been measured according to the rhythms of daylight, seasons, and the land. Caught up in rapid industrialization and factory automation, North American cities saw the remodelling of the social, political, and ecological landscape. Waves of immigrants arrived from other countries, and migrants from the countryside flooded into the cities to seek work. Urban growth could be disorderly, with pigs, cattle, and goats roaming the streets of the industrializing cities of Toronto and Montreal, where they supplemented the household food supply of the working class (MacDowell 2012, 83). During this era, a flourishing economy fuelled the notion that the application of technology, science, and business principles to human problems would lead to a good life for all. The professionalization of the sciences and public administration, coupled with public demands to deal with burgeoning health, safety, and environmental concerns, stimulated the growth of government regulation, public policy, and administration.

URBAN REFORM

Early local government was largely focused on maintaining social order and public safety. Services such as sewers, fire protection, waste removal, and policing were established primarily to protect private property and to deal with emergencies caused by devastating epidemics, fires, and mob violence. Poorer citizens often had to rely on the patronage of wealthy and powerful individuals who controlled city politics. In the closing decades of the nineteenth century, middle-class citizens agitated for reform in reaction to political corruption, unreliable government services, and urban decay. The urban reform movement was accompanied by some social assistance, housing, and improved health conditions for the poor.

Situated at the heart of the city dynamic were the members of a business community who served as active volunteers in local politics, education, and public works. Numerous community benefits would not have been achieved without the initiatives of local business associations. Notions of community development were linked to economic prosperity and liberal democracy. Largely unconsidered, however, were all the interests and problems that fell outside of the priorities of the dominating elites. As a result, the early days of urban development saw adverse health impacts due to poverty, social inequality, poor living conditions, and the environmental degradation caused by the emissions of smokestacks, poisonous wastewaters,

and the garbage that accumulated alongside residential housing. Women played an important role in the local politics of the day by shaping community standards and setting priorities. Yet the activities and concerns of women were seen as private, apolitical matters associated with the well-being of the family. In contrast, the concerns of men were public matters considered worthy of recording and made their way into historical accounts.

Urban reformers purported to establish apolitical, neutral systems of government and administration. Whatever the stated goal, their efforts helped to ensure that governments were responsive to the interests of one immensely powerful lobby group – the comfortable middle and upper class, which usually included a sizable number of local businessmen. The members of this community of interest could hardly be considered neutral in their aspirations for their cities. Early city policy and planning reflected the "progressive" business and technical mood of the day, including beliefs about the importance of efficient scientific planning and zoning. Zoning was adopted as a planning tool used to partition land in order to separate incompatible land uses and to foster the planning of parks, boulevards, tree planting, civic centres, and transportation routes. The zoning of land was undertaken in the name of the broader public interest. Whether members of the wider city populous had any role in helping to determine the shape and form of their cities is a question that was seldom, if ever, asked. This approach to governance also emphasized the need to develop the aesthetic beauty of a city in order to draw people to the community. Land developers, businessmen, and homeowners, whose shared views dominated municipal councils, reinforced the value placed on private property. Municipalities accelerated land development through policies that provided incentives for businesses and industry to locate in the city.

The general urban population also gained benefits from zoning decisions that included marked improvements in the provision of public spaces and gardens. Notable examples include Mount Royal Park in Montreal, designed by the renowned landscape architect Frederick Law Olmsted, the Garrison Reserve in Toronto, Stanley Park in Vancouver, and Point

Pleasant Park in Halifax. As Laurel Sefton MacDowell (2012, 90) notes, these parks were to be seen both as the "lungs of the city" and as something that would be accessible to everyone. Moreover, "confronted with filthy, smoky, and gloomy cities, reformers, poets, and social observers began to idealize country living" (91) – quite a different perspective from the view of European settlers that wilderness was a threat to be tamed and dominated.

The early political commitment to urban parks was reinforced by the establishment of administrative structures like the Toronto Committee of Public Works and Gardens in 1860 and by Canada's first election of a Board of Parks commissioner in Vancouver in 1888 (MacDowell 2012, 92). Notwithstanding the provision of some public spaces, the zoning used to separate land uses deemed incompatible also encouraged the ongoing segregation of groups of people into varying types of spatially separated enclaves – leading to neighbourhoods that ranged from the wealthy and influential to the economically, politically, and environmentally impoverished. Systemic and overt discrimination against racialized, ethnic, or specific religious groups was built into the social and political customs of the dominant elites (see Box 2.2).

EARLY PLANNING, CONSERVATION, AND PUBLIC HEALTH

Local governments have always relied heavily on property taxes to raise the revenue needed for the provision of services. Given this fiscal reality and the dominance of liberal capitalism, the priorities of municipalities have historically been directed more toward economic development than toward policy areas such as environmental conservation. The tempo of urban development has not been attuned to the rhythms of the organic world and its imperatives. Nevertheless, even a century ago, a few early radical planners, such as Thomas Adams, recognized that

> **BOX 2.2 Discrimination in Canada**
>
> Canada has a history of discrimination against various ethnic, racialized, religious, and other groups. One widely known example is the experience of businessperson Viola Desmond, an African Nova Scotian. Desmond was fined twenty-six dollars for a minor tax infraction in 1946 because she sat down in the main floor section of a New Glasgow movie theatre without paying the difference in price of one cent, an "amusement tax." Instead, she was supposed to have taken a seat in the balcony section, which was reserved for nonwhite people (Bingham 2013). The real reason for the fine, accompanied by a night in prison, was racial discrimination, as the box office had refused to sell her a main floor ticket despite her willingness to pay for one. Desmond appealed her conviction all the way to the Supreme Court of Nova Scotia. Although she ultimately lost the appeal, her actions inspired other African Nova Scotians and served as a touchstone for the Canadian civil rights movement. She is now featured on Canada's ten-dollar bill (Canadian Museum for Human Rights 2018).

planning should incorporate the goal of fostering a healthy social, living, and natural environment.

The goal of conservation was not entirely ignored by the governing bodies of the day. The Commission of Conservation was established as an advisory body to the Government of Canada in 1909. The commission's committee on public health linked conservation and urban planning. It invited British planning pioneer Thomas Adams to be the advisor on town planning in 1914 (Artibise and Stelter 1995). The roots of the city-planning profession in Canada can be traced to the commission's work (Gerecke 1977, 151). The province of Saskatchewan, created in 1905, was known for its advanced approaches to public health, and its progressive public policies provided an example to the commission. Its public health legislation required municipalities to provide all their plans for improvement or sewage construction to a new Commission of Public Health.

In 1910, the Commission of Conservation held a public health conference, where federal and provincial officials met with Dr. Charles Hodgetts, the commission's medical advisor. Hodgetts focused particularly on cities' contaminated water, which was associated with diseases like typhoid (Rutty and Sullivan 2010, 2.7). At this time, the Canadian Public Health Association was formed to address serious public health problems caused by events like the First World War and the devastating Influenza Pandemic of 1918–19; its cause is often referred to as the Spanish flu because it was first widely reported in Spain (2.19–2.20). With the arrival of the COVID-19 pandemic in 2020, lessons from history – including those derived from the 1918–19 pandemic – became much more salient for contemporary policy agendas.

In 1935, the research committee of the League for Social Reconstruction produced a proposal for social planning in Canada and for the creation of a National Planning Commission. The league was concerned that capitalism was the cause of "many urban ills," including "land speculation, insufficient housing, premature subdivision of land, inadequate parks and public buildings, shack towns and housing policy only for the well off" (Gerecke 1977, 159–60). Even though the proposal did not change the direction of professional planning, it heavily influenced the formation of the Co-operative Commonwealth Federation (now the New Democratic Party) and, in particular, oriented its members toward the importance of good housing standards for all (160). Discussions about the appropriate role of planning had to compete with more immediate concerns generated by the Depression and, later, by the Second World War. In the postwar period, housing developments became a top priority, and the profession of community planning once again began to pick up steam. In Ontario, the Department of Planning and Development was established, and 1946 saw the introduction of the province's Planning Act as well as its Conservation Authorities Act.

By the mid-twentieth century, the Depression and the Second World War had made it abundantly clear that individual enterprise and ingenuity were not going to solve the major social and economic challenges of the times. Governments became active in building the national and provincial economies and in providing social and health services. The growth of the welfare state shifted public attention to more senior levels of government, leaving municipalities with ever-diminished authority. Economies of scale and standardization were concepts that garnered favour with provincial ministries or departments of municipal affairs, which assumed more control over local governments. Authority for planning and education became increasingly centralized and rationalized. However, while these measures were being enacted, the responsibilities of local governments also expanded concomitant with burgeoning urban growth and diversifying public demands.

THE RISE OF ACTIVISM

The contours of political space are not fixed: we produce new political spaces through our own political activities. We scale politics to our purposes.

– Magnusson 2009, 106

By the 1960s and '70s, densely populated urban areas had sprung up beside the Great Lakes, stimulated by the postwar baby boom. Heavy industrial growth was accompanied by significant water, land, and air pollution. Industrial and municipal waste systems piped nonbiodegradable detergents into the lakes, threatening human health, aquatic life, and other ecological systems. During this era, the population boom led to a huge wave of property redevelopment in city centres and expanded suburban growth. Critics questioned municipal decision-making processes that promoted large real estate projects in the name of progress – decisions that came at the cost of dismantling older, small neighbourhoods. Before the massive property redevelopments, inner-city areas were not vacant but instead often consisted of old ethnic neighbourhoods, recently arrived immigrants, and new Canadians, as well as many lower-income people.

These decades were also known as a time of intense social activism. The rapid growth of communications and mass media facilitated the spread of a social movement throughout North America that was focused on human rights, environmental degradation, and poverty. Political activism was scaled up to the national and international levels and scaled down to grassroots community actions and protests. University student activism left an important environmental and social legacy that endures to this day. A lack of action on the government front stimulated the emergence of environmental groups such as Pollution Probe (see Box 2.3).

Citizen groups challenged the disruptive techniques of various urban developers and the lack of attention to alleviating the housing and health problems of the urban working class. It was becoming clear that citizens expected to be able to participate politically beyond the ballot box when decisions directly affected their interests. Community or neighbourhood associations formed throughout Canada. They rarely possessed any formal political authority, however, because they lacked financial resources, voting powers, and information about local decision-making processes and did not fit well within the decision-making hierarchy of local governments. Outside the operations of the municipal institutions, however, political debate in the larger cities tended to coalesce around two competing groups of interests: pro-development advocates versus populist activists fighting to protect the interests of city residents, the working class, and/or the inner-city poor. Local groups won some high-profile disputes, but many more neighbourhoods were lost. City governments were dominated by pro-development ideology and practice (Lorimer 1972; Sewell 1972).

As the inner-city debates carried on, sprawling suburban development also generated heated discussions. Rapid greenfield development fuelled the demand for extensive, expensive infrastructure and services, leading to other political debates about the proper allocation of resources between the urban core and its peripheries. Critics of suburban development ranged from those who wished to prevent the adverse impacts of unbridled development on rural and natural areas to those wishing to protect the vitality of the city cores. Large commercial projects on city peripheries contributed to the erosion of city centres. Shopping centres, box stores, and ultimately, power centres gobbled up land, resources, and retail dollars.

Assertions of property rights, the need for revenues, and rising housing demands continued to fuel outward pressures for growth. Many demands on local governments were related to land use, but others began to coalesce around social and health issues. At the same time, councils were hampered by diminished provincial grants and limited authority. Local governments began to rely more heavily on user-pay practices – fees, licences, and permits – in order to make up for revenue shortfalls.

GOVERNING FOR EFFICIENCY

Over the course of the twentieth century, municipalities experienced many changes in form and substance. The franchise had been broadened to include all adult Canadian citizens, with few restrictions. Many universal services were provided for the benefit of residents. However, the ability of citizens to participate effectively in local politics was still constrained by

---

BOX 2.3 Pollution Probe

In the 1960s, concerns about the impact of industrial growth, waste, and pollution led to the rise of environmental activism. A lack of action on the government front stimulated academics and students at the University of Toronto to organize into a protest group known as Pollution Probe (n.d.-b). This citizen group's public efforts, which targeted consumers, industry, and government habits, led to some very tangible results. The group's ability to achieve public awareness, aided by scientific evidence, allowed its members to be influential on a number of fronts, such as by testifying before the International Joint Commission set up by the United States and Canada under the Boundary Waters Treaty of 1909 and by contributing to the passage of both the Canadian Water Act of 1970 and the Great Lakes Water Quality Act of 1972 (Holden 2011; Forkey 2012, 97–98; C. Doberstein 2013; Bradford 2016; Francis 2016; Bradford and Baldwin 2018; Frantzeskaki et al. 2018). Many decades later, Pollution Probe has grown into a well-established public interest group that addresses a wide range of environmental issues while partnering with and lobbying different organizations and agencies. It identifies as "a leading agent of change at the intersection of communities, health and environment" (Pollution Probe n.d.-a).

economic, legal, social, and ideological forces. Local social agencies, neighbourhoods, and marginalized groups had limited resources with which to advance their causes. Perceived deficiencies in the policy and administration of public services, along with growing child poverty, inequality, and environmental problems, left many city residents skeptical about governments' ability to respond to public needs.

Squeezed for financial resources, municipalities relied on the private sector for alternative ways to deliver services. Narratives associated with economic liberalism dominated governing discourse even more forcefully in the 1980s and '90s than in the past. In some provinces, government responses to economic pressures, coupled with a conservative ideology, led to sweeping consolidations and to the amalgamation of cities. The largest of these came to be known as Megacity Toronto. This new city, comprised of 2.4 million people, was incorporated on January 1, 1998. The members of Citizens for Local Democracy (C4LD), many of whom were veterans of 1970s activism, had unsuccessfully fought a grassroots crusade against the proposed merger. Nevertheless, by the end of the twentieth century, public participation had become a central theme in politics. Speaking of the times, B. Guy Peters (1996, 47) stated, "This is clearly an age in which government finds it difficult to legitimate its actions without active public involvement."

By the turn of the twenty-first century, city councils – traditionally responsible for "hard" services – found themselves contending with crumbling infrastructure, waste management sites nearing capacity, and numerous environmental problems. In addition, they were confronted with the local impacts of an overwhelming range of unanticipated events related to global climate change, disruptive technologies, growing social inequality, and resource scarcity.

CITIES IN A GLOBAL ERA

In today's integrated, economic world, some may be skeptical that local governments and other political actors are capable of effectively fostering a democratic and sustainable community. Political scientist Caroline Andrew (1997, 147–48) has observed that economic globalization has strengthened the influence of the private sector at the expense of local actors,

but that said, the results are not necessarily predetermined: "Progressive local action is not easy or obvious, but it is not precluded by the working out of globalization." Warren Magnusson (2009, 113) also considers the impact of global forces on how the modern polity is shaped: "We seek to scale ourselves as well as others to the metric of an imagined modernity, a metric that demands that we 'live large' in a now globalized economy, participate in a globalized culture, and become good citizens of a state within a system of states." He suggests that it is possible to orient oneself to a different scale of living, one that has its own "internal vitality" (113). In fact, as discussed below and elsewhere in this book, there are people who have done just that.

Local activist groups are diversifying their agendas and gathering support from broad-based community movements. These grassroots groups often call for the decentralization of economic and political decision making and for rescaling politics to make way for sustainable localities, a process often referred to as "relocalization" or "degrowth." The seeds of these movements, sown in the activist years of the 1960s and '70s, started to take root in the 1990s. George Francis (2016, 143–44) has noted that these communities of interest, or "aspirational communities," associate themselves with a variety of labels and adjectives, including "biosphere, blue green, compassionate, creative, equal, fire smart, forest, green, healthy, human rights, inclusive, intelligent, learning, livable, resilient, safe, smart growth, strength, sustainable, transition, vibrant, and youth-friendly." Many of these communities of interest have overlapping goals with somewhat different emphases.

In 2005, the movement for more inclusive and collaborative local governing processes toward sustainability received tangible support in the form of the Federal Government Gas Tax Fund, which would support environmentally sustainable municipal projects. It was stipulated that municipalities would create Integrated Community Sustainability Plans (ICSPs). These long-term plans, formulated in consultation with community groups, would cover the environmental, social, cultural, and economic aspects of sustainability. The plans were to be approved by city councils and would commonly go through six stages:

(1) define the goals and establish the structure of the process; (2) gather input to create a long-term sustainability vision for the community; (3) describe the current realities and analyse them within the lens of the established sustainability vision; (4) develop a strategy, and identify and assign responsibilities; (5) [ask] city council formally to approve the ICS plan; and (6) implement, monitor, and review progress. (Stuart et al. 2016, 222)

The ICSPs encouraged collaborative approaches to sustainability planning in a number of cities throughout the country, leading to ongoing community-supported sustainability initiatives that receive varying degrees of emphasis on city websites. The initiatives that emerged from the collaborative planning processes are often linked to community climate action plans that have also complemented federal and provincial goals. In British Columbia, for example, the provincial government's Green Communities Committee formed a partnership with local representatives of the Union of BC Municipalities and the Fraser Basin Council. This partnership led the province to develop the BC Climate Action Toolkit in order to help local governments reduce greenhouse gas emissions and to support them in adopting an integrated approach to community planning for sustainability (Government of British Columbia n.d.-a, n.d.-b).

Inclusive, comprehensive community plans designed to respond to the circumstances of municipalities adhere in many ways to criteria delineated by sustainability scholars. However, they can become unwieldy instruments when local governments attempt to implement new policies. As one analysis reports:

Creating plans has benefitted local governments: it has enabled fiscal transfers to provide needed infrastructure, ensured compliance with regulatory regimes or kept cities in line with their competitors. In the long run, however, having to manage large numbers of plans creates coordination and implementation challenges. A planner ... noted, "There are various agencies each with their own jurisdiction and somehow everything must be tied together into a coherent whole." Rather than making planners' work easier, having more plans in place complicates implementation. (N. Hall, Grant, and Habib 2017, 255) (see Box 2.4)

Along with the practical concerns of integration, coordination, and the prioritization of issues come some more fundamental philosophical and ethical considerations. Tanya Markvart (2015, 171), in an assessment of ICSPs, states that the dominant perception of sustainability in local governments "conforms with the prevailing capitalist model of economic growth and development." Markvart contrasts the prevailing Cartesian-Newtonian mechanistic view of the world with that of the integrated and ecological complex

---

BOX 2.4 Proliferating urban plans

In a cautionary article that discusses the proliferation of plans in Canadian municipalities, Nathan Hall, Jill L. Grant, and Muhammad Ahsanul Habib (2017, 244) provide the following list, albeit possibly incomplete:

Regional plan, municipal plan, official plan, community plan, integrated community sustainability plan, growth plan, infrastructure plan, capital investment plan, transportation plan, transit plan, transit node plan, active transportation plan, cycling plan, pedestrian plan, sidewalk plan, heritage plan, cultural plan, youth equity strategy, seniors strategy, poverty reduction strategy, immigration plan, newcomers strategy, open-space plan, green plan, environmentally sensitive area plan, parks plan, urban forest plans, recreation plan, physical activity plan, climate change adaptation plan, energy plan, waste management plan, watershed plan, urban design strategy, economic development strategy, workforce development plan, downtown plan, housing plans, homelessness reduction strategy, structure plan, functional plan, secondary plan, neighborhood plan, strong neighborhoods strategy, district plan, emergency management plans, hazard plan, fire risk plans, flood management plan, vision plan, waterfront plan, regulating plan, plot plan.

systems perspective required for long-term sustainability (20). Shifting to an actual ecological approach to planning will require a transformative approach to local institutional learning.

CONCLUSION: FAST CITIES, SLOW CITIES

Long before colonization, the land now called Canada was inhabited by a thriving civilization with its own political, economic, and cultural traditions that were strongly associated with the land. These First Peoples and their ways of life were swept aside by colonial settlement, railways, roads, infrastructure, and industrialized cities. The introduction of local governments was meant to provide order and services, but these bodies were constrained by the legal and constitutional authority of both the federal government and the provinces and territories. In many ways – if not most – this remains the case today, as discussed in the next chapter. The rapid influx of migrants into ill-equipped cities generated health, social, and environmental issues that stimulated calls for urban reform, which was to be informed by notions of efficiency and scientific management. As Harold A. Innis (1951, 140), once noted, "Industrialism implies technology and the cutting of time into precise fragments suited to the needs of the engineer and the accountant." Stimulated by the enlargement of the welfare state, the growth of mass media, and increased access to higher education, social movements concerned with human rights and the environment emerged across the world in the last half of the twentieth century. Members of the interested public began to lobby for more inclusion in local decision-making processes. Now, in the twenty-first century, social and economic inequality and serious ecological concerns have underlined the need for transformative social and institutional change. The application of technological innovations is redesigning the built and natural environments. The fast pace of today's cities does not align well with the inclusive, integrated decision making and policy implementation that are required for long-term urban sustainability.

Society no longer beats in time with the rhythms of the land or even with the dictates of twentieth-century clockworks. Human interactions are now shaped by digital communications tapped out in bits and bytes and shared virtually and instantaneously.

Many social and economic communications are compressed into a small number of characters capable of being globally disseminated. In the process, both time use and its value also become increasingly compressed.

Liberal notions of time, communications, and technology facilitated the growth of the nation-state, centralization, and globalization – as well as the mobility of capital, information, and affluent individuals – in real and virtual spaces. As noted above, "time-space compression" (attributed to David Harvey 1989) refers to the compression of time through the liberal economic activity that drives globalization. The interconnectivity of cities is driving rapid changes that local governments are left to address despite lacking the fiscal and legal authority to respond to challenges, many of which exist at a global scale. The speed of the global economy and the disruptive impact of new technologies privilege certain types of decision making and structures over others. Certainly, it is worth considering the long-term impacts of such rapid change on the sustainability of desired social-ecological environments, as McEachern (2005, 278) has astutely observed:

> Good, liberal use of time means efficient use of resources, not only within a time span but in anticipation of our own future times, disregarding needs of future people – who are non-existent individuals ... Liberal time can be exposed as a concept that has mattered in our environmental relations just as much as space and materials and the rest of our culture. It has made a difference in our environmental history.

By their very nature, so-called fast cities might be defined as those that adapt most readily to these technological developments and to the dynamics associated with globalization. Some might also argue that these fast cities are able to harness information technology in order to foster more livable, creative, and smart cities. Such cities would have integrated transit and infrastructure systems and automated monitoring of energy, water, and material consumption. Functional, technical approaches are being embraced in many ways as governments search for green economic solutions that can generate wealth and conserve energy or other resources while presenting new business opportunities. One example is the once-proposed plan (now cancelled) by Sidewalk Labs, a branch of Alphabet, to redevelop Toronto's Quayside district as a smart community (see Box 10.3). Fast-city initiatives can come at the cost of social equity, privacy rights, and the social-ecological sustainability of desired systems.

In contrast, slow cities have been conceived in reaction to the frenetic speed at which change is taking place. Strongly associated with the slow food movement, slow cities emphasize the value of old traditions, heritage, and a slower pace of community life. They draw on the benefits associated with cultural traditions rooted in agrarian practices that follow the cadences of the land. At the same time, the illiberal elements of these old traditions can also result in an unwillingness to embrace new and innovative approaches to solving problems and to fostering social-ecological diversity.

Local decision makers frequently attempt to embrace both the slow and fast paradigms; they might introduce policies to encourage cultural celebrations and traditions of the past while nevertheless facilitating the development of livable, densely packed, fast-paced, digitized cities. Advocates of a combination of the fast and slow approaches to urban governance may see this alternative as the optimal way to achieve sustainability. Local decision makers, however, diverge considerably in the ways that they define sustainability, in the policy areas that they choose to emphasize, in the trade-offs made, and in the means used to achieve their goals.

Over the history of Canadian local government, the industrialization of cities, the introduction of new technologies, and competing social, economic, and political forces have altered societal conceptions of time and space. In the process, events, decisions, and actions have taken shape within the context of an increasingly interdependent set of governing arrangements, limiting the ability of local governments to plan their communities – each of which displays unique local responses to the dynamic and complex social-ecological systems that characterize the twenty-first century.

NOTES

1 Among the many well-known geography, social, or political theorists who consider questions of time and space are Torsten Hägerstrand, Henri Lefebvre, David Harvey, Anthony Giddens, and Canadian Harold A. Innis.

2 Readers are encouraged to read extensively from a rich and diverse literature by Indigenous scholars and communities that offers understandings of Indigenous knowledge systems and ways of supporting reconciliation.

3 Federalism and Multi-level Governance
Intergovernmental Relations

INTRODUCTION: GOVERNING DIVERSE COMMUNITIES

> Canada: "a railway in search of a country" –
> one where "the ties that bind are creosoted and
> six feet long."
>
> – Eric Nicol, humour columnist, depicting the
> disparate and vast territory that the founders
> of a new country needed to unite and settle in
> some tangible way (cited in Black 1975, 228)

In the 1880s, the leaders of the new Canadian federation built an intercontinental railway across the country, connecting towns and villages. It was a key element of an economic strategy aimed at building the manufacturing base (located primarily in the central industrial heartland) and at encouraging western expansion and settlement through immigration. Political expediency also invited a federal solution to accommodate the notable distinction between the French-speaking and the English-speaking populations.

A century ago, over half of Canada's 9 million inhabitants resided in rural areas spread out across immense expanses of wilderness (Statistics Canada 1951). Today, the northern territories of Nunavut, the Northwest Territories, and Yukon, which account for 39.3 percent of Canada's land mass, still contain only a little over 100,000 people, with more than half living in the territorial capitals. The provinces' northern regions are also sparsely populated. A large majority of Canada's almost 40 million people are clustered in the southernmost part of the country.

Two key factors have shaped Canadian local government. One is the enormous (and varied) social, cultural, and physical environments where municipalities are situated. The other is the Canadian federal system of government – a pragmatic political compromise devised to stitch together a vast territory populated by peoples holding diverse, often competing, interests and cultural and linguistic traditions. As Edwin R. Black (1975, 149) once stated in his book about divided political loyalties, "Confederation was a compromise that embraced not simply different geo-economic communities and separate political entities, but two distinctive cultures [i.e., French and English] rooted in historical enmities, antagonistic religions and different tongues." Until the British assumed control in 1763, a mostly French-speaking rural population inhabited Quebec, a former French colony. The Roman Catholic Church dominated political and social life. After the 1763 Treaty of Paris ended the contest between France and Great Britain for control of North America, a proclamation established new political and administrative structures. In 1969, Canada officially became a bilingual country, reflecting the dominance of the two original colonizing countries of France and England. Today, approximately one-fifth of the Canadian population speaks French. Outside of Quebec, there are also communities with sizable French-speaking populations, most notably in Ontario, Manitoba, and New Brunswick.

As for other linguistic groups, colonial governments employed policies that focused on extirpating

Indigenous languages, particularly through the residential school system. In the northern territories and elsewhere, efforts are now being made to sustain these traditional languages. Today, in Nunavut, Inuktut is recognized as an official language. As the Government of Nunavut (n.d.) states, "Our territorial language laws clearly affirm that Inuit in our territory have an inherent right to the use of Inuktut, in full equality with other official languages." The Northwest Territories (2022, 2) also officially recognizes French, English, and nine Indigenous languages, all of which may be used in the territorial legislature or in territorial courts. In local settings "where there is a significant demand for services from a region or community in one of the other Official Languages, members of the public also have a right to receive service in that language" (2). In Yukon, the public can use English, French, or a Yukon Indigenous language in the legislature.

Over its history, Canada has become increasingly multicultural. Almost 13 percent of the population now speak predominantly another language, and one in four people has a mother tongue other than English or French. This percentage has been growing over time, although more than 90 percent of Canadians speak either English or French on a regular basis (Statistics Canada 2022b).

Canada's economy was first powered by natural resources. Today, natural resources (the primary sector) are still an important part of the economy. So, too, are its manufacturing base (the secondary sector), its services industry (the tertiary sector), and its growing information and communications technology (ICT) industry (the quaternary sector). This diverse economic makeup is reflected in the demographic characteristics of local communities. Consider, for example, the remote resource-based communities, such as the pulp and paper town of La Tuque, situated in north-central Quebec. The city comprises a little more than 11,000 people but stretches over an area of 24,809 square kilometres. In contrast, North America's fourth most populous city, Toronto, was inhabited by approximately 2.8 million residents in 2021. Toronto, also referred to as a "world city" – with its large manufacturing, service, and technology industries – is nested within Metropolitan Toronto, which contains over 6.2 million residents living within 5,902.75 square

kilometres. In turn, Metropolitan Toronto is located in the Greater Golden Horseshoe, a densely inhabited, highly urbanized region of Canada with well over one-quarter of the Canadian population – approximately 10 million people.

Obviously, scale and location are important considerations with respect to questions of governing for sustainability. These factors are also germane to any discussion about political boundaries and jurisdictional authority. The tremendous physical, economic, political, and cultural variety of municipalities necessitates specific governing arrangements appropriate to their unique contexts. In Canada, constitutional authority is divided between one national and ten provincial governments. The national government has devolved some authority to the territorial governments. There are many overlapping responsibilities between these orders of government. Toward the end of the twentieth century, First Nations acquired certain rights of self-government under the 1982 Canadian Constitution. In Canada's parliamentary system, local governments have no independent constitutional (or legislative) authority.

In the twenty-first century, the concept *of multi-level governance* emerged to recognize that political influence extends far beyond formal institutional governing arrangements. Multi-level governance acknowledges that complex vertical and horizontal networks extending from the local to the global facilitate engagements between political actors, including those in the civil, nongovernmental, and private sectors. This chapter discusses the formal institutions of federalism that have been used to manage intergovernmental relations. It also explores the emergence of the multi-level governance model, which recognizes the influence of a wider diversity of political actors.

FEDERALISM

Confederation marked the start of Canadian federalism. The main goals of the union were to pave the way for economic growth, territorial expansion and national defence. However, many people wanted to keep existing governments and boundaries. There were various reasons for this. French Canadians held a strong majority in

> *Quebec. They did not want to place all powers in the hands of a central government in which they would be a minority. There was also a strong sense of identity in Nova Scotia and New Brunswick. Federalism was therefore a compromise for many.*
>
> – Stevenson 2006

Canada has a parliamentary, federal system of government. Formal authority is shared by two orders of government: the national (or federal) government and the ten provincial and three territorial governments. Jurisdictional powers between the federal and provincial orders of government are enumerated under Sections 91 and 92 of the Constitution Act. Constitutional powers are divided between the Canadian federal and provincial governments, with the latter having jurisdiction over local institutions, whereas the territories are under the ultimate legislative authority of the federal government. Indigenous peoples' governments, sometimes referred to as a third order of government, have distinct sets of legal and institutional arrangements that reflect their unique status in Canada.

Today, even though over 80 percent of Canada's population lives in medium or large cities, provincial and territorial governments have the constitutional authority to pass legislation regarding municipal affairs. As a result, cities are run by municipal governments that often lack the fiscal resources and legal authority necessary to meet the multiple demands and needs of their citizens. Some provincial governments have responded by revising pieces of legislation with the putative goal of giving municipalities the ability to make some limited decisions autonomously and to form partnerships. Some concessions have also been made in terms of taxation or granting programs, but the provinces retain strong overriding authority in many areas of local affairs. For its part, the federal government has relinquished some limited authority to the territories through a process called devolution. Overall, federal-provincial wrangling – a feature of politics throughout Canadian history – has left little negotiating room for municipal governments. Under a narrow interpretation of the formal written Con-

stitution, municipalities would have no rights of self-government. Provincial governments have often (but not always) applied this restrictive interpretation to define the responsibilities and boundaries of local governments (Z. Taylor 2019, 312). It is worth observing that provincial governments themselves do not favour this static historical interpretation of the Constitution when it comes to advancing their own jurisdictional authority.

Local governments are important political, social, and economic institutions with their own customs and practices that have evolved over time. The Constitution, with its division of powers, was written under governing conditions that do not reflect the contemporary challenges of modern society. Moreover, a focus on formal constitutional authority fails to recognize a well-known strand of thought in Canada's institutional makeup: that of cooperative federalism. This concept refers to numerous intergovernmental arrangements and agreements introduced to facilitate functional cooperation. Almost half a century ago, Black (1975) made a gentle plea for recognition of the value of flexibility and pragmatic collaboration between governments, with the Constitution seen as a living document that responds to changing dynamics. He argued that Canada's long history of formal and informal intergovernmental cooperation fostered functional working arrangements for programs offered by different orders of government. This type of administrative federalism, Black suggested, could strengthen both orders of government, thereby allowing them to achieve policy goals through joint action that neither could accomplish on its own and facilitating greater intergovernmental harmony. There are, of course, the inevitable trade-offs, as criticisms of this approach include questions of accountability and the diffusion of political responsibility (115).

Morton Grodzins, a scholar of federalism, introduced the "multiple-crack" thesis, which suggests that American federalism permits numerous interest groups, including local governments, to gain political access at various points so that they might influence the legislative/administrative system (Grodzins and Elazar 1984, 275). This thesis has also been considered in the Canadian context, where the federal system makes it possible for various policy communities to influence federal or provincial political agendas at different points (Rocher and M. Smith 2002, 3). Certainly, this case can be made in the context of climate change policy in both countries, where the federal governments, the Canadian provinces (and territories), and the American states have taken differing positions and actions on the issue.

The multiple-crack thesis might be "how the light gets in" (à la singer-songwriter Leonard Cohen's famous song "Anthem") in terms of both innovative policy making and the diffusion of ideas between jurisdictions, including local governments. Nevertheless, it can also inhibit or paralyze policy change through multiple veto points. As Eugénie Brouillet (2011, 607) observes, "The essence of federalism is a delicate exercise in the fair weighting of opposing forces. The flexibility offered by the federative principle makes it possible to imagine a panoply of legal arrangements more or less centralized or decentralized in response to the social, political, historical and cultural realities of the groups involved." This perspective on federalism is relevant today, as the diversity of actors in policy communities is increasing, socio-cultural, economic, and biophysical landscapes are radically changing, and governing responsibilities are becoming increasingly entangled. As a result, a more flexible, adaptive approach is required when interpreting the Constitution.

National and provincial legislation, regulations, and policies shape political dynamics between orders of government and between municipalities. It is misleading, however, to portray municipalities as passive recipients of exogenous political policies and processes. Municipalities take many decisions that have a much larger impact on the health and well-being of their cities than might be assumed given their formal jurisdictional authority. Local governments have often demonstrated more initiative than some senior governments when introducing strategies to deal with important issues. They are active players in global, national, and regional arenas. That said, external forces operating at many scales, from global imperatives to regional disputes over watershed-based issues, require a collaborative, strategic form of governance. Therefore, the ability of local governments to achieve their agendas depends a great deal on how well they can navigate intergovernmental efforts and collaborative partnerships.

Christopher Leo (2006) has coined the term "deep federalism," extending federalism's historical focus on federal-provincial institutional relationships to include urban regions and communities. He explores how truly national policies can be devised that take into "account the very significant differences among regions and communities" (483). Leo notes that communities have their own sets of resources and capacities as well as locational realities. For this reason, he stresses that it is important for these communities to have the authority, flexibility, and capacity to design their own economic strategies. Leo points out that in the "borderless world" characterizing this era of globalization, urban regions have become economic engines that require "a different set of governance arrangements" suited to a city's specific circumstances (490). This view contrasts with the historically understood notion of federalism, under which local governments have no role in structural/institutional understandings (490). Leo acknowledges that more thought must be given to "appropriate degrees of both federal oversight and community input" (503). Deep federalism, then, extends a flexible notion of federal-provincial relations that accommodates differences among regions to include local governments and civil society. This deepened understanding of Canadian federalism and multi-level governance in policy processes offers a useful and necessary framework if the desired outcome is sustainable social and ecological systems in local communities.

James Salzman and J.B. Ruhl (2010, 66) argue that the best way forward in response to contemporary challenges such as climate change and urban sprawl might be to embrace a form of "Dynamic Federalism." They advocate the more adaptive strategy of "whittling away" at complex, interconnected policy problems. This conception of federalism embraces jurisdictional redundancy and overlap by enabling government "to track" and respond to environmental issues across scales (105). This approach "allows governance adaptation to transpire more quickly and with less political jockeying than static, exclusive jurisdiction models" (105). It also embraces cooperation among interagency networks that have been established over time through meetings and through informal communications and practices, making the structure of "overlapping authorities" an evolving "organism" (108). As Harriet Bulkeley and colleagues (2018, 705) observe, "There is a growing recognition that to regard political organisation as a 'nested system' is to miss the critical ways in which political order and authority have been reconfigured across and within scales."

A related concept, introduced by Neil Bradford (2020, 2), is "place-based federalism." His work has identified, and helps to fill, a notable gap in the institutional literature by recognizing an important twenty-first-century reality: place matters, meaning that local communities have an important role to play in addressing the major social and ecological issues of our time. As Bradford asserts, "Economic, social, environmental, and health issues – once seen as the exclusive domain of national and provincial or state governments – find localized expression, requiring customized interventions that blend central resources with community knowledge and networks" (3). Chapter 8 returns to this discussion of place-based politics.

INTERGOVERNMENTAL RELATIONS

Federal-Local Relations

> *There is a growing awareness that today's major public policy challenges converge most profoundly in cities.*
>
> – Bradford 2018, 5

The federal government's role in local governance is not as obvious and direct as its role in provincial governance under Section 92 of the Canadian Constitution. Nevertheless, the federal government deeply influences local sustainability through its policies, trade and environmental decisions, program funding, taxation, regulations, and various tripartite agreements. Provincial governments, also in need of revenue, are more likely to tolerate federal intrusion into their jurisdictions when federal spending will help to finance costly urban projects (Stoney and Graham 2009, 375). In addition, as urban centres continue their rapid growth, municipal issues spill over into areas of

national jurisdictional concern and vice versa. Policy areas that may cross provincial and territorial boundaries include infrastructure, immigration, air and water quality, food, international trade, emergency measures, transportation, energy, and communications.

In 2015, the federal Liberal government introduced many large initiatives that Bradford (2018) refers to as an "implicit" national urban agenda. International organizations, including the United Nations Human Settlements Programme and the Organisation for Economic Co-operation and Development, have advocated the establishment of national urban agendas, signalling recognition that centralized resources and intergovernmental collaborations are required to address complex problems (6). Given the constitutional reality that municipalities fall under provincial jurisdiction, the federal government adopted more of a sector-specific approach that sidesteps an explicit intervention in provincial areas of authority.

The federal government has introduced programs that directly transfer federal funds to municipalities. Examples include the Green Municipal Fund, the Municipalities for Climate Innovation Program, the Municipal Asset Management Program, and the National Housing Strategy, the latter of which is discussed below. In the 2019 federal budget, additional money was allocated through the federal Gas Tax Fund (GTF) to address short-term infrastructure priorities in municipalities and First Nations communities (Infrastructure Canada 2019a). In March 2021, to aid economic recovery from the COVID-19 pandemic, the federal government renamed the GTF, calling it the Canada Community-Building Fund, which was accompanied by an additional increase in funding (Federation of Canadian Municipalities 2021). The GTF has been an ongoing source of revenue since 2005 and is earmarked for local infrastructure projects. Rural broadband was also singled out for funding support in order to connect rural and remote communities, the aim being to provide Canadians with universal Internet access (Department of Finance Canada 2019). In November 2022, the federal government allocated $1.6 billion to further shore up communities' resilience and infrastructure in the face of climate change as detailed in *Canada's National*

Adaptation Strategy: Building Resilient Communities and a Strong Economy (Environment and Climate Change Canada 2022a).

The federal government has also invested in a national collaborative food policy that, among other things, promotes food security in Canadian communities. The initiative includes a Local Food Infrastructure Fund and a Northern Isolated Communities Fund (Agriculture and Agri-Food Canada 2019). Other programs indirectly provide communities with funds through agreements between the provinces and territories, such as an integrated grey, green, and social infrastructure plan delivered through the Canada Investment Bank (Department of Finance Canada 2017). One of the earliest and best-known examples of an initiative to undertake federal activities in municipal affairs is the federal government's housing policy, which is overseen by the Canada Mortgage and Housing Corporation (CMHC). Throughout Canadian history, these initiatives and many others have been facilitated by delicate negotiations between the federal and provincial governments. The latter want funding assistance but are wary of federal intrusion on their jurisdictional powers (W. Kennedy, pers. comm., July 31, 2020).

Canada Mortgage and Housing Corporation

The CMHC came into operation in 1946 to promote the building of much-needed housing stock and to administer the National Housing Act of 1938. Housing construction has often been used to stimulate the economy, as was the case in postwar Canada. The primary goal of the CMHC was to increase the availability of low-cost housing through various types of financial assistance and incentives. The CMHC expanded gradually into other areas of urban renewal and neighbourhood improvement. Into the 1980s, it played a huge role in assisting with the building of new homes. Yet the initiative did not come without social or environmental costs. Leo (1995, 31) notes that the activities of the CMHC, combined with the regulatory and planning activities of provinces and municipalities, contributed considerably to suburban development and a planning regime that encouraged low-density planning and the use of the automobile at the expense of public transit. Today, the building

of new suburbs remains a common sight, as areas that were once wilderness or farmland continue to see greenfield development despite the current attempts of many urban planners to contain suburban sprawl and to encourage inner-city densification.

By the mid-1980s, the era of fiscal restraint, retrenchment, and privatization had taken its toll on government corporations. The CMHC's focus was narrowed primarily to low-income families and to nonprofit housing and housing rehabilitation. In the early 2000s, the federal government did engage in tri-level cooperation with an affordable housing program. In 2017, following a national strategy of public consultation, the Liberal federal government launched its National Housing Strategy, with a focus on human rights. With 1.7 million people lacking core housing, the ten-year, $40 billion strategy was announced to "help reduce homelessness and improve the availability and quality of housing for Canadians in need," as well as to "promote diverse communities and encourage the construction of homes that are sustainable, accessible, mixed-income, mixed-use, and located near transit, work, and public services," with 25 percent of the funds earmarked for projects directed at women, girls, and their families (CMHC 2017). The initiative was welcomed by many housing advocates. Critics raised a number of issues, including the plan to parcel funds out over a decade rather than making them immediately available, the strategy's repackaging of existing programs, and fears that middle- and lower-income workers would still be unable to afford housing in Canada's largest cities (e.g., see Press 2017; Coyne 2017; and Kalinowski 2017).

Parts of the housing strategy include the Canada Housing Benefit and the Federal Community Housing Initiative, both of which are jointly funded through an approach that relies on multi-level, collaborative-governance partnerships with the provinces and territories. During the COVID-19 pandemic, affordable housing shortages and rising housing prices continued to escalate. People who could not afford housing in Canada's metropolitan areas moved far afield to smaller municipalities, with the cascading effects being felt by those local economies and communities. Housing shortages stimulated further federal funding commitments. Many of these policy initiatives that directly affect municipalities have been facilitated by the Federation of Canadian Municipalities.

Federation of Canadian Municipalities

Municipalities have long recognized the need for a federal voice. The Federation of Canadian Municipalities (FCM) was formed in 1937 in an initiative to achieve unemployment relief from the federal government during the Depression. Its roots were planted in earlier national meetings of municipalities, one of which concerned a fight for more control over the activities of local utilities (Federation of Canadian Municipalities n.d.-a). Since its formation, the FCM has acted as a lobbyist for various municipal interests while working to connect municipalities, communicate important concerns, serve as a forum on issues that affect municipalities, and provide various programs.

The FCM's more than 2,000 members range from small rural communities to the largest urban centres and include twenty provincial and territorial associations. Together, they account for over 92 percent of the Canadian population (Federation of Canadian Municipalities n.d.-a). The organization represents municipalities in all areas of federal jurisdiction. It also tackles international and global issues related to trade negotiations. Given that the provinces hold constitutional jurisdiction over local government, it can be a challenge for a national organization to act on behalf of all members when municipalities have different interests. More recently, with the formation of the Big City Mayors' Caucus, the FCM has taken steps to ensure that the interests of large urban centres are recognized. These cities, which represent the bulk of the Canadian population, argue that they lack fiscal and political authority commensurate with their size. For their part, the smaller rural and northern communities also contribute significantly to the Canadian economy, society, and polity. As a result, within the FCM, forums have been created to address the specific issues of diverse municipalities.

The wide-ranging work of the FCM has extended to virtually all policy areas that might affect municipalities, including international affairs with respect to the impacts of climate change negotiations on municipalities, municipal-Indigenous relations, environmental issues, housing, infrastructure, urban strategies, and taxation. It should be noted that although the FCM is a national lobbying voice for municipalities, the provincial municipal associations are also active advocates of local governments.

Provincial-Local Relations

Few countries in the world have senior levels of government that have been so reluctant to loosen restraints and regulations from local governments, which have no formal protection under the Canadian constitution.

– A. Smith and Spicer 2018, 931

In Canada, legislation specifies the functions to be performed by local governments through provincial municipal acts. Municipalities are also governed by provincial planning acts, land-use acts, and legislation, regulations, and policies that directly affect them in areas such as transportation, environment, housing, health, education, and energy. Local governments vary in structure between and within provinces. They can be organized in one or two tiers. Two-tier governments consist of upper-tier metropolitan, regional, or district governments that provide services across a large geographic area and lower-tier municipalities within the region that deliver more local services. To address unique local circumstances, provincial governments have also created a variety of other public entities, including cities, towns, and villages as well as water boards, school boards, and others.

Creatures of the Province and Local Autonomy

Local governments are frequently referred to as "creatures of the province." It is a common refrain – one applied to them because of their lack of constitutional status, legislative authority, and fiscal resources. This appellation may be convenient for provincial governments wishing to override municipal authority. But it can also be reasonably viewed as a "legal and political fiction" (Good 2019). Rather, Canada's federation might best be understood in the context of possessing a living Constitution. As society evolves, so does the meaning of the Constitution – expanding and growing to reflect changing realities. As Kristin R. Good (2019) argues, "By creating municipalities, Canadian provinces establish local political institutions, delegate responsibilities, divide decision-making power and create systems of accountability to local citizens. They *constitute* a new level of government."

Provinces have used tools like incorporation, annexation, amalgamation, and dissolution to rearrange municipal governance in order to accomplish various provincial and local policy goals or to accommodate demographic changes. Approaches to the provincial imposition of policies on local governments vary between provinces and elected administrations. Ontario, Quebec, and Nova Scotia implemented the mandatory amalgamation of municipalities in the 1990s. In British Columbia, in contrast, under 2003 legislation known as the Community Charter, the province has been prohibited from forcing amalgamations on municipalities against their will. Alison Smith and Zachary Spicer (2018, 935–36) define local autonomy in Canada as "the ability to develop and implement policies at the local level, free from provincial institutional constraints." Using this definition, they have developed an index to assess the relative autonomy of the governments of the ten largest cities across the country. They conclude that all of the big Canadian cities have relatively low levels of autonomy from the provincial governments. Given the country's political and geographic diversity and its federal institutional composition, it is not surprising to discover that there are some variations. Vancouver, for example, has relatively more autonomy than its counterparts in other regions (949).

Over the past few decades, some provinces have implemented legislation, including community charters, that permit local governments more flexibility by giving them some spheres of authority where they might operate independently. The degree to which community charters support enhanced municipal autonomy might warrant skepticism. Cities must still conform to the rules of provincial municipal acts. In areas where there is no prohibiting legislation, provincial governments have been known to override municipal decisions, with the justification that the interests of the whole province must be considered.

One can highlight examples of provincial governments overriding municipal policies throughout the country. Ontario, particularly in recent years, offers the most striking instances of provincial actions that have undermined local democracy and autonomy. In 2017, the Ontario Liberal government overrode the City of Toronto's stated intention to introduce tolls on roads leading into the city. In 2018, Ontario's newly elected Progressive Conservative government imposed a forced council amalgamation on the City of Toronto, reducing the number of ward council seats from forty-four to twenty-five, a measure that was met with vociferous opposition both in the city and across the country, including from other municipal governments. The provincial government continued to wield a heavy legislative hand in other areas. It has used a tool known as a minister's zoning order to override local and regional plans on development activities, even in situations that may affect environmentally sensitive lands. In 2022, the same government passed the More Homes for Everyone Act, legislation that disregards local planning processes and limits time for public consultation and environmental assessments. Penalties were imposed on municipalities for their failure to pass development decisions within 120 days. That year, Ontario also passed the Strong Mayors, Building Homes Act, which authorizes the mayors of Toronto and Ottawa to override council insofar as the goal is consistent with the provincial agenda of building homes. These strong mayor powers would be extended to other municipalities in the months to come.

In addition, the provincial government passed the More Homes Built Faster Act in 2022. With the aim of streamlining approval processes in order to address the housing crisis and to build 1.5 million more houses in the next ten years, this legislation stripped municipalities and Conservation Authorities of many abilities to plan and protect the environment. Furthermore, the legislation freezes or reduces fees for building houses or exempts developers from paying these fees altogether. These exemptions amount to billions of dollars that municipalities can no longer use to pay for other services and to provide infrastructure. The loss of these revenues requires municipalities to raise money elsewhere or to cut services. Their choices are limited; property taxes are one of the few options. The Association of Municipalities Ontario (2022, 3) has said that the changes could leave municipalities short of revenues amounting to over $5 billion, shifting costs from developers to taxpayers. It also stated that the legislation strips municipalities of the ability to manage housing responsibly in an environmentally sound way. It raised concerns about the liveability of Ontario's communities and about the serious risks to the environment and human health "at a time when the impacts of climate change are evident and urgent" (3).

The government also reversed its pledge not to touch the protected Greenbelt in Ontario's Greater Golden Horseshoe. In November 2022, it proposed to remove 2,995 hectares from the Greenbelt (to be replaced with land from elsewhere). The Greenbelt Act of 2005 had been put in place to permanently protect farmland, communities, forests, wetlands and watersheds, and cultural heritage. Despite the fact that the Greenbelt was supposed to be protected under this legislation, it was reported that a number of developers had recently purchased land in the areas of the Greenbelt that the provincial administration planned to open up for housing development (Jones and Brockband 2022). Grassroots protests took place across Ontario. Reports by the provincial auditor general and the integrity commissioner looking into the issue found many irregularities in the provincial decision-making processes. The auditor general noted that the process was biased in favour of developers. In the fall of 2023, the Ontario government once again reversed its decision and said that it would not allow development on the Greenbelt after all. Subsequently, the Royal Canadian Mounted Police launched an investigation into the affair (Canadian Press 2023).

In late 2022, the provincial administration had also introduced the Better Municipal Governance Act, which allows the mayors of Toronto and Ottawa to pass bylaws with the approval of only one-third of council as long as the bylaws align with provincial priorities – a power that was soon extended to other municipalities. The provincial government also gave itself the power to appoint regional heads of government, who had previously been chosen by voters or by their elected representatives, and to appoint provincial facilitators to assess other regions.

This is only a brief and incomplete outline of the numerous steps taken to strip decision-making authority from local governing bodies. Widespread dismay and alarm concerning democracy, conservation, and overall good governance have been voiced by former mayors, other governments, and many other communities of interest (Crombie et al. 2022). Moreover, in the haste to push through the governing regime's priorities, local planning processes were thrown into chaos.

The need for affordable housing is undisputable. The imposition of chaos, however, has never been considered an efficient or effective tool for tackling serious issues, such as a housing crisis.

Local government processes are complex and often frustrating, but they can be improved through considered consultation and collaboration. The provincial approach, which favours reducing development charges or removing them from housing, will require municipalities to find the revenues elsewhere, such as through property taxes and user fees, or to decrease services (Found 2021, 2). Actions of this kind lead to unanticipated cascading negative effects on the environment, the economy, and those individuals most vulnerable. In the latter case, it would have made sense to consult those people at risk of being homeless – that is, those with lived experience – using bottom-up approaches rather than the converse. The issues vary according to their distinct political cultures and the government in power, but instances of provincial governments overriding municipal autonomy can be identified across the country.

In addition to legislative restraints, limited fiscal capacity constrains municipalities' abilities to effectively address complex social and ecological problems. In response, local governments have been undertaking partnerships with other political actors and engaging in strong lobbying efforts through their various municipal associations. It should be recognized that provincial governments do not always act as barriers to sustainable local change. Provinces and municipalities have often collaborated on initiatives – building greener infrastructures, protecting valued ecosystems, or fostering healthy built and social environments. The following chapters discuss examples of these projects, which were undertaken either in cooperation with or despite the efforts of local authorities.

Municipalities have a growing policy role in the Canadian federation. Intergovernmental reform, in a way that includes municipalities, is long overdue. Drawing on lessons from other countries, Tomas Hachard (2022, 1–2) offers four approaches to Canadian intergovernmental reform:

1. **Ensure municipalities have the capacity, voice, and structures to participate effectively in intergovernmental relations**. This can be achieved through investment in staff at the municipal level; investment in municipal associations; increased regional coordination and, ideally, new regional governance structures; and further horizontal coordination across the province among municipalities and municipal associations.
2. **Increase municipal involvement in provincial policymaking**. Potential models include a formal, institutionalized council for provincial-municipal relations, perhaps modelled on South Africa's extended cabinet; a set of intergovernmental councils focused on priority policy issues, supported by dedicated secretariats, and co-governed by the province and municipalities; or enforceable provincial requirements to consult municipalities on matters that affect them.
3. **Eliminate unfunded mandates** through, for example, provincial legislation or provincial-municipal intergovernmental agreements that require consultation on the fiscal impacts of draft legislation or regulation and that allow any disagreements to be taken to court.
4. **Strengthen trilateral relations**. Potential models include new location-specific or policy-specific [trilateral] agreements modelled on previous Urban Development Agreements; sector-specific trilateral intergovernmental councils that avoid top-down governance, meet regularly, and are supported by secretariats; or a general trilateral council, [which could be achieved] through reform of the structure of First Ministers' Meetings.

There is no shortage of considered recommendations for intergovernmental reform. Evidence suggests, however, that there is little, if any, appetite on the part of provincial governments to embrace such reforms. In fact, in 2022, governance appears to be increasingly centralized in the higher orders of government – paying short shrift to the essential role that municipalities play in providing livable cities.

Federal-Territorial Relations

The 1867 Constitution Act assigned constitutional authority over the territories to the federal government, not the provinces. In 1870, the federal government acquired the northern territories from the Hudson's Bay Company. The Indigenous peoples were primarily left to their traditional lifestyles until after the Second World War. Municipal government, applied as it was to settled areas, held no relevance to them. The Northwest Territories, although still a large area of land, has had its size reduced several times since the area was first ceded to the Crown in 1870. Manitoba, Yukon, Alberta, Saskatchewan, Quebec, Ontario, and, most recently, Nunavut have seen the extension of borders and the creation of new territories from the land that was once undifferentiated northern territory.

The responses that local governments in the territories require from senior governments are different from those required in other parts of the country. After 1960, some processes were initiated to devolve a measure of authority from the federal government to the territories. Over the decades, pressure on senior governments for increased self-governing authority and more revenue sharing has intensified throughout Canada, with arguments for the devolution of powers in the territories being bolstered by various unique factors – some cultural and others practical. Today, each territory – Yukon, Northwest Territories, and Nunavut – has its own legislative assembly and executive council and exercises "province-like powers" (Intergovernmental Affairs Canada 2022). Since the closing decades of the twentieth century, pressure for further devolution of authority from the territorial governments to local communities has accompanied the negotiation of treaties and self-government for Indigenous peoples. In addition to recognizing legal rights and cultural practices, there are also practical considerations that favour devolution, including the challenges that a centralized authority faces when attempting to govern isolated and remote communities. Given the sparse population spread over large territories and the specific geographic and diverse cultural imperatives of northern communities, they are not easily governed at a distance.

SUBSIDIARITY AND THE PRECAUTIONARY PRINCIPLE

The effective incorporation of local communities into a deeper form of federalism as envisioned by Leo (2006) and others could be facilitated by the formal or informal adoption of a principle known as subsidiarity. Subsidiarity suggests that authority and responsibility should be handed down to the smallest unit of government that can deal with the task most effectively and is formally included in European Community law. Subsidiarity also has been seen as a tenet in environmental law, an area where Europe has established itself as a global leader (van Zeben 2014). Brouillet (2011, 605) defines subsidiarity "as a principle by which the smallest possible social or political entities should have all the rights and powers they need to regulate their own affairs freely and effectively."

The principle of subsidiarity may seem to be a reasonable one for the purposes of democracy and efficiency. Yet, in practice, it does raise questions that are not readily dismissed. Scholars have noted the practical problems with disentangling the responsibilities of provincial and local governments and determining who should be responsible for what (K.A.H. Graham, Phillips, and Maslove 1998, 174). Moreover, agendas can be as readily captured by powerful local elites as they can by national ones; local democracy does not automatically follow the devolution of authority. The principle of subsidiarity may work very well in one case but not in another. Brouillet (2011, 632) also points to the possibility that "opportunistic reasoning" can be used in the courts when arguing jurisdictional questions. The application of the principle of subsidiarity might have effects that are not only decentralizing but also centralizing if it is determined that a higher order of government should intervene in the affairs of smaller units when deemed

necessary (605). Both federalism and subsidiarity are noted to be "dynamic and evolutive" concepts that require a "balance between respect for the freedom of small entities (diversity) and the need for social cohesion and state coherence (unity)" (608).

Court rulings have often had an impact on how municipal authority and jurisdiction might be interpreted (Mosonyi and Baker 2016). One decision that has some implications for municipal autonomy is *Spraytech v. Hudson* (2001), a Supreme Court of Canada case about a bylaw introduced by the City of Hudson, Quebec. On June 28, 2001, the court upheld Hudson's right to pass a bylaw that banned the cosmetic use of pesticides within municipal boundaries as long as the ban did not conflict with legislation at the provincial or federal levels. Companies that used pesticides had challenged the city's right to pass the bylaw. Many of the intervenors in the case represented environmental organizations with national scope or anti-pesticide groups in other communities (Canadian Environmental Law Association 2000). The case illustrates how local environmental groups can network with outside nongovernmental organizations, making them influential forces when dealing with other powerful actors. In this case, the environmental groups supported a local government's decision – one citing international law that emphasizes the Precautionary Principle, which upholds the right of local governments to take preventative action to stop environmental harm.[1] Jerry DeMarco (2001) also stressed the importance of this decision for local autonomy, quoting the following sections of the Supreme Court's ruling:

> The case arises in an era in which matters of governance are often examined through the lens of the principle of subsidiarity. This is the proposition that *law-making and implementation are often best achieved* at a level of government that is not only effective, but also *closest to the citizens affected* and thus most responsive to their needs, to local distinctiveness, and to population diversity ... The so-called "Brundtland Commission" recommended that "local governments [should be] empowered to exceed, but not to lower, national norms." (Para. 3, emphasis added)

A tradition of *strong local government* has become an important part of the Canadian democratic experience. This level of government usually appears more attuned to the immediate needs and concerns of the citizens. (Para. 49, emphasis added)

Over the years, the Supreme Court has made decisions that have at times centralized and at other times decentralized authority. The *Hudson* case illustrates the important function of courts in determining a municipality's relative degree of autonomy.

In a more recent case before the Superior Court of Quebec, *Gastem v. Ristigouche* (2018), the small Quebec village of Ristigouche Sud-Est also received a favourable ruling. The village had been sued by the oil and gas company Gastem for passing a municipal by-law that prevents the company from drilling within a no-drill zone located 2 kilometres away from the source of the town's drinking water. Although Gastem had secured a drilling permit from the province, the judge cited the Precautionary Principle, saying that the municipality had the right to protect its drinking water. At the time of the ruling, there was no overriding provincial law in place that defined these specific rules around water protection (Page 2018). Such principles are often discussed in the environmental literature and are even working their way into the preambles of some legislation (Tollefson 2012, 5–6).

Subsidiarity and the Precautionary Principle can offer the flexibility to resolve conflicts that frequently overlap jurisdictionally. However, in some rulings, as Brouillet (2011, 631) observes, the courts have prioritized the criterion of efficiency over other considerations. The vague nature of a principle that is not limited or well defined can contribute to a centralization of power just as readily as it can lead to decentralization (631). Moreover, the vagueness regarding such principles and how they should be interpreted and applied prevents them from being adopted in more than a discretionary way by the courts. With respect to the Precautionary Principle, Chris Tollefson (2012, 7) concludes,

When the principle is viewed as little more than "common sense," at best it provides little decisional guidance and at worst promotes uncertainty and

subjectivity. The principle must likewise respect the discretion of elected decision-makers to make judgments about the public good. Leaving aside concerns about interpretive uncertainty, courts are unlikely to adopt a principle that is perceived as fettering judicial discretion to balance competing interests.

Nevertheless, outside the formal legal system, these concepts can serve as guiding principles in decision-making arenas when considering questions of environmental management, social justice, and collaborative decision making.

CONCLUSION: MULTI-LEVEL GOVERNANCE

Globalization, urbanization, and the growing salience of the notion of *governance* rather than *government* have been identified as "tectonic shifts" requiring multi-level cooperation and reconsideration of legal-political governing models (Blank 2010, 510). Politically relevant activities do not take place only between governments. Many political actors – governments, nongovernmental organizations, the private sector, media, and members of the public operating at differing scales – notably influence public agendas. Multi-level governance has been defined by Martin Horak (2012, 339) as "a mode of policymaking that involves complex interactions among multiple levels of government and social forces." Some analysts prefer to use the term "orders" or "spheres" of government rather than "levels." Yishai Blank (2010, 524) asserts that the federal government is not a level of government *superior* to provinces; rather, under the Constitution, each of these orders of government is assigned different areas of jurisdictional authority.

Multi-level governance takes place in urban, rural, and remote areas of Canada. Horak posits that multi-level governance is particularly notable in Canada's largest cities, where complex questions go beyond the authority of the single government entity. Examples might include the provisioning of expensive infrastructure such as regional transit systems, addressing the fallout of a natural catastrophe requiring emergency management (Horak 2012, 340–44), or developing federally and provincially owned property, such as Toronto's waterfront, whose renewal is overseen by Waterfront Toronto, a corporation jointly created and funded by, and accountable to, the City of Toronto, the Province of Ontario, and the Government of Canada. Local governments' responsibilities over the years have also expanded into other areas reflecting new policy considerations (346–47). Those who are well acquainted with the politics of rural or remote regions might hasten to point out that governing disputes or collaborations can be as intricate, and potentially contentious, as those in large urban regions. One need only observe the complex jurisdictional and social-ecological questions raised by pipeline or mining development, fisheries, forestry – and the list goes on. Moreover, some rural and remote municipalities often collaborate at the regional level to share the cost of some services or facilities and to engage in regional economic development.

Multi-level governance includes informal agreements, cooperative partnerships, negotiations, and networks among policy communities. Governments require new decision-making frameworks in order to respond to the evolving needs of their constituencies, to deliver services in an effective and responsive manner, and to sustain healthy communities. Devolution of authority might be sought by those who see it as an essential element of the environmental agenda. Conversely, it could be argued that many environmental goals might be undermined by giving local agencies and interests more decision-making control. Politically influential local interest groups may be more preoccupied with defending their employment opportunities or economic interests than, for example, protecting their local wetlands. It is important to recognize, however, that it is the community's residents who are often most directly affected and who may have the most to lose if planning and development are not handled in a way that is socially or environmentally responsible. Bulkeley and colleagues (2018, 706) challenge the assumption that the quest for "urban autonomy necessarily means ceding power from the (central) state or that it would automatically entail empowering local communities." They suggest that "meaningful autonomy" might be found in various forms of collaboration and networking, among other strategies. Chapter 8 returns to this discussion of multi-level and polycentric governance.

The Canadian federation was founded on the principles of compromise and political expediency. The founders determined that dividing powers between different orders of government was the most politically acceptable way to stitch together a vast geography containing distinct political cultures. At that time, local governments were a constitutional side note, as they fell under the legislative control of provincial governments. For their part, the traditional systems of Indigenous peoples' governments were dismantled under the 1876 Indian Act. However, Indigenous peoples' rights to self-government were later affirmed in the 1982 Constitution Act.

BOX 3.1   A proposed multi-level governance model for Canada

Neil Bradford (2018, 8) proposes three models of multi-level governance, emphasizing collective action rather than top-down initiatives:

- *Federal-provincial/territorial agreements with municipal involvement:* Involves significant financial transfers negotiated between federal and provincial/territorial governments for major investments in public infrastructure. At the implementation stage, federal and provincial governments obtain municipal input on specific investments.
- *Direct federal-municipal/community programming:* Involves pan-Canadian federal programs whereby eligible municipal and/or community partners receive financial and/or technical assistance for locally identified projects that address national goals and meet federal criteria.
- *Federal-provincial-municipal policy adaptation:* Involves the three orders of government, often including community partners, working together to tackle "wicked problems" in selected urban areas exhibiting multiple signs of distress. Through seed financing, the governments establish joint action-planning tables and other mechanisms in order to adapt programs and services to local conditions.

Canada has a long history of negotiating intergovernmental relations among diverse political interests. The need to accommodate communities of interest has expanded beyond formal institutional actors with the recognition that nongovernmental actors, media, and members of the private sector all have a powerful role in influencing governing agendas. This influence goes beyond jurisdictional borders, stretching into global politics and down to local grassroots actors and citizens, where it gives rise to multi-level governance. Complex social, economic, and environmental challenges are frequently played out in urban settings. Strategies to address these challenges require multi-level collaboration (see Box 3.1).

Many studies and recommendations over the years have presented ways to strengthen local governance and autonomy. The Canadian Constitution, with its federal division of powers, did not mention local governments, except to assign responsibility for them to the provincial governments. That said, some constitutional scholars point to the concept of a living Constitution – one that takes into account the long recognition of municipalities under various pieces of legislation as constituting a level of government.

Politically, however, powerful centralizing forces within these two orders of government leave little room for local autonomy. The rise of authoritarian approaches to governance by some senior administrations runs counter to the principles of sustainability and good governance discussed in Box 1.1. For their part, local governments lack political agency as well as legal and fiscal capacity, all of which are important to the principles of sustainable good governance identified by the United Nations, among others. Nevertheless, these constraints do not preclude local governments from introducing public policies that can put them on a more sustainable path.

NOTE

1 The Precautionary Principle, also known as Principle 15 of the Rio Declaration on Environment and Development, which was adopted in 1992, declares that "where there are threats of serious or irreversible damage, lack of full scientific certainty shall not be used as a reason for postponing cost-effective measures to prevent environmental degradation" (Science Direct n.d.).

4 Governing Ourselves
Who Decides, How, and for Whom?

INTRODUCTION: FORMAL INSTITUTIONS OF LOCAL DEMOCRACY

Local governments directly affect the daily lives of people and their immediate surroundings. Their responsibilities are expanding far beyond their traditional property-related and service-provision mandates. Municipalities, however, are but one set of political actors among many. Political authority and influence are dispersed between various orders of government, a plethora of private and societal organizations, members of the community, and the media. Any quest for a healthy democratic society is necessarily one held in constant tension as people in various spheres promote their agendas. Competing priorities might include considerations of individual and group rights, economic development, revenue generation, societal needs and demands, cultural considerations, who should decide (and when and where), and biophysical sustainability. Local governments are also constrained and influenced by the complex, dynamic social and ecological systems in which they operate.

To focus only on governing institutions and their ability to influence change would be to ignore the political influence of the forces that comprise daily societal interactions and economic transactions, from the noteworthy to the mundane. As citizens move through their communities, interacting with them in myriad ways, they contribute to how these localities are governed. Nevertheless, local government remains a key member of the cast of influential political players. It is the institution that has much of the formal authority to represent the municipality as a whole. It manages local revenues and possesses decision-making authority that can shape the overall health of the community and the environment on which it depends. Therefore, a consideration of how democratic processes hold local governments publicly accountable is worthwhile.

If enough pressure and leverage are brought to bear, local institutions can be one of the more accessible political vehicles for advancing diverse public concerns and alternative views. Accomplishing this task is not easy. In the pursuit of economic wealth and environmental health, policy makers face challenges that are inherently contradictory and possibly irreconcilable. At the root of the conflict is a liberal-democratic system of values that, although founded on a philosophy of the collective interest, common property, and representative decision making, recognizes the rights of individuals to exercise certain freedoms, own property, and participate in the political process. The tension between collective interests and individual rights is particularly striking when we examine the concept of sustainable communities. North American cities have been planned around the demands of individuals and their rights related to private property. Environmental politics have been based on a philosophy of collective rights that, in market systems, have usually been subordinated to assertions of private and individual rights. In such systems, democratic politicians strive to achieve workable compromises among major interests. Local governments operate as representative democracies where citizens vote in regularly held elections to choose members of council and other local bodies to represent their interests and make decisions on their behalf.

THE ELECTORAL PROCESS

The right to elect one's government freely is considered a hallmark of even the narrowest of definitions of democracy. Earlier in Canada's history, women and members of certain ethnic, religious, and other groups were not permitted to vote. Today, the franchise is considerably more inclusive – although, as discussed below, there are still many barriers to meaningful political participation. The rules vary somewhat across Canada, but in general a voter in a municipal election is required to be a Canadian citizen, to be eighteen years of age or older, and to have lived in the city and/or province for a period of time (e.g., several months to a year). Historically, a "first past the post" municipal voting system has been used, with the candidate who gains the most votes winning the election regardless of the percentage of the votes that this candidate receives. A new system was put in place in Ontario for the October 2018 elections that allowed municipalities to adopt a ranked system, where voters could rank their top three preferences. In the ranked system, if no candidate has a majority of the votes, the candidate with the fewest votes is dropped, and their ballots are distributed to the remaining candidates until one candidate has at least 50 percent of the votes plus one. The rationale for this system is that it more democratically reflects the voters' preference and enhances the legitimacy of the outcome. In addition, it has been said to increase diversity by encouraging members of underrepresented groups to run, thereby enlarging the pool of candidates. In 2018, the first municipality in Canada to adopt the ranked system was London, Ontario. In general, the outcome of its election seemed to be a success (Pagliaro 2020). After the fall of 2020, Ontario's Progressive Conservative government forbade municipalities to choose a ranked system, requiring that they revert to or retain "first past the post" elections.

The central tenets of a representative democracy, such as the one in Canada, include accountable and responsive government. Voters choose candidates or parties that most closely reflect their policy preferences. In theory, a failure by the elected representatives to fulfill these expectations or promises may cause them to lose the next election. In practice, however, there are additional municipal variables (distinct from those affecting the other orders of government) that influence electoral outcomes. For example, Anthony Sayers and Jack Lucas (2017, 1) note that local governments are often characterized by high levels of incumbency and by low turnovers in council, with individuals quite often retaining the position of mayor or councillor for long periods of time. These factors may see representatives keep their positions through several electoral cycles. Sayers and Lucas suggest that this political stability makes it easier for the electorate to know the positions of the people running for council and to make decisions based on their past actions (2, 20). Moreover, with the exception of a few cities, municipalities often lack a party system that could give councils incentive to act as a collective by adopting a more consensual approach to decision making. Long-term stability has policy advantages, but it can also lead to policy inertia. These dynamics can be both an advantage and a disadvantage for municipalities that are striving for sustainability in an era of complexity and uncertainty. Like-minded councils may be better equipped to pursue long-term objectives and to follow through on important policy initiatives. Nevertheless, they may also be reluctant to embrace required changes or to make mid-course adaptations in response to unanticipated events in a rapidly changing environment.

In addition to voting for municipal councils and other local bodies, citizens can vote on plebiscites or referendums – a form of direct democracy in Canada that is sometimes used to gauge public support for an initiative. The results may or may not be binding, depending on the jurisdiction. They are also used municipally in conjunction with an election, but their frequency varies across the country. Plebiscites often deal with well-known contentious public issues such as adding fluoride to water, amalgamating municipalities, building large municipal facilities, and deciding on other large expenditures. The degree to which the use of plebiscites contributes to a more democratic local environment depends on the context, how they are held, how the debate is framed, and who determines the questions. A plebiscite, for example, might be a useful way to gauge public opinion about whether to invest millions of dollars in a large sports facility. More complicated decisions, however, are not easily reduced to a simple, closed question. Long-term land-use planning is such a case. In these situations, some other public consultation mechanisms would be more appropriate.

In general, on the basis of a ward system, an at-large system, or some combination of the two, local candidates for council are elected for a term that varies across the provinces and the territories, typically four years. The ward system operates with one or two councillors elected from a specific area within a city. At-large elections present all voters with the same set of councillor candidates, with those who succeed being elected to city council to represent the views of all the citizens in the city. The type of electoral system does influence the perceptions and behaviours of councils (Koop and Kraemer 2016). It can also influence the composition of councils and their representativeness. City-wide campaigning, for example, can be expensive and can favour the election of more privileged elites, whose residences may be concentrated in certain parts of the municipality. For their part, ward-based politicians may be interested primarily in advancing the interests of their own geographic areas at the expense of the broader community, with such a system possibly leading to divisive political debates. A ward-based system does not necessarily preclude privileged elites from capturing political agendas.

Municipal Elections

Can municipal electoral systems effectively promote democracy through locally elected councils and other governmental bodies? To a certain extent, the answer depends on one's ideological predispositions. Some might suggest that the system of formal, representational democracy that prevailed throughout most of Canada's history leads to the most desirable outcomes. Those who subscribe to a more inclusive form of local decision making or, more broadly, to the concept of

participatory or ecological democracy (as discussed in the next chapter) argue that democracy is best pursued through the active engagement of citizens and other communities of interest. In the latter perspective, civil society is viewed as the important centre of democratic activity. Directly or indirectly, citizens are influential participants in local governance. According to Darin Barney (2000, 14), "Democracy refers to a form of government in which citizens enjoy an equal ability to participate meaningfully in the decisions that closely affect their common lives as individuals in communities."

Such popular conceptions of democracy encompass a broader understanding of public engagement in political affairs than has been historically the case in Canada. Certainly, the ostensible opportunities for political participation have expanded considerably since the days of early municipal governments, as have the expectations of the public to be consulted on a variety of local issues. If they have the desire and capacity to do so, individual citizens can participate in local governance in many ways, such as voting for elected representatives or in a referendum or a plebiscite, running for office, lobbying council, and volunteering their time on several local boards, committees, and commissions. They can also influence political agendas indirectly by participating in various types of media, pressure groups, and social movements. Public demand for a more participatory democracy has encouraged governments to increase their legitimacy in the eyes of the public by going beyond consultation in order to engage citizens in the process of government decision making. The evolution of the Internet has expanded governments' potential to effectively include the public in policy processes if they have the political will to do so. Citizen activism and social movements also help to influence government agendas by organizing actions and communications that use social media, by mounting public protests, and by serving on government consultative bodies.

Local Party Politics

As discussed above, one of the distinguishing features of Canadian municipal governments, with a few notable exceptions, is that they are not based on a party system of representation. Canadian federal and provincial governments, in contrast, are styled after the British parliamentary model, which uses a party system, with the elected governing party seated in rows facing the party that forms the Official Opposition, thereby encouraging a more adversarial style of debate.[1] In city council chambers, seating arrangements are typically designed in a horseshoe shape, a format that can encourage consensus-style discussions.

A municipal party system has emerged in British Columbia and Quebec, two provinces whose legislation enables the formation of municipal parties (A.A. Moore 2017, 6). The most well known of these systems are in Vancouver and Montreal. The party systems in these large cities might help to address the constraints that citizens experience when trying to keep track of or interact with the various candidates due to the size of the electoral wards and the large population base of big urban centres. In these situations, it is easier for citizens to know which candidates they wish to support based on a party's electoral platform. Some advocates suggest that a civic party system imparts an element of competition and choice to local elections, which would otherwise be dominated by one group of decision makers, many of them incumbents – particularly in an at-large electoral system. Alternatively, a party system can exaggerate differences between parties (Tindal et al. 2013, 324) and lead to more adversarial politics, weakening agreement on initiatives that are introduced to serve the interests of the community as a whole. Municipal parties have historically aligned themselves with an agenda that is either pro-business and pro-development or left-progressive. In recent years, progressive parties have also increasingly positioned themselves as parties advocating for environmental protection, as was the case with Vision Vancouver (formed in 2005) and with Projet Montréal (formed in 2004). The leader of Projet Montréal, Valérie Plante, was elected as Montreal's first female mayor in the city in the 2017 municipal election and was re-elected in the fall of 2021. After the election, the new mayor quickly launched an active environmental agenda for the city and took a leadership role on climate change in the international arena. It is worth noting that even in large cities that are officially nonpartisan, voters tend to identify with representatives on a left-right political spectrum, as observed in the 2014 Toronto mayoral race (McGregor, A.A. Moore, and Stephenson 2016).

As noted above, the distinctive political dynamics found in municipalities tend to favour a more consensus-based decision-making style over the oppositional party-based systems in federal and provincial governments. Consensus-based approaches are worth pursuing in this era of ideological polarization when decision makers need to determine how to collectively address long-term concerns. As Sayers and Lucas (2017, 20) caution,

> Those wishing to engage our city councils in policy discussion should be aware of these unusual dynamics. Stability and unity suggest that long-term strategies of persuasion and an emphasis on common purpose – seeking consensus – may well be more effective than short-run attempts to dominate or divide council. Internal coalitions, where they do exist, are likely to be too unstable to provide a basis for long-term strategic behaviour.

To be sure, it can be a tricky juggling act. Today's environment requires governments to be capable of institutional learning, adaptiveness, and flexibility in a rapidly changing climate while seeking consensus and a measure of stability in order to achieve long-term sustainability (see Box 4.1).

ELECTED REPRESENTATIVES

The Mayor

In Canada, mayors are elected by popular vote and are members of their governing councils as well as the heads of their municipal corporations. Not every local government refers to its head as a mayor. The title varies according to the local structure in place. For example, a chairperson steers regional governments, whereas a reeve commonly fills this role in villages and townships. Although the general responsibilities associated with each of these positions vary somewhat, they remain essentially the same throughout the country. The primary functions of the office are to preside over council and maintain order, to act as a ceremonial leader of the community, to sign all bylaws

BOX 4.1 Consensus-based decision making

On October 20, 2018, eight of Vancouver's ten councillors were newly elected, along with a new independent mayor, Kennedy Stewart. For the previous decade, in this at-large electoral system, the council had been dominated by one party, Vision Vancouver, and its leader, Mayor Gregor Robertson. The new council included five members of the Non-Partisan Association, three members of the Green Party, and two members from two other parties.

Mayor Stewart stated that consensus-based decision making was the approach that would be implemented going forward, emphasizing the potential contributions of each councillor. As a mayor independent of a particular municipal party, he was well positioned to forge a consensus on the primary issues that he wanted to address, including homelessness, social housing, and affordable housing. He also wanted to tackle the crisis of opioid overdose by taking preventative measures, regulating a safe drug supply, and providing safe spaces (Stewart, pers. comm., May 29, 2019).

In his inaugural address, Stewart cited Peter J. Smith's (2017) distinction between a global and a globalist city. Stewart (pers. comm., May 29, 2019) wanted to see Vancouver in the latter camp, "leading the world in liveability; in social justice; in economic development; in tackling climate change; in cultural production; in fun; and in coolness." He noted that 50 percent of the ancestral roots of Vancouver's population were not officially represented on council. Concerned about that lack of diversity, he pledged that the city would reach out to these communities in order to make sure that their interests were heard and taken into account.

In October 2022, Ken Sim was elected mayor under the party banner of ABC Vancouver. This new party was formed by members of the old Non-Partisan Association, a party that has been aligned with the business community. ABC Vancouver was able to win a majority of seats on Vancouver City Council, the Vancouver Parks Board, and the Vancouver School Board. In a city where one in five residents identifies as ethnic Chinese, Sim is the first Chinese Canadian mayor.

and ensure that they are carried out, to effectively communicate information to council, the administration, citizens, other parties, and other governments, and to ensure the effective management of the corporation. In a formal institutional context, the ability of Canadian mayors to exercise authority and to make decisions may appear limited compared to the "strong mayor" approach used in some American cities. However, in 2022 and 2023, this situation changed dramatically in a number of Ontario cities when the provincial government, determined to pursue its agenda aided by like-minded mayors, used its constitutional authority over municipalities to grant these mayors more authority.

In September 2022, the Government of Ontario introduced a unique twist on the "strong mayor" model by passing the Strong Mayors, Building Homes Act. Under this legislation, the mayors of Toronto and Ottawa (with a planned expansion to other cities) have been given extensive veto powers in policy areas that align with provincial priorities. Further legislation introduced in November of that year, the Better Municipal Governance Act, enables these mayors to pass bylaws with the approval of only one-third of council. Under this legislation, substantial authority is vested in mayors over areas such as local agendas, administrative staff, budgeting, and council bylaws. Five former mayors of Toronto (who had collectively governed for over fifty years), wrote a public statement strongly opposing the legislation for being "profoundly undemocratic" and for eliminating "any meaningful role of city councillors and therefore the voice of the local residents who elect them." They noted that the legislation also positions the mayor to be the focus of powerful lobbyists and removes checks and balances that are meant to prevent power from being concentrated in the Office of the Mayor (Crombie et al. 2022). Some mayors from other Ontario cities also made statements opposing the move.

Although Canadian mayors may not possess the authority of their counterparts in the United States, they still wield considerable informal power and can shape political agendas, particularly with their access to information and their ability to network with other influential actors in the city and with the other orders of government. As Kate Graham (2018, 235) notes in her study of Canadian mayors, these elected municipal leaders may be able "to *influence, mobilize, empower, and lead other actors*" due to "the uniqueness of their election as mayor." Their authority can be enhanced if they also have the ability to lead and to gain the trust of others in the administration, community, or other governments. Graham notes that even though mayors may be more influential than has typically been thought, Canadian cities themselves are relatively weak vis-à-vis their position in Canadian federalism (237). As cities mobilize to act on climate change, however, it is notable that a number of former and current mayors have played a leadership role in international forums, including the mayors of some of Canada's biggest cities, such as David Miller (former mayor of Toronto), Gregor Robertson (former mayor of Vancouver), Valérie Plante (current mayor of Montreal), and Don Iveson (former mayor of Edmonton).

The Council

The elected municipal council as a whole possesses provincially delegated legal powers. These councils may range in size from a few individuals in small towns to over fifty members in large metropolitan areas. Councils can pass bylaws and resolutions within the limits laid down by provincial legislation. The responsibilities that come with such powers include the creation of an official community plan to guide land use, the authorization of funding for new municipal projects or other hard and soft services, the approval of changes to property bylaws as well as to bylaws dealing with municipal matters like the restriction of smoking in public places, the regulation of the public use of parks, and the development of city transportation policies. The council must also approve administrative appointments and pass bylaws governing the terms of appointments. Councillors regularly participate in standing committees that have been delegated some responsibilities. Typical examples include community services, economic development, planning, public safety, finance and administration, environment, and public works. Councillors meet with other groups and with members of their constituencies, who bring issues of local concern to the attention of the appropriate governing body. Councillors also serve as sources of information either through the media or by responding directly to the inquiries of citizens both at home and at city hall. They also make and attend presentations, attend the opening of new public facilities, schools, and parks, and participate in numerous other public functions. It can be a very time-consuming job. As one City of Toronto staff member (pers. comm., August 11, 2020) notes, "A request to remove a single tree from private property in Toronto can involve council if the request is denied and appealed." When one considers the size of Toronto and the huge constituency represented by each councillor, it is clear that a huge bureaucracy is needed to manage these types of daily activities – whether small or large.

How Representative Are Councils?

One of the hallmarks of a democratic society is that citizens can choose their leaders or run for office themselves. Yet how representative is the process if the most likely contenders often come from the same socio-economic background and share the same ideological perspectives and visions for their cities? It is true that women, members of different ethnic groups, and individuals from other groups that experience discrimination are now running for office more than in the past. However, barriers to holding elected positions are still real – many of which are related to gender, ethnic background, or socio-economic status. Despite some improvements, numerous ethnic groups, for example, continue to be underrepresented on city councils today, whether they are descended from the Indigenous peoples who first inhabited the continent or are newcomers. Before even considering a run for office, many face considerable challenges, such as finding adequate housing and schooling, health and safety concerns, food insecurity, systemic or overt discrimination, a sense of placelessness, and inadequate forms of employment. For marginalized people, therefore, finding time to participate in political life must come well after taking care of their basic necessities. Political representation is often a matter of who has the time, resources, and societal support to run for office. It also raises questions about who has the connections to raise funds and to establish a campaign team. Although campaign spending is not a sufficient measure in itself, some provinces attempt to generate a more equitable opportunity for people wishing to run for office by placing legal limits on the amount that candidates can spend. One study of municipal elections conducted in 100 of the larger Canadian cities between 2006 and 2017 found that women comprised only 15.69 percent of candidates contesting mayoral races and that half of all mayoral races had no female candidates (Breux, Couture, and Koop 2019, 177). In one study, a gender analysis of the country's 441 municipalities with a population of over 9,000 revealed that women held approximately one-third of a combined total of 3,756 council seats (Ogilvie 2020).

BOX 4.2   Halifax District 8 councillor Lindell Smith

Halifax councillor Lindell Smith brought a broad suite of abilities and interests to council in 2016. As a councillor, he was in a position to draw council's attention to the many diverse communities that comprise the City of Halifax. Smith, a music producer with deep roots in the community, was one of the youngest elected councillors. He brought a "social policy lens to the city," pressing it to address practices of systemic and overt racism, such as in hiring and policing practices (Kimber 2019).

Smith, as the co-founder of a nonprofit music studio, also represents youth through the promotion of art and music – important means of encouraging community engagement and belonging. His numerous awards include the Lieutenant Governor's Award for Education and Community Service, his selection as one of five Youth Rising Stars for Nova Scotia, the Abby Bryant (humanitarian) Award of Excellence, and the Black Business Initiative's Industry Development Award from the African Nova Scotian Music Association. He was re-elected to council in 2020 (L. Smith n.d.).

In local elections, the presence of candidates with diverse backgrounds might lead to a more representative, inclusive local government, but it can also result in affinity voting, which occurs when people vote for a candidate who shares their social or demographic characteristics, possibly based on the belief that their interests might be more effectively represented (Bird et al. 2016). Although studies in this area are sparse, Karen Bird and colleagues note that affinity voting took place in the 2014 City of Toronto mayoral race, where Olivia Chow,[2] a female Asian candidate, attracted notable support from nonwhite women voters. These researchers, however, also discovered that overall voter turnout among nonwhite women was lower in that election. This outcome could have had something to do with the perceived relevance of the local election to certain groups. The complexity of electoral and institutional systems in federal countries like Canada can also contribute to electoral apathy at the municipal level. Moreover, it is challenging for political newcomers to enter local electoral races or to generate support at the local level when better-known incumbents are contesting the election. Acclamations are not uncommon. The lack of municipal competitiveness can act as a barrier to an inclusive, representative democratic system. As Mariana Valverde (2018) observes, "Racialized young people and tenants, especially low-income tenants, often feel elections are not for or about them. This is the vicious circle of municipal politics: marginalized residents stay away from the polls because their issues are never the main priority, and they don't see themselves reflected in a council that is overwhelmingly white and property-owning."

Why is a diversity of perspectives on council important for sustainable governance? First and foremost, a just and inclusive system is a prerequisite for a healthy, thriving community. In addition, diverse voices bring different and innovative approaches to contemporary complex problems that have been created in part by entrenched, self-reinforcing past practices and ideological perspectives. Council diversity also reinforces the public legitimacy of the formal governance structures; without legitimacy, it is difficult to garner public support for important initiatives or to foster a civil democratic society. Moreover, without diverse representation, large segments (sometimes the majority) of the population may not see themselves reflected in the governing system, a situation that can erode a sense of belonging and a sense of responsibility toward the larger community. Youth, for example, are a constituency often underrepresented on municipal councils, even though they have the most invested in a sustainable, healthy future (see Box 4.2).

Problems of diversity in representation can be aggravated by small councils with huge constituencies. For example, the Ontario government's abrupt imposition of a new city council system in Toronto prior to the fall 2018 municipal election, which dramatically reduced the number of wards from forty-seven to twenty-five, potentially undermined democratic efforts on several fronts. The passage of the Efficient Local Government Act, 2018 assisted those who were already established in city politics to successfully stand for re-election given that incumbents tend to be favoured. The majority of councillors elected in the Toronto 2018 election were white, male, and middle-aged rather than being drawn from a diversity of candidates who might have more accurately reflected the multicultural, multilingual composition of the city (Beattie and Rider 2018). An estimated 200 different languages are spoken in Toronto, with almost half of the population speaking a mother language other than English and French (Endangered Language Alliance Toronto n.d.; Statistics Canada 2017). The lack of consultation and the short notice before the municipal election drew outrage from a large number of constituencies, organizations, and political voices throughout Canada. Many mayors spoke out once again about how little formal authority municipalities have if a provincial government chooses to exercise its power (Beattie 2018).

Local governments, however, have more authority than a cursory institutional view suggests. If a council has the political will, democratic and meaningful engagement of the general public in its decision-making processes is quite possible. Neighbourhood councils, for example, could readily be established (Eidelman 2018). That is only one of several ways that a city council can encourage more diverse participation

from a wide demographic, including underserved constituencies. C. Richard Tindal and colleagues (2013, 395) refer to such strategies of "localized government" as representing "a decision by government officials to decentralize decision-making authority over a specified geographic area to local residents." There have been some initiatives throughout Canada that were initially designed to delegate some meaningful authority to sublocal groups. Over time, however, many of these initiatives were either watered down or lacked substantive local government support and resources to constitute a notable shift in governing authority.

Community Councils

> *Effective self-government means more than political space and partial autonomy; it requires some measure of relative equality, genuine opportunities for self-realization, and a politics beyond the single policy to encompass a range of issues that matter. Genuine debates will most likely be rooted in the neighbourhoods of the world's cities.*
>
> – Lightbody 2006, 543

One investigation of widespread amalgamations in Ontario initiated in the 1990s and early 2000s has revealed that, in those places that underwent amalgamation, its effectiveness was limited by legislation and faced barriers by city councillors and city officials (Spicer 2016). In the case of Toronto, six municipalities and the regional municipality were amalgamated into one large city, with each of the former city governments becoming community councils that aligned with the former city boundaries. The newly formed city was given the authority to determine the roles of these six community councils (later reduced to four). Their authority on matters such as local planning, land use, and community issues was restricted solely to their geographic boundaries and precluded city-wide issues. Alexandra Flynn and Zachary Spicer (2017, 19) note that this division of authority is problematic because some issues designated as city-wide can have a localized impact and vice versa. Problem solving may also require multi-level governance that a local-level body may not have the authority, resources, or capacity to resolve.

Even if the political will were there to empower community councils, would they turn out to be as democratic and effective as might be envisioned by their advocates? If authority were dispersed to local representatives, what would the trade-offs be in terms of the provision of city-wide policies or services? Moreover, who would dominate these citizen-based, neighbourhood bodies? Would they be inclusive and have diverse representation, or would they be captured by a local privileged elite lobbying for their own agenda at the expense of other constituencies (Spicer 2016, 133)?

Quebec also went through a period of municipal consolidation at the turn of the twenty-first century. Borough councils were introduced into the new City of Montreal. These councils acquired authority to deliver services and to play a role in local decisions, becoming relevant political actors. They have elected borough mayors, who are also city councillors, and have elected borough and city councillors. These borough governments are responsible for housing, local roads, culture and recreation, some urban planning, and parts of social and community development (S. Katz and Roussopoulos 2017).

THE ABCS OF AGENCIES, BOARDS, AND COMMISSIONS

Beyond running for mayor or council, an individual can serve in a number of other locally elected or appointed positions. Agencies, boards, and commissions, popularly known as ABCs, have a semi-autonomous, permanent status in local government and have been created to fill a specific function or purpose. Police commissions, school boards, transit commissions, housing authorities, and Ontario's Conservation Authorities are all examples of special-purpose bodies with their own governing actors, semi-independent status, and designated budget. Some of these local authorities, such as school boards, are required under provincial statute, whereas others are established by local council. These special-purpose bodies can be traced back to the reform era of the early twentieth century, when some services were deemed too important to be subjected to the whims of elected councils. These bodies were given the authority to carry out their mandate without excessive political interference.

ABCs might be viewed negatively from the perspective of political accountability and transparency given that they fragment political authority and the coordination of services while reducing the role of elected council in making decisions on behalf of the whole community. Moreover, many positions on a number of special-purpose bodies are made by appointment rather than through election.

In a more positive light, ABCs can serve a useful function in cases where policy concerns spill over jurisdictional boundaries. When cities grow, one response of provincial governments is to deal with the expanding population by amalgamating municipalities into large units governed by fewer elected representatives. Unfortunately, amalgamation does not always tidily encompass all of the surrounding suburban communities, leaving inevitable issues of coordination. Some problems simply cannot be solved by amalgamation. Moreover, as discussed above, diverse citizen interests are not necessarily effectively represented by a formally elected city council. It is difficult for a council to be fully informed and responsive to the demands posed by numerous complex issues that can often spill across municipal boundaries. Special-purpose bodies allow members of civil society to become involved in topics that affect their environment through multiple avenues. Some issues cannot be dealt with by expanding municipal boundaries. For example, if the issue concerns a biophysical area such as a vital watershed, the most appropriate governing vehicle might be an intermunicipal or interjurisdictional body. These types of special-purpose bodies can encourage and allow for diverse participation in local governance and can bring different kinds of expertise to bear on problems. Individuals may be more inclined to contribute to their community as a member of a social housing board than as an elected member of local council. The same is true of boards of policing, planning, health, and so on. These boards also allow local governments to deal with issues that reflect their unique heritage and requirements, serving to strengthen, rather than weaken, the fabric of civil society.

Special-purpose bodies can command a sizable portion of a city budget. Jack Lucas (2016, 5) draws our attention to their integral role in communities:

The electricity in our homes, the police in our streets, the books in our libraries – all of these are administered by local special purpose bodies. When we send our children to school, roll up our sleeves for a flu shot, or spend a weekend at a local conservation area, we are, often without realizing it, engaging with ABCs.

These bodies, then, can undermine or, conversely, enhance local democracy, depending on one's perspective. On the one hand, not only are arm's-length bodies removed from the spotlight that is placed on local councils, but they can also further fragment responsibilities (lessening political accountability and policy coherence) and can be readily captured by local elites, all of which can weaken democratic processes. On the other hand, they open up additional avenues for citizen involvement in public decision making (K.A.H. Graham, Phillips, and Maslove 1998, 156). These understudied bodies, according to Lucas (2013), are "hidden in plain view" and merit closer

---

BOX 4.3 **Agencies, boards, and commissions/committees in three small Canadian cities, 2021**

City of Stratford, Ontario (population 33,232)

Accessibility Advisory Committee
Active Transportation Advisory Committee
Ad-Hoc Citizen's Committee on Council Remuneration
Board of Park Management
Committee of Adjustment
Communities in Bloom Committee
Downtown Stratford Business Improvement Area Board of Management
Energy and Environment Committee
Heritage Stratford Committee
Sports Wall of Fame Committee
Spruce Lodge Non-profit Housing Corporation
Stratford Police Services Board
Stratford Public Library Board
Stratford Town and Gown Advisory Committee
Stratfords of the World (Ontario) Committee
Upper Thames River Conservation Authority

(City of Stratford n.d.)

City of Prince Albert, Saskatchewan (population 37,756)

Boards
Board of Police Commissioners
Board of Revision
Development Appeals Board
Prince Albert Downtown Business Improvement District Board
Prince Albert Public Library Board
Property Maintenance Appeal Board

Committees
Airport Advisory Committee
Aquatic and Arenas Recreation Project Fundraising Committee
Aquatic and Arenas Recreation Project Steering Committee
Budget Committee
City and Peter Ballantyne Cree Nation Joint Planning Committee
City and School Boards Liaison Committee
Community Services Advisory Committee
Destination Marking Levy Advisory Committee
Executive Committee
Golf Course Advisory Committee
Management Committee
Planning Advisory Committee
Regional Co-operation Committee

(City of Prince Albert n.d.)

City of Boisbriand, Quebec (population 28,308)

Accountability Committee
Arts and Culture Committee
Committee on Communications and Citizen Relations
Committee on the Environment
Committee on Public Administration and Finance
Committee on Recreation, Culture and Community Life
Demolitions Control Committee
Family and Seniors Committee
Festive Decorations Evaluation Committee – Special Committee
Fire Safety and Civil Protection Commission
Human Resources, Ethics and Professional Conduct Committee
Information Technology Commission
Monitoring Committee of the Creation Centre's Internal Operations Management Agreement
Pension Committee
Planning and Place Names Advisory Committee
Public Works and Infrastructure Committee
Road Safety Committee
Safe City Commission
Strategic Orientation and Development Committee
Universal Accessibility Committee for the Integration of Persons with Disabilities
Youth Council Committee

(City of Boisbriand n.d.)

examination given that they play a diverse, dynamic, and important role in governance. Box 4.3 offers a comparative table of the agencies, boards, and commissions in three small Canadian cities. Some of these bodies, such as school boards, have been around for much of Canada's history, whereas others are relatively new, reflecting emerging priorities. Examples include accessibility committees, environment or sustainability committees, youth councils, smart city committees, and planning and service committees jointly formed by First Nations and municipalities.

CONCLUSION: WHO GOVERNS?

> *In a political system where nearly every adult may vote but where knowledge, wealth, social position, access to officials, and other resources are unequally distributed, who actually governs?*
>
> *The question has been asked, I imagine, wherever popular government has developed and intelligent citizens have reached the stage of critical self-consciousness concerning their society. It must've been put many times in Athens even before it was posed by Plato and Aristotle ...*
>
> *Now it has always been held that if equality of power among citizens is possible at all – a point on which many political philosophers have had grave doubts – then surely considerable equality of social conditions is a necessary prerequisite.*
>
> – Dahl 1961, 1, 3

Over the past century, formal representative institutions have remained fairly consistent in terms of overall structure. A mayor, reeve, or chair presides over council, whose members are seated in a horseshoe arrangement around the room. During regularly scheduled and publicized meetings, councillors discuss local issues for which they have responsibility under provincial and territorial legislation. Local media attend the meetings and report on the issues that are most likely to attract public interest. Citizens, members of the private sector, and various other interest groups petition to address council on matters of

personal or public concern. Special-purpose bodies such as school boards, water boards, and other agencies similarly hold regular meetings. But questions have been raised about how well these formal institutional arrangements represent the interests of the public as a whole.

In Ontario, the 2021 Municipal Democracy Index ranked the political health of the province's thirty-two largest municipalities, with Peterborough winning the highest ranking. The ranking was based on voter turnout, gender balance on council, racial diversity, and efforts made by each municipality to be more inclusive and inviting for ordinary citizens. Comparative efforts of this kind can provide helpful information for performance improvements. They can assess initiatives and successes against similar municipalities. Using the assumption that "things you measure tend to improve," the index reveals that local municipal democracy has considerable room for improvement: "The results are sobering and reveal a democratic deficiency, particularly in the areas of public participation and diverse representation" (Armstrong Strategy Group and Unlock Democracy Canada 2021).

As of 2022, a number of trends in the formal institutions of local government appear to be deepening and extending historical power structures. In local elections, long-term incumbents often retain power and are re-elected, voting turnout is low, and newcomers are hesitant to run for office. Those who would present platforms advocating change from the status quo or who would represent marginalized members of the community are often deterred from the prospect of public office. Running a campaign can be expensive and disheartening. Very personal attacks on social media and in public make a difficult and demanding job even less appealing. Discussions in city council meetings and among school board trustees are more visibly divisive along ideological lines.

Over sixty years ago, well-known political scientist Robert Dahl (1961) questioned the representativeness of democratic institutions in the absence of social equality. The relative ability of representative liberal democracies to deliver on their ideals has long been debated. Today, we see intensifying political debate about societal inequality and its implications for the health and democracy of communities. As discussed in the next chapter, in addition to enduring questions about how institutions might best foster a democratic, equitable society, the Anthropocene has generated questions about how local governing institutions might best support the rights of present and future generations and the long-term sustainability of vital social-ecological systems.

NOTES

1 Exceptions to the rule are the Governments of Nunavut and the Northwest Territories, which are based on a consensus-style approach, in keeping with the traditional ways of Indigenous peoples.

2 As this manuscript was in development in 2023, Olivia Chow ran again for mayor of Toronto, under a progressive platform, and won the election.

5 Expanding Civic Engagement
Local Democracy in the 2020s

INTRODUCTION: CONTEMPORARY NOTIONS OF LOCAL DEMOCRACY

> *Never doubt that a small group of thoughtful, committed citizens can change the world. Indeed, it is the only thing that ever has.*
>
> – Margaret Mead

When we repeatedly hear familiar refrains such as the one above, it is clear that they resonate with many people. Agency – the capacity to act, participate, and make choices – is fundamental to those interested in the active pursuit of a just, thriving society and a healthy environment. A politically inclusive governing system plays a critical part in building social capital, healthy civil societies, innovative political economies, and long-term sustainability. Among the wide variety of types and (overlapping or competing) definitions of democracy, the notion of "ecological democracy," as succinctly defined by Ross E. Mitchell (2006, 463), warrants mention:

Ecological democracy can be conceived as an alternative democratic model that: 1) strives to incorporate interested citizens into environmental decision-making, and 2) lacks structural features that systematically concentrate environmental amenities into the hands of particular social groups, while imposing environmental and ecological degradation on others. Ecological democracy appears whenever citizens are freely incorporated into

inclusive environmental decision-making – or, at minimum, those desiring to participate are provided with meaningful opportunities to do so, and their input well considered.

Environmental political theorist John S. Dryzek (2005) suggests that ecological democracy should be sensitive to the ecological context, recognizing that environmental issues transcend government boundaries. In addition, ecological democracy incorporates notions of inter- and intragenerational equity, building on the fundamental tenets of sustainable development first laid out by the Brundtland Commission (World Commission on Environment and Development 1987).

Democracy itself – what it *should* mean – is highly contested. The pursuit of ecological democracy is equally problematic, if not more so. Some objectives pursued in the name of ecological democracy may not be compatible with one another (Mitchell 2006). Consider, for example, the interconnected nature of social-ecological systems, where decisions taken at one place or time may have unexpected and unintended consequences in another place or at some other time. To be sure, the process of governing diverse societies and environments comes with both cost and contention. However, a political system that fails to consider important societal and ecological perspectives and values is much more counterproductive. Historically, local governments were not inclusive, nor did their agendas address large-scale, border-transcending issues such as global climate change, human migration, or other social-ecological matters. Furthermore, it is still debatable how many of city hall's daily responsibilities are devoted to such issues. One report on municipal climate change plans across Canada concludes that the initiatives overall are quite weak in terms of implementation, monitoring, evaluation, and stakeholder engagement (Guyadeen, Thistlethwaite, and Henstra 2018).

One city staff member working in a Canadian municipality stated that this point cannot be emphasized enough: "I've spoken to a number of municipal counterparts, and it's the same thing: council makes a climate change declaration but doesn't provide the tools or resources to achieve the overall goal. Often, the same old priorities take precedence" (pers. comm., August 11, 2020). We can also observe worrisome, and arguably oppressive, measures by some provincial governments that run roughshod over communities of interest, effectively marginalizing people. Nevertheless, in contrast, many Canadian municipalities have introduced participatory processes directed at defining and pursuing long-term sustainability goals.

Some observers suggest that our best hope for a healthy social-ecological environment rests with a form of societal-based governance – a system where grassroots organizations and social movements can articulate the needs of a diversity of public interests, including those of economically and socially disadvantaged groups. As scientist and peace activist Ursula M. Franklin (2006, 183) once said, "Law and regulation are considered *one* possible instrument of justice – not as *the* instrument of justice ... Other instruments of justice, such as compassion, tradition, common morality, and the notion of a common good are presently somewhat in eclipse, while economic instruments such as markets and tax systems are gaining ascendance as perceived tools for social justice." Local governments and the liberal-capitalist system in which they operate have been structured in some ways that limit or contain democracy rather than promoting it (Magnusson 1996, 21). As discussed in the previous chapter, there is an inequitable distribution of political power and influence; some groups have many more access points than others. Large segments of the population are effectively constrained from

participating in the formal political decisions that shape their social, economic, and physical environments. Inter- and intragenerational social equity has always been considered fundamental to a sustainable society since first being articulated by the Brundtland Commission (World Commission on Environment and Development 1987). How might local political institutions be influenced in a way that encourages a thriving civil society and healthy environment? For the purposes of this book, civil society is defined sociologically as "an intermediate associational realm situated between the state on the one side and the basic building blocks of society on the other ... inhabited by social organizations with some degree of autonomy and voluntary participation on the part of their members" (Manor, M. Robinson, and White 1999, 3).

Social movements and activism serve an important political function by challenging the status quo in ways that cause governments to respond to pressing public concerns. Civil society's organizations can contribute to better governance by calling for more transparency and greater access to information about government practices and policies and by taking on a public advocacy role (Manor, M. Robinson, and White 1999). Groups and associations also often perform useful public services that governments fail to provide. A strengthened sense of civic and community responsibility alone, however, cannot readily foster a broadly inclusive and effective local sustainability strategy. It should also be recognized that social movements can often be as regressive as they are progressive. But if citizens feel that they have been stripped of an effective voice in politics and society, government policies will ultimately fail, setting the stage for civil unrest.

Alternatively, governments could focus on providing safe environments for peaceful public political expression and consultation. They could adopt practices of institutional learning that would help them adapt to the unique and evolving needs of each community. As Warren Magnusson (2015, 247) observes, there is "no magic formula"; rather, he argues, "we need experimentation and innovation, informed by lateral communication between activists, politicians, and public officials in different communities." Some analysts like to use the metaphor of nature to illustrate

BOX 5.1   Diverse ecology and economy

According to renowned urban thinker Jane Jacobs (1985, 224),

Many of the root processes at work in natural ecologies and our economies are amazingly similar, and we can learn much about success and failure in our own arrangements by noticing, for example, that the more niches that are filled in a given natural ecology, other things being equal, the more efficiently it uses the energy it has at its disposal, and the richer it is in life and means of supporting life. Just so with our own economies: the more fully their various niches are filled, the richer they are in a means for supporting life. That is another way of saying that economies producing diversely and amply for their own people and producers, as well as for others, are better off than specialized economies ... In a natural ecology, the more diversity there is, the more flexibility too, because of what ecologists call its greatest numbers of homeostatic feedback loops, meaning that it includes greater numbers of feedback controls for automatic self-correction. It is the same with our economies.

This approach also applies to governing sustainable communities. Such diversity and flexibility allow for innovation, institutional learning, and an ability to adapt, depending on the signals feeding back into the political system.

how governing systems might be strengthened. For example, biological systems have built-in redundancies enhancing their resiliency (see Box 5.1).

Similarly, redundancies in governance and a diversity of societal institutions cooperating at different scales can also enhance effectiveness, equity, and economic efficiency. This is something that those provincial governments predominantly preoccupied with short-term cost efficiencies have largely overlooked. Their attempts to benefit from economies of scale can backfire when they impose one uniform service on all the people who inhabit a large geographic area, supplying the service regardless of a local need or desire for it. These attempts can raise service costs while reducing effectiveness and failing to realize the immediate objectives. It can be difficult, for example, to provide the same cost-efficient services for a whole region when a provincial government

amalgamates rural towns with highly urbanized municipalities. This is particularly the case in complex systems where no single government can effectively tackle the entangled and costly social-ecological challenges caused by climate change, global health crises, and social inequity, to name just a few.

It is worth cautioning, however, that proposals using nature as an exemplar for governing systems should be viewed metaphorically because human systems frequently operate very differently from the biophysical world. Moreover, building redundancy into a human-generated system to enhance resiliency can also backfire if the system in question is undesirable and counterproductive. Robert Michels's famous "iron law of oligarchy" springs to mind when one envisions fortresses of powerful, change-resistant, bureaucratic organizations reinforced by reams of red tape (cited in Diefenbach 2019, 545).

The principle of subsidiarity merits consideration with respect to its potential role as a general principle to advance the goal of an equitable and democratic civil society. One analyst has referred to subsidiarity as the "principled tendency toward solving problems at the local level and empowering individuals, families and voluntary associations to act more efficaciously in their own lives" (Vischer 2001, 116). A tendency toward a principle, however, does not call for wholesale devolution or the dismantling of regulatory systems. Rather, it recognizes that local governing institutions and organizations make valuable potential contributions to fostering a healthy, sustainable community.

Nevertheless, if governments are to be effective, they must also have the capacity to effect meaningful change. Judith E. Innis and David E. Booher (2003, 7) posit that a "governance system with capacity can learn, experiment, and adapt creatively to threats and opportunities. It is characterized by regular inter-action among diverse players who solve problems or complete complex new tasks by working together." In these times of uncertainty and change, governing systems need to be capable of institutional and social learning and adaptation. They also require the par-ticipation of a diversity of stakeholders both to gener-ate innovative ideas and to respond to a variety of differing complex imperatives.

EXPANDING CIVIC ENGAGEMENT

Local democracy is best achieved if at least four condi-tions are realized. First, local government requires a measure of political authority with sufficient resources if it is to cope effectively with the onslaught of global social-ecological imperatives, federal-provincial off-loading, and citizen demands. Second, in a democratic society, the institutional accrual of resources and authority needs to be accompanied by a strength-ening of the transparency and public accountability of the governing system. Third, strong, diverse, and informed networks of politically active groups and individuals must have the capacity to participate politically – that is, as a lively civil society able to engage with a degree of autonomy from the formal governing institutions. As Magnusson (2015, 5) ob-serves, "Political equality, which is what democracy is about, depends on closing the gap between the rulers and the ruled, the governors and the governed." Fourth, political participants operating within the context of multi-level governance must be capable of collaboration, self-reflection, learning, and adapting their practices in the context of a dynamic, changing environment. Achieving some of these goals will in-volve inevitable trade-offs. For example, a networked, collaborative approach to decision making inevitably involves a blurring of political lines of accountability. These trade-offs, therefore, need to be transparent so that decision makers and citizens alike are aware of the implications of their choices.

Strategies to encourage more inclusive forms of public participation in local government cannot be achieved without systemic changes in the formal pol-itical institutions and in society at large. Voter turnout in municipal elections, which averages just over 60 percent, is lower than at the federal or provincial levels. Moreover, an electoral system cannot adequately re-flect the variety of interests contained within modern, often heterogeneous, communities. Low levels of participation and a perceived lack of public trust in governments have helped to motivate local decision makers to adopt a variety of public participatory mech-anisms. These mechanisms can range from relatively weak, comprising one-way government public infor-mation sessions, to very robust efforts at engagement where citizens are encouraged to participate in col-laborative, direct decision making or co-management. Municipalities can facilitate citizen participation through various citizen forums, including delibera-tive mini-publics, citizen assemblies, citizen panels, and citizen juries. Some Canadian municipalities (and many others around the world) have engaged in these kinds of efforts over the years. For example, delibera-tive mini-publics include small groups of citizens who are selected to be a representative subset of the wider community. They are gathered to discuss an important policy and governance issue and to offer their input on local decisions (Curato et al. 2021).

In sum, for local governments to serve as effective democratic institutions, they need to engage a wider diversity of the public in community decision-making processes. The inclusion of diverse voices brings more perspectives to the table, providing a broader range of potential solutions to complex problems. The decision-making process also acquires further legitimacy. Moreover, a sense of political efficacy, particularly among those who have typically been underserved by government institutions, can help to strengthen a sense of belonging and to foster healthy communities.

Public Consultation

Municipalities, either by provincial requirement or local initiative, frequently reach out to the public for input on two major aspects of community decision making: the official community plan and the muni-cipal budget. Other common topics for public con-sultation include transit planning, new residential developments, and climate change plans. These pro-cesses have taken place either in public forums or online. The introduction of public engagement initiatives is only part of the equation. Other crucial aspects include answers to the following questions: to what degree do citizens from a diversity of backgrounds avail themselves of the opportunity to provide input, do local governments take their responses seriously, and do these citizen contributions effectively translate into policy action and implementation? One 2017 Ipsos survey of public involvement in municipal consultations revealed a low level of participation, with only 9 percent of respondents saying that they were "very likely" to participate in future public consultations. The percentage rose to 39 percent when combined with respondents indicating that they were "somewhat likely" to participate in the future (cited in Knaus 2018). In terms of how the public is most likely to participate, online and mail surveys generated the most positive interest. At the end of the day, the elected council is formally accountable for the decisions taken. Its members also need to take accountability in the context of provincial legislation and regulation, existing priorities and strategies, financial and technical limitations, and other considerations.

Participatory Democracy

As noted above, democracy in all its variations is a highly contested notion. Its application holds different meanings between and within communities. This caveat also applies to the notion of participatory democracy. However, there are some basic tenets, or pillars, that participatory democracies share: (1) "equal rights and access to justice," (2) "representative and accountable institutions and processes," and (3) "citizen initiative and participation" (Kemp and Jiménez 2013, 18). As explained by the International Institute for Democracy and Electoral Assistance (IDEA) in its framework for local democracy,

> Citizenship is understood as a set of equal rights and liberties, complemented by equal access to justice (Pillar 1), which are on the one hand bestowed and facilitated by representative and accountable institutions and processes (Pillar 2), and on the other hand claimed and realized through the agency and actions of people themselves (Pillar 3). (22)

Throughout Canada, local governments appoint citizens to special committees to advise the government on issues of local concern. Where these appointments are semi-permanent, a city will advertise openings of several voluntary citizen advisory positions available to the public after an election. In some municipalities, participants may be recruited on the basis of friendships or networks previously developed with council or city hall in general (see Box 5.2). Those recruited citizens may very well be asked to participate on the basis of their own expertise with respect to the policy issue at hand. The practice, however, can limit the opportunities for diverse public input into local decisions.

Committees might deal with broad policy areas like parks and recreation, environment, arts, heritage, or social services. An advisory body may also be formed to deal with a

---

BOX 5.2 Who speaks for whom? Local participatory roundtables

A narrative based on a true story

A group of citizens was asked by a city government to participate on a local advisory committee tasked with finding ways to foster a healthy community. One of the topics under consideration was housing for homeless citizens. Looking around at the group, one of the participants noted that it would be difficult for the committee to effectively discuss homelessness and to offer meaningful advice given that there were no real experts in the room. Puzzled, the committee chair looked at the assembled group composed of social workers, health professionals, housing advocates, city staff, and academics. The chair waited for further elaboration. The committee member explained, "None of us here in this room is homeless. Someone who is homeless could give us the expert insights needed to make really helpful recommendations." Today, some local governments have recognized that an effective, participatory, inclusive democracy is one where citizens with lived experience have important contributions to make in civil discussions.

specific project, such as cleaning up a polluted water-way, revitalizing a downtown area, or developing bicycle trails. Large Canadian cities often have dozens of citizen advisory committees, whereas small municipalities may have only a few. A review of city websites across the country reveals how differing municipalities highlight locally specific issues and the degree of effort invested in encouraging citizens to sign up for advisory committees. It is worth remembering, however, that these committees are advisory only in nature. City hall officials may choose not to follow the advice – a choice that obviously discourages citizen engagement.

Members of the public also participate in local governance through groups and nonprofit organizations, some of which provide services with funding from local government (and often from provincial and federal governments as well), the private sector, and elsewhere. As with the advisory committees, these organizations focus on a variety of social and environmental aspects of the city. The aim is to assist those organizations that are perceived to be of benefit to the city.

Traditional methods of participation fall well within the umbrella of a "decisional" view of government, where the role of the elected representative government is to be the final arbiter of the public interest and to take decisions (Peters 1996, 69). Citizens might vote, but at the end of the day, councils decide. However, collaborative policy processes that include the public are becoming more widely used. These more participatory processes generally take the form of discursive roundtables comprising groups of citizens who come forward as individual volunteers, are nominated by a community of interest, and/or are recruited by local governments. Timothy D. Sisk (2001, 148) writes,

> *Collaboration* is defined as a process in which the diverse interests that exist in a community are brought together in a structured process of joint decision-making. Often, third parties are involved in helping facilitate agreement ... Collaborative decision-making is linked to efforts to prevent disputes by involving everyone in decisions before conflicts arise, to manage ongoing differences,

and to settle disputes that threaten the health and cohesion of a community.

In the participatory approach, the public interest is created through citizen-based forums that bargain with each other and with government representatives. In contrast, "in the decisional view the capacity to produce decisions, rather than the ability to create consensus, is the characteristic mark of governance" (Peters 1996, 69). Extensive consultation with citizens and interest groups also means that once these exercises have taken place, governments will encounter political difficulties if they do not appear to take seriously the recommendations of public consultation. Governments must find policy and administrative mechanisms to coordinate their own activities with other departments and governments in a way that constitutes an acceptable response to diverse constituencies. This objective is not easily achieved. The more broadly inclusive the initiative, the more difficult it becomes to reach and implement timely policy decisions. Yet it could also be argued that a process will be viewed as illegitimate if it includes only select members of interest groups (57).

In addition to government representatives, these consensus-based processes often involve diverse communities of interest. Roundtables have been employed regularly by government decision makers to resolve contentious political disputes over public resources. Much of the literature suggests that these roundtables or public consultation processes make policy processes more accountable, transparent, and democratic. However, the formal mechanisms of modern representative democracies and public administrations were created to address the need to govern large populations using hierarchical, decisional representative structures. Participatory processes such as roundtables are frequently considered in the context of small gatherings of people. These processes will flounder if they do not have effective administrative, political, or public support.

In recent decades, the concept of networking governance has emerged around the world. Decision-making forums in this context include government representatives and nonelected members of civil society, who can wield a fair amount of informal political influence as a result of their participation. As these forums are convened to tackle complex, multi-scale issues, they inevitably give rise to concerns about political accountability and democracy. Metagovernance – a process by which complex governance arrangements can be managed – offers ways to address such democratic concerns. Carey Doberstein's (2013, 585) study on the metagovernance of Canadian communities reveals that "government remains the principle public authority at the (figurative and literal) table." Doberstein notes that although networking governance has been said to "marginalize elected officials, other understandings suggest that government can actually use the involvement of civil society actors in policy development and implementation to enhance democracy by providing a check on centralized power and promoting compromise" (588).

MAKING SPACE AND TIME FOR PUBLIC PARTICIPATION

In addition to collaborative policy making, forms of public engagement include deliberative democracy, participatory budgeting, citizen juries, and crowd-sourced policy making (Longo 2017, 521). Justin Longo points out that these "new governance models" are centred "on the emergence of horizontal networks of public, private, and non-profit organizations, superseding traditional, hierarchical control by governments," and that the interpersonal communication and participation of these nongovernmental actors are facilitated by the Internet and by advances in digital technology (521). One example is CivicAction, an organization focused on contemporary policy challenges in the Greater Toronto and Hamilton Area. CivicAction has the goal of building civic leadership for the future by "engaging young, emerging and under-represented leaders." The organization aims to remove barriers encountered by people who have been politically or socially marginalized and to develop the region based on the principles of accessibility, equality, and inclusivity. The organization's goal is to "leverage partnerships" across the region with a wide diversity of stakeholders, including NGOs, government, and the private sector (CivicAction n.d.).

Participatory democracy can engage citizens in direct forms of political decision making, thereby facilitating a sense of belonging and civic responsibility while encouraging stewardship toward one's community and the encompassing social-ecological environment. In discussing "place governance," Patsy Healey (2018, 69) asserts that if "political communities ... claim to be democracies and to promote the flourishing of all citizens, governing conceptions have to be justified in terms of some idea of a collective concern with how to shape the commons of a community." Negotiating how a shared public space is to be delineated and governed requires considerable navigational skills in building relationships "across a churning institutional landscape" (70). Nevertheless, as Healey states, bringing together members of civil society who hold diverse perspectives to discuss a shared place – the commons – can help to strengthen local democracy:

> Through processes of active debate and lively public discussion, of continual interaction where the personal and the political are in play in face-to-face interaction, through joint exploration of possibilities and potentials, a public may get to form which has some sense of shared destiny, some trust and even pride in what is being done collectively in their community to manage the qualities of the place they share. (72)

Direct citizen engagement in formal government decision processes can introduce a measure of innovation through the inclusion of a diversity of perspectives while striving toward consensus and collaborative forms of governance. To be effective, instruments for social and institutional learning – even transformative learning – need to be incorporated into the decision-making processes of local governments, as well as into civil society writ large (Fischer 2004, 2006; Dryzek and Pickering 2017). *Deliberative democracy* is a concept often proffered as a way to include citizens directly in government decision making through public deliberation. David R.H. Moscrop and Mark E. Warren (2016, 1) offer the following definition:

> "Deliberative democracy" is a compound term. In both theory and practice, it connects deliberative influence through reason-giving, reciprocity, and

publicity to a family of political systems that broadly enable popular control of the state and government through empowerments such as voting, petitioning, and contesting, as well as the electoral and judicial systems that enable them. These empowerments are democratic when they are distributed to, and usable by, those affected by collective decisions in ways that are both equal and equitable.

As Moscrop and Warren note, not all deliberation is democratic, nor are all democratic practices deliberative. Deliberative democracy, they argue, is characterized by "*equality* in opportunities for participation, and *equity* in processes and outcomes" (2). To achieve these ends, the principles of equality and equity must be present not only during deliberations but also before the process begins, when determinations are made about who sets the agenda and about who gets to participate, with an emphasis on those most affected.

Deliberative democracy has been promoted as a way to include the public in governing processes, but it is also seen as a mechanism for addressing the serious contemporary policy challenges of complex systems. John S. Dryzek and Jonathan Pickering (2017, 353) suggest that for institutions to effectively address pressing social and ecological problems, individuals and institutions must have the capacity "to function as deliberate, self-critical agents of change in social-ecological systems." Given the serious environmental questions of this era, these analysts emphasize the need to be self-reflexive and able to question foundations and assumptions in order to "monitor the impacts of institutions on ecosystems and vice versa, and to rethink and reshape core values and practices accordingly" (353). One way of doing so is through public deliberation and "collective reasoning" (354). The book's conclusion returns to this notion of reflexive governance.

Deliberative democracy comes with numerous challenges that require the management of competing tensions. Examples include attempts to facilitate a public participation process that respects the contributions of both lay knowledge and expert knowledge, the accommodation of diverse perspectives while achieving a consensus, the juggling of polycentricity and centralizing political forces, and the ability to be flexible enough to respond to changing demands while ensuring that there is the requisite stability to see a plan carried through in the long term (Dryzek and Pickering 2017, 359).

Moreover, questions of scale cannot be glossed over. Representative democracy came about to manage and respond to large populations, whereas deliberative democracy is typically seen as face-to-face communications operating at a small scale. Deliberative democracy may supplement, but is unlikely to replace, representative democracy (Flynn and Spicer 2017). Graham Wright (2019, 2) further contributes to the debate by questioning whether the decision-making outcomes of deliberative democracy are necessarily better than those produced by a voting system. Questions of power are also raised with respect to the nature of the debate, as a deliberative system that favours rational discourse over other types of participation, such as storytelling, will privilege certain participants while marginalizing others (3).

Given the potential limitations of deliberative democracy, Wright (2019) offers the alternative of *integrative democracy,* first posited by Mary Parker Follett. Unlike deliberative democracy, where participants seek to persuade each other, integrative democracy is more accommodating of diverse perspectives and "demands co-created solutions" (11). Participants air their differences and arrive at a joint agreement while ensuring that potentially marginalized voices are heard. The emphasis is placed on arriving at a solution that "reflects a diversity of perspectives and approaches" (14). As a method of civil engagement, Wright argues, integrative democracy "instills in participants a stronger sense of collaboration and collective identity than persuasion-based deliberation" (15). Although this conception holds promise, the question of how it would work in a large, modern municipality remains to be answered. However, with certain issues, such as place-based or neighbourhood concerns that most directly affect a specific group of people, the concept of integrative democracy may well be worth consideration.

INCLUSIVE DEMOCRATIC SPACES
As discussed throughout this book, the fostering of diverse environments is necessary for healthy sustainable

5.1 Twins Mary Dooher and Pauline Stewart at the Toronto Gay Pride Parade, 2014 | Courtesy of MJ Dooher

communities, but it does not come without conflict and tension between competing interests. In an age of rapid urban growth, migration, and multiculturalism, a salient policy concern is how to create an enlightened and democratically inclusive society for people with different cultures, languages, and socio-economic backgrounds. Universally designed public spaces, community festivals, and annual parades help to foster a healthy, democratic society (see Figure 5.1).

Many analysts have wrestled with the question of how best to politically accommodate social diversity, particularly in this age of globalization. Given the country's linguistic and cultural diversity, political theorists Will Kymlicka and Kathryn Walker (2012, 3) advance the notion of "rooted cosmopolitanism," which they define as "a postcolonial cosmopolitanism, divorced from ideas of either cultural homogenization or political unification, accepting of cultural diversity and of the rights of the world's peoples to local autonomy." Contrary to historical liberal notions of cosmopolitanism as something that "transcends" the local (1), rooted cosmopolitanism recognizes the value of local cultures, which can help to foster a sense of belonging. As Kymlicka and Walker write,

> In a sense, rooted cosmopolitanism can be seen as the flip side of enlightened localism. Rooted cosmopolitanism seeks to overcome the limitations of traditional forms of cosmopolitanism by highlighting the significance of local autonomy and cultural difference; enlightened localism seeks to overcome the limitations of traditional forms of "parochial localism" by highlighting how the claims of outsiders can "enlighten" local practices and make them more encompassing. (23n1)

Governing ideals might include recognizing diversity through the adoption of inclusive, effective, accountable, and transparent decision-making processes. The ultimate goal is to create just and tolerant communities that encourage civic trust, learning, innovation, and adaptability. However, these arguments for more enlightened forms of cosmopolitanism or localism also need to be tempered by recognition of the ecological requirement that we transition to a low-carbon future. Citing German sociologist and economist Ferdinand Tönnies (1887), Stephen Quilley (2013, 275) argues,

> Tönnies famously characterised the process of modernisation in terms of a shift from "gemeinschaft" to "gesellschaft" – from place-bound "communities of fate" to more mobile communities of choice. Cosmopolitan, liberal, gesellschaftliche societies emerged on the back of a one-off bounty of fossil fuel and are synonymous with the ever faster circulation of people, information and commodities. It is hard to conceive of a "low-energy cosmopolitanism."

Later chapters more fully discuss attempts across the country to transition society to a low-carbon or post-carbon future. The question here is how to foster inclusive democracies in an globally interconnected world. David Hayes and Andrew Dobson (2008) offer an observation similar to that made by Quilley: "The progressive, inclusive politics of the past two centuries has been accompanied by a fossil-fuelled energy binge. As society powers down, what will become of the outward-looking social and political advances that have accompanied the age of energy excess?" They suggest that any transition that has a hope of success will require the creation of a managed approach to change. The aim will be to create a mediating structure that avoids the "centralist-corporatist politics of the 1970s" while not relying on a "thorough-going localism." They argue that collective interests need to be organized and defined in the "democratic public realm," where "relations between citizen and state can and should be reformed," and that "every opportunity should be taken to revitalise it, and to fortify the democratic institutions."

Prominent political scientist Robert D. Putnam (2020) has argued that a democratically inclusive society cannot be achieved without trust and what he refers to as "social capital." Both the term "social capital" and the ideas associated with it have generated a fair share of academic debate. Critics have pointed out the limits to Putnam's theory, noting its lack of attention to the undue influence of powerful macro-political and macro-economic actors, as well as the ways that competition within and between social networks can undermine possibilities for cooperation and reciprocity (Gelderblom 2018, 1309). However, the point of Putnam's work is to emphasize the importance of social networks in building trust and reciprocity (or mutual trust) in order to foster a democratic society (1313). Some types of social networks can also lead to undesirable and exclusionary effects, undermining inclusive decision making and a sense of belonging in a plural society. This consideration has given rise to the notions of "bonding" and "bridging" networks as ways to circumvent such effects: "Bonding networks that connect folks who are similar sustain particularized (in-group) reciprocity. Bridging networks that connect individuals who are diverse sustain generalized reciprocity" (Putnam 2020). Both types of networks can include people from a diversity of backgrounds and can promote a sense of

belonging, or they can include social organizations that bring together people from all walks of life and encourage a sense of community.

Such tenacious, citizen-based organizations can thrive without the support of macro-actors. Local governments, however, can encourage civic efforts by taking influential public positions on issues, and they can make policies that influence the sociopolitical environment of a community. Public statements that declare a municipality's political stance can influence the collective and individual behaviour of community members. One such statement is the City of Vancouver's (2018) *Women's Equity Strategy 2018–2028*, which promises "an intersectional approach to our work to ensure that all residents, including all women, have equitable access, inclusion and participation in the life of the city." Another example might be official municipal recognition that a city has been built on the traditional territory of First Nations. However, public political statements aimed at fostering diversity and inclusivity are not sufficient and can be met with a measure of skepticism. Despite public statements of support, these communities, like all others, are subject to various forms of overt and systemic discrimination. To be effective, such public statements need to be followed by meaningful policy action and implementation. Nevertheless, they can be used to foster a democratic ethos and to ensure that local decision makers follow up on their publicly stated goals.

Citizens may be encouraged to participate in a variety of initiatives, such as signing petitions, joining neighbourhood associations, engaging in information exchange with the local government, participating in consultative exercises or advisory committees, serving on arm's-length bodies that have received municipal funding, or taking part in collaborative decision making. The use of information and communications technologies (ICTs) to consult citizens and to foster a form of e-democracy is also under discussion in various municipalities. One of the challenges of encouraging participation is motivating those residents who do not participate for a variety of reasons, such as feeling alienated by the governing process, which might seem complex, time-consuming, intimidating, exclusionary, or technocratic (Fischer 2004); feeling as though one lacks the requisite knowledge or aware-ness of local issues; or simply being indifferent to the issue unless one's immediate interests are threatened (Sancton 2011, 217).

An additional emerging complexity of public participation is related to a number of democratic dilemmas associated with the growing use of the Internet for governance, public communications, and political discourse. The digital divide between the information-rich and the information-poor reflects other concerns about the social inequality caused by economic and political marginalization. Even for those who have access to the Internet, a growing reli-ance on social media can expose people to political information that is not based on evidence or facts, undermining public faith in governing institutions and in formal democratic processes.

CONCLUSION: DEMOCRATIC FOUNDATIONS OF LOCAL SUSTAINABILITY

As Margaret Mead and so many others have noted, important societal change takes place when civil society pressures governments to respond to its con-cerns. Since the 1960s, grassroots actions on environ-mental issues and human rights have been a force behind widespread policy changes at all levels of governance. It has often been said that local gov-ernments are closest to the people. As discussed in Chapter 3, local governments do possess a degree of autonomy and can take important steps toward sus-tainability despite some institutional, legal, and finan-cial constraints. To do so, however, they must engage members of civil society in the governing process. It is important for local residents to have a sense of be-longing, inclusion, trust, capacity, and agency if they are to feel responsible for the stewardship of their community. Public trust and the perception that gov-erning institutions have legitimacy require transparent processes that are responsive to the needs of diverse segments of society. Some of this trust can be gained through regularly held municipal elections, but an elected council must also have a culture of open decision-making processes, one that freely shares government information, and it must be receptive to public petitions and lobbying, all supported by re-sponsive administrative offices at city hall.

However, the demographic composition of those elected to Canadian city councils does not reflect the widely disparate groups of people who comprise any given municipality. If members of civil society do not identify with their elected representatives or with the agendas that dominate city council, these local gov-ernments will not be perceived as legitimate or demo-cratic. In response, analysts of local politics have proposed various solutions, including the adoption of neighbourhood councils, citizen juries, and delib-erative approaches to democracy. The catch here is that local elites can also capture and dominate the political agenda when participating in these proposed entities.

The liberal-progressive politics that thrived in an era of global capitalist growth powered by abundant natural resources could easily give way to reaction-ary populist forces during times of constraint, limited resources, economic disparity, and social polariza-tion. Today, we are experiencing the emergence of these forces throughout the world. Such circumstances challenge Kymlicka and Walker's (2012, 3) vision of a localized, "rooted cosmopolitanism."

Needed more than ever is the introduction of an inclusive form of ecological democracy where differ-ences are aired, diverse forms of communication are considered legitimate, and the resulting agreements reflect these interests. Time, political will, and capacity are needed to foster inclusive forms of democracy that rely on thoughtful communicative practices and deliberations. Where these discussions take place also matters, as do considerations of scale and scope. What shape inclusive democracy would take in a modern Canadian municipality is still debated or, at best, a matter of experimentation. Currently, in addition to running for local mayor or council, citizens might participate on some local boards, agencies, commis-sions, or advisory committees. Meaningful change can and does happen through these formal political av-enues as councils strive to address diverse issues such as climate change, affordable housing, and sanita-tion. More inclusive participation may be found in some Canadian localities that have adopted collabora-tive forms of governance, co-management, and joint agreements, particularly with respect to resource use. For the most part, however, citizens are governed through a representative system of democracy, with the former encouraged to bring their concerns to city hall, where their issues may or may not be satisfactorily addressed.

Formal responsibility for local decisions may be seen to rest with the mayor and elected council. In practice, however, the vast majority of day-to-day decisions rest outside of chambers in the unelected administrative arm of municipal government. Although these large and complex bureaucratic organizations are ostensibly responsible to the elected city council, they do take many independent decisions that shape the local community and environment. The significant – some would say determining – role that they play in fostering a sustainable community is the topic of the next chapter.

6 Decision Making at City Hall
The Machinery of Government

INTRODUCTION: LOCAL PUBLIC ADMINISTRATION

Historically, good municipal government has been equated with efficiency, often in terms of service delivery; many still view it in such terms. As Brian W. Head and John Alford (2015, 712) note, governments have generally been reasonably good at delivering services when the tasks involved are "standardized, routine and high volume." However, Zack Taylor (2016, 26) observes that although this utilitarian view may speak to a kind of administrative efficiency, it tells us little about the local government's ability to deliver on overall government objectives related to a thriving and healthy community – that is, about the effectiveness of its governance. As noted in Chapter 3, the notion of *governance* rather than *government* better reflects the complexity that characterizes the processes of public decision making and implementation and the political role of other constituencies.

What constitutes good governance is a matter of debate. Moreover, there are always trade-offs between considerations like short-term efficiency and consensus-based decision making or between transparent, accountable decision processes and speedy outcomes. With these caveats in mind, Taylor (2016, 9) offers a description of good governance that captures many contemporary understandings of its implementation:

> In general, good governance is identified with a high degree of inclusivity, robust accountability, impartial and competent administration, the capacity to assimilate knowledge and learn from

experience, and timely action. These dimensions are underpinned by supportive formal rules and social and organizational norms, as well as sufficient human and institutional capacities to perform assigned tasks.

In municipalities, city councils (and other public bodies) are elected to provide good, competent governance, and they are supported by nonelected staff who implement, or administer, policies and programs – that is, by the *public administration*. The tasks undertaken by this administration include planning, organizing, coordinating, and advising elected officials. Increasingly, city staff also engage and consult with members of the public. City halls contain the core administrative bodies of municipal governments. Situated in prominent locations, they possess architecture and historical characteristics that emphasize their symbolic importance as political city centres that administer the public's interest (see Figure 6.1).

Conventional understandings of public administration are rooted in a hierarchical and bureaucratic model of political accountability. In the late 1800s, during its nascent years, public administration was referred to as the "practical science of administration" (Wilson 1887, 197). Public administration was informed by the assumption that the application of the principles of rationality, efficiency, and scientific management could most effectively serve the public interest (e.g., see the work of Frederick W. Taylor, including Taylor 1915). However, administering the public interest cannot be scientifically managed according to some universally understood concept of rationality. Given their differing values, goals, and objectives, many people possess competing views of what constitutes a rational or logical way to proceed administratively. Specific bounded notions about financial and resource efficiency, for example, have often been equated with rational public administration. Focusing solely on a narrowly defined concept of efficiency can work at cross-purposes with other principles, such as effectiveness, equity, and sustainability. For instance, cost-cutting measures in the name of short-term efficiency can prove extremely expensive and inefficient in the long term. Many examples show the harmful effects of short-sighted measures aimed at fiscal constraint, such as the devastating and costly impacts of not addressing climate change, homelessness, and social discrimination, to name just a few. The application of public management principles can help local governments to produce favourable patterns of organizational behaviour, achieve managerial objectives, or deliver policies mandated by elected city councils. However, the warning signs go up when the goal itself is the implementation of these principles rather than their use as tools to serve the public interest.

Despite the dramatic events that local governments face and the pressures placed on them, the traditional model of public administration mostly prevails. An observer of the local government scene fifty years ago would be reasonably familiar with the same municipal legal-administrative structures, jurisdictional authority, financial constraints, rules of council, and emphasis on accountability, efficiency, and effectiveness that we see today. What has changed is that members of the interested public are much less content to be passive observers. Local governments must find new ways to accommodate some form of participatory democracy through governing structures originally based on classical notions of representative liberal democracy. In addition, the range of responsibilities has expanded tremendously since the early days of municipal government, when providing hard services and "boosting" the local economy were the primary preoccupations of city councils.

6.1   City Hall at Quebec City, Quebec, 2017

THE PRINCIPLES OF PUBLIC ADMINISTRATION

The foundational principles and structures of public administration provide a useful starting point for understanding how city government operates in theory – if not necessarily in practice. The overview presented here serves as a springboard to Chapter 7's discussion of the contemporary realities and complexities of governing in the twenty-first century. The formal model of public administration that prevailed throughout the previous century – referred to as the Weberian model – is based on notions of accountability that organize the nonelected arms of government (or the bureaucracy) into silos structured hierarchically so that they report to the elected arm of government above. Formally, all local governments are organized to hold the activities of civic employees and departments ultimately accountable to the city council. As a collective, council is responsible for representing the public interest. A well-organized working bureaucratic apparatus is needed to ensure transparent processes and to coordinate operations and activities. City staff carry out a multiplicity of tasks dictated by provincial laws and regulations. Not only do they administer local bylaws, policies, and guidelines, but they also respond to the demands, requests, and concerns of the public and council. The ideal of a traditional public administration is one where professional, well-educated employees administer the laws and policies of the elected government in a neutral, apolitical manner, with the elected officials presumed accountable for the outcomes.

In practice, the formal model of public administration falls short. City councillors do not have the time or capability to monitor all the activities of the type of large bureaucratic apparatus that governs the modern municipality. These elected councillors frequently rely on professional administrators for their advice, knowledge, and expertise when making policy decisions. As a result, city staff necessarily make most of the day-to-day decisions regarding a city's ongoing operations. They regularly make important choices when allocating responsibilities, prioritizing tasks, and operationalizing service delivery.

Although these issues may appear dull on an individual basis, they have a collective effect on the governance and shape of local communities. At the heart of daily administrative activities lie political decisions about who should get what and how. Those in charge of these administrative decisions wield considerable political influence. One cannot understand local politics, therefore, without knowing how city hall operates given the considerable political influence of the local public administration. This organization is responsible for helping to create, deliver, and implement local policies and services. City staff also play an important role in determining which issues achieve salience on council's agenda, as well as which initiatives should be encouraged or funded. Although staff frequently make recommendations that are readily accepted by council, their recommendations are often drafted with the knowledge that certain types of recommendations are not politically acceptable. So knowledge of a council's politics tends to shape the recommendations presented to council by staff, who will discard politically unacceptable recommendations and focus on suggestions that are likely to be accepted (W. Kennedy, pers. comm., July 31, 2020). City staff are influential in all such decisions. Governments might also make a deliberate choice not to act. The actions that governments take and the issues that they choose to focus on or to ignore, as well as the processes used to make and implement decisions, tell us much about what is valued and prioritized. Governments, in turn, are influenced by dominating systems of belief about how the public's interest, as they understand it, can best be administered.

One enduring and pervasive ideological belief is that local governments would be more effective and efficient if they adopted business principles. This belief has been reinforced in practice through the close relationship that local councils have with private interests (frequently in land development) or with other decision-making elites. Related to this perspective is an argument that the application of economic principles to municipal government also stimulates local innovation and competitiveness. In the closing decades of the twentieth century, local decision makers continued to seek ways to maximize economic efficiency as service costs increased and public demands rose. Bert George and colleagues (2018, 15) comment, "After the implosion of the unsustainable, oversized, bureaucratic and procedural government of the Weberian bureaucracy, there was a need for a parsimonious approach to resource allocation as well as a focus on output and results in public organizations." This quest led to a renewed emphasis on the use of business-type principles in decision making and to a focus on alternative service delivery, customer service, and total quality management. Introduced in the latter part of the twentieth century as New Public Management (NPM), this approach sought to confine government activities to narrowly prescribed limits while assessing outcomes using performance targets. B. Guy Peters (1996, 23) suggests that at the heart of this approach is the belief that markets are the most efficient mechanism for allocating resources within a society. Laura Ryser and colleagues (2023, 152) provide this perspective: "Neoliberal public policies were mobilized via New Public Management (NPM) ideologies. NPM is defined as policy reforms that mobilize institutional rules and regulations to exert control over public sector organizations, with a focus on cost reduction, devolution or transfer of responsibilities, cost recovery, accountability, performance, and generating greater efficiencies through incentives and market-based strategies."

Some of the NPM mechanisms may be effective at assessing outcomes in terms of productivity and quality and at giving councils a means to supervise the decisions made by staff (W. Kennedy, pers. comm., July 31, 2020). However, governments are not businesses, and they are delivering public goods and services that are not meaningfully measured using conventional metrics.

The application of business principles in government reduces citizens to customers and councils to boards of directors. In a healthy civic society, citizens are not just passive recipients of cost-effective services but individuals who have responsibilities as well as rights. There is also the questionable assumption that businesses actually do deliver the most effective services for the cost. Businesses must factor in how to make a competitive profit for their shareholders, an imperative that comes with its own set of costs and trade-offs. This market model of government may be responding to the wrong signals if success is measured only by examining the immediate bottom line. As Peters (1996, 43) has observed, in such models, outputs are what count, not the procedures by which governments make decisions or how and by whom. Finally, a business model is often a poor fit for the requirements of public administration. Governments must offer services in areas where the private sector would not find it profitable to do so. This is the case when public goods are universally shared for the benefit of the whole community, such as public parks, policing, public health, and the natural environment. Without the stabilizing effect of governments, the community – including its business enterprises – would not thrive.

INSIDE CITY HALL: THE MACHINERY

The formal model of public administration presents many challenges when applied to daily realities. One of the most important is how to hold government accountable for its actions. Given the many decisions that must be made in a large, modern government, it is difficult to hold any individual accountable for mistakes, particularly if a previously elected government made them. It is also hard to hold elected officials accountable since they rely on professional administrators for advice, knowledge, and expertise when making detailed financial or other policy decisions. Moreover, in the case of smaller local governments, serving as a member of council is often considered to be a part-time occupation. Administrators, then, necessarily make many important decisions, particularly when politicians do not have the capability to monitor all the activities of a large bureaucratic apparatus.

Accountability, Efficiency, and Effectiveness

Accountability is an important concept in public administration. Governments are structured, administered, and run based to a great extent on ensuring that they can be held accountable for their actions and can be seen to serve the public interest. In federal or provincial governments, in particular, the neutral civil servant is thought to be shielded from public view. The role of civil servants is to serve the elected politicians who make government policy decisions for which they alone must answer to the public. Civil servants are not directly accountable to external actors like pressure groups, news media, and the general public. In contrast, at the local government level, there is an absence of line departments for which individual councillors are formally responsible, although they may sit on committees that oversee the work of one or more departments. What is more, the public is much more likely to encounter and interact with local members of the civic administration. The multiple community responsibilities of civic employees, politicians, and citizen volunteers make it difficult to maintain distinct lines of accountability.

The structure of government also influences the accountability of civic employees. In Canada, local governments are organized in diverse ways that affect the lines of accountability. The internal administrative structures reflect some of the priorities of the government and how it views the mandates of different departments. In some communities, for example, departmental reorganization has taken place with the goal of seeing municipal corporations operate in a more business-like fashion. Recently, some municipalities have been restructured to reflect the need to foster interdepartmental, interagency, or collaborative partnerships with political actors outside of city hall.

Administrative Models

In addition to creating cities, towns, and villages, provincial governments have responded in a number of ways to unique local situations by establishing water boards, regions or districts, and school boards as well as other agencies, boards, and commissions. As noted above, appointed staff make recommendations to the elected council and administer programs and policies. Each of these governing bodies is based on a hierarchy (although some pyramids are flatter than others), and all are ultimately accountable to elected representatives.

Throughout Canada's history, a variety of localities have adopted different administrative structures, including council committees, boards of management, and executive committees, as well as different administrative roles, including chief officers, city managers, and commissioners (see Tindal et al. 2017, ch. 8). In addition, local governments may experiment with their own innovations. A system that relies on a city manager or chief administrative officer (CAO) places one primary administrator at the apex of the administrative hierarchy. This type of system is now used both in small cities, where relatively few officials are expected to handle a diversity of tasks, and in larger municipalities, which have much more capacity and administrations that are staffed with people who have specialized skills. Managing public services in a very large metropolitan city like Toronto, with over 35,000 employees, poses its own set of challenges. That said, all municipalities have structural similarities.

The city manager or CAO is responsible for the coordination of all the city departments, for overseeing the activities of one or more departments, and for reporting back to council with recommendations. Department heads also interact with members of council as well as through the city manager or CAO, who in turn is expected to be accountable to the mayor and council. The elected mayor and council have the authority to hire and fire senior staff members, although it does not happen easily or cheaply, and the process is governed by provincial legislation. The city manager or CAO is the most visible member of the administrative staff and is expected to be able to account for the operations of the whole city administration. This role includes one of the most important responsibilities – the preparation and submission of the budget.

Each city department or body is designed to fulfill a specific policy or service function. Throughout Canada, departments fall under the authority of a few senior staff, such as directors or managers, who are generally responsible for delivering the same basic services efficiently and effectively. Nevertheless, how these services are prioritized and grouped within the bureaucracy reveals how the government conceptualizes their roles. Typically, local governments group services based on their main responsibilities. One example is corporate services, such as the municipal corporation's human relations, legislative services, management of information and communications technologies (ICTs), and public procurement, finance, and administration. Additional examples are transportation, public works, and engineering; public health; public safety (i.e., fire, police, and other emergency services); community planning and development; environmental services; and community services related to families, seniors, housing, and income support.

Some municipalities are moving away from conventional organizational structures and toward outcome-based approaches that emphasize the health and sustainability of communities. Within each department, municipalities cluster various organizational units or introduce new ones to reflect current priorities. For example, cities facing climate emergencies are developing corporate climate action plans to ensure that their corporate activities address climate change.

Local governments' primary responsibilities revolve around land use and associated considerations. An official plan (also known as a community plan) is generally required of municipalities by provincial and territorial governments and must operate within the legislative guidelines set out by provincial or territorial planning acts. All development is expected to conform to the community plan, which is typically reviewed every five years and revised every decade. The plan reflects the vision that the community holds in terms of its future evolution. The ability of local governments to deliver on this vision depends a great deal on political will, capacity, and authority. Beyond that, little can be achieved in terms of implementing municipal agendas without the requisite resources. Given this reality, departments of finance play a key role in local public administration.

Local Finance

Municipalities are squeezed for revenues. Traditionally, their main sources of revenue have been property taxes, grants from senior governments, and fees. They have limited alternatives to the property tax, which covers an ever-diminishing share of a municipality's costs. Meanwhile, local governments are increasingly responsible for expenses that are not related to property, including the costs of climate change, rising poverty and homelessness, and environmental degradation. William Kennedy (pers. comm., July 31, 2020) notes that local government's reliance on one or two major sources of revenue makes it difficult for it to tailor the financial impact of an expenditure to the nature of a project (see Box 6.1). Government grants have not kept up with the growing responsibilities of municipalities.

Smaller rural and resource-based municipalities have been particularly hard-hit by senior-government cutbacks: "The capacity of staples-dependent municipalities to respond to change has been eroded by decades of cutbacks and consolidation of services in rural regions, outdated municipal tax structures, and limited municipal jurisdiction" (Ryser et al. 2023, 152).

Some provinces have granted their larger cities enhanced status under legislation that permits them additional leeway when raising revenues. Harry Kitchen, Enid Slack, and Tomas Hachard (2019, 9) provide a detailed account of the Canadian system of municipal property taxation, suggesting that local governments, specifically in the largest cities and

BOX 6.1 Municipal finance

As explained by William Kennedy (pers. comm., July 31, 2020), former director of finance, City of Prince George, British Columbia,

> Authority, responsibility, and financial powers should be aligned. The financial structure of local government, because of its emphasis on property tax and user fees, reflects a focus on services to property and local residents. It is only recently that wider concerns about environment, social issues, sustainability, etc., have come to the fore, yet the financial structure has remained mired in the past. Municipalities need wider taxation policies so that spending and taxation decisions can be properly linked (to enhance accountability). Local sales and income taxes, for example, have been used in some parts of the United States.

metropolitan centres, should have a wider range of tax choices and that the type of revenue should match the expenditure funded. Additional revenues include access to road toll taxes, congestion charges, various types of sales taxes, and personal income taxes. Newer sources of funding have been provided by senior governments to support sustainability initiatives. For instance, the federal government established a permanent federal gas tax fund to help municipalities address their infrastructural deficits. Municipalities can also apply for funding under programs such as the Green Municipal Fund (GMF). The GMF, initiated in 2000, was originally a $625 million program funded by the Government of Canada and delivered by the Federation of Canadian Municipalities. The GMF supports innovative municipal environmental initiatives to improve air, water, and land quality, to reduce greenhouse gas emissions, and to provide benefits for local communities. Lessons learned are shared with other municipalities (Federation of Canadian Municipalities 2019). In the 2019 federal budget, the government committed $1 billion to funding social-environmental programs in municipalities. Provinces also provide municipalities with grants and funding. One example is Alberta's Municipal Sustainability Initiative, introduced in 2007 to assist with the construction or rehabilitation of infrastructural services, facilities, and other local projects (Government of Alberta n.d.).

An additional source of funding for municipalities comes from municipal bonds or other forms of debt, such as leases or short-term loans, usually subject to approval of the provincial government. Bonds are a source of funding, but they must be paid back out of future streams of revenue. Since 2007, a number of cities around the world have been issuing municipal green bonds or green city bonds to fund environmental projects or to mitigate the impacts of climate change and greenhouse gases. Ottawa was reported to be the first to do so when it issued such a bond to fund its new light-rail transit system (Critchley 2017). By 2019, communities were increasingly framing their priorities within the context of climate change action plans and sustainability. Analysts began looking at how the new planning realities will be financed. In addition to green bonds, possible funding sources include environmental impact bonds, catastrophe bonds, and green banks (Carvalho 2018). Subsequently, the COVID-19 pandemic also pummelled the world. Local finances took on yet another layer of complexity, raising questions about what to prioritize and how to finance these plans. Senior governments obviously have been stepping in, but these major events call for paradigmatic shifts in financial models, at least in the short term. Public finance is fundamentally about political choices.

Choices about how to allocate revenues for the provision of particular public goods and services tell the observer a great deal about which goals and objectives decision makers think are most important. One need only consider how resources are allocated to various services, such as economic development, public transit, urban forests, homeless shelters, multicultural centres, festivals, recreational complexes, and opera houses. Who should pay for and deliver the services that promote a social and ecologically sustainable community? Finance departments play a key role in advising council and in implementing these kinds of local decisions and any others involving financial considerations.

The activities of a finance department stretch horizontally across municipal departments; it is not uncommon for financial and municipal corporate services to be grouped together. Given its key administrative and policy role, recommendations coming from the finance department play a pivotal role in environmental sustainability. One example pertains to the choices that administrations make about public procurement – the process by which governments purchase goods, services, or public works. Public procurement can also be used as a policy instrument to encourage innovative and more sustainable practices. Policy analyst Liesbeth Casier (2019) defines sustainable public procurement (SPP) as follows:

> SPP is about delivering the best value for taxpayer money when buying goods, services, and public works. It means moving away from buying based only on the cheapest price, and instead incorporating other socioeconomic, social and environmental values ...
>
> Green procurement is an environmentally friendly approach to SPP: it entails buying products, infrastructure and services that have a low-carbon footprint and that reduce impacts on biodiversity, decrease greenhouse gas emissions, and reduce pollution and pressure on natural resources.
>
> Social procurement encourages buying products, infrastructure and services that take into account working conditions, gender equality and respect for human rights throughout their operations and production processes.

From its influence on procurement practices to its budgeting process and tax system, the activities of a finance department merit close attention with respect to sustainable communities. The primary role of a finance department is to keep the government solvent. The department oversees the preparation of the annual budget used to finance municipal programs and objectives that reflect the city's priorities. The department will also participate in medium- and long-range financial planning to ensure that the municipality's financial situation is sustainable. Provinces exercise significant control over service provision and spending, and taxes must be collected for special purpose bodies and to service debt charges. Local governments generally are not allowed to run deficits in their operating budgets, although they can incur a debt for capital expenditures subject to certain guidelines. At the time of writing, how these rules will be enforced in the aftermath of the COVID-19 pandemic or another major disruptive event is open to question.

In those areas of finance where a municipality does have discretion, the allocation of monies has typically been the responsibility of city hall. Today, a budgeting process also often contains public consultation to ascertain public priorities. These consultations, which take many forms, can be as simple as an online questionnaire or as comprehensive as a participatory budgeting process. First introduced in Brazil, the concept of consultations has gained popularity in cities around the world, giving members of the public a direct say in allocating a portion of the budget. One of the challenges, as always, is how to ensure that the process is truly inclusive and representative of all societal groups (Friendly 2016).

Property Taxes, Grants, and Fees: Fair and Green
Other important political decisions associated with finance have to do with how revenues are raised to pay for services. To pay for shared community services, local governments have traditionally relied on property taxes and user fees as their main revenue sources, along with some grants from senior levels of governments. Municipalities depend heavily on such grants to provide major infrastructure. The property tax, based on the assessed value of a property, accounts for about 30 to 60 percent of municipal revenues, depending on the jurisdiction (Kitchen, Slack, and Hachard 2019, 3).

Municipalities can also impose special charges on a property to cover infrastructural or other costs, including special assessments, municipal bonusing, and development charges.[1] Development charges are levied to pay for the capital costs of additional required services, such as new infrastructure for a particular development. In the case of housing, these development charges can even improve housing accessibility by using "one-time fees levied on development to recover municipal growth-related capital costs"

(Found 2021, 2). When the alternative of raising property taxes or user fees is pursued, "the timing disparity between the initial capital investment and the receipt of growth-related revenue forces the municipality to raise property taxes and user fees above efficient levels" (2).

User fees cover a range of municipal services, including waste, water, transit, parking, and parks and recreation. Some of these fees are tied to consumption, whereas others are fixed. Fees can be used to encourage conservation of a resource and to reduce consumption, such as household use of water and disposal of waste. They can also improve accountability by tying the service to the cost of providing it. Some services are offered universally as a public good, but others include a partial fee or full fee for the cost of providing the service. For example, a park in the centre of town might be a public good that is freely and universally available to people as a place to stroll or sit on a bench. A sports league that plays cricket or baseball in that park may pay user fees to help cover the cost of maintaining the fields and bleachers. A group taking yoga classes in that park may pay full fees for the cost of the instructors if they are hired by the city recreation department. Almos Tassonyi and Harry Kitchen (2021, 3) suggest that user fees "are ideal for funding services for which specific beneficiaries can be identified, non-users can be excluded, and the quantity of service consumed can be measured. These are services with 'private goods' characteristics – such as water, sewers, solid waste collection and disposal, and public transit." In public finance, the goal is to tie the cost of the service to those who receive the benefits. The argument is that when such linkages are achieved, the basic goals of public finance are satisfied: "efficiency, accountability, transparency, fairness, and ease of administration" (4). As frequently stated here and elsewhere in this book, trade-offs must be considered. Paying for a service, particularly if your neighbour consumes more of the service, may appear to be an unfair system. However, this view does not address the issue of poverty, namely that some members of the community can afford to pay for services, whereas others cannot. Acknowledging that the question of affordability is an important concern, some public finance analysts argue that the financial burden should be addressed through other means. The alternative possibilities might be "income transfers from a senior level of government or social assistance programs targeted to individuals in need" (18).

As noted above, the traditional approach to taxation suggests that it should be governed by the principles of "fairness based on benefits received from local services, accountability, and efficiency ... Fairness exists when properties of equal value pay the same amount of property tax, because each of these properties has access to the same municipal services" (Kitchen, Slack, and Hachard 2019, 5, 7). This notion of fairness is viewed as a mechanism to foster transparency and accountability, important aspects of a healthy democratic governing system – which, in turn, is a core element of a sustainable community. However, it has also been argued that a "fair" tax system should include considerations of the principle of social equity, another important attribute of a healthy community. The gap in income disparity has been widening in recent decades, and some have argued that property taxes, rather than being fair, are regressive. The argument is that property taxes do not account for differential levels of personal income since those with lower incomes spend a higher proportion of their income on property taxes. Moreover, although renters do not pay property taxes, these taxes are usually reflected in their rent (D. Thompson et al. 2014, 27).

The choices of local governments with respect to setting a property tax rate, subsidizing a service, or imposing a user fee all have implications for social equity, ecological sustainability, and economic development. Which services should be paid for by all taxpayers and which ones should be paid for entirely or partially on a user-pay basis when considering the core elements of a sustainable community? In terms of the ecological sustainability of vital physical systems, some might argue that user fees could be imposed to promote behaviour that would reduce waste and unnecessary consumption. According to this green-economics perspective, users could be required to pay the actual life-cycle costs of services like waste disposal and water and energy provision in order to encourage conservation. Others, however, might argue that such a system would discriminate against the poor and would not necessarily encourage

conservation among the rich, who may be the largest consumers of the environmental good. Some municipalities employ a blend of approaches, applying a flat basic consumption rate but levying additional charges when use is exceeded. Municipalities may also offer relief programs for low-income earners in order to address questions of income inequality, as did the City of Toronto (n.d.) with its property tax and its water and waste relief programs. User fees, however, do undermine an important principle of equity, namely that everyone should have access to universally provided services.

Approaches to assessing property taxes also influence how property is developed. Pamela Blais (2010, 38), for example, notes that property taxes have historically had the perverse effect of encouraging urban sprawl and greenfield development, given that such land is less expensive, rather than facilitating more compact urban development. She argues that property taxes should reflect the marginal costs of providing a service to efficiently allocate resources, which is not the case in the prevailing system, where property taxes are based on market value (106). Tightly packed urban areas, Blais says, are much more cost-efficient than the traditionally sprawling suburban areas with respect to infrastructure and services, although suburban areas are now also becoming more densely built or infilled. She urges us to consider the per-unit costs of providing infrastructure for single-family homes on a city's periphery rather than for dwellings in the downtown area of a densely inhabited city (8–9).

William Kennedy (pers. comm., December 30, 2020), however, cautions that such comparative analyses between different types of planned communities can be challenging to conduct in practice because urban and suburban areas have unique service requirements, whose costs are not easily allocated to different types of property. Denser, urban areas can have distinct additional costs, for example, due to the greater need for traffic lights, water mains, fire-protection services, and regulations associated with governing compact, highly populated centres. In turn, suburban or rural areas may incur higher costs for items such as snow removal, street lighting, and road maintenance.

A final question when considering municipal finance in the context of sustainability is whether the variables under consideration and the means of assessment applied are the right indicators for the desired outcomes. For example, conventional cost-benefit analyses are not designed to incorporate ecosystem services into calculations when assessing the outcomes of policies and projects. In contrast, ecological-economics models, which are now being explored and in some places adopted, can take these considerations into account. In addition, an argument achieving salience around the world is that community well-being should be measured not by using liberal economic growth models but by implementing alternative means of assessment. One example is the Canadian Index of Wellbeing (n.d.). Given these complexities, urban finance can no longer rely on the use of conventional liberal economic assumptions if the goal is to foster long-term community sustainability.

CONCLUSION: LOCAL GOVERNING SYSTEMS

Public administration is important in any study of local government. Day-to-day management and decision making rest, in large part, in the hands of the administrative staff. The challenges facing local administrations vary considerably across Canada due to factors such as a city's size, political history, culture, economy, and environment. The degree to which administrators are influential depends, in part, on a number of factors, including organizational structure, available resources, means of communication, governing system, political will, and legal and regulatory restrictions. As important, however, is the informal authority that individuals wield by virtue of leadership ability, professional and personal values, knowledge, power structures, and capacity. Public servants do not operate in a vacuum. The information they bring to the decision-making environment is necessarily informed by their own experiences and set of values. Who should be influencing these experiences and values to ensure that city hall reflects the needs and desires of citizens?

Given that much of the authority granted to municipalities by provincial and territorial governments has traditionally focused on land use and property decisions, the private sector and developers have been influential actors in local governance. Property taxes, moreover, are a primary source of revenues for local governments as they seek to provide for an ever-expanding array of services that are not property-related. However, the growth in demand for a diversity of services, as well as mounting public calls for increased consultation, are pressuring governments to be more inclusive and open in their decision-making processes in order to meet political goals in a wider range of government activities. This inclusiveness applies not only to politically active nongovernmental organizations and interested members of civil society but also to those who have often been underserved or marginalized by local institutions. Healthy communities require an active, well-informed civil society, as well as a measure of reciprocal trust between political stakeholders.

Hierarchical organizational structures in government will continue to exist for all kinds of functional and democratic reasons. This reality, however, does not preclude the fact that local governments are now facing complex issues that require them to stretch horizontally, cut across hierarchies, and reach beyond their own jurisdictional spheres. They are now adopting some forms of networked, collaborative, multi-scaled forms of governance. As discussed in Part 2, these new forms of governance are emerging in response to numerous challenges – not the least of which is the need to sustain the vital social-ecological systems on which humans depend.

NOTE

1 In 2022, the Ontario provincial government imposed constraints on how local governments can apply development charges.

PART TWO

P.2 City Hall at Woodstock, Ontario, 2019

Networks and Partnerships
Connected Cities and Overlapping Responsibilities

The ability of local governments to respond effectively to complex problems relies a great deal on their political institutional culture, capacity to govern, administrative and policy approaches, and willingness to learn, collaborate, innovate, and develop networks. Today, the decisions of governments spill over political and physical boundaries as social and environmental issues become ever more entangled. Within and between municipalities, decision-making processes are diversifying as more political actors vie for influence. Polycentric forms of governance with local elements of autonomy are becoming recognized as important constructs for facilitating political consensus on shared areas of concern. Horizontal collaborations between government departments, bodies, other municipalities, and political actors are now common, and multi-level governance processes are now employed to navigate complex, overlapping issues (see Chapters 7 and 8).

The complexity of governing for sustainable social and ecological systems has been accompanied by the recognition that standardized institutional fixes are inadequate for the task. Moreover, the interdependence of social and biophysical systems calls for place-based forms of governance, policies, and approaches that are more responsive to the requirements of the unique social, political, and geographical contexts of diverse localities. The ecological services provided by watersheds or by unique geographical or cultural features require multi-scale collaborations. New institutions that can bridge political, knowledge, or social boundaries are more able to adapt to dynamic, shifting environments (see Chapter 8).

Beyond national borders, global events are reaching into local communities, necessitating international municipal cooperation to address the implications of wide-ranging developments such as climate change, pandemics, resource depletion, global economic competition, human migration, social injustice, 5G (or fifth-generation) technology, and the proliferation of social media. Climate change and the COVID-19 pandemic highlight that global and local issues are mutually dependent, necessitating both multi-level collaboration and place-based governance (see Chapter 9).

Governments are also challenged to harness and respond to exponential developments in the application of information and communications technologies (ICTs). Sustainability and, for that matter, any significant policy area of local governance cannot be addressed effectively without also considering the implications of the local adoption of innovations such as smart grids, artificial intelligence, digital transit systems, and government-employed surveillance tools. Decision makers also find themselves responding to the introduction of "disruptive" technologies that have cascading implications for city planning and policy. For instance, what are the implications of driverless vehicles for cities that have been planned around the automobile and its driver for the past century or longer? All aspects of city planning will be affected since this one innovation will have an impact, for example, on parking, cyclists, pedestrians and public transit, and traffic flow, not to mention all the other innovations that will co-evolve alongside driverless vehicles, such as the so-called sharing economy (see Chapter 10).

In this age – now popularly referred to as the Human Epoch or the Anthropocene, a time when humans have significantly altered life-supporting earth systems –

local governments are at the centre of the maelstrom. In a relatively short time, their mandates have expanded from a focus primarily on property-related issues and the provision of local services to a focus on the dynamic and multi-scale requirements needed to sustain healthy communities.

7 Bridging the Silos
Systems Thinking at City Hall

INTRODUCTION: HIERARCHIES AND HYBRIDS

The structural apparatus through which programs and services are delivered influences how the public interest is served. Attempts to address multi-scale, systemic, environmental problems when using a traditional, bureaucratic silo approach fall far from the mark. The silo approach or mentality is analogous to grain silos that dot the rural countryside. It has been so named in reference to the bureaucratic habit of government officials operating solely within their own mandates in order to maintain lines of vertical accountability and communications, without adequately consulting with their counterparts in other relevant departments or agencies.

Complex, interrelated social-environmental problems cannot effectively be addressed when institutional responses lack coordination between different departments. Today, changing perceptions regarding the most effective forms of governance in a complex environment are contributing to new forms of decision-making processes. Systems theories are attracting attention as one way to map interactions between social and ecological systems and to evaluate how changes in one variable may affect others. Multiple interactions between actors and systems will lead to positive and negative feedback loops. The key to understanding local political influence is to identify which combination of variables will lead to what kinds of desirable and undesirable system responses. This analytical perspective has led to new prescriptions for more integrated decision-making approaches that can address a wide variety of municipal concerns, such as infrastructure development, revenue generation, community health, and watershed planning,

Over the past several decades, various local governing bodies have incorporated some holistic approaches to decision making. One example is the Healthy Cities and Communities movement, initiated in the 1980s, which recognizes the interdependent relationship between social, economic, and biophysical health. Although local governments were quick to pick up the "vision" of this movement – one that includes public roundtables – they have been slow to internalize its implications for public administration and local governance. Conventional approaches to administration and policy making frequently founder on the shoals of complex, cumulative administrative and policy challenges. All too often, decision makers determine that an issue can be readily navigated by tackling only identifiable, tangible objects rather than those lying beneath the surface. Hierarchical reporting systems, traditional administrative approaches, and the overall lack of capacity of local governments all contribute to an inability to think about and resolve problems that are not easily reduced to discrete objectives that can be dealt with separately. A politically visible response to waste management, for example, may be to build a new landfill, providing tangible evidence to the electorate that the government is taking action. In contrast, a whole-systems approach to managing the flow of urban materials for long-term sustainability is not politically appealing because it is much more complex and time-consuming.

Community sustainability requires a new way of looking at governance – one that understands actors and social-ecological systems in terms of their dynamic interactions and effects. Systems approaches to governance are premised on the understanding that influence is wielded by a multiplicity of actors through a complex network of interacting variables that are operating at different spatial and temporal scales. Biophysical, socio-economic, and cultural factors all play into the mix. The challenge is to foster institutions that are both responsive to multiple competing demands and capable of dealing with layers of complexity. At the same time, they need to maintain clear lines of accountability and transparent decision-making processes. Such governing complexity has encouraged some analysts to advocate new forms of hybrid governance arrangements, what one group of researchers terms "smart hybridity" (Koppenjan, Karré, and Termeer 2019b). Rather than inventing new forms of governing structures, smart hybridity draws on existing structures and introduces small-scale innovations and changes, adjusting where necessary. As these researchers suggest, "These new forms of organization and governance rely on informal mechanisms and 'softer' governance methods and manage to bridge the gaps between individuals, organizations, domains and administrative levels in today's hyperfragmented organizational, economic, political and social environment" (Koppenjan, Karré, and Termeer 2019a, 15).

PATH-DEPENDENT BEHAVIOURS AND RESISTANCE TO CHANGE

Institutional and governance changes are not easily accomplished. "Path-dependent behaviour," "dispositional immobility," and "resistance to change" are all labels ascribed to barriers that cause public officials to block the introduction of organizational and policy innovations. Path-dependent behaviour refers to the difficulty of changing a pattern of behaviour or practice once it is established, particularly if the economic and social costs are "prohibitively high" (Markvart 2015, 67). In the case of local governments, change-resistant behaviours are reinforced when elected incumbents or city officials have held their positions for long periods. Dispositional immobility refers to the nondecisions of governments (i.e., decisions not to do

something), which effectively maintain the status quo. James Lightbody and Lisa Kline (2016, 1) suggest that this kind of "administrative stasis" can create "tactical political barriers to innovation, and policy inaction becomes a deliberate response." Such a situation can occur when efforts to maintain the status quo reinforce the entrenched interests and perspectives of the dominant governing elites, including those who work at city hall.

Long-time employees holding the same organizational position can provide the stability essential to the smooth operation of the municipality while elected governments come and go. That said, city staff may become so set in their own ways of doing things that they resist changes to the administrative system. These employees acquire a tremendous amount of influence by virtue of their knowledge and many years of working in the same job. As a result, depending on the personalities involved, it can be difficult for newly elected politicians – who rely on city staff for information – to assert and maintain control over any initiative throughout its life cycle.

Nonelected city employees exercise considerable discretion on a daily basis with respect to public decisions. From a democratic perspective, the interactions of elected members with staff and citizens may not be optimal given the multiplicity of other tasks that consume their time. In addition, the interactions of city staff with members of the private sector or with other members of civic society need to be properly recognized, understood, and taken into account in institutional structures and processes. Among other things, doing so could mean drawing up more stringent conflict of interest guidelines and introducing more transparency into decision-making processes. For example, many times throughout history, concerns have been raised about instances of corruption related to questionable relationships between private land developers and city hall (Anderson 2013).

Regulations have often been introduced to address concerns about a lack of transparency and secretive deals. Examples include the requirement that council meetings be open to the public (with some exceptions) and the establishment of an impartial municipal or provincial ombudsman to hear complaints about council conduct, to improve municipal services, or to address ethical issues related to the activities of members of the elected or nonelected arms of city hall. Other measures might be access to information legislation, integrity commissioners, open-data policies that make government documents publicly available online, and results-based accountability with a focus on the end goals or outcomes of a policy.

Despite entrenched organizational forces, change can happen. Administrative and policy innovations might come about as a result of efforts to legitimize public decisions, the election of new councils, the hiring of new city hall employees, the diffusion of policy ideas, or institutional learning. These developments may be incremental due to various institutional and individual constraints, such as limitations in capacity, the preferences of the political elite, a plurality of perspectives that require accommodation, and simply, inertia. Change may also come about as a result of policy layering, "where new policy goals are added to, or layered onto, an existing policy commitment without removing others" (Carey, Kay, and Nevile 2019, 493). Looking at public decision making as a complex system, one could argue that change can come about as a result of interactions of a multiplicity of factors and actors, including "tipping points, network effects, combinational effects, bandwagon effects, reinforcement, emergence, and ... layering" (494). Change within an organization can result from a sudden exogenous event, but as Michael Howlett and Andrea Migone (2011, 60n11) observe, it is just as likely that "a large amount of institutional change may come about in a gradual endogenous fashion."

POLICY SHOCKS AND PUNCTUATED EQUILIBRIUM

Administrative or policy change, however, can also occur suddenly if a certain threshold is crossed, such as when an exogenous policy shock occurs. According to Frank R. Baumgartner and colleagues (2009, 608), sudden policy shifts "are contingent themselves on a network of interacting variables, causing context to matter." They have adopted the term "punctuated equilibrium" to explain sudden policy change. The term was first coined in the field of paleontology to explain how a long term of stability can prevail followed by a period of rapid change, leading to the emergence of new species. The COVID-19 pandemic might be termed a period of punctuated equilibrium if, in fact, it does lead to new policy innovations (Nikitas et al. 2021).

Other examples of exogenous forces that might influence internal administrative practices are natural disasters (e.g., floods, fires, and hurricanes) and the effects of climate change. Canada and the world are now experiencing more frequent and intense natural disasters. Devastating wildfires, catastrophic floods, heatwaves, and droughts are now regular occurrences, and natural disasters are forecast to intensify in the years to come.

Municipal governments have been developing strategies to address the impacts of global climate change. For example, in Ontario, the Region of Waterloo has devised an action plan in collaboration with a diverse group of community and organizational partners coalescing under the banner of ClimateActionWR (n.d.). Other examples include Toronto's Green Standard and Transform TO and Vancouver's Climate Emergency Action Plan.

The dire global impacts and consequences of climate change, coupled with global activism by nongovernmental organizations and thousands of scientists, have also stimulated governments to declare climate emergencies (Climate Emergency Declaration Organization 2023). Throughout the world in 2019, specifically in highly developed economies, numerous governments supported climate emergency declarations with a sharpening of their strategic policy on combating greenhouse gas (GHG) emissions and mitigating the impacts of climate change (see Chapter 9). Canada was no exception, with the national government and about 500 municipalities (in partnership with local organizations) declaring climate emergencies. In 2022, the Government of Canada committed $1.6 billion (in addition to other existing federal funds) to its new Adaptation Action Plan in order to help communities in five strategic areas: "improving health and well-being," "building and maintaining resilient public infrastructure," "protecting and restoring nature and biodiversity," "supporting the economy and workers," and "reducing the impacts of climate-related disasters" (Environment and Climate Change Canada 2022a).

A network of municipalities has committed to reducing its carbon emissions and the impacts of GHG emissions using a framework laid out by the Partners for Climate Protection (PCP) and implemented with the assistance of the Federation of Canadian Municipalities (FCM) and ICLEI – Local Governments for Sustainability through its Building Adaptive and Resilient Communities program. As of 2022, over 420 projects aimed at reducing GHG emissions had been developed in over 500 Canadian municipalities under the PCP network, which contains a communications hub. The PCP Hub is a "peer-to-peer online network" offering a platform for municipalities to ask questions, share successes, and gain access to expertise and technical advice and help. It receives funding both from ICLEI and from the FCM's Green Municipal Fund, which is financed by the federal government (Partners for Climate Protection 2021).

For instance, the Region of Waterloo, which is an upper tier of government, and its local municipalities and townships have all declared climate emergencies and introduced a climate action strategy to reduce GHG emissions by 80 percent from 2010 levels by 2050. In Kitchener, one of the region's municipalities, Mayor Berry Vrbanovic has long been involved in promoting action on sustainability and climate change. He has participated in policy forums, from the local to the global levels of governance, and has served as the treasurer and the co-president of the world organization United Cities and Local Governments (UCLG).[1] In 2011–12, Vrbanovic served as the president of the FCM and sat on its Green Municipal Fund Council. In February 2020, he introduced the City of Kitchener's (2019) first sustainability report, which provides an accounting of action taken the previous year on its Corporate Climate Action Plan, with a focus on areas under its municipal control (see Box 7.1). The city is working to reduce its carbon emissions and the impacts of its GHG emissions (5). It promotes collaborative and partnership approaches that draw on the framework provided by the United Nations Sustainable Development Goals (SDGs) (United Nations General Assembly 2015). These initiatives to guide the activities of the city's corporate operations are only part of a broader sustainability plan that will incorporate and coordinate many diverse municipal objectives into the city's governance as a whole (City of Kitchener n.d.).

Other complementary efforts include the Low Carbon Cities Canada (LC3) (n.d.) network, a part-

---

BOX 7.1   The City of Kitchener's Corporate Climate Action Plan

The aim of the City of Kitchener's (2019, 5) Corporate Climate Action Plan is to work toward eight goals:

1. Maximize facility-level efficiency and resilience.
2. Optimize and innovating City fleet through technology, alternative fuels and electrification.
3. Upgrade and standardizing outdoor lighting to LED technology; where applicable, with controls.
4. Complete a comprehensive review of the existing waste program to improve and expand diversion.
5. Plan and implement climate adaptation initiatives through engagement, policy and projects that improve resiliency to impacts that pose risk to the corporation.
6. Generate and manage robust data to analyze, forecast, and report on findings and trends to inform strategic planning, business operations and project level performance.
7. Guide decision making for broad support of greenhouse gas emission reduction and resiliency to climate change.
8. Improve engagement and two-way communication between corporate stakeholders by optimizing existing channels and creating new ones.

"The City of Kitchener's Corporate Climate Action Plan (CorCAP) aims to achieve meaningful and measurable carbon emission reductions throughout its operation, while also adapting to impacts resulting from climate change. An absolute greenhouse gas (GHG) reduction target of 8% by 2026, over 2016 levels" (City of Kitchener 2019, 6).

nership among seven of Canada's largest cities that is supported through the Federation of Canadian Municipalities. Its endowment of $183 million from the Canadian federal government through the Green Municipal Fund finances its mission of supporting municipalities "as they reach their carbon emissions reduction potential while improving public health, creating jobs and building resilient communities" (Simon Fraser University 2021).

Cities are also collaborating along with educational institutions to develop regional strategies for climate change adaptation. For example, Niagara Adapts is a partnership between seven municipalities in the Niagara Region of Ontario and Brock University's Environmental Sustainability Research Centre (n.d.). These kinds of partnership efforts strengthen the ability of local governments to learn from each other and to build synergies that would have been difficult to achieve individually.

MUNICIPAL EMERGENCY MANAGEMENT
Historically, governments and individuals have placed a relatively low priority on disaster preparedness and mitigation efforts, with individuals tending to psychologically minimize and underestimate the potential risks from environmental hazards (Henstra and McBean 2004, 2). With the rising intensity and frequency of natural disasters over the past few decades, local governments throughout Canada are now being challenged to reconsider their approaches. This is particularly the case in those communities that have been devastated by extreme weather occurrences like floods, wildfires, and hurricanes. Traditional hazard management approaches have been based on assumptions of rarer occurrences of disasters, with the goal being to protect or separate people from potential hazards. Newer policy alternatives draw on risk management principles that go beyond protection to consider the consequences of hazards using a range of policy tools, including "mitigation, response, and recovery. The shift towards risk management involves an expansion of the government and non-government stakeholders involved in designing and implementing policy" (Henstra and Thistlethwaite 2017, 2). This approach also entails sharing the risks and costs of a disaster with other partners; in the case of municipal-

ities, for example, these costs are also shared with other levels of government (2). Upper-level governments play key roles in providing municipalities with financial, information, and capacity-building resources, particularly with respect to adaptation planning (Vogel, Henstra, and McBean 2018).

METABOLIC RISK AND GOVERNANCE
Another way to conceptualize risk is through an analysis of social metabolism. Like biological metabolism, the social metabolism of a complex social-ecological system such as a city draws on material and energy from the biophysical environment in order to sustain itself and evolve. The system's social metabolism may be at risk or reach a tipping point and collapse as a result of climate-related changes. It could also be at risk from the overuse of natural resources, extreme weather events, socio-economic degradation and polarization, or a combination of these factors. Simron Jit Singh and colleagues (2022) argue that a social-metabolic risk governance strategy can be employed to guide decision-making processes and to manage metabolic risk. The application of a risk-governance framework can help decision makers to understand and reconfigure resource use and service delivery in complex social-ecological systems such as cities (see Box 7.2).

Natural and human-made disasters are now causing governments throughout Canada to rethink how they address challenges related to climate change and how they build social-ecological resiliency. According to one government official in Alberta's forestry department, the biggest improvement in emergency preparedness across three major wildfire events was the strengthened cooperation and coordination between the stakeholders, who worked together rather than in silos (cited in Graney 2019). Partnerships that avoid silos is an approach that has rapidly gained ground in municipal circles.

In 2019, major local, regional, and provincial agencies, along with academia and other bodies, including those responsible for planning, energy, transportation, water management, construction, and conservation, signed a charter to collaborate on the reduction of flooding and extreme rain events. The Flood Resilient Toronto Charter was developed to

BOX 7.2   Risk governance and managing social-metabolic risk (SMR)

Governing for social-metabolic systemic risks such as climate change might be best approached using a "risk governance" framework. As Simron Jit Singh and colleagues (2022, 2) state, SMR is "systemic risk associated with the availability of critical resources, the integrity of material circulation, and the (in)equitable distribution of derived products and societal services in a socio-ecological system." Metabolic risk governance, the authors argue, must therefore, "embrace societal goals with the boundaries set by metabolic flows" (8).

To manage SMR and avoid metabolic collapse, mechanisms and strategies to reconfigure resource-use patterns and associated services that are sustainable and socially equitable are crucial ... Some of the strategies include resource-localization where possible, shortening supply chains, increase resource circularity rates by closing material cycles, and optimizing spatial planning that promotes multifunctional infrastructure use and align to nature-based solutions guidelines. Strategies will also need to consider the distribution of costs and benefits (beyond just monetary) of specific resource-use configuration across different segments and sectors of the society ...

Governing SMR and tipping points ... would mean governing metabolic flows so that potential disruptions in the circulation of critical resource can be avoided ... Policies in this context are based on envisioning potential future trajectories and value judgments about their social and ecological implications. Furthermore, the inclusion of stakeholders and the public insights provides orientation for policies targeted towards positive tipping points (Franzke et al. 2022). In that context, known experiences reflecting water, energy, food security and infrastructure dimensions needs to be reoriented towards interdisciplinary and cross-sectoral cooperation, and the engagement of scientists, regulators and other stakeholders must be steered to foster effective risk governance. (Singh et al. 2022, 8, 9)

encourage city resilience and innovation in flood protection (Welsh 2019). Previously, the City of Toronto had joined the international collective 100 Resilient Cities (Rockefeller Foundation n.d.), which had inspired the city's resilience strategy and the creation of a resilience office. The strategy is more inclusive, encourages civic engagement, and prioritizes the needs of the most vulnerable people by integrating equity into the process. An important overarching objective is to "institutionalize resilience" and to embed new practices in city decision making. Resilience initiatives include the Don River Naturalization and the Food Resilience Strategy of Toronto Public Heath (City of Toronto 2019, 142, 143).

Another way to build resiliency and to avoid risk in the face of climate change and natural disasters is to adopt planning strategies that include preparations for extreme climate-related events. One approach, for example, is the PARA framework – protect, accommodate, retreat, and avoid – which can be used for flood risk reduction. Elements of all these strategies have been employed at different times and places, with the appropriate strategy being context-dependent. However, it is becoming manifestly apparent that precaution and risk management strategies need to be employed in advance of, rather than in response to, natural disasters (see Box 7.3).

When a catastrophe or crisis point leads to major disruptions, such as those that cause towns or cities to be rebuilt, new partnerships and collaborative forms of governance may arise. Emergency responses call upon the combined efforts of all relevant stakeholders and volunteers. These "high-profile unexpected shock events" may have the effect of pushing other important issues – such as slow-onset events – off decision-making agendas. A slow-onset event, one that occurs gradually but does not seem to require immediate attention, is often pushed to the bottom of a government's agenda. Public bureaucracies play a key role in managing gradual but vitally important events, such as climate change (Tosun and Howlett 2021).

During the crises of the COVID-19 pandemic, many observers expressed worry that the pandemic was pushing climate change off governments' immediate agendas. One could argue, however, that shock events of this kind can also have the reverse effect by highlighting the significance of slow-onset events. The pandemic, for example, caused a spotlight to be directed at long-standing issues in the health care system, and climate change may now receive more attention due to catastrophic weather events.

These policy shocks or punctuations do not possess uniform characteristics, nor do they have the same effect. Different types of exogenous and endogenous policy punctuations can lead to path-breaking policy changes, but they can also reinforce existing policy paths. John Hogan, Michael Howlett, and Mary Murphy (2022, 9) observe that a crisis or policy failure does not necessarily lead to policy change, with the COVID-19 pandemic being an example:

It was a truly exogenous shock on a par with a tsunami, massive earthquake, or medium-sized meteor impact but with a long-lasting and continuing impact on society and the economy. Responses to it have highlighted the inadequacies and fault lines in some existing institutions but have not themselves been adequate to drive significant policy change across multiple sectors where that change had not already begun. It was rather in many cases at best a "path clearing event," a kind of policy punctuation which serves as an accelerator that can lead to change in proximate areas where change was already underway.

Elected governments are able to respond only to a limited number of issues at any one time. Jale Tosun and Michael Howlett (2021) suggest that public bureaucracies can perform an important role in ensuring that slow-

onset events are addressed and maintained on decision agendas over time. Whether they can do so effectively depends a great deal on what the analysts refer to as their functional capacity (i.e., material resources, professionalization of bureaucrats, and autonomy from political principals) and their analytical competence (i.e., substantive knowledge, analytical tools and techniques, and communications) (see Tosun and Howlett 2021, 46, fig. 1). Of course, the ability of public service officials to exercise these capabilities depends on the context in which they operate, including the degree of assistance, resistance, or indifference offered by the political regime in power. The policy-making abilities of local governments are limited by their historically assigned responsibilities, such as the provision of property-related services like hard infrastructure, by their lack of legislative authority, and by their limited tax base. The following outlines how local governments are structured and have changed over time, particularly with respect to how they address questions of sustainability.

BOX 7.3 **Protect, accommodate, retreat, and avoid: The PARA framework**

PARA is one planning strategy aimed at reducing risks from natural disaster emergencies. Brent Doberstein, Joanne Fitzgibbons, and Carrie Mitchell (2019, 32–33) discuss PARA's four main approaches:

Protect approaches involve the construction of engineered structures and systems (e.g. dikes, floodwalls, diversion structures, etc.) designed to keep flood waters away from homes, communities, critical facilities, and valued infrastructure. *Accommodate* approaches are those adaptive strategies which are designed to allow continued use of flood-prone areas by improving the resilience of communities or valued facilities/infrastructure to occasional flooding, or by limiting damage in these areas (e.g. raising structures, flood proofing foundations, etc.). *Retreat* approaches are those where homes, communities, facilities and infrastructure that are subject to repeat flooding are relocated permanently to safer areas. *Avoid* approaches are those which attempt to proactively prevent homes, communities, facilities or infrastructure from being built in flood-prone areas in the first place.

NEW MODELS OF GOVERNANCE

A new model of governance has emerged on the heels of New Public Management (NPM), which prevailed in many administrations in the last decades of the twentieth century. This new model, known as New Public Governance (NPG), recognizes the need to address the complex nature of policy making and the interdependencies of many governing actors and factors operating at different temporal and spatial scales. Rooted in organizational sociology and network theory, it "lays emphasis on the design and evaluation of enduring interorganizational relationships, where trust, relational capital and relational contracts act as the core governance mechanisms" (Osborne 2006, 384). NPG also recognizes the effectiveness and efficiencies offered through the provision of services in collaboration with nongovernmental and other organizations (Vinokur-Kaplan 2018).

BOX 7.4 Collaborative decision-making processes

Tanya Markvart (pers. comm., October 18, 2020; see also 2015), a community sustainability planning practitioner in Waterloo, Ontario, explains the collaborative decision-making process:

Many advocates of sustainability have called for forms of decision making that are inclusive, discursive, and include participants who contribute a diversity of perspectives equitably without domination by any one group. Collaborative and other forms of discursive decision making emerged in response to this call, which rang loudly within the environmental movement over the latter half of the 20th century. There has been a strong shared belief among advocates of sustainability that complex environmental problems require forms of decision making that are sensitive to the perspectives, types of knowledge and uncertainty inherent in complex environmental problems. According to many sustainability theorists, decentralized and discursive decision-making processes are capable of attending to this inherent plurality and uncertainty and, therefore, they contribute to more equitable and ecologically rational decision outcomes. The basic assumption has been that collaborative decision making encourages stakeholders from diverse backgrounds to build trusting relationships, learn from each other, critically reflect on a range of values and impacts, reach consensus on complex issues, and develop a sense of shared responsibility over decision results. Good collaborative processes feature:

- openings for participation in decision making that are inclusive of all interested and/or affected stakeholders;
- critical reflection and reciprocal understanding of the variety of interests at stake;
- collective decision making that appeals to the common good as opposed to self-interest;
- equal opportunity to participate;
- deliberations are free from coercive power;
- planners are (neutral) facilitators as opposed to experts;
- citizens are fully informed;
- a concern for social learning and change; and
- consideration of all alternatives.

Whether or not deliberative processes lead to greater sustainability is a matter of much debate. Indeed, examples of good collaborative processes are still relatively rare. An evaluation of municipal sustainability planning in Canada revealed that many contextual factors may shape the design of decision-making processes. These include, to name a few, budget and time constraints, entrenched attitudes, and the local context in terms of the range of sustainability issues at stake. One exemplary case of sustainability planning in Canada is the City of Kingston's Strategic Sustainability Plan [*Sustainable Kingston Plan* (2010)], which involved direct citizen control over implementation through an arm's length non-profit organization. In this case, planning practitioners acknowledged the need for change with respect to the design of decision-making processes and they consciously raised the bar on practice by facilitating a strong citizen-led initiative.

Collaborative governance has been defined as "a specific mode of interaction that is deliberative, multilateral, consensus-seeking, and oriented toward joint production of results and solutions" (Ansell and Torfing 2015, 316). In this model, the collaborative decision-making processes aimed at sustainability require new approaches.

Municipal initiatives to undertake collaborative and participatory sustainability planning are now becoming well known. Tanya Markvart, for example, investigated sixty-five municipal exercises in Canada focused on strategic sustainability planning. Although many such initiatives have been implemented, they may not necessarily achieve their intended goals. As these collaborative efforts become increasingly common, case studies such as those undertaken by Markvart offer important insights about what constitutes a good and effective decision-making process to foster sustainability (see Box 7.4).

Collaborative processes are seen as desirable for social, political, and practical purposes in the context of "wicked" problems and issues that may cross functional, political, temporal, and spatial scales.

Moreover, formal representative governing institutions possess their own limitations when it comes to questions of transparent decision making and public accountability. Eva Sørensen and Jacob Torfing (2021, 1–2), who refer to this situation as "*thin accountability*," advocate collaborative networked systems of governance that would instead promote "*thick accountability*":

> Hence, as we define it, *thick accountability* refers to a dialogical accountability relationship in which: (1) account givers have both capacity and opportunity to provide precise and adequate accounts about particular governance decisions and the mission-related results that are obtained; and (2) account holders have both skills and competences to critically assess and sanction these accounts vis-à-vis a broad set of norms, values and obligations. Performing these roles in thick accountability processes requires mutual trust.

The conventional, hierarchical assessment of accountability using performance measurements, Charles Conteh (2016) argues, was based on a mechanistic understanding of government as a closed system rather than an open, fluid, and complex system, which more accurately portrays the government decision-making environment. He advocates for a form of accountability that emphasizes principles of "trust, openness and reciprocity rather than mechanical instruments of control" (237). All parties are to be mutually accountable – or to have "social accountability" – with an emphasis on the importance of institutional learning and adaptation, public reporting and peer review, deliberative forums, and processes that are consensual and reciprocal.

New Public Governance approaches, however, can be subject to problems of exclusion, a lack of transparency, high transaction costs, and limitations in the ability of societal actors to self-govern (Koppenjan, Karré, and Termeer 2019a, 13). One unresolved issue with respect to NPG models is how to address the questions of accountability, efficiency, and effectiveness that the original bureaucratic, hierarchical model was designed to address. Horizontal collaborations and networked systems can blur the lines of accountability. Recognizing these challenges, Sørensen and Torfing (2021, 15) promote the adoption of a "double-loop social accountability model" that employs metagovernance oversight in support of bottom-up accountability. They suggest that such an approach would supplement, rather than supplant, traditional institutional forms of accountability.

Since no single model of governance can address wicked problems, Joop Koppenjan, Philip Marcel Karré, and Katrien Termeer (2019a, 16) advocate hybrid approaches:

> Hybrid, and thus smart governance involves bringing the right parties together at the right moment and stimulating their collective problem-solving capability as well as finding new governance arrangements in the space that exists between government, market and society. These are often hybrid forms of governance based on smart combinations of existing organizational and governance methods.

These analysts recognize that no panacea or grand model can address shifting social-ecological dynamics.

What is needed, they suggest, are organizations that are able to adapt, change, and innovate in order to respond to new and sometimes unanticipated issues. To be sure, institutional and governance changes are not easily accomplished. Indeed, in multi-scale systems, governing in ways that ensure the positive alignment of outcomes at various times and in diverse places is an impressive feat. Moreover, this undertaking assumes that the political players are willing and able to operate in such a multi-dimensional arena. Although local decision makers often resist change and find ways to avoid disrupting past practices, numerous examples of collaborative approaches can be found at different scales and in distinct policy areas. Changing municipal priorities related to sustainability also influence emerging planning and management practices. Beyond the political will to make it happen, sustainability requires the identification of new priorities and goals, institutional restructuring to reflect these priorities, the allocation of resources to deliver them, and an organizational transformation that reflects "embedded sustainability" (Zeemering 2018, 136). Public-sector sustainable planning and management can substantially influence both service and policy delivery. Eric S. Zeemering cautions against "bolt-on" sustainability – that is, adding sustainability programs using existing management and organizational practices. Rather, he suggests that local governments should develop overall sustainability approaches and should embrace opportunities and strategies for social learning by working collaboratively. He argues that "local governments, as the providers of public services, can use sustainability strategy to rethink service delivery approaches, including the social and environmental externalities of the production technologies and choices they make" (145).

Local governments have typically been structured based on hierarchical models, with linear departments overseeing responsibilities such as corporate services, community services, economic development, planning,

---

BOX 7.5 Restructuring city hall toward a sustainable community

Some municipalities across the country are restructuring their bureaucracies to reflect emerging governing challenges and concerns about long-term sustainability rather than automatically following traditional organizational clusters. The following examples are illustrative of this approach.

Saint John, New Brunswick, underwent a reorganization in 2016 and updated it in 2022. The city aligned the roles of its departments with the aspirational goal of leading "the nation as an example of a sustainable community" and with the organizational goal of functioning as a "service-based, results-oriented, high-performance public service organization." Services are clustered together to effectively deliver these goals and to focus on issues of particular concern to the city, namely growth and community services, fire and emergency management services, transportation and public works, utilities and public infrastructure, finance and administration, and strategic and corporate services (City of Saint John 2022).

Edmonton implemented an organizational departmental grouping called Integrated Infrastructure Services, which aims to foster citizen and stakeholder engagement, create healthy communities, and introduce renewable energy systems, facilitated in part through its Building Great Neighbourhoods Branch (City of Edmonton n.d.-c).

Montreal, Canada's second largest city, has created some new departmental units, such as the Laboratoire de l'innovation urbaine de Montréal. Its goal is to address urban challenges by developing innovative solutions, such as driverless vehicles, open data, and public Wi-Fi (City of Montreal n.d.-b). The city has also introduced a departmental grouping that focuses on quality of life, "to improve the lives of Montrealers with respect to the environment, arts and culture, the economy and society" (City of Montreal n.d.-a). Two of the clusters in this department are social diversity and inclusion and ecological transition and resilience.

public safety, and public works. These departments then report to a central administrative office or to a chief administrative officer accountable to city council. Some local governments, however, have been restructuring to emphasize sustainability, with services clustered together to achieve the goal of creating livable cities (see Box 7.5).

In British Columbia, local asset management has been reframed within the context of climate change and sustainability by municipal associations, and the province has adopted a governing approach based on practices of collaboration and continuous learning to ensure that community services are delivered in a socially, economically, and environmentally responsible manner. The plan emphasizes the important role of the natural and built infrastructural assets in sustaining existing communities for use by future generations (Asset Management BC n.d.).

PARTNERSHIPS

> *When actors with different resources, competences, and ideas are brought together in processes of creative problem solving, they are likely to produce a better understanding of the problem at hand, and engage in processes of mutual learning through which they can develop and test new and bold solutions while building a joint sense of ownership for their project.*
>
> – Sørensen and Torfing 2018, 389

Local governments have engaged in partnerships with other organizations and groups to address complex challenges and to provide services given their limited municipal sources of revenues. These entities include the private sector, nongovernmental organizations, volunteers from civil society, and other governmental bodies.

The Private Sector

From its early days, one of the primary roles of local government has been to manage relations with the business sector, which is primarily property-related. Local governments have long been viewed as responsible for providing hard services such as infrastructure

and for making land-use and development decisions. Regardless of whether the motivation is altruistic or self-serving, the ideological orientation of business heavily influences local councils. Councils, in turn, base their decisions on a set of assumptions that advance certain interests at the expense of others. Leaders of the local private sector often serve on city council, promoting public services that are also useful to their own interests. These efforts frequently provide the community with necessary services, such as a sewage system, clean water, public transit, and electricity. Sometimes, however, city officials and businesspeople are reluctant to undertake initiatives that might deal with other important public matters, such as addressing the adverse environmental and social impacts that could accompany industrial development. Local governments have always sought business development to provide much-needed revenues. In both its positive and negative manifestations, this public-private relationship has important implications for the social and ecological health of a municipality and for the way that these considerations are viewed and treated.

Public-Private Partnerships

One approach that became influential in the 1990s was alternative service delivery (ASD), which was used at all levels of government in an attempt to reduce the size of administrations by having some services and other activities delivered by private-sector organizations. Given the limited options of local governments, they had little choice but to pursue alternative avenues for funding and delivering services. One of these mechanisms was public-private partnerships (P3s), which are now frequently used to fund public infrastructure projects. These partnerships operate "on a continuum between full privatisation and traditional government procurement" and include "a myriad of structures that facilitate the participation of the private sector in the provision of public infrastructure and services" (Colverson and Perera 2011, 2). P3s are seen to have advantages like distributing costs and risks between the partners as well as bringing private-sector investment, time efficiencies, innovation, and expertise to the initiative. The use of the private sector to provide public services such as waste management and snow removal has generated concerns about high tendering and transaction costs, complex contracts, transparency, and democratic accountability (Colverson and Perera 2011; Valverde and A.A. Moore 2018). Questions about the public transparency of these partnerships have led local governments to mandate the release of project information. However, as Mariana Valverde and Aaron A. Moore (2018) caution, such information does not necessarily lead to democratic accountability if the information is not readily comprehensible by a typical citizen or does not provide meaningful understanding of the projects in the context of other governing priorities or approaches.

Historically, the development sector has had a dominant effect on local planning processes. Private-sector actors can include landowners, real estate developers, mortgage bankers, realtors, construction companies and contractors, cement works, sand and gravel companies, and building suppliers. New subdivisions, for example, are often proposed by a private-sector developer, who must submit a subdivision plan to the city. Elected officials, planners, and other members of city government consider whether these new subdivisions conform to the official plan and whether there are sufficient revenues to cover any costs that the city might incur. City staff also determine the applicable zoning codes, building permits, and land-use regulations, and they oversee the construction of roads, sewers, and other necessary infrastructure. Councillors are keenly aware of the much-needed revenues that developers might bring to the community. However, in recent years, community plans have been increasingly framed within the sustainability discourse, as can be seen with the introduction of Integrated Community Sustainability Plans (ICSPs). Although many actors are usually involved in the process of designing the community plan, municipal planners play an important role in implementing this vision.

Community Benefits Agreements

Some argue that in order to address concerns about the accountability, social equity, legitimacy, and transparency of partnership agreements, community members should be brought into the negotiations. One

mechanism for doing that is the Community Benefits Agreement (CBA). As explained by policy analyst Andrew Galley (2015, 8),

> Community Benefits Agreements are formal agreements between a real estate or infrastructure developer and a coalition that reflects and represents people who are affected by a large development project. The agreement outlines the benefits the community will enjoy from the project. These benefits usually include some combination of jobs, training or apprenticeships, business opportunities as well as neighbourhood improvements. Where the development includes residential construction, affordable housing can be a benefit negotiated through this process. Most agreements reflect the interests of people who are not already benefiting from economic growth, such as young workers, newcomers, foreign-trained professionals and low-income communities, and send opportunities their way.

CBAs have been operationalized in various parts of North America since the turn of the twenty-first century, although they started to gain steam only toward the end of the 2010s. In 2018, British Columbia established a Crown corporation, BC Infrastructure Benefits, not only "to partner in the successful delivery of projects, mobilize and grow a safe, diverse and skilled workforce and honour community strength by building on local assets, knowledge and potential" but also to "ensure priority hiring is given to equally qualified local residents, Indigenous people, and other underrepresented groups" (n.d.-c). That year, Vancouver implemented a city-wide CBA policy.

In 2019, the City of Toronto also adopted a new Community Benefits Framework, which provides training and job opportunities for Toronto residents "from historically disadvantaged communities and equity seeking groups" and fosters opportunities for diverse, local business and social organizations to access city contracts. The framework applies to city-led projects and city-owned lands, offering financial incentives for private developments while promoting voluntary discussions between community groups and developers about the community benefits of developments on private land. The framework sets out targets for workforce development, a community benefits coordinator monitors, tracks, and reports on achievements and targets, a multi-stakeholder advisory group provides advice and promotes transparency and accountability, and a job-skills training centre has been established "to assist job candidates from equity seeking groups, including Indigenous peoples" (Toronto Community Benefits Network n.d.). CBAs offer the possibility of including citizens in the development process. However, there are negative possibilities to consider, such as co-optation and corporatism undermining transparency and the democratic decision-making processes undertaken by elected representatives. CBAs are not designed as forums for discussing a community's long-term sustainability goals. CBAs offer one avenue for citizen volunteers, but there are many other arenas where volunteers play a vital role in shaping local communities.

Volunteers

Citizens and interest groups are active players in local governance. When local residents are engaged, they perform important communications, political, and democratic functions by helping to articulate the concerns and interests of less politically active members of the public, making them influential shapers of the local political culture. In conjunction with local administrators and city staff, citizens often help to inform, design, administer, and implement programs. Civic participation spans activities like contributing individually to helping neighbours or the wider community, voting and serving on government advisory committees, keeping politically aware and informed, and forming organizations such as nonprofits, neighbourhood associations, unions, local food roundtables, environmental groups, multicultural associations, and recreation and leisure clubs.

In this era when climate change emergencies and natural disasters are becoming more frequent, volunteers are viewed by local governments as essential participants in efforts at all stages of the disaster, from preparation through to recovery efforts. There are, however, power and capacity differentials among volunteer groups. All types of political participation may not be equally lauded by local governments, with the work of some groups considered unimportant or

disruptive to the daily flow of established city patterns. Initiatives by activists – marches, parades and rallies related to social, political, or environmental causes – are not conventionally seen as important volunteer work. Without their efforts, however, governments may lack the political will or the necessary public support to act on any number of social and environmental concerns.

Volunteer work includes the efforts of those who live on the economic margins but whose contributions lie below the political radar. Such efforts might include cooperating on daily living responsibilities, collaborating to maintain safe housing and healthy neighbourhoods, or organizing shared child care. These types of activities may be differently packaged, presented, and perceived. Nevertheless, they do constitute a voluntary contribution directed at improving overall community sustainability and strengthening the civil community culture.

However, governments might also see volunteers and their efforts as an opportunity to offload responsibilities and cut public funding for a service. This is contrary to the goal of governments, other organizations, and citizens working cooperatively in order to ensure that sufficient resources and political support are in place to achieve collaboratively designed, sustainable communities. It is also important to keep in mind, when addressing local political questions, that the scope of volunteer initiatives is not necessarily confined to a municipal boundary. They can network and cooperate across many political and geographic scales in ways that are sometimes at cross-purposes and sometimes mutually reinforcing (Laforest 2011, 72). The role of civil society participation and how it is perceived are also undergoing transformation. Chris Ansell and Jacob Torfing (2015, 327) wonder what competencies and capacities governments and leaders will need in this emerging period of "interactive governance" as participants learn "to shift scale or to manage across or at multiple scales." Neil Bradford and Michelle Baldwin (2018, 20), for example, identify a new form of civic leadership that is intended to transform cities into more inclusive, innovative, and sustainable communities through the use of "change catalysts," "civic entrepreneurs," and "institutional intermediaries." In the process of encouraging such forms of public participation, decision makers might do well to be mindful that these civic agents could be very influential in shaping cities even though they are not elected representatives. Attention also needs to be given to the accountability and transparency of such groups.

CONCLUSION: GOVERNANCE SYSTEMS

Conceptualizing governments as systems is not a new phenomenon. In the mid-twentieth century, David Easton (1953, 1965) introduced one well-known perspective rooted in political science systems. Easton portrayed a political system as the flow of interactions between the government and a public made up of a plurality of interests vying for influence. The public provides inputs into the government through a series of demands and supports. Governments respond to these demands by converting them into laws and policies, or outputs. Easton argued that a political system is never in a state of equilibrium but always dynamic, as it must be open to change in response to factors in the political environment. Public inputs are converted into policy as they are interpreted and weighed by a variety of decision makers, who are influenced in turn by a number of other forces, actors, and systems (Easton 1953, 1965).

The patterns of influence in a political system are more complex than a simple model portraying inputs and outputs might suggest. Instead, this system should be understood as a complex network of interactions between actors and the systems in which they participate. Among these actors are government decision makers, interest groups, and the attentive public. Included in a policy community of interest formed around urban transit, for example, would be elected officials; the relevant government departments and agencies, such as public works, planning, engineering, and perhaps a transit commission; other federal, provincial or territorial, and regional governments; citizens' groups and individuals; users' advisory committees; the local business association; the local media; and maybe an interested academic or two. These actors are part of shifting constituencies that reconfigure to respond to different sets of pressures and problems.

Municipal governments are reaching out to various communities of interest to help them achieve their policy goals. Certain private-sector actors, particularly those involved in property development, are very influential in municipal decision making, as has always been the case since senior governments tend to privilege their interests. Municipalities also regularly consult members of the public about city planning and policy making.

Aspirations for sustainability cannot be realized by departments operating in silos. Social-ecological sustainability requires complex systems thinking, horizontal decision making, and team approaches at city hall, in the community, and beyond. Municipal climate change plans, for example, require coordination among departments and operations. The City of Kitchener's Corporate Climate Action Plan focuses on reducing municipal corporate greenhouse gas emissions, promoting sustainability in the community, and preparing the city for the impacts of climate change. In the process, the city has considered the municipal fleet and facilities, lighting, air quality, transportation, nature and biodiversity, adaptation, equity and social justice, and community climate action (City of Kitchener 2021). In turn, these actions are coordinated with the Climate Action Strategy of the Region of Waterloo and with other municipalities in the region. Beyond that, Kitchener has joined a network of other municipalities in the national Partners for Climate Protection program. The city is also one of twenty-five Canadian cities chosen as a showcase city in the area of climate change action as part of the Global Covenant of Mayors for Climate and Energy.

The approach of initiatives such as Kitchener's climate action plan are directed at addressing many of the elements of local governing strategies for sustainability (see Box 1.1), including the United Nations Sustainable Development Goals, which are aimed at improving internal governance and accountability structures (City of Kitchener 2021). It also displays many of the characteristics of successful sustainability initiatives. The sustainability strategy has benefited from having a municipal champion as its mayor, who is a leader at global, national, and local forums, and it has succeeded by taking a systems approach, creating tools and indicators to assess outcomes, receiving financial and institutional support from the federal government, networking with other organizations (from the local to the global), adopting a learning culture, and making use of digital and other forms of communications. These efforts all have traction and are becoming entrenched within local government. Moreover, they have support at the international and national levels of government.

That said, local governments are frequently treated as "creatures of the province" under the Constitution. Provincial governments can wield heavy hammers on local initiatives. In Ontario, where many examples readily spring to mind, the momentum that municipalities have achieved may be significantly slowed by the rapid passage of sweeping, undemocratic legislation. In 2021–22, Ontario introduced legislation with the stated intention of addressing the critical issue of housing accessibility. Adopting a business-market approach, this legislation smoothed the way for developers to build housing. In the process, the provincial government undermined the important role of Conservation Authorities in flood control and in the protection of environmentally sensitive areas. It also weakened municipal policies that require energy-efficient houses and green building design. The provincial approach will both contribute to GHG emissions and raise the costs of home heating. The province has centralized decision making in a way that reduces the ability of local governments to provide services in an efficient, fair, and effective manner – basic tenets of any measure of good governance. In sum, jostling for pre-eminence in some areas of Canada are two very strong political trends: top-down, reactionary government and incremental, networked, inclusive systems of governance. As discussed in the next chapter, collaborative and place-based models of polycentric governance have been emerging to address complexity and sustainability in a variety of political arenas.

NOTE

1 UCLG is a global network of cities and local, regional, and metropolitan governments and their associations.

8 Beyond Boundaries
Network Governance

INTRODUCTION: COLLABORATIVE AND PLACE-BASED GOVERNANCE

Social, ecological, political, and economic issues not only spill over departmental and agency boundaries (as discussed in the previous chapter) but also the municipal boundaries that constrain the ability of local governments to autonomously make and implement decisions. Historically, some provincial governments have dealt with purported inefficiencies and service fragmentation by taking the formal institutional, "consolidationist" approach of amalgamating or annexing neighbouring municipalities (Spicer 2022b, 3–4) or by creating regional governments. An alternative is informal types of voluntary intermunicipal cooperation that create networks between governments through cooperative arrangements. British Columbia, for example, has been using intermunicipal collaboration to provide basic infrastructural services since the early 1900s. Self-organizing arrangements where municipalities cooperate to deliver joint services are quite commonly used across the country. These efforts allow local governments to share the costs of a service and to ensure service continuity (Spicer 2015, 7). Beyond voluntary forms of cooperation between neighbouring municipalities, many local governments also have entered into collaborative arrangements with Indigenous governments, which have distinct, legally recognized spheres of jurisdiction.

Other types of governing entities include networks comprised of governments, political groups, nongovernmental organizations, and societal actors operating at different system scales. Network governance emphasizes the importance of process, dialogue, partnerships, trust-based communications, and collaborative learning (Meuleman 2018, 29). Network governance can involve place-based oversight bodies known as bridging organizations, such as those responsible for biosphere reserves and community forests, or it might take the form of watershed-based governing systems. These bodies span political boundaries to sustain valued ecosystems and are nested within larger systems. Social-ecological systems do not recognize political boundaries. Governance through networking and collaboration is considered a prerequisite if these valued systems are to be sustained. Their good governance, however, will require that these decision-making processes be designed and managed with power dynamics in mind and that they follow the principles of transparency, accountability, efficiency, and effectiveness. Some offer the concept of metagovernance as one possible way to navigate this complex task.

POLYCENTRICITY AND SELF-ORGANIZATION

The concept of polycentric governance *is best understood when juxtaposed with monocentric governance [V. Ostrom, Tiebout, and Warren 1961]. An ideal-type* monocentric *system is one controlled by a central predominant authority (e.g. a comprehensive governmental authority or private monopoly responsible for all goods and services). By contrast, a* polycentric *system comprises multiple governing authorities*

*at different scales which do not stand in
hierarchical relationship to each other but are
engaged in self-organisation and mutual
adjustment [E. Ostrom 2010].*

— T.H. Morrison et al. 2019, 1

Over fifty years ago, political scientist Vincent Ostrom introduced the concept of polycentric governance to characterize the multiple, overlapping decision-making centres of metropolitan areas, although the concept's potential application to other kinds of governing arrangements, such as water authorities, was not noted. Ostrom and his colleagues challenged the dominant assumption of the times that these kinds of political arrangements were necessarily undesirable: "Contrary to the frequent assertion about the lack of a 'metropolitan framework' for dealing with metropolitan problems, most metropolitan areas have a very rich and intricate 'framework' for negotiating, adjudicating and deciding questions that affect their diverse public interests" (V. Ostrom, Tiebout, and Warren 1961, 842). In the ensuing decades, he was joined by Elinor Ostrom in further exploring and developing the possibilities offered by polycentricity. In later years, Elinor Ostrom's (1990) path-breaking work on the polycentric governance of common-pool resources laid the groundwork for understanding environmental governance in the context of social-ecological systems.

Polycentric arrangements have been advocated in environmental governance approaches, as they are seen to be flexible and adaptable and to encourage policy innovation. They are also regarded as more capable of addressing "wicked," complex problems than formal, hierarchical, monocentric forms of government. However, these arrangements can be limiting in terms of accountability and inconsistent in terms of outcomes, paralysis, and stalemates. They can also possess uneven power dynamics that have, until recently, received limited critical attention in both literature and practice (T.H. Morrison et al. 2019, 2).

Efforts to address some of these limitations include concepts such as metagovernance, which is a way to produce "a degree of coordinated governance, by designing and managing sound combinations of hierarchical, market and network governance to achieve the best possible outcome" (Meuleman 2018, 74). This approach has been applied to different governance styles both within organizations and between organizations and actors engaged in network governance arrangements (76). As Carey Doberstein (2013, 587) states, "Metagovernance is thus a concept capturing the management of governance networks, serving as a framework to study how government crafts and steers non-traditional hierarchical public decision making through governance networks."

Polycentric systems might be particularly appropriate to environmental issues such as climate change, allowing governance efforts to be directed in a way that addresses the problem at the appropriate scale, from the local to the global. Some analysts emphasize the important role that state actors play in polycentric governance arrangements:

> While modes of governance have been shifting from more hierarchical/bureaucratic models to more polycentric/networked structures, it is important not to underestimate the power and unique role of the state within modern networked governance systems. State actors are unique in their ability to make and enforce rules, roles which cannot be fulfilled by any combination of non-state actors. (Winfield et al. 2021, 37, citing Setzer and Nachmany 2018)

Conversely, if provincial governments are unsupportive of polycentric arrangements, their legislation and regulations can undermine such efforts.

NEW REGIONALISM

New regionalism is a collaborative, integrative approach to regional development. According to Sean Markey (2011, 3), it "offers opportunities to address the complexities of territorial planning and mobilize the strategic competitive advantages of place-based assets within a globalized economy." Over a period of several decades, some senior governments in various parts of the country retreated from a top-down approach to regional development. Stimulated by a process of political and economic restructuring, new regionalism emerged to fill the policy gap. This region-based approach emphasizes partnerships, adaptive learning, and the identification of opportunities within a territory (Minnes et al. 2018, 76).

Political scientist C. Richard Tindal and colleagues (2013, 178) distinguish between traditional, or old, regionalism and new regionalism. The traditional approaches relied heavily on structural and institutional tools to address questions of overlapping boundaries. One favoured approach was to enlarge the actual boundaries of municipalities in attempts to create one overarching governing municipal or regional authority, as was the case in several provinces in the 1990s (M.L. McAllister 2004, 88–117).

In contrast, the new regionalism prioritizes *governance* as opposed to *government*, process rather than structure, and open boundaries, collaboration, coalitions, and trust building by "moving away from a focus on power and how it is allocated among levels of government and shifting to an emphasis on empowering neighbourhoods and communities" (Tindal et al. 2013, 178). The possible drawbacks of this approach include limited local capacity to act effectively, a lack of recognition of a broader public interest that goes beyond the immediate territory in question, and parochialism. Zachary Spicer (2022b, 12) observes that "inter-local agreements tend to have very few traditional accountability mechanisms embedded, meaning that public knowledge of the agreement or ability to independently assess the performance of the agreement is low."

New regionalism is complemented in many ways by new localism. Bruce Katz (2017b) explains that the concept was designed to acknowledge the difficulties that cities face in dealing with contemporary issues such as competitiveness and questions of social inclusion, diversity, and environmental sustainability. Reliant on a "new class" of city leaders, new localism is based on the view that "to solve challenges in a multidisciplinary way, local governments and their leaders must deploy the hard power of their governmental authority to regulate, tax, educate, and plan, but also the soft power to convene the broad networks of actors within their communities who often do the legwork of delivering change" (B. Katz 2017b). The emphasis on "soft power" and cooperation has some historical precedents in Canadian institutional cultural traditions. Zack Taylor (2019,

241) offers the example of Vancouver's long history of regionally collaborating with other municipalities. Carey Doberstein (2013, 585) also observes that there is quite an extensive history of networking in Canada at the local level, although "such governance networks are always on some sort of 'leash'" in relation to senior governments. However, "it is generally understood," she adds, "that governance networks require some basic regulation in order to function efficiently, and that the state is the most appropriate mediator, institutional designer, and integrator" (590). Informal authority, networking, and collaboration can go a long way toward achieving some important policy goals, particularly when formal institutional structures are not responsive to case-based and place-specific matters.

POLITICS OF PLACE

Place matters. Governing to sustain vital social-ecological systems requires multi-scale decision making that can more readily address complex, diverse environments. Canadian local governing systems cannot be fully understood outside of the widely diverse geographies and ecologies in which they operate. Iqaluit, the capital of Nunavut, one of Canada's three northern territories, features a small population that experiences harsh arctic winters and short summers, a rugged northern terrain, and a socio-political culture strongly influenced by both Inuit and Western ways. In terms of land mass, Nunavut covers one-fifth of Canada. Its population is scattered throughout the territory, mostly in little hamlets. In contrast, Charlottetown is the capital city of Canada's smallest province, Prince Edward Island. This eastern maritime province and its small communities rely heavily on farming, fishing, and tourism. Equally distinct is Toronto, Canada's most populated city and North America's fourth largest. It is situated within the rapidly growing Greater Golden Horseshoe, which boasts over 10 million inhabitants and is also in a category of its own. For comparison, Canada's population in 2023 was approximately 40 million people. Toronto has been labelled a "global" city, a designation given to those cities purported to have a global reach and influence. Canada also has many mid-sized to large cities, with populations ranging from 100,000 to over 1 million. Each Canadian municipality, with its environmental footprint, has emerged from a unique set of circumstances related to its geography, colonial past, and settlement patterns (see Table 8.1).

For all their diversity, Canadian municipalities are embedded in systems operating at various scales politically, socially, and physically. Cities require a flexible multi-scaled system of governance facilitated by organizations that can bridge temporal and spatial scales and knowledge sources. Multi-sectoral and multi-level partnerships characterize this emerging governance paradigm and are increasingly seen as legitimate entities in public decision-making arenas. Related to the concept of *multi-level governance,* which is employed in political science to refer to the interactions among political actors and institutions, is the concept *of multi-scale governance,* which is often used in environmental studies, geography, or literature on integrated resource management that considers spatial or temporal scale and social-ecological systems dynamics. Multi-scale governance is used particularly to address issues that transcend political jurisdictions and the boundaries of ecological systems. Human interactions with ecological systems require management and monitoring at different temporal and spatial scales.[1] Multi-scale governance emerged when it became increasingly apparent that the twentieth century's expert-based, scientific approaches to resource and environmental management were ill-equipped to sustainably manage human interactions with dynamic, uncertain, complex social-ecological systems.

Falling within the framework of multi-scale governance are place-based and adaptive co-management approaches used for many purposes:

- to facilitate an understanding of the local impacts of social-ecological challenges
- to generate policy responses to context-specific issues
- to foster participatory, inclusive democracy and a sense of belonging
- to serve as settings for stimulating social learning and community-based policy innovations.

Place-based studies can also contribute to a network of shared knowledge that facilitates knowledge integration across cases, with some policy solutions

TABLE 8.1 Comparison of the population and land area of provincial and territorial capital cities in 2021

	Population	Land area (km²)	Population density (per km²)
Municipality			
City of Iqaluit	7,429	51.58	144.0
City of Charlottetown	38,809	44.27	876.6
City of Toronto	2,794,356	631.10	4,427.8
Province or territory			
Nunavut	36,858	1,836,993.78	0.0
Prince Edward Island	154,331	5,681.18	27.2
Ontario	14,223,942	892,411.76	15.9

being scaled up and applied to other areas or larger regions (E.M. Bennett et al. 2021). For its part, adaptive co-management is used to manage human interactions with social-ecological systems in an era of uncertainty and change.

Adaptive co-management is a flexible, place-specific approach that has emerged in attempts to deal with shifting dynamics and to nudge desired systems toward a sustainable trajectory. It includes strategies that facilitate "dialogue among interested groups and actors (local/national); the development of complex, redundant, and layered institutions; and a combination of institutional types, designs, and strategies that facilitate experimentation and learning through change" (Armitage, Berkes, and Doubleday 2007, 5). Co-management can promote the public legitimacy of governmental decisions while increasing compliance with public policies and regulations. Fikret Berkes (2009, 1692) observes, "Justice, equity, and empowerment are also relevant because the basic idea behind co-management is that people whose livelihoods are affected by management decisions should have a say in how those decisions are made."

INDIGENOUS GOVERNMENTS AND LOCAL GOVERNMENTS

Indigenous governments throughout Canada have distinct governing arrangements and are not considered local governments. When Indigenous governments engage in negotiations, they do so on a nation-to-nation and government-to-government basis. Moreover, Indigenous peoples have distinct rights under Section 35 of the 1982 Constitution Act.

From time to time, First Nations whose reserves are located near municipalities engage in discussions on issues of mutual interest or concern. Formal agreements have taken place as far back as 1928 (Alcantara and Nelles 2016, 15). In recent years, however, there has been renewed attention to agreements between reserves and municipalities. Some of these discussions have emerged out of conflicting values and goals related to a range of social-ecological concerns, such as resource development, land use, environmental stewardship, and social injustice.

Many Indigenous people, subject to overt and systemic forms of discrimination, have experienced extreme poverty, inadequate housing, and substandard living conditions, including broken infrastructure, unsafe water, and compromised physical and social environments.[2] Christopher Alcantara and Jen Nelles (2016) document numerous partnership agreements between Indigenous peoples and local governments throughout Canada, most of them in British Columbia, Saskatchewan, and Ontario. These agreements vary considerably: whereas some involve forging "deep and lasting partnerships" and/or efforts to decolonize their relationship in order to foster equality and to improve intercultural communications, others are "business-oriented transactions involving municipal service provision" (11).

For example, following a devastating wildfire that destroyed approximately one-third of the town of Slave Lake in northern Alberta, a tri-council was formed to facilitate the recovery. Made up of elected officials from the Sawridge First Nation, the Municipal District of Lesser Slave River No. 124, and the Town of Slave Lake, the tri-council adopted a consensus-based approach to develop a regional fire-recovery plan and subsequently moved on to other collaborative initiatives of mutual benefit, including economic development, emergency management, and wellness (Municipal District of Lesser Slave River No. 124 2018).

The lack of coordinated leadership from senior levels of government has been critiqued with respect to local and urban Indigenous issues (Alcantara and Nelles 2016, 6), although some programs have been instigated by provincial and federal governments. One such effort is the First Nation–Municipal Community Economic Development Initiative (CEDI), operated through a partnership between the Federation of Canadian Municipalities (FCM) and Cando (Council for the Advancement of Native Development Officers), an organization staffed and overseen by Indigenous people. The initiative, which began with Phase 1 in 2013, was directed at fostering joint community-development partnerships between First Nations governments and nearby municipal bodies.

The Truth and Reconciliation Commission of Canada

At the time of Confederation, an explicit federal policy was implemented to eliminate Indigenous governments and to assimilate First Peoples using the brutal mechanisms of physical violence and cultural genocide. A main element of the policy was residential schools, where children who had been removed from their parents and communities were not only forced to abandon their traditional ways but were also severely abused or killed (Truth and Reconciliation Commission of Canada 2015, 2–3) (see Figure 8.1).

The government-funded and church-run schools opened in the late 1800s and operated for over a century. As part of a class-action settlement, a Truth and Reconciliation Commission was established with a mandate to document and communicate what happened at these schools based on the hope that doing so might "guide and inspire First Nations, Inuit, and Métis peoples and Canadians in a process of truth and healing leading toward reconciliation and renewed relationships based on mutual understanding and respect" (Truth and Reconciliation Commission of Canada n.d.). Following six years of hearings and the testimony of survivors, the commission released a final report in 2015 that contains numerous calls to action, many of which could help municipal governments "to advance the process of reconciliation at the local level" (Union of BC Municipalities 2015). In 2013, the City of Vancouver became the first municipality to declare a Year of Reconciliation, which entailed "building cultural competency, strengthening relations, and developing efficient decision-making within the City's service provision" as well as formally acknowledging that "it sits on the unceded traditional territory of the Musqueam, Squamish and Tsleil-Waututh First Nations" (Union of BC Municipalities 2015). Subsequently, other municipalities in British Columbia and elsewhere in the country engaged in some reconciliation processes and were provided with tools and approaches by the Truth and Reconciliation Commission and by organizations such as Reconciliation Canada and the FCM.

Urban Reserves

Urban reserves, located in or next to cities, have come about either as a result of municipal expansion around a pre-existing reserve or through a First Nation's acquisition of land in a city. These urban reserves have specific governing arrangements and can provide First Nation bands with business opportunities that would not be possible on a rural or remote reserve. Negotiated agreements between First Nations bands and municipal councils are often undertaken to address questions of cooperation and compensation (Indigenous Corporate Training Inc. 2015). At the time of writing, there were well over 100 urban reserves, with the oldest being the Muskeg Cree Lake Nation, established in 1988. These reserves can take many forms, one example being an urban reserve dedicated specifically to education. The urban reserve of Star Blanket Cree Nation encompasses the 32.05 acres of land that contain the First Nations University of Canada in Regina, Saskatchewan. The evolving relationships between Indigenous and other governments require collaborative forms of governance capable of managing complex arrangements.

8.1 Reconciliation Pole. On April 1, 2017, the Reconciliation Pole was raised at the University of British Columbia, located in the unceded traditional territory of the Musqueam, Squamish, and Tsleil-Waututh First Nations. The pole, carved by Haida hereditary chief and master carver James Hart, shares the terrible story of the residential schools, which operated from the 1800s to 1996. The thousands of copper nails that survivors have hammered into the pole's replica of a schoolhouse represent the thousands of Indigenous children who died in the schools.

PLACE-BASED GOVERNANCE AND BRIDGING ORGANIZATIONS

Place-based governance promotes a local sense of place and community development without the constraints posed by political boundaries. Mike Raco and John Flint (2001, 590) suggest that the concept of *place* can be understood as representing "humanised spaces in which intentions, engagements and associations are established and developed." In contrast, formal institutions, such as provincial and local governments, lack these elements of place. Rather, "units of spatial (state) organisation tend to be established for the purposes of wider administrative efficiency and the assertion of state power" (591). Place-based governance can provide arenas for collaboration among a variety of stakeholders, including governments, private-sector interests, volunteer organizations, and citizen groups. The outcomes may not necessarily be desired by all of the participants. Efforts to sustain valued social-ecological systems and how they are defined will not satisfy all participants.

Politics is the art of negotiation and consensus. Trade-offs are inevitable. Consider one scenario. When on holiday, entranced by the natural scenery, particularly by an ecologically diverse forest, a visitor from a big city decides to relocate to a rural community. Upon arrival, this new resident, who also happens to be an ecologist, discovers that a large section of the forest is slated to be logged. The land is to be developed into a community recreation centre. The goal is to reduce vandalism in the town centre by keeping restless teenagers close to home. However, the newcomer wants to educate the community about the ecological importance of natural areas. Many residents, including the elected council, are anxious to keep the teenagers from engaging in unhealthy activities. They would rather build the recreation centre and are not receptive to the outsider's perspective. Nevertheless, well-managed governance processes allow for the sharing of knowledge between the municipal government and a diversity of participants, including local fishers and hunters, social workers, youth, business owners, and the ecologist. A compromise might be developed that permits the construction of the recreation centre using sustainable building design principles

while also preserving the integrity of the forest. In the process, the newcomer will learn from local knowledge and vice versa.

Bridging organizations facilitate place-based governance by helping to overcome barriers to cooperation among disparate communities of interest. These barriers can include intergroup communications difficulties, such as when what sustainability means to someone in community development is very different from what it means to a field ecologist; the political jurisdictional considerations that arise with multi-level governance; competing objectives; and conceptual disciplinary silos (Abernethy 2016). Berkes (2009, 1695) asserts that bridging organizations "provide an arena for knowledge co-production, trust building, sense making, learning, vertical and horizontal collaboration, and conflict resolution." These organizations can also help to address problems posed by a lack of *governance fit,* which is "the failure of an institution or a set of institutions to take adequately into account the nature, functionality, and dynamics of the specific ecosystem it influences" (Ekstrom and Young 2009, 15).

Two examples of these bridging organizations are those responsible for the oversight of biosphere reserves and model forests, both of which require a place-based form of governance. In these cases, the area governed is more likely to be delineated by geographical and biophysical characteristics rather than by political boundaries.

Biosphere Reserves

Biosphere reserves are "learning places for sustainable development." They are sites for testing interdisciplinary approaches to understanding and managing changes and interactions between social and ecological systems, including conflict prevention and management of biodiversity. They are places that provide local solutions to global challenges. Biosphere reserves include terrestrial, marine and coastal ecosystems. Each site promotes solutions reconciling the conservation of biodiversity with its sustainable use.

– UNESCO n.d.-b

Biosphere reserves (BRs) were created by the United Nations Educational, Scientific and Cultural Organization (UNESCO) in the 1970s as natural-science research sites. Over time, they have evolved into place-based models for sustaining desired social-ecological systems. They are nominated by national governments and receive designations as BRs from UNESCO. They remain under the sovereign jurisdiction of the nations where they are located. Each reserve must contain land that has been set aside for conservation. These BRs have three primary functions: "conservation of biodiversity and cultural diversity"; "economic development that is socio-culturally and environmentally sustainable"; and "logistic support underpinning development through research, monitoring, education and training" (UNESCO n.d.-b). As of 2023, 748 BRs were designated in 134 countries, including 23 transboundary sites throughout the world (UNESCO n.d.-c).

In Canada, at the time of writing, there are nineteen reserves. The first is Mont Saint-Hilaire, Quebec, designated in 1978, and the most recent is Átl'ka7tsem/Howe Sound Biosphere Reserve, British Columbia, designated in 2021 (UNESCO n.d.-a). Cooperation among these reserves is facilitated by the Canadian Biosphere Reserve Association (n.d.). The BRs are managed through community-based efforts, and a local convenor group must be in place to act as a proponent. BRs vary considerably in size, governance structure, social dynamics, and physical characteristics. Operated as nonprofits, BRs rely heavily on volunteers and unpredictable sources of funding. Nevertheless, they accomplish a number of goals. For example, the Charlevoix Biosphere Reserve, founded in 1988 and headquartered in Baie-Saint-Paul, Quebec, is engaged in a range of activities, such as holding public events to foster environmental sustainability, providing advice and eco-education for citizens and organizations, offering certification and recognition programs, partnering with other organizations on waste management, sustaining valued landscapes and ecosystems while managing climate change, and promoting awareness of Charlevoix's natural and cultural heritage and local crafts (see Figure 8.2).

8.2 Hautes-Gorges-de-la-Rivière-Malbaie National Park, Charlevoix Biosphere Reserve, Quebec, 2022

Networked partnerships help to strengthen the resilience of the organizations that oversee biosphere reserves. For example, the Clayoquot Biosphere Trust (n.d.), a registered charity, is the only body that oversees a biosphere reserve, the Clayoquot Sound UNESCO Biosphere Region, and functions as a community foundation.

Model Forests

Model forests were established in the 1990s by the federal government to foster sustainable forestry practices, an effort that eventually shifted to promoting "soft skill" development in forest-dependent communities (C. George and Reed 2017, 1110). The organizations that oversee these sites continue to face operational challenges as their original focus moves from natural-science research to inclusive community-based initiatives:

> The stakeholder process, although helpful for broadening participation, offers few avenues for addressing three imperatives for place-based governance: (i) understanding of community issues and priorities, (ii) achieving empowerment through authentic community engagement and ownership, and (iii) tailored approaches that improve community capacities and achieve effective outcomes. Effective place-based governance, however, requires additional structures and procedures to encourage community engagement. (1120)

Questions about the accountability, transparency, and funding of these organizations inevitably emerge when local governing institutions constitute only one of several participating stakeholders. Their authority, in turn, is constrained by jurisdictional mandates and by the regulatory authority of other governments and other bodies. Ryan Bullock, Kathryn Jastremski, and Maureen G. Reed (2017) observe that the model-forest program has been credited with advancing the concepts of sustainable forest management and with building partnership networks at scales ranging from the local to the international. Nevertheless, they write, "there was not a means by which socio-economic dimensions and community sustainability themes, projects, and researchers could influence forest management or policy" (164). In addition, evaluating the success or failure of discrete sustainability initiatives undertaken within the auspices of these bridging organizations can be challenging. Given that social-ecological systems operate at different temporal and spatial scales, a success at one scale may not be deemed a success at another. However, in their studies of biosphere reserves, a number of researchers have concluded that well-facilitated, collaborative, and place-based learning processes used in adaptive co-management approaches are associated with more positive sustainability outcomes overall (Plummer et al. 2017). Nevertheless, the ability of these sustainability initiatives to achieve trans-

formative outcomes is contingent on a variety of factors, including receptive institutional environments and the presence of well-designed and facilitated processes (Reed and Abernethy 2018).

Citizen and Community-Based Science

Citizen participation and citizen science are considered essential elements in these multi-stakeholder partnerships. Citizen science is becoming a globally recognized field of studies in trans- and interdisciplinary research. It works to bridge science, society, and policy. If well designed and managed to ensure the quality of data and meaningful citizen engagement, citizen science can support scientific findings and policy decision making (Hecker et al. 2018). It can contribute to community sustainability through valuable local knowledge of environmental trends, establish collaborative knowledge-exchange networks, use crowd sourcing to identify and monitor species considered important in cultural and biodiversity studies, assist in monitoring water or air quality, conduct citizen-based scientific projects, contribute to ecological restoration, and work with scientists to test their findings and extend their results. In the process, members of civil society frequently become environmental stewards. They can share their knowledge and learning with the rest of a community and can assist in making decisions about local land use and environmental impacts. Citizen science can engage the public in social movements and can galvanize collective action on issues of global concern like climate change (Groulx et al. 2017). As people become involved in environmental projects, they may also experience a deeper sense of place and belonging. A sense of connection to one's landscape can foster environmental stewardship, healthy communities, and responsible citizenship (Hooykaas 2021). Citizen knowledge and volunteerism have often been engaged at the level of watershed governance.

Community-based science is also seen as an important part of local transitions toward sustainability:

> Community science is a form of place-based social learning, one that is both the process and product of collective scientific inquiry at the community level ... The key to community science lies in its roots

in the place-based relationship between the community's experiential local ecological knowledge holders and instrumental scientific knowledge holders. In an iterative and cyclical transformation process, participants in community science plan both forms of knowledge in the practice of communication and learning about their local socio-ecological system and the flow of ecosystem services. (Loucks et al. 2017, 45)

Community-based science helps to foster social learning in governing processes aimed at problem solving in a dynamic, shifting, and complex environment.

WATERSHED GOVERNANCE
Integrated approaches to the governance of social-ecological systems are being adopted to varying degrees by some governments. Integrated watershed management, for example, requires collaborative governance not only because water, unlike private property, is a commonly shared commodity but also because the vitality of all ecosystems directly depends on water. Over the past fifty years, however, domestic and industrial water use increased at a rate disproportionate to population growth. Canadians are prolific users of water. This use is partly a reflection of the country's economic dependence on the production of raw resources since primary industries like agriculture, oil extraction, and mining rely extensively on water. Despite being considered a freshwater-rich country, many Canadian municipalities are encountering serious challenges related to drought and floods. Accompanying this trend has been a rise in contaminants being directly introduced into freshwater supplies or as seepage into aquifers. Possible contaminants include road salt, pesticides, fertilizers, heavy metals, and radioactive materials. The sources of contamination include leaking septic tanks, aging city infrastructure, landfill sites, and the improper disposal of hazardous containers. The hydrologic cycle does not readily lend itself to site-specific cleanup or remedial action. Pollutants may travel a long way, making it difficult to contain the effects of a particular contaminant.

Climate change has also contributed to stresses on water quality and quantity by causing record-level droughts and floods across the country. Exacerbating the situation are developments that destroy natural habitat by covering surfaces with hardscape, thereby reducing wetlands as well as forested and other types of vegetation that could absorb excess water during flooding and mitigate the impact of drought. The adverse impacts of degraded water supplies have not been distributed equitably. Across Canada, for example, remote First Nations communities have been affected by contaminated drinking water, and many have lived for years under "boil water" advisories.

End-of-pipe approaches, such as building hard infrastructure and taking remedial actions to deal with potential emergencies, including water contamination and floods, offer only limited, short-term benefits and are extremely costly. One alternative in the case of water management is the application of "soft path" approaches:

The "soft path" is a planning approach for fresh water that differs fundamentally from conventional, supply-focussed water planning. It starts by changing the conception of water demand. Instead of viewing water as an end-product, the soft path views water as the means to accomplish certain tasks. The role of water management changes from building and maintaining water supply infrastructure to providing water related services, such as new forms of sanitation, drought-resistant landscapes, urban redesign for conservation and rain-fed ways to grow crops. (Brandes and Brooks 2007, 1)

Based on managing demand rather than supply, this approach works within ecological limits, includes civic participation, and significantly reduces water consumption and degradation by "changing water-use habits, technologies, and practices" (1). Green-blue infrastructure, which uses environmental solutions, also employ soft path approaches, such as daylighting streams, a process that restores or naturalizes a former waterway – one that has been buried underground or diverted into culverts – as a means to mitigate the impact of climate change and extreme weather while improving local social-ecological ecosystems.

Preventative planning related to community watersheds is an essential part of a strategy to achieve and sustain a safe, potable water supply. David Waltner-Toews (2004, 111) suggests that socio-economic, cultural, and ecological contexts must be understood at different scales, beginning with the community and landscape ecology and then working upward and downward from there. Efficient, effective, and equitable water management ultimately depends on whether local governments have the ability, will, and resources to adopt ecosystem-based policies. It also depends on whether they are granted the requisite authority to coordinate and harmonize policies with other governments and other resource users.

In the past half century, many governments and organizations have jointly managed regional watersheds, defined as "an area that drains all precipitation received as a runoff or base flow (groundwater sources) into a particular river or set of rivers" (Natural Resources Canada 2017). Watershed-based organizations have been established to coordinate overlapping areas of responsibility, facilitate public participation, and accommodate the natural boundaries of the watersheds themselves. These organizations, which enter into continental and international agreements, include local watershed advisory councils that make recommendations, as in Alberta and Saskatchewan, and special-purpose governing bodies, such as Ontario's long-established Conservation Authorities.

In 1946, the Province of Ontario created thirty-six Conservation Authorities that have boundaries determined by natural watersheds rather than by political jurisdictions. These bodies are described as "community-based watershed management agencies, whose mandate is to undertake watershed-based programs to protect people and property from flooding, and other natural hazards, and to conserve natural resources for economic, social and environmental benefits" (Conservation Ontario n.d.-a). Ontario uses an Integrated Water Management approach to address environmental concerns, climate change, and rapid urban growth (Conservation Ontario n.d.-b). The Conservation Authorities work with local municipalities, provincial agencies, and community organizations. Each governing board is comprised of representatives from municipalities located in the watershed. In 2020, Ontario moved to significantly reduce the scope and comprehensiveness of its internationally recognized Conservation Authorities, which had been lauded for their watershed-based approach to river basin management (see Box 8.1).

One of the criticisms levelled at the Integrated Water Management approach over the years is that its very complexity may render it impractical (Worte 2017, 365). In addition to jurisdictional, legislative, and regulatory fragmentation, a multiplicity of actors operate at different levels related to ecosystems at multiple scales, funding is chronically insufficient, and priorities change with each newly elected government. In such a scenario, sustainability goals may appear more aspirational than achievable. Yet notable initiatives should not be glossed over. In Toronto, for example, the Don River had degraded over the centuries "from a complex and rich wildlife community to a highly industrialized, artificial waterscape with low ecological diversity and limited public value" (Toronto and Region Conservation Authority n.d.). The Toronto and Region Conservation Authority, in cooperation with Waterfront Toronto and the City of Toronto, initiated one of the largest infrastructure projects in the city's history when, based on an Environmental Assessment, it resolved to naturalize and revitalize the mouth of the Don River by reconnecting it to Lake Ontario, thereby protecting the Port Lands from flooding (Toronto and Region Conservation Authority n.d.). This green-blue infrastructure project is an indication of the progress that can be achieved in the context of multi-stakeholder approaches to the management of complex ecosystems if political will, institutional capacity, and resources are made available to see them to fruition. However, when a provincial government is in power that prioritizes development over environmental protection, these initiatives can be critically undermined.

Bilateral Water Governance

In addition to their global partnerships, Canadian and American cities work together on many initiatives. With the United States being Canada's major trading partner and with the two nations sharing the world's longest border, Canadian cities are directly affected by the actions of their closest international neighbour,

BOX 8.1 Ontario's Conservation Authorities and collaborative governance

Greg Michalenko (pers. comm., March 11, 2020), a member of the Grand River Environmental Network, describes the work of Conservation Authorities:

The Conservation Authorities were initiated at a time (1946) when there were serious looming environmental and health-threatening problems in Ontario: widespread deforestation and erosion, critical water quality and water provision problems, depleted wildlife populations, widespread threats of flooding. By and large, the work of the conservation authorities has been effective. For example, under the care of the Grand River Conservation Authority (GRCA)[,] our local Grand River has been transformed from a seriously polluted and industrially contaminated stream to a watershed with greatly reduced flood threats [and] vastly improved water quality to the extent that the sports fishery is once again flourishing; [it is] a place where river otters can once again be seen within the city limits of Kitchener-Waterloo, and once-threatened bald eagles are now happily nesting along the river.

The benefits of these programs are also financial. Earlier professional studies indicated that an expensive water pipeline would have to be built to bring water from Lake Erie to bolster the limited water resources of Kitchener, Waterloo, Cambridge, and Brantford. These communities, with a total population of over 700,000, [in] one of the fastest growing urban areas of Canada, [are some of] the most dependent on groundwater for domestic and industrial needs. Fortunately, under the leadership and wisely chosen policies and programs of the Grand River Conservation Authority in collaboration with the municipalities, the goodwill of residents was easily recruited to address water consumption. The result has been a 50% reduction in per capita water use and an estimated $2 billion expenditure has been averted: we don't need the pipeline after all! These should be viewed correctly as long-term investments in a sustainable future – and not [as] yearly expenditures.

Much of this success is due to the evolution of the conservation authorities from their original top-down administrative format to a far more constructive, effective, and financially economical model that recognizes that successful outcomes of leading-edge management of large river basin systems only occur if there is widespread public acceptance of and involvement in the programs of the authorities. The Ontario Conservation Authorities have been so successful in this regard that they are now viewed – quite rightly – as world leaders in river basin management. In 2000, the Grand River Conservation Authority was selected as the recipient of the most prestigious international award for river basin management, the Thiess International Riverprize. The GRCA relies on hundreds of partnerships to identify priorities for action and address issues. Fostered through monthly newsletters, special events along the river and the Grand Action Registry, these committed partnerships have strengthened a sense of community ownership in the stewardship of the river. The enlightened approach, of proven effectiveness, is to engage the community, not ignore it. Liaising and collaborating with farmers, outdoor and environmental educators, clubs, and students, municipalities, anglers, conservationists, school boards, 4H clubs, health authorities, Girl Guides and Boy Scouts, outdoors clubs and enthusiasts, heritage advocates, First Nations, service clubs, scientists, and myriad others is core for successful outcomes, not peripheral.

Note: In 2022, Ontario's Progressive Conservative government passed sweeping legislation that has undermined many accomplishments of these Conservation Authorities as well as other environmental-protection initiatives.

including negotiated and regulated trade agreements. By the start of the twentieth century, the notion of a continental commons had emerged, and resources shared between the United States and Canada were regulated by international treaty (Forkey 2012, 34). Extensive ties between the two countries over the course of their history have deeply affected the sustainability of North American cities. This is the case whether the issue is economics and trade, as with the North American Free Trade Agreement between Canada, the United States, and Mexico; the physical environment, such as air, water, and fisheries; security along the undefended Canada-US border; or social well-being, such as immigration policies and their cultural impacts.

Municipal actions are circumscribed in several ways by Canada's obligations under international trading agreements. Examples include zoning, environmental regulation, municipal government procurement, public-private partnerships, and financial assistance such as tax breaks to encourage investment or to support local business. Trade liberalization has been promoted by the federal government, which argues that this approach has raised the standard of living for Canadians through stable and efficient access to markets (Global Affairs Canada 2021). Be that as it may, intensified competition in the global economy pressures municipalities to support the interests of business communities, reducing the bargaining leverage of local governments (Tindal et al. 2013, 418).

Given that the physical environment does not recognize borders, long-term sustainability requires environmental agreements between countries, regions, and cities, along with agencies to implement them. One such organization is the International Joint Commission. Recognizing that the waters shared by Canada and the United States could lead to transboundary disputes, the two nations signed a Boundary Waters Treaty in 1909. The commission was formed to regulate, investigate and recommend solutions to a wide range of binational issues arising from the use of shared waters, "including drinking water, commercial shipping, hydroelectric power generation, agriculture, industry, fishing, recreational boating and shoreline property" (International Joint Commission n.d.).

The Great Lakes and St. Lawrence Cities Initiative

Cities dependent on the Great Lakes and the St. Lawrence River in both Canada and the United States have formed numerous partnerships over the years, one of which is the Great Lakes and St. Lawrence Cities Initiative (GLSLCI). The initiative was founded in 2003 by the mayor of Chicago, Richard M. Daley. The Canadian chair was David Miller, a former mayor of Toronto. This coalition of over 130 municipalities representing over 14 million people was formed to ensure both the protection and the restoration of this freshwater resource – one of the largest in the world. The water resources of the Great Lakes and the St. Lawrence are the focus of the initiative, but given the interdependent relationships within social-ecological systems, it also encompasses wide-ranging agendas related to mitigating the impact of pollutants, international climate change agreements, and local economic development. Discussions have also addressed the argument that the Great Lakes–St. Lawrence River Basin should be designated a UNESCO biosphere reserve given that it is a "unique ecosystem of worldwide significance" (Great Lakes and St. Lawrence Cities Initiative 2017).

This collaborative effort involves networking between mayors, representatives from other levels of government, Indigenous peoples' representatives, and various organizations, such as the International Joint Commission and its Water Quality Board, the Great Lakes Commission, the United States Environmental Protection Agency, Environment Canada, the Great Lakes Fishery Commission, the Great Lakes Executive Committee, the Chicago Area Waterway System Advisory Committee, and the Great Lakes Advisory Board (Great Lakes and St. Lawrence Cities Initiative n.d.). International environmental initiatives and agreements of this kind have been proliferating, particularly in recent years (Johns, Thorn, and Van-Nijnatten 2018). In June 2018, the GLSLCI used its collective voice as the representative of a region with a huge economy and 20 percent of the world's freshwater resources to shun the US Republican administration's move toward isolationism in the management of shared waters:

"The mayors of the Great Lakes and St. Lawrence region are the keepers of the flame of our special cross border relationship," said Paul Dyster, mayor of Niagara Falls NY and immediate past president of the Cities Initiative, "American mayors of the Cities Initiative stand shoulder to shoulder with our Canadian cousins in the face of escalating rhetoric that threatens to damage 200 years of peace and economic prosperity in the region. (Great Lakes and St. Lawrence Cities Initiative 2018)

In 2022, the GLSLCI approved its 2022–25 strategic initiatives, which emphasize equitable access to water resources for municipalities and their citizens, ecosystem protection, the promotion of a sustainable blue economy, and resilience (McKinney 2022).

CONCLUSION: MULTI-SCALE GOVERNANCE

Climate change, social polarization, and other boundary-crossing issues are now generating "wicked" problems that need to be grappled with in the context of multi-scale problems. Polycentric forms of governance and bridging organizations have emerged to fill gaps in institutional, scientific, and social knowledge and in decision-making capacity. Collaborations extend to other types of governing arrangements that address environmental considerations, including regional watershed bodies, biosphere reserves, and community forests. Such arrangements are based on a growing understanding of the complex governing challenges involved in sustaining crucial social-ecological systems that vary in different social, political, and biophysical spatial contexts. New frameworks for governance are emerging – ones that recognize that *place matters.*

Throughout history, various observers have noted that when land or a resource is shared "in common," with no entity taking responsibility for its management, the end result appears to be environmental and resource degradation. Adverse economic consequences follow. Garrett Hardin popularized this concern in 1968 with his article "The Tragedy of the Commons," written at a time when environmental issues were gaining notable salience on public agendas. In Canada, this reality hit home with the collapse of the eastern cod fisheries, devastating many local coastal communities in 1993. Throughout Canada and the rest of the world, other commonly shared resources have been severely affected by overharvesting and environmental degradation. In response, governments have typically taken one of two conventional approaches: top-down government regulatory control or privatization through the marketplace (E. Ostrom 1990, 1).

Elinor Ostrom presents another approach, recommending ways that resources can be collectively and sustainably managed by communities rather than by centralized government or market forces. Through collective action, Ostrom (1990) argues, people can self-organize and develop their own governance mechanisms. Until those approaches are developed and accepted, "major policy decisions will continue to be undertaken with a presumption that individuals cannot organize themselves and always need to be organized by external authorities" (25). Ostrom observes that, throughout the world and throughout history, there are numerous examples of local communities successfully managing shared resources (C.C. Gibson, E. Ostrom, and Ahn 2000, 421). Conversely, top-down quotas and state-managed systems have often proven unsuccessful in sustaining resources.

Vincent and Elinor Ostrom have been credited with introducing and developing the concept of *polycentricity,* which refers to complex governing systems with multiple decision-making centres all operating with a degree of autonomy (Carlisle and Gruby 2019, 928). Keith Carlisle and Rebecca L. Gruby have suggested "that a polycentric governance system ... may exist if the decision-making centers take each other into account in competitive and cooperative relationships and are capable of resolving conflicts" (928). Polycentricity, as a concept, has its own share of limitations. It offers no guarantees that outcomes will be any more sustainable or successful than other models of governance. A lack of political accountability, a lack of decision-making transparency, and inequitable power dynamics are all variables that can undermine efforts to navigate complex governance regimes. Certainly, much more empirical and case-based work is needed to develop frameworks and models for applying and assessing these multi-scale governing approaches (Partelow et al. 2020). However, drawing on "recent empirical studies," Carlisle and Gruby (2019, 928) conclude "that polycentric governance systems may be more likely than monocentric or centralized governance to exhibit enhanced adaptive capacity and therewith lead to better environmental and social outcomes."

Existing, dominant legal-political governing models are being nudged to accommodate multi-scale governance approaches capable of dealing with wicked problems (see Chapter 1), including climate change (see Chapter 9), loss of biodiversity (see Chapter 11), and pandemics or homelessness (see Chapter 13). Bridging organizations that foster collaborations by connecting stakeholders have emerged to address these evolving challenges. But multi-scale governing approaches still have a long way to go from theoretical precept to mainstream thinking and application. This is particularly the case in jurisdictions where a formal institutional approach is wielded with a heavy hand and where complex systems thinking – if at all contemplated – is not regarded as politically expedient. Despite these seemingly intractable problems, as discussed in the next chapter, municipalities are increasingly recognized as important players in international governing regimes. This view is not surprising when one considers an issue like climate change – a wicked problem to which cities, the biggest contributors, have directed concerted efforts of mitigation and adaptation.

NOTES

1 Clark C. Gibson, Elinor Ostrom, and T.K. Ahn (2000, 218) make a useful distinction between *scale* and *level,* referring to scale as "the spatial, temporal, quantitative, or analytical dimensions used to measure and study any phenomenon," whereas level indicates "the units of analysis that are located at the same position on a scale."

2 A growing body of literature discusses the rich cultures, valued traditional knowledge, and ways of governing that have endured and contributed to sustaining Indigenous peoples and communities as well as the environment.

9 Changing Climates
Local to Global Interactions

INTRODUCTION: GOING GLOBAL

Cities are proving themselves to be important political players at all scales of governance. Today, cities such as New York, London, Paris, and Tokyo are important nodes in the dynamic global economic network. Discussing the proactive global role that cities can take, Peter J. Smith (2017, 186) makes a useful distinction between "globalized" and "globalist" cities, suggesting that globalized cities might be seen as those affected by global forces, whereas globalist cities can take a more proactive role as "players in the world on issues such as peace; aid and development; social, environmental and economic sustainability; and good democratic governance."

Toronto might be regarded as a "global" or "alpha" city given its size and demographic diversity (see Figure 9.1). Either way, as the fourth largest metropolis in North America, Toronto has a global reach extending far beyond what its formal municipal status might indicate, falling as it does under provincial constitutional jurisdiction. Under the City of Toronto Act, 2006, the city was granted some additional flexibility by the province to raise revenues and to enter into agreements with other governments given its size and socio-economic impact. In addition, in 2022, Toronto was awarded "strong mayor" powers under the Strong Mayors, Building Homes Act, which allows the mayor to make senior appointments, assign functions, make many policy decisions, and exercise veto powers. Also introduced in 2022, the Better Municipal Governance Act gives the mayor the further power to pass bylaws supported by only one-third of council as long as they align with provincial priorities. The mayor's unprecedented power over a metropolis of this size reduces the power of council, posing a serious threat to local democracy. Nevertheless, the municipality is still constrained from acting on various initiatives by many legal and institutional factors. Toronto's influence as a global city, therefore, is often wielded by other means.

Sociologist Saskia Sassen (2016), for example, does not place or rank these global cities in a formal institutional hierarchy somewhere below the national government. Rather, she views them as entities that bypass national governments altogether by directly engaging at the global scale. Sassen, describes the transformation of these large urban centres into "highly specialized and dedicated knowledge systems":

> It needed a space where professionals and executives coming from diverse countries and knowledge cultures wound up picking up knowledge bits from each other even if they did not intend to do so. I saw in this process the making of a distinctive "urban knowledge capital," a kind of capital that could only be made via a mix of conditions among which was the city itself with its diverse knowledge and experiential vectors. (99)

With this "urban knowledge capital," global cities might attract investment from transnational corporations and their establishment of head offices. However, their presence is also accompanied by social-ecological impacts. The rapidly rising costs of housing

9.1 City of Toronto waterfront, 2017

and growing social inequality, as well as physical pressures on environmental services, readily spring to mind. Nevertheless, Sassen (2016, 107) argues that, alongside the rise of these powerful corporate entities, it is possible to see the emergence of a global civil society "partly enacted in a network of localities deep inside cities."

Another game-changing element that has decentralized traditional, formal institutional relations is the rapid domination of the digital information economy. Senior governments no longer act as conduits of information to cities and rural communities and, in the process, control important types of political information. As Davide P. Cargnello and Maryantonett Flumian (2017, 608) observe,

> Where these traditional institutions once played an indispensable role, governments, courts, and parliaments now operate in an era where networks can spontaneously form and reform around complex issues with the help of digital technologies, where new voices expect to be heard, and where the role

of traditional governing institutions is sometimes called into question. Substantial distribution of information combined with near-instantaneous global connectedness means that no one institution, organization or government can any longer hold a monopoly on information, decision-making or even convening capacity.

The dizzying transformations in governance arrangements, spurred on by digital technologies and other decentralizing factors, are also accompanied by what Cargnello and Flumian refer to as "distributed" and/or "disintermediated" forms of governance (611). What was once handled by traditional ministerial departments may now be distributed to other stakeholders, such as private or nongovernmental actors, agencies, and local bodies as well as Indigenous governments.

Civil networks at play within cities emerge around any number of topics, including land use, taxation, public education, health and safety, economic development, the arts, social justice, the environment, and most recently, the deadly COVID-19 pandemic.

Municipal organizations and communities of interest are partnering and networking within neighbourhoods, cities, city regions, and globally. Madeleine
Stout and colleagues (2018, 2) write, "There are diverse
globally networked policies that speak to (social) sustainability and livability, with varied lineages and degrees of traction: a partial list includes the WHO-led
Healthy Cities and Age-Friendly Cities initiatives, the
Child-Friendly Cities movement, and the widespread
adoption of Pedestrian Charters. These policy fields
share commitments to mobility, safety, inclusion, and
opportunity, especially at the neighbourhood scale."
In the context of the international reach of municipalities and their ability to collaborate globally, this chapter considers the collective abilities of local governments
to address questions of sustainability, most notably
climate change.

GLOBAL MUNICIPAL FORUMS AND SUSTAINABILITY

Municipalities are active in many international forums
and have been so for a much longer time than may be
commonly assumed. The International Municipal
Movement marked its centenary in 2013. This movement took various forms before eventually becoming
United Cities and Local Governments (UCLG 2015),
with a mission to "be the united voice and world
advocate of democratic local self-government, promoting its values, objectives and interests, through
cooperation between local governments, and within
the wider international community." The organization
promotes strengthening the capacity of local governments through networking, partnerships, and sharing
information.

Using a sustainability framework, UCLG's
(2021a) global agenda contains three sets of recom-
mendations. The first set emphasizes the local actions
of subnational governments to address the United
Nations Sustainable Development Goals (SDGs)
(United Nations General Assembly 2015), the 2015
Paris Agreement on climate change (United Nations
Framework Convention on Climate Change Secre-
tariat n.d.), and the *New Urban Agenda* (United
Nations Conference on Housing and Sustainable
Urban Development 2017), which outlines a global
standard for sustainable urban development. In

addition, it stresses the importance of the *Global
Charter-Agenda for Human Rights in the City* (UCLG
2012) and the policy document *Right to the City*
(UCLG 2019a).

The second set of recommendations focuses on
national legal, institutional, and policy reforms, and
the third set addresses the global scale of governance,
finance, and decentralized cooperation (UCLG
2021a). The set of recommendations directed at the
national level of government emphasizes a partnership approach of multi-level governance, as discussed
in Chapter 3, and is consistent with Christopher Leo's
(2006) approach of "deep federalism." There is also a
call for "effective decentralization" and for financing
local governments in a way that supports sustainability goals (UCLG 2021a). UCLG asserts that this
agenda cannot be achieved without the enhanced
participation of local governments, which represent
approximately 70 percent of the global population
and 240,000 towns, cities, regions, and metropolises
(UCLG 2016, 2021b).

Canada has an active role in UCLG through the
Federation of Canadian Municipalities (FCM), a na-
tional organization that chairs the North American
Section of UCLG. The mayor of Kitchener, Ontario,
Berry Vrbanovic, served in leadership and presiden-
tial roles in FCM and UCLG.

Municipal governments globally, including in
Canada, are key players in conceptualizing what is
meant by sustainable development and how it might
be applied. Globally, the concept of sustainable development first became widely known with the dissemination of the report *Our Common Future* by the
World Commission on Environment and Development (1987), also referred to as the Brundtland Commission. First defined as "development that meets the
needs of the present without compromising the ability
of future generations to meet their own needs" (37),
the contested concept has been intensively debated,
expanded, and refined. In 1992, the United Nations
Conference on Environment and Development, or the
Earth Summit, held in Rio de Janeiro, released a program for action titled *Agenda 21*, which was adopted
by 178 governments. The voluntary action plan covers
the social, economic, and biophysical aspects of sustainable development. Chapter 28 of this plan was the

foundation for "a local Agenda 21" plan of action for sustainable development by local governments (United Nations Conference on Environment and Development 1992, sec. 28.2), whose inclusion is explained as follows:

> Because so many of the problems and solutions being addressed by Agenda 21 have their roots in local activities, the participation and cooperation of local authorities will be a determining factor in fulfilling its objectives. Local authorities construct, operate and maintain economic, social and environmental infrastructure, oversee planning processes, establish local environmental policies and regulations, and assist in implementing national and subnational environmental policies. As the level of governance closest to the people, they play a vital role in educating, mobilizing and responding to the public to promote sustainable development. (Sec. 28.1)

This action plan was coordinated by ICLEI – Local Governments for Sustainability, an organization founded in 1990 as the International Council for Local Environmental Initiatives. ICLEI, comprised of more than 1,500 cities and regions around the world, has a commitment to sustainable development. The goal of ICLEI (n.d.-b) is to "address the local impacts of unprecedented global change, from urbanization to biodiversity loss to climate change, aiming for urban development to have the least possible impact on global systems and to build people-centered and equitable communities." The Canadian office, located in Toronto, promotes local sustainability by providing technical support, knowledge, and networking opportunities and by emphasizing issues such as the management of energy and greenhouse gas (GHG) emissions, climate change adaptation, green procurement, and urban biodiversity (ICLEI n.d.-a, n.d.-c, n.d.-d).

Since the Earth Summit, many global conferences and agreements have focused on sustainability. In 2012, the United Nations Conference on Sustainable Development, known as Rio+20, initiated the Sustainable Development Goals (see Figure 9.2), which were to build on what had been known as the

9.2   United Nations Sustainable Development Goals (SDGs) | United Nations General Assembly (2015), 14

1. No poverty
2. Zero hunger
3. Good health and well-being
4. Quality education
5. Gender equality
6. Clean water and sanitation
7. Affordable and clean energy
8. Decent work and economic growth
9. Industry, innovation and infrastructure
10. Reduced inequalities
11. Sustainable cities and communities
12. Responsible consumption and production
13. Climate action
14. Life below water
15. Life on land
16. Peace, justice and strong institutions
17. Partnerships for the goals

Millennium Development Goals. In 2015, the United Nations General Assembly (2015) adopted a plan of action titled *Transforming Our World: The 2030 Agenda for Sustainable Development*. This agenda includes 17 SDGs and 169 targets for eradicating global poverty and fostering sustainable development – to be tackled over a period of fifteen years (1). SDG 11 aims to "make cities and human settlements inclusive, safe, resilient and sustainable" (21). In Quito, Ecuador, on October 20, 2016, the *New Urban Agenda* was adopted at the United Nations Conference on Housing and Sustainable Urban Development (2017). The action-oriented agenda is intended "to leverage the key role of cities and human settlements as drivers of sustainable development in an increasingly urbanized world" (9). Global collaborations continue, and the lists of initiatives grow.

CITY LEADERSHIP IN CLIMATE CHANGE

> *We can't eat money or drink oil.*
>
> – Autumn Peltier, an Anishinaabekwe member of the Wikwemikong First Nation on Manitoulin Island, Ontario, addressing the Global Landscapes forum at the United Nations, September 28, 2019

The changing power and governance dynamics of local governments are underscored when considered in the context of climate change. The issues are not confined to the boundaries of a municipality's political jurisdiction, nor is their resolution:

> Global city networks to address urban climate change mitigation offer a good example. The network members are metropolitan cities, but they interact globally, for the purpose of achieving local solutions. Even more complex networks will combine multiple scales on a single dimension. Members may be organised at local, national, or transnational scale and also interact at multiple scales and have multiple strategic horizons. (Ansell and Torfing 2015, 319)

Cities are vitally important in the pursuit of a global transformation toward sustainability (Wolfram 2016; Castán Broto et al. 2019, 449). However, given that they are embedded in interconnected governing and social-ecological systems networks, the changes required go far beyond the auspices of local governments. Moreover, entrenched path-dependent governing behaviours, informed by a capitalist-growth economic model, are not easily budged. As a result, it is reasonable to question whether local governments have the capacity to effect transformative change (A.W. Moore et al. 2018; Castán Broto et al. 2019). Some communities of interest, therefore, are working outside the formal structures of government in hopes of finding a more sustainable way forward. Their efforts are helping to encourage local governments to take a more assertive role on the international stage, particularly when senior governments fail to take the initiative.

Young people have also been calling for a radical global transformation of our social, political, and economic practices. Autumn Peltier, an internationally recognized teenaged activist, has been advocating for clean water for Indigenous communities and others, saying that it is time to "warrior up" and defend the planet (Kent 2018). In the fall of 2019, millions of adults left work to join youthful protesters who had been inspired by a young Swedish activist, Greta Thunberg, to walk out of school in order to call for urgent and transformative measures that can address the climate change crisis (see Figure 9.3). Four years later, in 2023, youth in Canada and around the world continued to be at the forefront of protests, demanding action on climate change, launching lawsuits against senior governments, and keeping the issue on the public agenda.

Current trajectories show that Canada and other countries are falling far short of their commitments under the 2015 Paris Agreement, which is part of the United Nations Framework Convention on Climate Change, an initiative that deals in part with GHG emissions. Throughout Canada, protesters have marched to city halls and legislatures in order to demand governmental action. Public concern is tangible, and the effects of climate change are palpable, but what is required for a meaningful transition? The goal of the climate change agenda is a low-carbon or no-carbon economy with a socially just distribution of resources.

9.3 Climate change strike in Waterloo, Ontario, September 27, 2019

In December 2015, the United Nations Climate Change Conference resulted in the Paris Agreement, a global agreement to combat climate change and to work toward a low-carbon future (United Nations Framework Convention on Climate Change Secretariat n.d.). This was viewed as a landmark agreement to limit global warming to 1.5 °C. Global scientific consensus warns that a failure to do so will lead to catastrophic global human and ecological consequences:

> Addressing climate change and implementing responses to 1.5°C-consistent pathways would require engagement between various levels and types of governance ...
>
> Local governance faces the challenge of reconciling local concerns with global objectives. Local governments could coordinate and develop effective local responses, and they could pursue procedural justice in ensuring community engagement and more effective policies around energy and vulnerability reduction They can enable more participative decision-making. (IPCC 2018, 352, 354)

The Paris Agreement recognizes the important contributions that cities can make to tackling climate change. At the conference, mayors and city leaders from around the world participated in the Climate Summit for Local Leaders and signed the Paris City Hall Declaration, reaffirming their commitment to tackle climate change (Cities for Climate 2015). At the time of writing, the scientific consensus is that global actions to date indicate that the world is *not* on track to meet the required targets, including a failure by wealthy countries to deliver on their collective $100 billion climate finance commitment to countries with less developed economies. At the conclusion of the United Nations Climate Change Conference in November 2021, the results were widely recognized as a political compromise. The UN secretary-general declared, "We are still knocking on the door of climate catastrophe. It is time to go into emergency mode – or our chance of reaching net zero will itself be zero" (United Nations 2021). In 2022, the conference was oriented toward moving beyond pledges and focusing on implementation and climate justice (United Nations 2022).

In 2016, along with climate change conferences, the United Nations held the Conference on Housing and Sustainable Urban Development, leading to the *New Urban Agenda* (2017). The *New Urban Agenda* is referred to as the "urbanization action blueprint" (UN-Habitat n.d.) and supports the Sustainable Development Goals, particularly SDG 11's focus on ensuring that cities are "inclusive, safe, resilient and sustainable" (United Nations General Assembly 2015, 21). The emphasis is on social inclusion; environmental sustainability; governance that is integrated, participatory, accountable, and transparent; spatial development that is balanced and supportive of development at all scales; and urban prosperity, including human well-being and sustainable economic growth.

As mentioned above, networks of municipalities and related organizations are actively involved globally in tackling questions related to sustainability – even in the absence of national leadership (C40 Cities 2018). Local governments are now important political actors and are able to effect change without their national governments as intermediaries – or despite them! One striking example is the role of cities in implementing the 2015 Paris Agreement to tackle climate change, which has been facilitated by a network of the mayors of the world's largest cities that was formed in 2005 to develop policies and programs aimed at "measurable reductions in both greenhouse gas emissions and climate risks" (Security and Sustainability Guide n.d.). In 2006, the organization was named C40 Cities to represent the forty participants. Toronto's mayor, David Miller, served as its chair from 2008 to 2010. By 2023, C40 Cities had grown to ninety-six affiliated members, including Vancouver, Toronto, and Montreal, with the latter city's mayor, Valérie Plante, serving on the Steering Committee.

In the spring of 2016, C40 Cities and ICLEI led the campaign #CitiesIPCC, which asked the United Nations Intergovernmental Panel on Climate Change (IPCC) to focus more on the role of cities in climate change by affording them new opportunities to collaborate with the international scientific community. The IPCC agreed to organize a scientific conference on climate change with a specific focus on cities. Urban advocates noted that the conference provided "a significant opportunity to enhance the scientific evidence on cities and climate change, including the impacts of climate change on cities such as regional impacts, adaptation and mitigation opportunities in cities; including sectoral actions (land use, transport, buildings, waste); and the evidence of successful actions, cross-cutting issues such as governance, financing and the integration of sustainable development" (Cities-IPCC 2018). The aim of the 2016 conference, hosted by the City of Edmonton, Alberta, was to stimulate climate change research, partnerships, and knowledge co-production and to establish a global research agenda (Cities-IPCC 2018). This conference led to the Change for Climate – Edmonton Declaration, which was co-developed by the mayor of Edmonton, Don Iveson, and the Global Covenant of Mayors with input from the Federation of Canadian Municipalities, United Cities and Local Governments, C40 Cities, and ICLEI. Signed by global mayors, it emphasizes the importance of cities in climate change and calls upon all levels of government and the scientific community to take immediate action. The Edmonton Declaration and the work that emerges from the initiative are intended to assist cities in garnering support from other levels of government, the scientific community, and other relevant stakeholders (City of Edmonton n.d.-a).

From an intergovernmental perspective, the more influence, networks, and international ties that a city has in these broad policy areas – all of which have an interdependent relationship with climate change – the more ability it will have to negotiate and to effect change in its own urban centre.

In 2017, Donald Trump's newly elected Republican administration in the United States withdrew national support from the Paris Agreement.[1] In response, US cities intensified their efforts to ensure that their country meets the targeted reductions in GHG emissions by 2025. The mayor of Chicago held the North American Climate Summit, which resulted in mayors across North America signing the Chicago Climate Charter (n.d.), a vow to meet the country's Paris Agreement commitments even in the absence

BOX 9.1 The City of Montreal's commitment to climate leadership

The City of Montreal has positioned itself as a global leader in climate change action. It has demonstrated its commitment to reductions in GHG emissions through participation in the Carbon Disclosure Project (CDP), Global Covenant of Mayors, and C40 Cities, and endorsement of the Paris Agreement at the UN Climate Change Conference in 2015, COP21.

In 2005, Montreal, as a municipal corporation, committed to reducing its carbon emissions by 20 percent by 2012 compared to 2002 levels, and it achieved that objective in 2010. In 2013, it committed to reducing its emissions by 30 percent by 2030 (City of Montreal 2019).

In December 2015, the Montreal administration endorsed the declaration from the Climate Summit for Local Leaders, held in Paris as part of COP21, aiming to reduce city GHG emissions by 80 percent by 2050. The city signed the Chicago Climate Charter in December 2017. In May 2018, Montreal mayor Valérie Plante announced that the city would be participating in the Women4Climate Mentorship Programme, a C40 Cities initiative focused on increasing women's participation in addressing climate change. That same year, the city endorsed the Edmonton Declaration, and at the San Francisco Global Action Climate Summit in September 2018, Plante declared that all buildings in the city would be carbon neutral by 2050 (City of Montreal 2019; Scott 2019).

In an address to the UN Summit on Climate Change in September 2019, Plante committed the city to reducing its carbon emissions by 55 percent by 2030. Plante noted that cities are on the front lines of the crisis and that their actions would have the greatest impact. Montreal's plans to reduce GHG emissions included electrification of transportation, enlarging city green spaces, and banning oil and gas heaters, and taking an inclusive approach that recognizes the importance of environmental justice (Scott 2019).

of the support of the national government. Over fifty cities from around the world signed the charter. As former Toronto mayor David Miller notes, the US mayors showed leadership after the Trump administration had failed to do so and had even "set up roadblocks" (cited in C40 Cities 2018). Among Miller's other international leadership roles, he is currently the managing director of the C40 Centre for City Climate Policy and Economy. Along with other Canadian municipal leaders, Mayor Valérie Plante has also taken a strong climate stance on behalf of the City of Montreal (see Box 9.1). In February 2022, Plante was elected vice-chair of the C40 Steering Committee, the governing body that provides strategic direction for the global network of ninety-seven cities committed to addressing climate change.

Another international initiative, the Global Covenant of Mayors for Climate and Energy (n.d.), which included 12,629 cities in 2022, focuses on developing and gathering knowledge, data, tools, and technical support to help cities achieve their goals of a resilient and low-emissions society. As of 2022, fifty-seven municipalities were members of the Canadian branch. Twenty-five municipalities were selected to serve as showcase municipalities and are slated to receive "intensive support" in addressing climate change and GHG emissions (Federation of Canadian Municipalities n.d.-b). In May 2019, former Vancouver mayor Gregor Robertson, who had previously served on the board, was named the organization's ambassador. Robertson had focused his ten-year tenure as mayor on making Vancouver the greenest city in the world. In 2022, the mayor of Guelph, Ontario, Cam Guthrie, was appointed to the organization's Board of Mayors as the representative of North America. The UN Biodiversity Conference was held in Montreal in December 2022, with Plante encouraging other mayors around the world to sign *The Montreal Pledge* (City of Montreal 2022), which includes fifteen actions to protect biodiversity (Lowrie 2022).

As noted by Harriet Bulkeley and colleagues (2018), Saskia Sassen (2016), and other analysts, multi-level governance indicates a changing and fluid dynamic in the instrumental role that city actors play at different political, economic, and social-ecological scales. These trends refute increasingly dated notions that the relative importance of these actors might be ascertained solely by an examination of their formal institutional (or legal) authority.

Today's sustainability initiatives, partnerships, and networks comprise a mosaic of diverse and frequently overlapping efforts by political actors and systems operating at different spatial and temporal scales (i.e., multi-scale governance). As Bruce Katz (2017a) observes,

> Across the world, cities are grappling with climate change. While half of the world's population now lives in cities, more than 70 percent of carbon emissions originate in cities. The 2015 Paris Climate Agreement, the UN's 2016 Sustainable Development Goals, and the recent UN Climate Change Conference in Bonn, Germany have all recognized that cities will need to be a key part of the world's response to climate change.
>
> While, in many cases, the solutions for cities are clear, the challenge lies in deploying them at scale across cities with radically different regimes of government and governance. Major interventions in the transport, buildings, and energy sectors, in particular, will be necessary. Transport and buildings constitute the bulk of greenhouse gas emissions in cities and cities consume over two-thirds of the world's energy, primarily through non-renewable sources ...
>
> Cities provide a natural experiment since they undertake the same projects with radically different stakeholders and approaches. This enables us to assess benefits and drawbacks, identify best practices that might be ripe for adaptation and replication and move closer to norms of behaviour and financing that can be easily routinized. The path to sustainable urbanization, in short, lies in granular application as much as grand policy.

Many municipal partnerships and initiatives have been pursued globally under the name of sustainable development. However, other large transnational agendas are also at work, with economic development continuing to trump sustainability efforts both socially and ecologically. Although these impacts are globally shared, neither the economic benefits nor the environmental damages are distributed evenly. As James Lightbody (2006, 523, 525) once cogently pointed out, "One gift from the neo-liberal world about which apologists and critics can agree is that capitalist emulation has raised gross wealth accumulation ... Sadly for cities, alongside grand wealth has come great inequality."

International initiatives to address sustainability and climate change not only require multilateral and bilateral cooperation but also call on individual municipalities to implement integrated sustainability policies within their own jurisdictions. Local efforts to support equitable housing, inclusive cities, healthy communities, sustainable ecosystems, and green economic initiatives alongside a host of other environmental initiatives are essential elements of the global Sustainable Development Goals (see Figure 9.2). Most large cities and many other municipalities have integrated sustainability policy initiatives into their strategic plans.

One global issue associated with these mounting natural disasters is climate-related human migration. As sea levels rise and drought and pollution render parts of the world uninhabitable, large numbers of people will need refuge in their own and other countries. The World Bank (2023) estimates that its member countries could see a total displacement of 216 million people. Canadian municipalities are ill-prepared to deal with the influx of climate-related migrants both internally and externally. Many municipalities are designing their own emergency management plans with climate change events like local floods and wildfires in mind. These plans also need to incorporate the reality of migrations into municipalities from other areas in Canada and beyond.

CONCLUSION: GLOBAL COOPERATION
Climate change is often referred to as the defining issue of our times. In 2019, the world was hit with the global COVID-19 pandemic, which destroyed or devastated hundreds of thousands of lives and punched holes in already volatile, highly interconnected socio-economic systems. Throughout the world, governments declared global emergencies at all scales. Once again, global mayors acted quickly, and C40 Cities rallied to address this newest threat.

On April 15, 2020, C40 Cities (2020) announced that more than forty mayors and city leaders in twenty-five countries had come together to form the Global Mayors COVID-19 Recovery Task Force:

Leading mayors worldwide [will] collaborate to achieve an economic recovery from COVID-19 that enables people to get back to work, while preventing climate breakdown from becoming an even bigger crisis that halts the global economy and threatens the lives and livelihoods of people everywhere ...

The mayors will discuss how to use huge public investment in the recovery to create a "new normal" for city economies, based on eliminating pollution and poverty, improving public health and increasing resilience to shocks.

C40 Cities was but one of the plethora of collaborative initiatives – undertaken at governance levels ranging from the global to the local – that enabled people to address every aspect of the pandemic's impact on society, the economy, and the environment. All of this collaboration took place primarily through the use of "virtual" communications while people were coping with unprecedented levels of physical isolation.

Political scientist Anthony Perl (pers. comm., June 12, 2023) has astutely referred to COVID-19's impact on climate change as an inconvenient truth:

The empirical reality is that the COVID-19 disruption did more to slow climate change than all the local and national climate plans, strategies, and commitments before or since the pandemic. In 2021, global GHG emissions collapsed along with travel, and particularly air travel between cities and automobile travel within cities. Quarantines and lockdowns left cities around the world with cleaner air from less motor vehicle traffic in 2021. Perhaps global disruptions like the pandemic, war, and other (worse) ruptures in tourism, travel, and trade to come will clear constraints for local sustainability initiatives. During the pandemic, municipalities took road space and redistributed it from the automobile to cycling, walking, and outdoor space for local businesses, from restaurants to food markets.

The rising rate and scale of serious or catastrophic disasters with cascading effects are driving home the need for governments to rethink their past practices. Given the disruptive nature of these events, it is evident that old path-dependent behaviours and approaches cannot address new realities. In terms of emergency preparedness, governments are beginning to shift away from siloed approaches to ones of partnership, inclusion, and coordination within a multi-level governance framework. The need to adopt more holistic strategies throughout the four stages of emergency management – prevention/mitigation, preparedness, response, and recovery – and the need for continuous institutional learning have been consistently illustrated by these disasters. Incorporating scale is an important part of these considerations, which should take into account political boundaries and multi-level decision making as well as how ecological systems are altered by the cascading effects of climate change, from the global to the local. Temporally, planning must incorporate slow- and fast-onset disaster events that result from climate change. Understanding how to develop and apply risk governance strategies using complex systems frameworks in order to avoid undesirable tipping points that lead to system collapse is part of the ongoing learning process. Ultimately, the goal is to build communities and social-ecological systems that can withstand shock and recover. A critical element in any sustainability strategy is open, effective communications systems, as discussed in the next chapter.

NOTE

1 When the US Democratic Party, under Joe Biden, replaced the Republicans, the United States officially rejoined the Paris Agreement in 2021.

10 Networked Cities
Communications and Smart Cities

INTRODUCTION: POWER AND COMMUNICATIONS NETWORKS

The understanding that knowledge is power has resonated down through the ages. Knowledge is a powerful political tool, and information is communicated in myriad ways. As famously argued by economic historian Harold A. Innis (1951) and by communications theorist Marshall McLuhan (with Fiore and Agel 1967) power is embedded in the carriers of communications – the vehicles or media that convey the information – as well as in the content of the messages. A striking example is the widespread shutdown experienced in the summer of 2022 by Rogers Communications, one of the three dominant telecommunications carriers in Canada. The shutdown caused major disruptions to vital public services, from health to transportation, business, and banking, affecting over 12 million subscribers. The event revitalized the national conversation about the dangers of oligopolies, the need for better built-in system redundancies, and the concerns with private influence over a sector of national interest. Months later, however, public concern appeared to dissipate, and Rogers Communications was granted final regulatory approval to take over western-based Shaw Communications. Two major Canadian telecommunications companies merged into one. More so than ever, the question of who controls the means and content of communications is an important political topic. But who is paying attention?

The information (or digital, or computer) age arrived in the latter part of the twentieth century. Sociologist Manuel Castells (2016, 8) argues that power is multi-dimensional and exercised through networks comprised of both dominating and countervailing forces:

> Global financial markets are built on electronic networks processing financial transactions in real time. The Internet is a network of computer networks, a network of networks ... Indeed, we can consider globalization as the process of global networking in every domain of human activity. Governance relies on the articulation between different levels of institutional decision making linked up by information networks. And the most dynamic social movements are connected via the Internet and wireless communication across the city, the country, and the world.

These networks, supported by information and communications technologies (ICTs), influence the dynamics of power in both visible and invisible ways. How these networks interact can reinforce existing patterns of inequality or foster a more inclusive, democratic society. The outcome of these interactions may be the result of intended design, but their complexity can also lead to surprising outcomes. Communication networks collectively lay down electronic pathways that shape cities and their politics in unexpected, and possibly undesirable, ways. The idea of a community as territorially constrained has come into question with the expansion of "virtual communities," which frequently transcend institutional boundaries.

The advent of the Internet of Things, artificial intelligence, 5G technology, and smart cities requires yet a new conceptual understanding of the ubiquitous role of communications in a city. Jennifer Gabrys (2010, 57) argues that it is time to shift our analytical perspective away from considering channels of communications and toward "an atmosphere of communications." Gabrys refers to "smart dust" (a term coined by electrical engineer Kristofer Pister) that permeates a city (48) and to "the simultaneity, instantaneity, and smartness of wireless communications," arguing that "it is possible to imagine information transformed into landscapes – environments and cities (57). An atmospheric mode of communication – like the ether, telepathic and electric – delineates a particular type of urban space that is composed not of distance and duration" but instead of an "etheric density that gives rise to new forms of presence." Mass communications, social media, and the ICTs that are used to convey them, as well as all other forms of communications, comprise powerful forces when it comes to determining *who* sets agendas at city hall and *how*. The power of mass communications also raises important questions about social equity in terms of the information-rich and information-poor, or the "digital divide." Those who are adept at using computer technologies and are readily able to access them have a distinct socio-economic and political advantage over others.

LOCAL POLITICAL COMMUNICATIONS

Political communication refers to the whole range of messages that deal with public governance. The information conveyed by these messages may be spoken, written, sent via electronic media, communicated using symbols, represented by public sculptures and statues, or even acted out in body language. Mayors, for instance, use a gavel or wear a chain of office to communicate their official role in council. A political communication can be signalled by the prominent placement of a statue of a historically influential political figure or a thought-provoking sculpture.

In 2020, for example, a sculpture called "Banana" depicting a gorilla looking at a smart phone was erected on private property on the main street of Waterloo, Ontario. The sculpture's artist said that the work was reflective of Waterloo Region as a main

10.1 "Banana," by Timothy Schmalz, Waterloo, Ontario, 2020 – a humorous depiction of people's reliance on cell phones

technology hub in Canada and was intended to be a playful take on people's heavy reliance on cell phones. According to artist Timothy Schmalz, "Laughter and fun can be a great instigator of positive change – especially if we all laugh together" (cited in Villella 2020) (see Figure 10.1). This is a good point: the sculpture is engaging, clever, and evocative. However, given that the sculpture is situated in a public location on the main street, city approval was required before it could be legally erected. The developer who commissioned the work was quoted by the local paper as saying, "Having a 12-person committee make decisions on public art, or taking proposals to the community for reaction and then making a decision, do not always lead to good outcomes" (cited in Pender 2020). This is an interesting assumption, but public art chosen by a single private entity does not guarantee a good outcome for the community either. Who should determine which symbols represent the city in a democratic society, particularly if the goal is to have an inclusive participatory approach to public decisions that affect the whole community? And what of the people who are most directly affected, those who see the sculpture on a daily basis?

Public communications can reinforce a sense of community, place, and belonging, or they can alienate and marginalize people. The presence of statues and street names that celebrate influential historical political leaders, for example, may be seen in a positive light by some who relate to them. For others, they may be a daily reminder that their municipality has given a place of honour to historic figures who actively promoted racist and discriminatory policies that became embedded in institutional practices and policies. In sum, the communications that local governments convey – verbal, nonverbal, written, or visual – have a compelling impact on how they choose to interact with their communities, their citizens, and the world.

Political communications also go far beyond messages exchanged between citizen and elected government. They include information that flows between and among governments, program staff members, pressure groups, media, citizens, and private-sector actors and their networks. They are carried through the supporting communications infrastructures, interacting at different temporal and spatial scales. The messages sent and received, along with the media used to send them, reflect value-laden decisions that affect public agendas and the priorities of opinion influencers and political leaders. Who has control over these communications networks? What are the ways that political actors, from the local to the global, participate in these information networks to achieve their goals? Members of the media, the private sector, the public, and governments all act as gatekeepers of political information. People who are not informed – those who do not have ready access to information, technology, or the media and do not possess the linguistic or technical literacy required to understand it – cannot actively participate in political decision making.

The proliferation and application of different ICTs in a variety of public and private settings affect relationships between governments, elites, citizens, the information-rich and the information-poor. They are also being applied in ways that have fundamental implications for concepts of community, giving rise to buzzwords such as "smart communities" and "virtual communities." One of the most important questions is the extent to which ICTs are changing the existing structures of political influence. Access to these technologies, such as social media, might make it possible for less influential citizens and communities to achieve a greater measure of authority and self-governance. Alternatively, it might be argued that although less prominent actors may be able to effect some political change through these media, their efforts can be overshadowed by more dominant networks controlled by economic and political elites. These elites, after all, will have at least as many of the same tools to advance their interests and are more likely to have the resources and abilities to exploit these media most effectively.

Optimists, advocating readily available forms of ICT, might argue that new technologies can lead to a revitalized sense of community and to a direct connection between citizens and their government. Neighbourhood Facebook groups can strengthen the sense of place and community among neighbours. During the COVID-19 pandemic, for example, local groups across Canada and the world used local media sites to reach out to neighbours in need, particularly the most vulnerable, who could not get out for food or supplies. These social media sites make it possible to announce local neighbourhood events and fundraising efforts. These sites also provide ready information on how to gain access to necessary local resources, how to address bylaw questions, or how to contact city hall and local elected representatives.

Access to public and local information also offers increased opportunities to influence municipal decision making. City governments use the Internet to consult citizens about their opinions on many local issues, particularly with respect to community planning. Theoretically, ease of access and convenience could even broaden the base of citizen participation. Widely available information may enhance participation by those who are predisposed to get involved in local issues but have been dissuaded by the inconvenience of having to go to city hall or to wade through layers of bureaucracy. The type and comprehensiveness of information provided on a given city's website demonstrates the level of government commitment to facilitating public access to electronically provided information. Use of the Internet – social media, local websites, and email – does bring about new patterns of political involvement. For example, ICTs make it possible for local governments to consult large groups of people inexpensively through virtual conferences and other methods of engagement. The use of such technologies was particularly evident during the COVID-19 lockdowns, when people could not attend public meetings in person.

The use of integrated ICTs to improve communications between governments and citizens depends on the availability of other avenues that can serve the same purpose. Whether information technology, such as email, actually provides a means of increased interaction between government and citizens is debatable. The volume of e-communications – texting, tweeting, emails, and so on – may be such that citizen requests and comments get buried every bit as much as do telephone calls and other traditional forms of communication. Moreover, certain actors are in a position to control and influence conduits of political information, whereas others are effectively shut out of meaningful political discussions. Some individuals are better positioned than others to be gatekeepers of information and, therefore, more able to determine the content of decision-making agendas.

Local decisions depend on the weight given to certain information at particular times. Moreover, although seemingly neutral, biases are embedded within how government statistics, data, and information are collected and used. These sources of knowledge are affected by the assumptions and biases of those who decide which bits and pieces will be accumulated and recorded. Each piece of information, once placed within a particular context, carries its own set of internal biases, most of which are not evident to users (Black 1982). A communication system is a technology embedded in a set of social arrangements that imply power, purpose, and organization. All social subsystems come complete with political biases and ideologies, no matter how high-tech or scientific they may be. Every information system favours one place over others, one set of values over others, and one group of people over others. Canadian municipal governments rely on such data and information for day-to-day work and planning. Yet they often do so without much awareness of the built-in biases of their data systems. Regardless of whether they are supplied by senior governments, chambers of commerce, or social activists, the data that are fed into local government channels are as biased as the communication systems as a whole.

The formal structures of a local government remain important in a communication-focused inquiry, but it is equally important not to confuse the formal accountability structure with the effective power structure. They are rarely the same. All governmental and political organizations comprise a series of interrelated networks, some of which are dominant, others subordinate, and many subject to changes as we move from one issue to another (Castells 2016). Although every opinion or interest group has its own focus, not many of them can get their issues on the agenda of local decision makers. Doing so depends on their access to the various information channels. The power to decide what gets on the agenda is at least as important as directing the decisions themselves. Often local councillors find that their time is almost entirely consumed by grappling with agenda items virtually dictated by supervising governments and their own senior managers. Even the ability to get city hall talking about a group's preferred issues depends on the alignment of socio-political forces, from the local to the global. These forces, in turn, are heavily influenced by the content and the type of media that inform the opinions of politically influential actors – whether they are members of government, private organizations, activist groups, or the general public. One of the important roles of the media is related to the question of civic literacy and public engagement in political issues.

E-GOVERNMENT AND E-DEMOCRACY

Being adequately informed about government initiatives is an important part of a citizen's ability to hold governments accountable and to influence the decision-making processes. Today, most governments provide general information to the public on their website. E-government might be defined most simply as the use of ICTs by governments to administer the public's interests more effectively and efficiently. The COVID-19 pandemic prompted more municipalities to adopt live stream webcasting of their council meetings. Many citizens use the Internet to carry out routine transactions, such as buying licences, checking garbage pickup dates, and looking for updates on power outages. Increasingly, websites and downloadable apps for mobile devices are important public resources not just for daily interactions but also in emergencies, when citizens may need to check how governments are dealing with the crisis and get assistance. Beyond information and service provision, all governments routinely use communications to persuade the public to comply with local bylaws, support community goals, embrace a civic spirit, participate in volunteer activities, and act as local entrepreneurs.

Critics might view the funding of communications departments as free advertising for the existing council, which allows it to increase its own legitimacy at taxpayers' expense. However, these departments also serve important functions, such as ensuring that communications are running smoothly within the municipal organization and improving the administration of the public interest. Uninformed citizens cannot hold governments accountable for their activities. It is the communications departments that provide the public with important civic information. Communications departments have historically operated to disseminate information to the public rather than to engage the public in an interactive process.

Government efforts to communicate with the citizenry have often been unidirectional. In the past, public consultation exercises were seen as separate initiatives and handled through advisory committees or through other vehicles. Recent years, however, have seen governments use their websites as useful tools to extend citizen-government networking. Moreover, provincial regulations require some form of public consultation. Large and small municipalities across the country have introduced some form of online initiative to engage public participation in local decision making. Many, if not most, municipalities across the country have set up interactive web-based initiatives to allow for a degree of citizen participation. St. John's, Newfoundland, for example,

uses a readily accessible, easily navigable website to encourage citizen participation and to gather feedback on its major initiatives (City of St. John's n.d.).

However, such websites and online initiatives are only tools. In and of themselves, they do not make governments more or less accessible. They may provide more convenient and readily available information that can lead to a more informed citizenry if the public chooses to avail itself of the services. It is also up to local governments to determine the extent to which their websites are accessible and interactive. Moreover, these websites need to have adequate resources and need to be staffed by people knowledgeable about the kinds of information and the levels of service that are offered. These gatekeepers of information play an important role in shaping citizens perspectives of their local government. They also help to determine whether the information provided improves or limits the accessibility of citizens to city hall.

Related to e-government is e-democracy:

Against the background of increasing political disenchantment among citizens, the perceived disconnection between citizens and politicians, and the loss of trust in political institutions that can be observed in established democracies in recent decades, e-democracy has been regarded (and often overstated) as a panacea capable of curing democratic fatigue and revitalizing or modernizing democratic processes. (Kneuer 2016, 667)

As a concept, e-democracy is as contested as other general notions of a democratic or sustainable society. It is frequently stated that digital communications can be used to facilitate more democratic governance by adopting ICTs to encourage citizen engagement. With the growing use of digital media by governments to interact with their citizens, one can readily enumerate the possible opportunities to facilitate forms of public participation. Examples include broadening access to government more generally, as well as opening up access to information (and to the Internet), enhancing public participation by reaching a larger and more diverse citizenry, encouraging online public deliberations and consultations, and using online petitions, referendums, or voting. More than half of Ontario's municipal elections are conducted with either online or phone voting. These efforts could increase administrative efficiency and voter participation. However, that did not prove to be the case in the 2022 Ontario municipal elections, when there were many acclamations of uncontested seats and the voter turnout was 33 percent, even lower than the turnout of 38 percent in 2018. Other limitations with respect to e-democracy include uneven public access to reliable Internet services, the need to ensure that the media and the public are well informed about the online voting processes, questions related to security and digital literacy, and issues of capacity and cost, particularly for smaller municipalities (Goodman and Spicer 2019).

E-democracy might be seen as a way to renew trust in democratic governance, but a degree of skepticism is warranted. ICTs could be used to facilitate democratic governance. But they could just as readily be used to reinforce existing power imbalances or used for social control. They do not necessarily introduce a new democratic system. As Marianne Kneuer (2016, 669) states, "Here, e-democracy is not understood as a possible future model for a different kind of democracy but ... as an overarching concept, namely the use of ICT by political actors (government, elected officials, media, political/societal organizations, and citizens) within political and governance processes in today's representative democracy." One observes local governments pursuing the same liberal-democratic goals as in the past (discussed in earlier chapters), with all the associated limitations and benefits, but now they do so within the context of digital communications.

MEDIA AS WATCHDOG?

Beyond local government communications, media freedom has often been an important part of liberal thinking when it comes to promoting notions of democracy. A free press is often referred to as the fourth estate, extending the older European concept of the three estates of the realm: the clergy, nobility, and commoners. Today, more recent forms of communication, including blogs and social media, are referred to as the fifth estate, which may be seen by some as means of promoting participatory democracy because it allows general members of the public to present their views and possibly to gain influence with a large audience. These influencers need not be members of the governing elite. However, if they have not been elected to represent the views of the wider public or if they present opinions on mis- or disinformation that lack consensus, what are the implications for democracy?

Old and new forms of media – most notably social media – are collectively playing a powerful role in shaping the political landscape. As Pierre François Docquir and Maria Luisa Stasi (2020) point out,

> Major social media platforms have empowered individuals who were previously unable to make their ideas visible on a large scale. They have dramatically altered the advertising markets by directly serving news to users to the detriment of media brands – thereby diverting an important source of income from news media. They have built users' profiles through the accumulation of traces of online navigation and drawn them in targeted advertising. And they have accelerated the dissemination of various kinds of harmful content such as hate speech and disinformation. As a result, policy makers everywhere are working in haste to effectively regulate the digital leviathans – but in the rush, the protection of fundamental rights is at risk of being overlooked.

The lack of accurate information spread through social media adversely affects democratic governance. In addition, clicktivism is also viewed as a trend that undermines civic engagement. Clicktivism refers to the rapid growth of online petitions that involve little effort or commitment on the part of the person signing the petition. The concern is that this movement undermines the physical presence of community organizations seeking to shape their local environment and to stimulate a collective civic culture. Conversely, others suggest that there is no reason to assume that clicktivism necessarily replaces the physical forms of local engagement, such as public protests or citizen petitions presented to city council. It can be seen as an additional avenue by which the public contributes. Certainly, recent years have seen a surge in both physical and online public protests and local events in response to vitally important issues such as climate change, Indigenous peoples' rights, and the Black Lives Matter and #MeToo movements (Fisher 2020).

Another consideration about the implications of press/media freedom is the democratic principle of government accountability. Historically, within popular liberal ideology, the media have been seen as the watchdogs of the state, as they perform the essential service of holding governments accountable for their actions. However, with the global concentration of digital media, as well as the decline of public support for independent community newspapers (digital or otherwise), comes an inevitable follow-up question: who is watching the watchdog?

A poorly informed electorate that relies on dubious, unverified sources of information that proliferate through social media networks will have a difficult time holding its governments accountable. The media's public service in holding governments somewhat accountable should be tempered with the realization that it is even harder to hold the media accountable for their own actions. Laws that deal with official secrets, libel, and slander may not be enough of a constraint. It is hard to control or regulate irresponsible or sensational posts or blogs. The best defence against this problem is to ensure that diverse news sources and opinions are publicly available so that the media, to a certain extent, are self-regulating. That is why, over the past fifty years, governments and the public have become concerned about global media behemoths, which threaten the public's ability to obtain the kind of information needed to hold governments, media, and other opinion leaders responsible for their activities.

Mass media ownership is becoming more concentrated, technologies are converging, and social media privately owned by massive global corporations – such as Meta, Alphabet, and X – are directing the ways that the vast majority of individuals connect and communicate. The lack of well-informed journalism has obvious implications for democracy and for the ability of citizens to make educated decisions. The decline of reliable local media has generated campaigns to support independent journalism (Ink-Stained Wretches n.d.).

None of these developments are new. The medium might vary, but communications have always been a powerful tool of the marketplace. That said, the scope, pace, and intensity of these changes in the flow of information make it difficult to regulate and assess the implications for governance. Users are unwittingly steered and tracked as they surf the web. Unwary customers are technologically assisted in making particular consumer choices. Individuals are encouraged to sacrifice privacy for convenience and economy. Consumer, political, and social preferences are readily tracked, often through the voluntary release of personal information. All of these trends suggest a level of private-sector control that was not previously possible and is difficult to limit – assuming governments even wish to take action.

Governments often look to the private sector to provide a number of public services, including surveillance technologies that assist with seemingly benign tasks like monitoring traffic flow, energy conservation, and speeding. However, the cumulative impact of these technologies has serious societal implications. Information technology is a powerful tool in the hands of those who have the economic resources to invest in it. One outcome, Vincent Mosco (1989) has argued, is that the applications of information technology can deepen and extend existing inequalities in society. This trend can further restrict citizens' access to information that is vital to informed democratic participation. Without such access, it is difficult for the public to hold governments and powerful private-sector actors accountable for their activities. Members of the private sector are influential players in bringing ICTs, infrastructure, and mass media (and often the message as well) to communities.

With cross-media ownership and integrated communications systems, private-sector interests are in a powerful position. Moreover, access to community information is challenged by the closure of local news media across the country as more people choose to use social media for their news rather than subscribing to local newspapers. At one time, these local papers were able to use resources from advertising and subscriptions to independently investigate the activities of governments and other influential political actors. The fact that some independent media still exist demonstrates that online, nimble organizations can survive in this globally competitive environment.

One example is Village Media (n.d.), a networked organization of community-based media that has expanded to include communities throughout North America.

ACCESS TO INFORMATION AND OPEN DATA

An ability to influence political decisions requires access to relevant information. This age-old truth was recognized by church and state long before the broad dissemination of the printed word was made possible by Johannes Gutenberg's invention of the movable-type printing press in the mid-fifteenth century. Governments have always used information to organize and control behaviour. In fact, well-placed administrators who have insider knowledge and can tap the right communications networks are often more influential than their elected political bosses. As a result, political office is particularly tough for people just elected for the first time. They usually lack both the knowledge of how governments really work and the time to figure it out. This problem can be intensified when jobs are deemed to be part-time or partially voluntary, as is often the case in small municipalities. Conversely, in larger cities, councillors are responsible to huge constituencies and have large policy portfolios. This situation forces elected representatives to rely heavily on the administrative staff for both information and political guidance, which places considerable power in the hands of unelected staff if councils pay attention to the advice.

Members of the public are at an even greater disadvantage. Whatever chance they have of calling governments to account depends on their knowledge of how public decisions are made. In Canada, throughout the 1980s and '90s, this concern led to the adoption of federal, provincial, and municipal laws on access to information and privacy. Ideally, good laws on access to information enable citizens to find out how governments spend their tax dollars, to see whether administrators have adhered to their own laws and regulations, such as environmental and human rights laws, and to reveal the incompetence of governments or their failure to fulfill their mandates. In practice, however, it is not easy to gain ready access to all of the information that one might want, even assuming that one has time and the interest to track

it down. In the past, a great many local governments were small enough that it was easy to maintain personal contact between citizens and elected representatives. Councillors would see their constituents regularly on the street. The volume of public interest could be handled through telephone calls, petitions to council, public meetings, and so on. But just as cities and their governments have grown, so too have citizens' expectations that they be kept informed. Some local governments have taken these concerns seriously. Direct contact with councillors and government departments through consultative exercises and volunteering continues to be a part of local politics. Today, governments increasingly rely on the Internet to extend their reach to more members of the community.

In countries throughout the world, many governments have adopted an open-data policy, whereby government documents and data are made publicly available. Open data specifically refers to data that can be freely used, reused, shared, and built on. The putative objective is to enhance transparency and accountability while encouraging the participation of a more informed and knowledgeable citizenry. In 2014, to open its data to the public, the Government of Canada introduced an "Open Government portal." Subsequently, the government established a multi-jurisdictional partnership – the Canada Open Government Working Group – to share information with provinces and municipalities across the country and to collaborate with them on promoting open data and information as well as public engagement using best practices. The working group also "shares, enhances, and develops common tools, platforms, practices, and policies to help Canadian governments increase the availability of their data and information to Canadians" (Government of Canada 2023).

In collaboration with the World Council on City Data, Canada has announced a pilot project of fifteen municipalities to be certified under ISO 37120, the first international standard for city data "that measures quality of life and delivery of municipal services ... This data will enable Canadian municipalities to compare their progress against their counterparts across the country and around the world in a number of domains. These domains include the environment, economy, education, governance, finance and transportation" (Infrastructure Canada 2019c). The project was completed in 2021.

Numerous municipalities across the country have open-data policies. The most accessible open-data sets include geographic information systems, government budget information, public facilities and parks, and zoning. Less accessible data sets relate to areas outside the control of the municipality, such as health, education, and air quality. The software and consulting firm PSD Citywide (n.d.) uses an Open Cities Index to benchmark the openness of municipal data across Canada, an initiative that has expanded to the rest of North America. Guelph-Wellington has introduced a Data Utility Project designed on the principles of openness, protection of privacy, and distributed governance (see Box 10.1).

Such principles align well with the local governing strategies for sustainability listed in Box 1.1 and comprise part of the municipal initiative "to build a circular food economy" (City of Guelph and Wellington County n.d.). Access to evidence-based municipal data is considered a key component of a smart city.

SMART CITIES

The "smart city" has been defined as a city that "uses digital technology to connect, protect, and enhance the lives of citizens. IoT [Internet of Things] sensors, video cameras, social media, and other inputs act as a nervous system, providing the city operator and citizens with constant feedback so they can make informed decisions" (Cisco n.d.). A smart city may offer certain benefits that improve public services and decision making and that engage citizens, fostering participatory democracy. Examples may include the application of smart technologies to manage natural assets, integrate infrastructure, and monitor air

> **BOX 10.1 Guelph-Wellington Civic Data Utility Project – Guiding Principles**
>
> 1. **Open and non-sensitive data sets** will be the core of our catalogue.
> 2. Our initial projects will work to **support the circular food economy goals of Our Food Future.**
> 3. **When we collect, share and publish data, we'll have an understood purpose** for how those activities will support our project priorities and advance the public interest.
> 4. **The Data Utility project is an experiment**, and we'll develop a framework to evaluate new experiments and collaborations, including working with private or profit generating ventures.
> 5. The Data Utility will be designed around distributed governance. **Data Custodians (the ones who first collected the data) will remain in control over who has access to their data and how their data is used.**
> 6. **Maintaining the privacy of residents is a priority**, and the Data Utility will adopt a Privacy Impact Assessment process.
> 7. While our initial collaborators are public sector entities, **we are building a framework that we hope will serve a range of public, private and not-for-profit collaborators.**
> 8. All Data Utility activities will be conducted **transparently** and **in the open according to democratic principles.** (City of Guelph and Wellington County n.d.)

quality, lighting, energy consumption, water use, traffic flows and public mobility, crime rates, and emergency response times.

Since the turn of the twenty-first century, cities have been engaged in developing both the content of their electronically mediated information and the carriers of this data with the help of the federal and provincial governments and the private sector. In 2019, the federal government announced the winners of its Smart Cities Challenge, with the goal of empowering "communities to adopt a smart cities approach to improve the lives of their residents through innovation, data and connected technology" (Infrastructure Canada n.d.). As can be seen from the winners, emphasis was placed on using technology to improve community quality of life (see Box 10.2).

The use of 5G technology, with faster downloadable speeds, facilitates almost immediate access to

- **Town of Bridgewater, Nova Scotia** – $5 million prize for its proposal to reduce energy poverty.
- **Nunavut Communities, Nunavut** – $10 million prize for its proposal to use a life promotion approach to suicide prevention [one that "will leverage digital access and connectivity to increase the availability and accessibility to mental health resources and support systems" (Infrastructure Canada 2019d)].
- **City of Guelph and Wellington County, Ontario** – $10 million prize for its proposal to create a Circular Food Economy. [For further discussion of this initiative, see Chapter 11, p. 164.]
- **City of Montréal, Quebec** – $50 million prize for its proposal to improve mobility and access to food. (Infrastructure Canada 2019b)

real-time government data. As noted above, the ready availability of such information could contribute to more effective and efficient public administration in many ways. Government data can be used to innovate, stimulate civic engagement, hold government accountable, improve service delivery, and foster sustainable communities.

There are alternative perspectives to consider. One smart cities discourse finding its way onto political agendas is based on the ideology of neoliberal urbanism. This corporatist discourse overwhelmingly promotes a digitally integrated city as a panacea for many contemporary urban problems while privatizing what were once public services. In the process, companies benefit from the data contained within the digitalized communications infrastructure by mining and marketing this information (Mosco 2019).

Surveillance Cities

Smart city approaches that lack careful consideration of the biases that are built into a city's communications infrastructure can generate consequences that threaten both local democracy and the social-

ecological sustainability of cities. One of the primary concerns, but by no means the only one, is the protection of a citizen's privacy: "The Smart City pulls surveillance-tech from our smart phone, walks it out the front door of our smart home, and embeds it into the built environment. And the controversy about Sidewalk Labs and Waterfront Toronto was at the heart of the conversation" (Lachman 2020).

Tech corporations frequently monetize and sell their users' personal data. Governments can use ICTs for a variety of types of social control, including video surveillance, collecting personal data on citizens, and undertaking web searches on specific individuals. Those least in a position to defend themselves are most likely to be targeted. Numerous studies, activist groups, and media stories have detailed how a preponderance of people subjected to such investigations are members of racialized and marginalized groups. These ongoing overt and systemic forms of racism embedded in public, private, and social institutions have led to worldwide protests and calls for government reform and police defunding. For instance, a report by the Ontario Human Rights Commission (2020) confirms that "Black people [are] disproportionately arrested, charged, [and] subjected to use of force by Toronto police." This finding is only one example of racist practices in Canada's largest city, but such discrimination has been identified in municipalities across the country.

A survey undertaken in 2018 noted that 88 percent of respondents were concerned about their level of privacy with respect to the advent of smart cities (Bannerman and Orasch 2020). This survey was undertaken to assess people's concerns about privacy in the wake of a proposed high-tech smart city development near Toronto's waterfront. The project was to be undertaken by Sidewalk Labs, a branch of Alphabet, the parent company of Google (see Box 10.3).

There are broader implications. Smart city initiatives typically involve public-private partnerships between government and tech corporations. The promotion of smart cities has emphasized using ICTs to increase efficiency in service provision, encourage innovation and creativity, and most recently, achieve environmental sustainability goals (McLaren and

BOX 10.3 Sidewalk Labs: A smart city

The brownfields redevelopment of the Quayside district near Toronto's waterfront was a private-sector project proposed by Sidewalk Labs. This "living lab" project was aimed at embedding a variety of ICTs in city infrastructure. The proposal captured many people's imagination of an eco-technological, futuristic city. Aarian Marshall (2017) reports,

> Sidewalk Labs promises to embed all sorts of sensors everywhere possible, sucking up a constant stream of information about traffic flow, noise levels, air quality, energy usage, travel patterns, and waste output. Cameras will help the company nail down the more intangible: Are people enjoying this public furniture arrangement in that green space? Are residents using the popup clinic when flu season strikes? Is that corner the optimal spot for a grocery store? Are its shoppers locals or people coming in from outside the neighborhood?

This proposed initiative also raised the specter of Big Brother for a great number of concerned observers. Richard Lachman (2020) posits,

> Imagine, as Sidewalk Labs did, an intersection camera capable of identifying a senior in a walker, able to increase the time given to cross before the lights change. Question: Who has access to that camera? Is the video-feed stored? Can law enforcement access it? Or immigration officials? Truancy officers? Civil tort lawyers? Sidewalk is a New-York-based entity; would the data be stored in Canada, subject to Canadian laws around search, seizure, and monitoring, or in the US, subject to American law and interests?

The initiative also generated numerous questions from observers about the possible adverse implications of a global corporation having a powerful influence over local government. Who benefits from the introduction of smart cities? Do they improve the quality of city life? What are the implications of these technologies for security, and what unanticipated vulnerabilities might they introduce? Does the technological complexity of smart cities lead to more problems or fewer? In 2020, Alphabet pulled out of the project, citing the poor real estate market during COVID-19, although the proposal had been subjected to extensive public criticisms.

Agyeman 2019, 170). One of the concerns is that the main determinants of urban design might be framed by ICT experts with their own sets of biases, which may not coincide with those of the residents of the municipality in question:

> The fundamental question of what kind of cities do we want to create and live in is largely reduced to the instrumental level within smart city discourse, in which it is assumed that tackling such issues is inherently of universal benefit. More profound framings with respect to fairness, equity, justice, citizenship, democracy, governance and political economy are either ignored or are understood in a pragmatic way within a neoliberal framing that renders them post-political in nature – that is, commonsensical and beyond challenge and contestation. (Kitchin 2019, 220)

Cities are complex places that have grown organically over time with inputs from a diversity of actors, factors, and systems. Their benefits and challenges related to sustainability cannot be adequately addressed solely by a series of technological applications. Zachary Spicer (2022a, i) concludes, "The introduction of new digital platforms into community life – including 'smart-city' technologies and firms like Uber and Airbnb – has raised the service expectations of residents, created new challenges relating to data governance and privacy, and introduced cyberthreats into the daily business of municipal administration."

CONCLUSION: VIRTUAL COMMUNITIES?

> *I wish to draw attention to the under-acknowledged relevance of language and seeking sustainability ... Humans operate to a large extent through linguistic symbols, which interpret the world in particular ways that have associated performative consequences.*
>
> – Larson 2011, 100

It has long been observed that information is power, and this is certainly the case today. The application of information and communications technologies is shaping cities in both intended and unanticipated ways. The promise of smart technologies to encourage the conservation of resources or to foster digital democracy by providing access to open data tells us only part of the story. The use of ICTs can also reinforce inequality by creating a digital-literacy divide and lead to inequitable policy choices. Smart cities may also give the impression that they prioritize intended design and the placement of information technology tools firmly in the hands of local decision makers and citizens. However, communication devices – such as personal hand-helds, public webcams, computers, and digital recorders – lay down digital pathways that shape cities in unanticipated ways, as surely as do the informal dirt-trodden footpaths laid down by pedestrians. As Gabrys (2010, 59) observes, "With the billions of motes forming detailed sensory networks, an increasing amount of information may be extracted from the urban environment. Smart dust finally offers the possibility of all-encompassing sense technologies that can continually scan, generate data from, and even regulate and modify, our natural-cultural environments."

The Internet gives citizens a handy tool with which to organize political associations and communities outside of the established institutions. Such citizen-based web networks or virtual communities are instances of a new politically influential form of community within local politics – one that is unconstrained by the rules imposed by jurisdictional boundaries and territorially based governments. The new technologies have implications for how citizens form political identities, as well as for how they perceive and interact with existing structures of government. The rapid adoption of information technology in homes, cars, businesses, public places, and government is leading to a reconceptualization of community and its boundaries. As Canadian political scientist Roger Gibbins (2000, 667) observes, "Home is where the cell is, and not the heart. Newsgroups create virtual communities unbounded by territory ... Simply put, ICTs have the potential to erode, and erode rapidly, the territorial foundations of our lives."

What are the implications of these new networks for local political identities that have been shaped by shared territory, history, culture, and economic circumstances? We may not see political loyalties shift from one jurisdiction to another or from a physical to a virtual space. To be sure, information technology and increased societal mobility have changed and broadened the type and nature of communities to which any one individual might belong. But Canadians have always had multiple political identities, one of the outcomes of their federal system. It is possible to be a Winnipegger, a Manitoban, and a Canadian while also being a member of various cultural communities and associations. The availability of multiple communities – some territorial and others reaching around the globe via digital media – may inspire political identities that are transient and fluid, readily shifting as circumstances change. Citizens may well gravitate to those private and public networks perceived to have the most power to fulfill their needs. It is not easy to predict the implications of ICTs for political identity and community. In the past, physical territory was defined and governed by political, social, and economic institutions. Today, communities of interest can exist outside of a physical territory as Internet-based communities or virtual communities. ICTs have introduced a new dynamic to the mix. They may provide citizens – at least those who have access to technology – with more political choices, public information, and influence in shaping political agendas. But others might see the new technologies as little more than tools of the private sector or the dominant elite that exclude their interests. A more worrying trend for questions of effective governance and democracy has been the proliferation of dis- and misinformation via social media and other outlets that citizens quote as fact without the necessary supporting evidence. Local governments lack access to the data collected by global digital platforms even though these platforms directly affect city governance.

Different actors influence the public agenda in a variety of ways, with members of the media acting as watchdogs or advocates, governments as social controllers or service providers, citizens as decision makers or critics, and businesses as investors. As the Sidewalk Labs example casts into sharp relief, an examination of how these gatekeepers collect, use, and control the dissemination of public and private information tells us much about who has influence in local politics and ultimately how municipalities are governed and cities are designed. Information has always played an important role in political interactions.

Now in this third decade of the twenty-first century, governments are expected to grapple with the imperatives of integrated systems, digital networks, interconnected policy communities, complex ecosystems, multifaceted global-local interactions, and conflicting notions about paradoxical trends leading to peculiar nomenclature such as "virtual communities." These challenges can be daunting. ICTs can offer valuable governing tools to assist municipalities in providing public services and responding to a multiplicity of demands. Open-data policies and practices and the adoption of ICTs can be used to address social-ecological concerns such as mobility, food provisioning, public health, and poverty as well as to encourage public civic engagement.

As indicated by the local governing strategies for sustainability listed in Box 1.1, ICTs can assist cities in sustaining vital social-ecological systems. They are tools that can facilitate public engagement, political transparency, access to government information, and knowledge sharing and collaboration within and between municipalities. They can also be used to make, implement, and monitor more efficient and effective decisions through smart city designs and to measure material flows in the urban metabolism, among other applications.

The converse, however, is also true. A digital communications system is of political benefit only to those that know how to access, interact with, and manipulate it. Canada's most vulnerable populations are not able to take advantage of these purported benefits and find themselves on the wrong side of the digital divide. Moreover, a technological infrastructure that monitors every aspect of city life poses a significant threat to local governance and democracy, as well as to a community's long-term health and sustainability. Without appropriate safeguards, ICTs can erode civil liberties and can narrow the range of possible solutions to contemporary governing challenges. Communications media and technologies can facilitate the rapid pace at which decisions are made – decisions that may very well require slower and more careful considerations of the policy implications for sustainable systems. Integrated, technocratic approaches woven into a municipality's infrastructure do not necessarily lead to innovation in governance, and technical approaches are not always the most appropriate response to every situation. To put it simply, one can cite American psychologist Abraham H. Maslow's (1966, 15–16) famous adage, "It is tempting, if the only tool you have is a hammer, to treat everything as if it were a nail."

It is also important to be attuned to the political biases built into these technologies – biases that inevitably reflect the interests of those who build and use these communications systems. If he were alive today, economic historian Harold A. Innis would remind us that such biases have always been built into political communications – going back to the era of the stone tablet. Given their powerful role in shaping local governance, political communications and the digital communications infrastructure that convey them merit close attention in the pursuit of sustainable communities.

PART THREE

P.3 "Tribute to Youth," by Edward Epp, Kiwanis Memorial Park, City of Saskatoon, Saskatchewan, 2015

Reimagining Local Governance
Transitioning toward Sustainability

The ability of governments to nurture sustainable communities rests largely on the way that they shape their biophysical and social landscapes. A biophysical environment is composed of interacting living and nonliving entities: air, water, organisms, and the earth's crust (or lithosphere), along with its biosphere, hydrosphere, and atmosphere. A landscape's biophysical structure is "an ecological system: an integrated whole made up of plants and animals interacting with the physical environment to compete for resources and engage in the chemically interactive processes of energy transformation and material cycling" (Murphy 2016, 80). Sustainable landscapes, both natural and built, are composed of resilient desired ecosystems operating at different scales. They have an intrinsic value that cannot be readily captured by economic models. In addition, they provide the ecological goods and services that people require not just to survive but also to sustain a measure of personal security and well-being. As discussed in Chapter 11, local governments historically viewed these ecological goods and services as resources to support property development and associated infrastructure. Beyond that, natural resources were seen as providing valued amenities such as parks and trails, golf courses, and public gardens. Today, the biophysical environment is becoming recognized for its vital life-supporting services, as well as for its natural resources, which are used for economic development. It also sustains human well-being by offering "cultural ecosystem" services in the form of aesthetic, spiritual, and health benefits (Ridding et al. 2018).

Biophysical systems and social systems interact, co-evolving and impacting each other in "ways that can be both beneficial and harmful" (Dunlap 2016, ix; see also Haberl et al. 2016b). Social-ecological systems are conceptualized in a way that

captures the complexities of societies, their biophysical environments *and* the interactions between the two. Employing concepts such as social metabolism as a link between societies and their environments, colonization as the process by which societies modify their environments to meet their needs and socioecological transitions as crucial historical transformations in human use of the environment (termed sociometabolic regimes) ... provides a powerful set of lenses for viewing the relationships between societies and their environments. (Dunlap 2016, ix)

In recent years, local governments have been made aware of the acute need to sustain vital social-ecological systems in ways that go far beyond their immediate anthropocentric utility. City staff have begun to grapple with the task of incorporating systems dynamics into their planning models and strategies. These approaches must accommodate interactions and ecosystem changes over time and across space. Other considerations include potential hazards, unanticipated catastrophic events, and human activities, which frequently conflict with natural systems (Murphy 2016, 59–60). They are all moving pieces on a multi-dimensional chessboard where local decision making must now be played out in the interests of long-term sustainability.

This task is rendered even more complex by the fact that local governments need to restore already damaged or collapsing ecosystems. For some time now, the human ecological footprint, particularly in urban centres, has outstripped the carrying capacity of the available environmental goods and services. Nevertheless, initiatives to work within ecosystem thresholds are becoming a feature, if not the foundation, of urban decision making. The management of natural assets, for example, has become part of municipal asset management, along with conventional municipal assets, such as built infrastructure, throughout their life cycle. Recognizing the impact of development decisions on valued ecosystems, some municipalities have acknowledged the need for integrative management of both their natural and built assets. Given the complex biophysical interactions that occur at different temporal and spatial scales, this type of management must take place in the context of multi-scale governance and collaborative planning.

As discussed in Chapter 12, local governments must also contend with the challenge of providing the required infrastructure to support the built environment. Single-function "grey" or "hard" infrastructure has typically been built to provide energy, waste, water, transportation, or building services. The conventional large, rigid, and centralized approach to the provision of infrastructure has resulted in a massive twenty-first-century problem. Urban infrastructure is crumbling and expensive to build and repair. It is also now vulnerable to widespread service failures, has inadequate defences against extreme natural events, and poses serious social-environmental problems. "Blue-green" infrastructure has emerged as an approach to tackle some of these challenges.

Blue-green infrastructure might be defined as a low-impact, multi-functional approach that combines "ecosystem services and human well-being to realize an efficient and sustainable use of spaces" (Wang and Banzhaf 2018, 758). For example, stormwater runoff is now managed using blue-green infrastructure, including natural buffers, rain gardens,

permeable pavement, and bioswales that channel runoff and help to filter pollutants. Other examples include efforts to reduce energy costs by expanding the use of green roofs, green building design, gardens, urban forests, community gardens, and parks to reduce cooling or heating costs and to mitigate urban contributions to climate change. Sustainable local foodscapes make up part of this blue-green landscape or infrastructure. Although life-sustaining, food is not "just food" (see Box 11.4); it is much more than that. A sustainable foodscape can knit together the fabric of a community, enabling people to collectively share and celebrate diverse cultures and traditions through a sustainable, just system of food provisioning – from seed to fork. At the same time, it can contribute to the local economy and foster a sense of belonging while strengthening civil society.

Concomitant with the adoption of blue-green infrastructure approaches is the introduction of alternative, decentralized, renewable, and low-carbon forms of energy, such as solar and wind power. Integrated management systems emphasize the importance of holistic, comprehensive approaches to providing waste, energy, water, construction, transportation, and other services. The emphasis has been on mitigating the ecosystem damages caused by industrial activities. A more aspirational approach is regenerative sustainability, which goes beyond simply limiting physical ecological damage. Regenerative sustainability conceptualizes building design as a socially and physically positive development approach. As John Robinson and Raymond J. Cole (2015, 3) argue, an important element of regenerative sustainability is the "primacy of process considerations" over "predetermined goals" – the preference for procedural approaches that emphasize collective decision making through "processes of reflection, feedback and dialogue."

Chapter 13 discusses the need to plan sustainable landscapes in a way that includes considerations of the physical and mental aspects of a healthy human environment. The COVID-19 pandemic reinforced public awareness of the importance of human health, but it has also deepened and extended existing inequalities and injustices, casting a harsh light on how political and social systems marginalize the most vulnerable among us. Ultimately, society as a whole must pay a high price for its lack of foresight. As the old saying goes, "We are only as strong as our weakest link." A sense of civic responsibility for the well-being of one's neighbour and community does not occur in the absence of a sense of belonging, place, and political efficacy. Inclusive policies and universal design are all building blocks of a vibrant civic culture and social landscape. The shared spaces of the commons have long been seen as an important part of a civic culture that enables people to congregate in public, express themselves politically, and strengthen social connections. Such places might include markets, waterfront areas, community or public gardens, recreational facilities, town squares, city halls, and other public venues. The collective public interest has often conflicted with Western notions of individual liberalism and private property rights.

Highly prized areas, such as commercially valuable spaces in a city core and waterfront property, are difficult to retain as public spaces since cash-strapped local governments look to property development to support public services. Beyond the loss and compartmentalization of public spaces as a result of private land ownership, municipalities have used zoning, design, and bylaws to separate "incompatible" land uses. These efforts have often been the result of public health initiatives aimed at separating noxious industrial activities from residential areas. In the process, however, they have also prevented certain economically or socially marginalized groups from accessing the more desirable and healthier neighbourhoods of a city. A "right to the city," as conceptualized by David Harvey (2003, 941), "is not merely a right of access to what the property speculators and state planners define, but an active right to make the city different, to shape it more in accord with our heart's desire, and to re-make ourselves thereby in a different image."

Local economic development has played a major role in determining the shape of urban landscapes. Municipalities rely heavily on revenues from property development to deliver public services. Moreover, their decision-making processes are heavily influenced by conventional liberal economic theories, as well as by the system of global capitalism in which they operate. Traditionally, prosperity and success have been equated with conventional measures determined by economic growth models. It has become apparent, however, that these models are incompatible both ecologically and socially with the requirements of long-term sustainability. Ecological economics and other alternative forms of valuation can be employed to capture the importance of social and ecological goods and services more effectively. Quality-of-life indicators are also being developed to account for the plurality of variables that affect the sustainability of communities into the future. In various communities, these indicators are now used to assist local decision makers in prioritizing policies that promote social equity, the biophysical viability of valued systems, and local economic vitality.

A sea change is required if local governments are to make progress toward disrupting embedded, unsustainable, path-dependent decision-making practices. Dominant entrenched economic and political interests must make way for a plurality of participants who bring new ideas and innovation to the governing process. A culture of institutional and societal learning, reflexivity, adaptiveness, and collaborative knowledge building are all essential to redirecting municipalities toward a more sustainable future (see Chapter 15).

All of these disparate interests require adaptable, flexible governing regimes capable of dealing with complexity (Dryzek 2014). Unfortunately, none of these requirements may readily be applied to current practices of local governments and their administrations.

11 Sustainable Landscapes
Ecosystem Services, Natural Assets, and Food Systems

INTRODUCTION: THE NATURE OF CITIES

In the end, a city remains "natural" precisely because it preserves the interplay between the unencompassability of wildness and the very essence of being human. There is no thematic prescription to draw upon, for the mystery of a natural city cannot be reduced to a neatly circumscribed inventory of sustainability principles, nor is it a static accomplishment. Instead, as evolving and historically implaced, a natural city must pay heed to our essential, often taken for granted connection with the earth and with other living beings with whom we are sharing our time.

– Leman Stefanovic 2000, 29

Today's urban landscapes would have been unrecognizable a hundred years ago, let alone when explorers and colonists first arrived in Canada. But these early incursions set in motion a process that shaped the social and physical contours of human settlements for centuries to come. When they arrived in Canada, Europeans brought with them a dominant ideological perspective that nature should be conquered by humans and used for their purposes. This human-centred (or anthropocentric) perspective was as foreign to the continent's original inhabitants as the other ideas introduced by Europeans. The early colonists, however, not only imported their European ideas and perspectives to the Americas but also brought with

them shiploads of material goods, such as tools, weapons, and blankets, as well as diseases and deadly epidemics that devastated Indigenous communities. Moreover, when they crossed the ocean to trade and settle, Europeans brought along botanical specimens and seeds – leaving a biological footprint throughout the colonized territories and beyond. Their cumulative social, material, and ecological impact irreversibly transformed the landscape.

In contrast to the European perspective, the spiritual world view of Indigenous peoples was much more eco-centric, as they viewed humans as only a small part of a complex web of life. Both in Europe and later in North America, there were iconoclastic thinkers – philosophers, scientists, and planners – who subscribed to an ecological view of nature, and their work strongly influenced subsequent environmental thought and planning. As North American cities took shape, however, they were designed according to the prevailing European notion that natural areas should be tamed, orderly, and contained. Boulevards, well-designed blocks, and groomed public gardens became accepted principles in urban planning. This idea of "improving" natural areas for human use was compatible with the science of administration and with the classical principles of bureaucracy, as discussed in Chapter 5. At the turn of the twentieth century, natural resources were viewed as goods to be managed "wisely" in order to ensure that they could be withdrawn, harvested, or extracted into the indefinite future. These strategies have failed to ensure long-term sustainability. Ecosystem scientists,

11.1   Nechako River in winter, Prince George, British Columbia | William Kennedy

along with an associated policy community, are calling for immediate and decisive action to protect and sustain urban forests, soils, watersheds, airsheds, and grasslands in order to avoid undesirable and devastating ecological impacts.

Over the past half-century, the field of local governance and politics has expanded considerably and now covers interdisciplinary areas of keen interest to those concerned with environmental sustainability. Clean water, air, and energy as well as biodiverse urban forests, agri-ecological food systems, wetlands and grasslands, parks, and other public and private lands are all critical ecological goods and services on which cities depend. Long-lasting and often unanticipated damages can occur if these goods and services are not well managed. To a greater or lesser extent, the issues facing local governments include water and soil contamination, public health threats, natural disasters, the effects of urban heat islands, energy brownouts, air quality alerts, greenfield developments that gobble up arable land, congestion, climate change, and food insecurity. Canadians are becoming aware of the ecological price to be paid for decades of rapid growth and careless development. City decision makers are increasingly adopting strategies that incorporate ecosystem approaches, including multi-scaled governance, co-management and partnerships, biodiversity planning, natural asset management, integrated ecosystem planning and restoration, and local food systems.

It is important to note that decisions made to sustain these vital systems must necessarily include their interactions with social systems. As Hilary Cunningham (2012, 159) observes, "The natural city cannot simply leap over social and economic questions to a sustainable urban space. Rather, it must trudge through the muddy ravines of poverty, social inequality, racism and other forms of discrimination, along the way asking the question of how 'the social' is being articulated in the quest for a natural urban landscape." Decisions to prioritize the preferences of certain societal groups can come at the expense of people who are neither politically influential nor privileged and at the cost of a diminished ecosystem function – possibly at a different spatial or temporal scale.

Finally, it is important to reiterate that *place matters*. The contexts in which sustainable landscapes are fostered require local and regional strategies that reflect the varying ecological requirements in communities across Canada (see Figure 11.1). One need only consider the social-ecological diversity throughout the vast expanses of Canada to recognize the important role that place-based policies play in effective biophysical and social ecosystem management. The major biomes that characterize different parts of Canada – aquatic, grassland, forest, desert, and tundra – can be further subdivided in numerous ways, including the temperature extremes that range from 40 °C in prairie summers to –70 °C in the far north. Added to the mix are the diversity of human interactions with those systems over time and across space.

THE COLONIZATION OF ECOSYSTEMS

In Western civilization, from the era of Aristotle to the Enlightenment, the pre-eminent view of nature was that it should be subjected to human will and thereby ordered, dominated, subdued, and used. Ecologist and environmental philosopher Brendon Larson (2011, 111) observes, "The dominant managerial approach to problem setting stresses the mechanistic and reductionist approach to finding solutions

... We commonly understand life as a mechanism, and biologists often seek mechanistic explanations in their research practices."

This anthropocentric view, exported around the world, has continued to hold sway throughout modern history, but it has also long been questioned by a few notable and well-respected scientists. Alexander von Humboldt, a well-known eighteenth-century German scientist and polymath, identified the complexity of the inextricable interconnection between nature and its inhabitants. His enormous breadth of knowledge and holistic approach influenced historical leaders in the sciences, the arts, politics, and the humanities. In his extensive travels, he observed that industrial and colonial practices like wasteful resource extraction had resulted in ecological devastation and social injustice. Humboldt believed that "the natural world was linked to the 'political and moral history of humanity,' from imperial ambitions that exploited colonial crops to the migration of plants along the paths of ancient civilizations" (cited in Wulf 2015, 288). Humboldt was also influenced by his encounters in South America with Indigenous people, who "regarded nature as sacred" (326). Humboldt's work helped to shape the writings and politics of key North American environmental figures such as Henry David Thoreau, George Perkins Marsh, and John Muir, among others (Wulf 2015).

In the early twentieth century, American president Theodore Roosevelt and his chief forester, Gifford Pinchot, were noted as being influential in the establishment of the Canadian Commission of Conservation (1909–21) and the North American forest and park systems. Under the direction of Clifford Sifton, the commission was to provide scientific advice on the wise management of natural and human resources. Its broad and interconnected range of topics for investigation included forests and fisheries conservation, fire protection, silviculture, agriculture, mining, game, rural and urban planning, social reform, and public health (Forkey 2012, 60–61). The commission's work produced many comprehensive and informative studies. However, it did not have the force of law behind it and could only produce recommendations.

The first decades of the twentieth century did not provide a receptive environment for conservation. A heavy emphasis on utilitarian principles and the economic utilization of natural resources dominated the political agenda (Gillis and Roach 1986, 169). This disregard for conservation proved to be a prevailing theme throughout modern history and an inadequate foundation for securing economic, social, and ecological health for the twenty-first century. Integrated, social-ecological system approaches to governance are increasingly coming to the forefront of policy discussions – although they still are not meaningfully embraced in many politically influential circles. This is the case in the context of municipalities, where economic prosperity has historically been coupled with land-use development. The "colonization of natural systems" (Haberl et al. 2016a, l), defined as the "intended and sustained transformation of natural systems" (Fischer-Kowalski and Erb 2016, 46), has taken place throughout history. In the context of global agribusiness, it has taken place with a lack of regard for the unsustainable, social-ecological consequences. Ecosystem services have yet to be properly valued, an oversight that is proving to have prohibitive costs.

URBAN ECOLOGY

> An ecosystem is a dynamic complex of plant, animal, and microorganism communities and the nonliving environment interacting as a functional unit. Humans are an integral part of ecosystems. Ecosystems vary enormously in size; a temporary pond in a tree hollow and an ocean basin can both be ecosystems.
>
> – Millennium Ecosystem Assessment 2003, 3

Aspirations to design cities in harmony with natural processes (see Box 11.1) can be found in a burgeoning academic and popular literature and in civic vision statements.

Despite such advocacy and notable advances in the ecosystem sciences, we lack a comprehensive understanding of the dynamic interactions of humans with ecosystems and landscapes that have been restructured by urbanization and industrial activity. The field of urban ecology, which explores these interactions, contains significant knowledge gaps. For

BOX 11.1   Designing cities with ecological integrity

Ingrid Leman Stefanovic (2012, 15) has observed that cities might be viewed as part of, rather than separate from, a natural system: "As celebrated anthropologist Margaret Mead once observed, cities are to humans what hives are to bees and dens are to foxes; cities can thus be viewed not as environmental aberrations, but rather as necessary movements in the unfolding of the human story. As such, they can be positive and ecologically sustainable, rather than environmentally malignant, developments – provided ecological integrity is both preserved and fostered within city limits."

example, it has no clear understanding of how species adapt to and evolve in cities in ways that often lead to the creation of novel ecosystems: "We still know little about how the supply and demand of biodiversity, ecosystem function, and ecosystem services are related in urban environments and, indeed, how ecosystem services can be defined in cities" (McPhearson et al. 2016, 210). Among the many impacts of the urban built environment on urban ecosystems are altered hydrological systems, the elimination of natural flood controls, reduced biodiversity, and the heat island effect, which is caused by a preponderance of pavement and buildings (Johnson and Munshi-South 2017).

The acceleration of human impacts is causing global changes in most major ecosystem controls: climate (e.g., global climate change), soil and water resources (e.g., nitrogen deposition, erosion, and diversions), disturbance regime (e.g., land-use change and fire control), and functional types of organisms (e.g., species introductions and extinctions). All ecosystems are experiencing directional changes in ecosystem controls that create novel conditions and, in many cases, amplify feedbacks, accelerating changes to new types of ecosystems. These changes in interactive controls inevitably alter the properties of ecosystems, often to the detriment of society (Chapin, Matson, and Vitousek 2011, 423).

Confronted by such imperatives, scientists and decision makers are developing new assessment tools to capture how anthropogenic activities affect the functioning of ecosystems and to understand and recognize the value of ecosystem services.

BIODIVERSITY

The Convention on Biological Diversity was signed in 1992 by many countries at the United Nations Conference on Environment and Development in Rio de Janeiro. The convention signalled the vital importance of biodiversity in sustaining ecosystem function and all life that depends upon it. Although most understandings of biodiversity include a recognition of species richness and abundance, there are competing and increasingly nuanced definitions. However, the relevance of any set of biodiversity patterns depends a great deal on scale and context (see Box 11.2).

At the United Nations Biodiversity Conference held in Montreal in December 2022, representatives of 188 governments – 95 percent of all 196 parties to the United Nations Convention on Biological Diversity, as well as two nonparties (i.e., the United States and the Vatican) – signed an agreement to take measures to arrest the ongoing loss of biodiversity, to protect 30 percent of the planet by 2030 while restoring degraded ecosystems, and to protect Indigenous rights. At the encouragement of Montreal mayor Valérie Plante, the mayors of many cities in Canada's largest provinces and the mayors of cities around the world signed a fifteen-point action plan entitled *The Montreal Pledge* (City of Montreal 2022), which is aimed at protecting green spaces and reducing pesticide use (Lowrie 2022). The political will of these very densely populated global cities and states to protect green spaces stands in marked contrast to positions taken by administrations such as the Progressive Conservative government in Ontario, which has overtly undermined such biodiversity efforts. As preparations for the Biodiversity Conference were underway, Ontario's administration passed unnecessary legislation to allow housing development on thousands of acres of Ontario's previously protected Greenbelt, a decision that was later reversed under intense public pressure and investigations by the provincial attorney general and the integrity commissioner (Hepburn 2022).

Biodiversity provides for ecosystem functions and, by extension, ecosystem services: "Although there is evidence that diversity increases the stability of ecosystems, it is also clear that it is not biodiversity per se that is responsible for this relationship but rather the other species (groups) or functional groups, which can react to environmental changes in different ways" (Plutzar et al. 2016, 378). Societal "colonizing" interventions, such as land-use development or flood control, alter natural structures and processes. These interventions have taken place historically without an understanding of their possible impacts on biodiversity and ecosystem stability. Moreover, "In addition to colonizing interventions, socioeconomic activities related to sociometabolic processes have an impact on biodiversity, such as the release of greenhouse gases (GHGs) and the climate change associated with it; hunting and fishing; and pollution due to toxins, heavy metals and acid emissions" (380). These interventions may introduce temporal or spatial discontinuities, or "decoupling," with the intervention occurring in one place or time and the consequence, such as the extinction of a species, happening elsewhere or at another time. From a decision-making perspective, these problems may indicate a poor functional fit between governing institutions and the ecosystems that they influence. Julia A. Ekstrom and Oran R. Young (2009, 15) define this poor governance fit as "the failure of an institution or a set of institutions to take adequately into account the

nature, functionality, and dynamics of the specific ecosystem it influences." The result is the deterioration of ecosystems and the services that they offer.

In cities today, natural habitats are frequently corralled in remnant woodlots, fragmented grasslands, partially buried and redirected wetlands, and patches of vegetation. Biodiversity is an essential element in sustaining healthy and productive urban ecosystems. Many municipalities now employ landscape designers to plan urban areas in ways that maintain essential ecological functions. As Michael D. Murphy (2016) explains, urban landscape designers attempt to foster biodiversity by developing designs that reflect a holistic understanding of the ecological structure and function of a landscape. Urban greenway corridors, for example, maintain connectivity between the patches, encouraging the flow of water, nutrients, energy, and species. The goal is to have "urban systems integrate with the landscape to sustain biological diversity, consume energy and matter creatively, and maintain vital ecosystem networks and material recycling" (85–86). Urban landscape design, policy interventions, and sound management practices that are focused on ecosystem function and biodiversity can help to improve degraded systems. It is hoped that through such initiatives, it will be possible to sustain essential ecosystem services.

Across Canada, large and small cities have developed and incorporated biodiversity strategies into

---

BOX 11.2 Biodiversity: The importance of scale and context

Species diversity in and of itself ... is valuable because the presence of a variety of species helps to increase the capability of an ecosystem to be resilient in the face of a changing environment. At the same time, an individual component of that diversity, such as a particular food plant species, may be valuable as a biological resource. The consequences of changes in

biodiversity for people can stem both from a change in the diversity per se and a change in a particular component of biodiversity. Each of these aspects of biodiversity deserves its own attention from decisionmakers, and each often requires its own (albeit connected) management goals and policies.

Second, because biodiversity refers to diversity at multiple

scales of biological organization (genes, populations, species, and ecosystems) and can be considered at any geographic scale (local, regional, or global), it is generally important to specify the specific level of organization and scale of concern. (Millennium Ecosystem Assessment 2005, 2) their decision-making processes, emphasizing the importance of multi-sectoral partnerships, institutional change, and civic engagement. The City of Edmonton, for example, took a leadership role in 2008 as one of twenty-one local government signatories of *The Durban Commitment: Local Government for Biodiversity* (ICLEI 2008). It has also created the Office of Biodiversity to coordinate with other departments in supporting and managing a network of natural areas and systems throughout the city (City of Edmonton n.d.-b).

With vital ecosystem components showing the effects of environmental degradation and climate change, decision makers are gaining awareness of the role that physical ecosystems play in sustaining human society, the economy, and the wider environment. Ecosystem services, also referred to as natural assets or natural capital, are now included in local policy and management plans. Among these services, defined as "the benefits people obtain from ecosystems," are "provisioning services such as food and water; regulating services such as regulation of floods, drought, land degradation, and disease; supporting services such as soil formation and nutrient cycling; and cultural services such as recreational, spiritual, religious and other nonmaterial benefits" (Millennium Ecosystem Assessment 2003, 3). Ecosystem services are now used in eco-economic modelling to better capture the indicators that most comprehensively account for human well-being and prosperity.

NATURAL ASSETS AND BLUE-GREEN INFRASTRUCTURE

Without natural assets, we have no economies – or life for that matter. The concept of natural assets is "used as an economic metaphor for the limited stocks of physical and biological resources found on earth. A complex web of biological, chemical, and physical processes produce ecosystem goods and services that flow like interest or dividends from those stocks, supporting all life on earth and deeply influencing the quality of human life" (O'Neill and Cairns 2017, 5). Historically, cities used the environment as a resource to be exploited and delivered services by relying on grey infrastructure, such as hydro utilities, sewer pipes, water treatment plants, waste management

systems, roads, and bridges. In contrast, innovative approaches to the sustainable management and delivery of services include blue-green infrastructure, which uses natural assets (i.e., ecological goods and services) in urban design and engineering. Examples include rain gardens, stormwater ponds, permeable pavement, urban parks, and green roofs (6).

MUNICIPAL NATURAL ASSET MANAGEMENT

Local governments have been allocated responsibility for land-use planning and management under provincial planning acts and regulations and for maintaining and managing local publicly owned assets. As Caleb Moss and Christina Benty (2020, 12–13) note,

These assets are comprised of the built environment and the necessary equipment, natural ecosystems and other resources required to support what we have built. Our water, sewer and storm drain systems, our transportation networks, our parks, trails, green spaces and public gathering places, our arts and cultural facilities, our emergency services infrastructure and equipment, all provide important services. These assets each perform a function which provides our residents' value. They have come to expect these services as part of their everyday experiences. In other words, residents receive value for service from these publicly-owned assets. These assets provide our community with value.

In 2014, the town of Gibsons, British Columbia, became the first municipality in North America to implement an asset management program that ranks natural assets and engineered infrastructure as equally important (O'Neill and Cairns 2017, 10). There are practical differences between the management of municipal assets and the management of municipal *natural* assets. Building, maintaining, and managing large built infrastructure involves collaboration only between governing authorities or public-private partnerships. In contrast, given that ecosystems do not operate in a way that respects political or social boundaries, the management of municipal natural assets requires a multi-scale collaborative approach that involves multiple decision-making authorities, other organizations, and citizens. Moreover, unlike single-purpose built infrastructure, a natural asset performs many services. A wetland, for example, provides "water storage, water filtration, groundwater recharge, flood mitigation, natural habitat for wildlife, carbon sequestration and recreation" (O'Neill and Cairns 2018, 5). These resources also deliver important benefits by mitigating the impact of climate change, which has caused a host of environmental impacts, including extreme weather events.

Decisions about which elements of an ecosystem should be prioritized and which trade-offs should be made to achieve certain objectives are not determined by scientists and public decision makers alone. Members of the public influence policy decisions and outcomes. To be effective, human-wildlife interactions require good public communications and consultation strategies. For example, the introduction of wildlife corridors and buffer zones can enhance ecosystem health, but these natural elements might also encourage the presence of animals that may not be universally welcomed. To offer a few illustrations, in contemporary Canadian cities, foxes can occasionally be seen roaming city playgrounds (see Figure 11.2); coyotes have been known to stalk small pets; and in northern towns, bears have been chased out of residential apple trees. These predatory animals and all the others down the food chain play an important role in maintaining ecosystem function, but their presence can conflict with the desires of citizens who influence land-use decisions. Alternatively, the existence of diverse flora and fauna plays an important role in human health and well-being. As a result, holistic natural asset management includes social equity considerations. As public resources, natural assets might be perceived as universally accessible and of benefit to a whole municipality. Certainly, that can appear to be the case when natural assets are managed to mitigate the impact of floods and extreme weather events or to develop public parks or community gardens.

Nevertheless, despite the "public" designation of these areas, the benefits are inequitably distributed. People with lower incomes, for example, often live in the more degraded areas of a city, such as those closer to industrial and possibly toxic sites, or they live in neighbourhoods that might be considered less

11.2 Fox in playground, Waterloo, Ontario, 2020. Wildlife sightings were particularly prevalent during the height of the COVID-19 lockdowns. Animals emerged when the human presence lessened. | Paul Habsch

desirable both environmentally and in terms of quality of life. Certain areas of a city that might otherwise seem desirable, such as neighbourhoods with urban parks or forests, often fetch high real estate prices, leading to the development of wealthy enclaves. These environments often have tangible and intangible barriers to people who cannot afford to live there. The lack of effective access to green areas has a direct impact on physical and mental health. Municipal plans that effectively address these inequities can contribute to the stock of a community's natural and social assets. Social asset building can be employed to foster a healthier, greener community. This outcome can be facilitated by municipal planning that values local neighbourhood knowledge and recognizes the potential assets that all community members can offer in helping to enhance the natural and living environment. Municipal parks and gardens are one example. Not only do they contribute green spaces to an urban centre, but they are also seen as important to public health and a sense of community (Hooykaas 2012).

PUBLIC PLACES AND PRIVATE SPACES

The public realm – defined here as spaces freely accessible to the general public – is an important element of a healthy community. Public space can contain valued places where all members of the community have an opportunity to gather together, exchange goods, share political opinions, celebrate the arts, and enjoy the environment. The ancient Greek agora has often been highlighted as one of these gathering places. Well before the advent of mass media, a valued democratic tradition was the Speakers' Corner, where citizens could trumpet their views loudly to passersby. Public parks, gardens, waterfront beaches, trails, and green spaces have long been viewed as essential elements of a healthy community. The privatization of what were once universally accessible places is apparent in the advent of gated communities, homogenous box stores, privatized beachfront areas, and user fees and licensing for access to what were once publicly available facilities. In effect, the privatization of these spaces limits the public's right of access to the city.

Not only does the loss of public gathering places and valued environmental spaces affect a city's democratic health, but it can also erode a sense of belonging and community and can be harmful to one's health. Environmental philosopher Glenn Albrecht (2019, 38–39) has coined the term "solastalgia" to refer to this phenomenon:

> I define "solastalgia" as the pain or distress caused by the ongoing loss of solace and the sense of desolation connected to the present state of one's home and territory. It is the existential and lived experience of negative environmental change, manifest as an attack on one's sense of place. It is characteristically a chronic condition, tied to the gradual erosion of identity created by the sense of belonging to a particular loved place and a feeling of distress, or psychological desolation, about its unwanted transformation. In direct contrast to the dislocated spatial dimensions of traditionally defined nostalgia, solastalgia is the homesickness you have when you are still located within your home environment.

"Solastalgia" is an apt term when describing the First Peoples' loss of a sense of place and the unwanted transformation of valued and sacred places. It also holds meaning for other people who identify with the degradation of the special places that they have long cherished. For example, a notable theme in Canadian literature, art, and music is the loss of familiar landscapes to encroaching development and environmental degradation (see Box 11.3).

BOX 11.3 "There Used to Be a Train"

Autobiographical song by northern Ontario bluegrass singer-songwriter Merv Mulligan

There used to be a train that ran through my backyard
The engineer, he would blow that whistle long and hard
I'd like to wave when he roared by, I'd watch the steam and the cinders fly
I'd dream about where he could go, and then
He'd roll back again.
My Grandpa used to meet the train to get the mail
He'd drive his team of horses and a wagon down the trail
I'd tag along and I'd go with him, never thought those days would end
But time waits for no one I guess that's true
Not even me and you.

1956 they pulled up the rails,
Tore down the station, stopped bringing the mail
All that's left of the railway now, is a trail for the hiking crowd
They march along eating peanuts and granola bars
on their way back to their cars.

... Hummers ... Big V8s ... Four-wheel drives

It used to take us a day to get into town
With four lanes now in a minute you are speeding down
but the soda shoppe is there no more, in its place is a cannabis store
And a Walmart looms on the edge of town
to me that was like hallowed ground

there used to be a train that ran through my backyard
there used to be a train that ran through my backyard
there used to be a train that ran through my backyard

Others have spoken about the negative impact on children's health when cities fail to plan for their well-being (C. McAllister 2011). Richard Louv (2008) refers to some of the associated mental health impacts as "nature-deficit disorder." However, grassroots public campaigns to prevent the loss of these valued places are difficult to sustain over time, particularly when development is incremental, and they often require government support. Expanding these public spaces and sustaining these social and natural assets offers an opportunity to reconnect people with their physical environment while building a sense of community.

New initiatives are also encouraging a sense of place and belonging within social-ecological landscapes. One example is the design and implementation of local foodscapes.

FOODSCAPES

Consider the places and spaces where you acquire food, prepare food, talk about food, or generally gather some sort of meaning from food. This is your foodscape. The concept originated in the field of geography and is widely used in urban studies and public health to refer to urban food environments. Sociologists have extended the concept to include the institutional arrangements, cultural spaces, and discourses that mediate our relationship with our food.

– MacKendrick 2014, 16

In a contemporary Canadian municipality, one's foodscape might consist predominantly of food outlets that offer highly processed and expensive imported foods, or it might be a "food desert," defined as an area that lacks access to healthy foods. At the other end of the food-provisioning spectrum, a sustainable local foodscape is comprised of culturally appropriate, affordable, accessible, nutritious food. Such places might be characterized by local food networks, urban agriculture, local food markets and community gardens (see Figure 11.3), community-supported agriculture, direct-farm marketing, and food forests where a wealth of edible foods are freely available in an ecologically diverse environment.

11.3 Community garden in Parry Sound, Ontario, 2014 | Paivi Abernethy

The global agro-industrial food system, which is currently unsustainable, consumes enormous amounts of fossil fuels, contributes significantly to climate change, degrades habitats, water systems, and soils, and contributes to food insecurity, waste, and social instability. In this system, food has been "transformed into a highly branded, packaged and de-spatialized commodity severed from time (e.g. season), space (e.g. landscape) and culture (e.g. meaning)" (Padró et al. 2017, 134). Economies of scale, which have frequently been offered as justification for this global food regime, have generated massive "dis-ecologies of scale."[1] Growing alarm about the social-ecological unsustainability of global agro-industrial practices has given rise to widespread calls for the establishment of alternative food networks based on a sustainable food system (see Box 11.4). It has also generated a global movement for the re-localization of food systems and for the distribution of food using short supply chains.

The goal of the movement is to reduce intermediaries between farmers and consumers by implementing a decentralized food-production model – a contrast to the centralized global system, where food is shipped long distances to the consumer. In such a model, food relations are "re-socialized" and "re-spatialized," and food is traceable to a particular farmer (Blay-Palmer et al. 2018, 5). Also positioning itself as an alternative to the global agri-food industry is an approach championed by advocates of agroecology:

Agroecology is described as the science, practice, and social movement that interweaves ecological and cultural knowledge and political values with agriculture ... Originating from an integration of ongoing research and experiences and from Indigenous knowledge practices, agroecology is at the core of a food sovereignty approach that is increasingly gaining attention across the globe. Proponents argue that incorporating equity and sustainability into agricultural production requires the consideration of human health, workers' rights and safety, animal welfare, and biodiversity as well as both scientific and place-based knowledge systems on the farm and within the broader food system. (Laforge and Levkoe 2018, 991)

Sustainable foodscape planning is also characterized by "land sharing," an approach designed to accommodate food production activities, to protect biodiversity, and to maintain ecosystem services by providing "a complex agricultural matrix" that also connects natural sites, thus fostering "high species richness" (Tello and González de Molina 2017, 31). This method contrasts with "land sparing," where land is set aside to be conserved in protected areas and is therefore exempt from the development, resource extraction, or intensive agricultural practices allowed in other areas (31). To be sure, it is a complex task to determine where land should be shared and/or spared and how to make the inevitable trade-offs. These ecological considerations require new forms of inclusive, networked, and collaborative governance, as discussed in the first two parts of this book.

MULTI-SCALE FOOD SYSTEMS

The global agri-food system may become sustainable if it is able to meet the food needs of all human beings in a fair manner through the biomass produce obtained from cropland,

pastureland and woodland, while at the same time keeping all agri-ecosystems on Earth in a reproducible and healthy ecological state, so as to ensure that they will be able to keep satisfying the needs of future generations.

– Tello and González de Molina 2017, 32

The efforts needed to transition toward a sustainable food system go far beyond what can be accomplished solely at a local level. Indeed, producing food only at a community level is not always the more sustainable approach. Some food production and distribution activities may best offer social, economic, and ecological benefits if they are pursued at a larger, more inclusive scale. Alison Blay-Palmer and colleagues (2018, 10), for example, discuss the City-Regional Food System (CRFS), an approach that conceptualizes a food system in terms of the interactions between an urban core and its semi-urban and rural hinterland:

CRFS offers a unifying approach to align multiple goals to the mutual benefit of all people in rural, peri-urban, and urban spaces. It provides both the assessment potential and focus of other analytical approaches such as alternative food networks, short food supply chains, or rural-urban linkages, and also deliberately includes sustainability and supply chain consideration ... CRFS also provides the focus needed to develop multi-scale policies and programs. For example, in the case of the SDGs [global Sustainable Development Goals], food provides a cross-cutting entry point to support all the goals and can play a central role in achieving both local and global sustainability.

As applied to Toronto, the CRFS encompasses what is known as the Greater Golden Horseshoe, which includes cities as well as peri-urban and rural areas and has a population of well over 9 million (Blay-Palmer et al. 2018, 18). The Toronto Food Strategy, established in 2010 and led by Toronto Public Health, serves an important function in this system. The strategy has adopted the premise that food should be seen as a public good and a part of the collective commons rather than as a commodified good. The goal is to ensure that food-provisioning systems benefit the common good above all. To that end, its activities and ambitions extend far beyond ensuring the availability of nutritious food to consider the role that a sustainable food system can play in achieving many objectives associated with a sustainable city. A food system has been defined as the "full cycle of how food is grown, produced, processed, distributed, consumed and disposed of" (Toronto Public Health 2018, 4).

A multi-stakeholder Toronto Food Policy Council was established to advise the City of Toronto on the many cross-cutting issues related to its food system (Toronto Public Health 2018, 3, 8). The activities of the council reach into many of the City of Toronto's departments, which view food as an important "lever" in social and community development, sustainability, and health (19). These activities stretch into waste and energy management, land use, emergency planning, economic development (8), and employment as implemented through programs such as Community Food Works for Newcomer Settlement, Community Food Works, and Urban Agriculture Indicators (22–23). Beyond the city, the efforts of the Toronto Food Strategy extend into collaborations with the larger region, such as the Golden Horseshoe Food and Farming Alliance (23), upper levels of government (8), and global partners (10). A sustainable food system is multi-scaled and requires the concerted, collaborative effort of citizens, social and private sector groups, and governments at many levels, from the local to the global.

Canadian governments are beginning to acknowledge in their policies that food is vital to human health and social equity, and they are engaging in co-governing strategies related to food provisioning (Martorell and Andrée 2019, 276–77). Agriculture and Agri-Food Canada (2019, 3) invested more than $134 million in a national food policy entitled *Food Policy for Canada: Everyone at the Table,* which is predicated on the following vision: "All people in Canada are able to access a sufficient amount of safe, nutritious and culturally diverse food. Canada's food system is resilient and innovative, sustains our environment, and supports our economy" (5). The short-term actions outlined in this policy are intended to "help Canadian communities access healthy food," "make Canadian food the top choice at home and abroad," "support food security in northern and Indigenous communities," and "reduce food waste" (9). Food Secure Canada (n.d.), "a pan-Canadian alliance of organizations and individuals working together to advance food security and food sovereignty," has heralded this initiative as "an important first step" and commended its establishment of a multi-stakeholder Canadian Food Policy Council along with its other initiatives. The organization cautions, however, that the national policy alone will not transform the existing food system (Food Secure Canada 2019).

The process of ensuring that Canadians across the country are food secure cannot happen without the recognition that food provisioning needs to be contextualized and appropriate to its local environment, which requires drawing on the "knowledge and experience that emerge from place-based interrelationships between human and ecological systems" (Nelson, Levkoe, and Kakegamic 2018, 266). Given that each local foodscape is unique, a place-based food policy needs to be prioritized.

In the Canadian north, local food security presents its own challenges. Although many inhabitants still supplement their diet with "country food," obtained by hunting and foraging, this way of life is threatened. The ability of people to rely on the land for their food is threatened by the loss of traditional knowledge, climate change, environmental degradation, and the historical imposition of colonial culture and values. The importation of processed food from regions far to the south has created its own set of ecological, social, and health costs. Northern communities, with some government grants, have pursued alternative approaches to local food production that include community gardens, greenhouses, and training for agriculture appropriate to the unique conditions of northern regions.

"JUST" FOOD? FOOD SECURITY AND FOOD SOVEREIGNTY

> *Food security exists when all people, at all times, have physical and economic access to sufficient safe and nutritious food that meets their dietary*

needs and food preferences for an active and healthy life.

— Food and Agriculture Organization of the
United Nations 2008

Food security is seen as the goal, and food sovereignty is seen as the means to get there. The global peasant movement La Via Campesina defines food sovereignty as "the right of peoples to healthy and culturally appropriate food produced through ecologically sound and sustainable methods, and their right to define their own food and agriculture systems" (cited in Food Secure Canada 2013). Adhering to what are described as "seven pillars," food sovereignty (1) "focuses on food for people," (2) "builds knowledge and skills," (3) "works with nature," (4) "values food providers," (5) "localizes food systems," (6) "puts control locally," and (7) recognizes that "food is sacred" (Food Secure Canada 2013).

Toronto was an early leader with its food strategy, but cities across Canada are also introducing initiatives to promote sustainable food systems and to address questions of food security and food sovereignty. That said, although important and notable achievements have taken place, the Canadian foodscape continues to be shaped predominantly by the global agro-industry and by large corporate interests. From metropolitan areas to remote communities, many people throughout Canada suffer from food insecurity and a lack of food sovereignty (see Box 11.4).

Food is not *just* food but rather an integral part of the social-ecological fabric of any community. In another sense of the term, the distribution of food throughout Canada and the world is not socially *just* but highly inequitable. According to one research group, "In 2022, 18.4% of people in the ten provinces lived in a food-insecure household. That amounts to 6.9 million people, including almost 1.8 million children, living in households that struggled to afford the food they need. This is a considerable increase from 2021 during a period of unprecedented inflation" (PROOF 2023).

Other groups also suffer disproportionately from food insecurity. As explained by Paul Taylor, the executive director of FoodShare, a Toronto nonprofit,

research undertaken with a team from the University of Toronto in 2019 revealed the food insecurity of Black people in Canada:

Black people are 3.56 times more likely to be food insecure than White people in Canada. We also found that 36 per cent of Black kids live in food-insecure households, compared to just 12 per cent of White kids. The majority of people who are food-insecure get their income from employment, but when we looked at income from social assistance, we found that White folks actually receive more money than their Black counterparts. And we thought, how could that be? It turned out those numbers included disability income, suggesting that either White people are more likely to be approved for disability or that they're approved for more money than Black people are. All of these factors affect who has food to eat and who doesn't. At FoodShare, we realize that our work can't just be about making food accessible. It has to be about dismantling the systems that lead to food insecurity in the first place – things like racism and colonialism. (Cited in "'When You're Black'" 2020)

Food security also varies geographically. In 2017–18, the northern territory of Nunavut had the highest reported level of moderate to severe food insecurity (49.4 percent). Other regions were reported to have higher levels of food insecurity than the national average of 8.8 percent: the Northwest Territories (15.9 percent), Yukon (12.6 percent), Nova Scotia (10.9 percent), and Manitoba (10.2 percent) (Statistics Canada 2020b). Particularly affected are those Indigenous communities reported to experience four times the level of food insecurity found in the rest of the country. Indigenous food sovereignty and security require acknowledgment and redress of the inequitable and unjust historical practices embedded in dominant governing systems. Indigenous scholar Dawn Morrison (2020, 27) notes that a balanced approach is required to address "underlying structural issues and inequality in privilege and power in the policy, planning, and governance of our ancestral homelands, where we hunt, fish, farm, and gather our foods." Many new immigrants to Canada also suffer from food insecurity

BOX 11.4 It's not just food: Sustainable food security for immigrants

Program and policy development specialist Yousaf Khan (2011, 81–83) writes,

> Food security is an important issue to everyone but it also has personal meaning. I grew up in a small rural village [in Northern Pakistan] that relied on farming to live. Ninety percent of the population of [the] village was farmers working hard on their own little farms. The majority of our food, except some pulses, was fresh, produced inside the village. All the food was produced within 5 miles radius of the village ...
>
> Leaving that village, I immigrated here to Canada and settled in Waterloo Region along with my family. Coming here was a surprising change: a change in weather, language, culture, food, food ways, and access to jobs. Everything seemed very strange. After finding a suitable place to live, the next step was to look for appropriate food. First of all, I had to ask somebody (usually a friend) to take me to the grocery store, because I was not able to walk to the store in harsh weather and even if the weather was good, it was difficult to bring home groceries in a bus, changing stops and consuming too much time; it was a real challenge. Inside the grocery store, our family was astonished by not seeing our familiar vegetables in the store. There was also no halal meat, and milk was packed coming from a company instead of a local farmer. This was a surprise for us. Most of the available fruits and vegetables were found to be imported with labels like *"Product of Mexico, Product of California etc."* I saw frozen vegetables for the first time in my life. We picked some of the vegetables within the range of available choices and milk. To get halal meat we had to go to a small ethnic food retailer. Inside the ethnic store I was pleased to find some familiar foods, but halal meat and my familiar vegetables were much too expensive.
>
> A year later I learned about a farm, and by visiting the farm, I saw at least some fresh tomatoes, green chilies and cabbage which did not need to be continuously sprayed with water to keep their look fresh, as it is happening in all supermarkets ... My family picked our own tomatoes and green chilies and experienced the soil and farming for the first time since we came here. It was then that I realized that to eat healthy, culturally-familiar food ... it is necessary to have a policy that ensures economic and physical access to food that satisfies the cultural and spiritual needs of people.

as they navigate language barriers, economic concerns, and search for culturally appropriate food (see Box 11.4).

MUNICIPAL ACTIONS TOWARD SUSTAINABLE FOOD SYSTEMS

Local governments can play a direct role in creating food systems that are sustainable, which in turn contributes to many other municipal goals, such as reducing the impact of climate change, protecting ecosystem services, and promoting healthy communities. Effective land-use planning and design can encourage the development of a local foodscape that is ecologically diverse. Municipalities can remove impediments caused by restrictive bylaws and zoning. They can facilitate local food production by encouraging community food systems through education, public workshops, public engagement in food provisioning, and community events. Local governing approaches to promoting and developing sustainable foodscapes can lead to a physical, social, and cultural mosaic comprised of community gardens, edible forests, peri-urban and urban agriculture, local markets, and distributed access to nutritious food sources. In addition, the adoption of "food democracy" policies can stimulate civic engagement in the development of food charters and public participation in food councils. Attention to questions of diverse food cultures could help to enhance a sense of place and belonging among the various cultures present in Canadian municipalities. In the process, new opportunities for small business and efforts toward sustainable livelihoods might be supported while enriching the cultural fabric of the community as a whole.

An enormous amount of food waste in Canada is leading to huge social-ecological costs. Much of this waste could be avoided (Nikkel et al. 2019). The food-rescue charity Second Harvest (2019) notes,

> Nearly 60 percent of food produced in Canada – amounting to 35.5 million metric tonnes – is lost and wasted annually. Of that, 32 percent – equalling 11.2 million metric tonnes of lost food – is avoidable and is edible food that could be redirected to support people in our communities. The total financial value of this potentially rescuable lost and wasted food is a staggering $49.46 billion.

Municipalities, along with other governments, can reduce food waste by introducing new landfill policies and redistribution infrastructure or by adopting an all-encompassing integrative approach to food.

The City of Guelph and Wellington County (2019), for example, aim to create Canada's first "circular food economy" (see Figure 11.4).

In 2019, the Guelph-Wellington initiative Our Food Future received federal smart city funding of $10 million to implement plans for a circular food economy, which is a closed system that reuses materials and reduces waste (see Box 11.5). Assisted by technology, this initiative aims to achieve a 50 percent increase in access to affordable, nutritious food, to foster circular food businesses, collaborations, and social enterprises, and to increase economic revenues by reducing food waste (City of Guelph and Wellington County n.d.). This systems approach is based on the framework of a circular economy.

In sum, urban food systems can be used as a form of blue-green infrastructure by making use of and sustaining ecological goods and services, including "cultural ecosystem" services (Ridding et al. 2018). The conventional agro-industrial food system has removed people from the process of their own food production and provisioning. It is worth noting that this system has also freed people from a labour-intensive process, thereby allowing them to engage in other activities. However, by taking a market-based retail approach that distances people from their food sources, it has generated a unique set of social-environmental problems. These outcomes are major contributing factors to global climate change, a catastrophic reduction in biodiversity (due to the mass production of single food crops), growing food insecurity and social inequity, and many other problems with their own sets of cascading effects. A key component of a sustainable landscape, therefore, is a thriving, local foodscape.

CONCLUSION: RECONCEPTUALIZING LOCAL LANDSCAPES

Historically, decision makers in Canadian cities prioritized compartmentalizing incompatible activities and

11.4 Our Food Future | City of Guelph and Wellington County, 2019

BOX 11.5 Our Food Future: A circular food economy initiative

The City of Guelph and Wellington County have adopted a collaborative, place-based approach that uses a circular economy to tackle concerns associated with equitable access to nutritious food, waste management, climate change, and local economic development. Although food has been the focus of the initiative, it was scaled up in 2021 to include other municipalities and other aspects of the food and environmental sectors in southern Ontario through a network called the Circular Opportunity Innovation Launchpad (COIL). The City of Guelph and Wellington County (2022, 21) discuss their approach in a mid-term report:

Our approach:

- begins with the creation of the circular food system because changes in the food system have the power to reshape economies, create healthy connected communities, and rebalance our relationship with the environment
- takes a whole of system and place-based approach where through local testing and learning, we will demonstrate the art of the possible
- employs a distributed governance and community capacity building approach where we co-create projects that address the impacts of today's linear economic system

- uses circular principles and practices, smart data and technology, and city building approaches to effect system change and implement our shared vision
- builds a regenerative economic system that is grounded in place and culture in Guelph-Wellington but connected to national and global supply chains
- measures our success with a quadruple bottom line that values purpose, planet, people and prosperity.

Ultimately, these changes will create a **roadmap for a larger, inclusive circular culture, and regenerative economy.**

maximizing economic development to promote the health and economic prosperity of their denizens. These priorities continue to have a high degree of salience for local agendas, but in the past, "wise use" approaches to the environment and conservation, such as scientific management and zoning to conserve and protect areas, were deemed to have special importance. This land-sparing approach led to a loss of species diversity as protected areas became islands in a sea of unsustainable urban, industrial, and agricultural development that threatened ecological diversity and ecosystem services. Although protected areas and ecologically sensitive areas are essential elements of a sustainable landscape, protecting these areas alone will not sustain vital ecosystems. Emerging approaches to creating more sustainable landscapes emphasize a land-sharing, multi-scaled model in order to protect biodiversity and valued social, cultural, and physical ecosystems. Local governments play an important role in planning, governing, and collaborating to promote sustainable landscapes in a

manner that effectively recognizes the value of natural assets. Blue-green infrastructure and sustainable foodscapes comprise important elements of such a strategy.

As pressures on land continue to intensify, Canada needs a housing policy that can address current shortages, which many have referred to as a crisis situation. Public spaces continue to be diminished, whittled away in favour of private land development. However, creative approaches to land-use planning remain possible. Cities still mow large swaths of public land along roads, infrastructure, and boulevards rather than mandating ecological options. Within city hall, institutional learning is an important step in transitioning staff away from conventional "city beautiful" approaches that attempt to groom nature. Natural corridors, community gardens, micro-forests, and food forests all offer easy alternatives. Reframing municipal assets to include *natural* assets offers new ways to think about urban design that are harmonious with desirable ecosystems. Public education programs and supportive bylaws can encourage more ecologically diverse plantings on private residential and corporate land. Guelph-Wellington's expanding circular food economy initiative is one example of many efforts across the country to shorten supply chains, reduce waste, and facilitate local, sustainable food production. Information and communications technologies (ICTs) can be used to facilitate the efficient use and monitoring of energy and water, to track metabolic flows within the municipality, and to share lessons learned from innovations. This discussion continues in the next chapter, with an emphasis on sustainable approaches to the built infrastructure of a city – the systems that play a large part in controlling the stocks and flows of energy, transportation, water, waste, and other human-biophysical urban interactions.

NOTE

1 In ecological economics, "we can talk about *scale disecologies* when the widening of the spatial scope of biophysical flows entail[s] an increase in the environmental load per unit of product – always taking into account the different dimensions involved and the multi-scale character of this complex issue" (Tello and González de Molina 2017, 34–35).

12 Regenerative Infrastructure
Linear to Circular Systems

INTRODUCTION: REGENERATIVE SUSTAINABLE CITIES

Cities breathe like leaves, though in a different manner. Cities grow by storing resources as buildings, roads, infrastructure, and technologies. They absorb flows of energy and matter to build and maintain ordered functional structures. Cities are crisscrossed by networks of energy, water, gas, and information, like fine capillaries. Their networks draw from many sources and absorb in order to store, replace, repair, and consume. Other equally important networks dissipate. The wastes of cities are emitted and dispersed in the atmosphere, soil, and water and return to their sources

– Pulselli and Tiezzi 2009, 58–59

The urban built landscape is crumbling, desired ecosystems are degrading, and global greenhouse gas (GHG) emissions are rising as municipalities consider how best to replace or renew aging grey infrastructure. The task is prohibitively expensive. However, it does offer decision makers an opportunity to rethink the provisioning of services in ways that harness ecosystem services, build circular economies, and introduce more self-sustaining alternatives. Linear, single-task, grey infrastructure might be replaced with multi-dimensional and multi-purpose closed-loop systems. Municipal approaches to the provision of services like energy, water, waste management, transportation, and broadband are being reconceptualized. In addition, the challenges caused by variables such as extreme weather events, natural disasters, power outages, hazardous waste, and traffic congestion require immediate responses from local government with the support of the other levels of government. Considerations related to quality of life include adequate transit services, housing, community-health centres, recreation centres, and the equitable distribution of environmental goods and services. Responses might include the development of blue-green smart infrastructure, robust levels of public engagement, and collaborative forms of multi-level governance.

In 2016, the federal government rolled out its national Investing in Canada Plan, a multi-billion-dollar twelve-year, integrated grey, green, and social infrastructure initiative. The plan, managed by Infrastructure Canada, is designed to be implemented in collaboration with other orders of government. The aim is to provide stable funding over a twelve-year period in order to tackle water and air pollution in communities, reduce the impacts of climate change and build resilience, encourage a "clean-growth economy," and foster dynamic, inclusive communities supported by reliable and modern infrastructure and services (Infrastructure Canada 2023). In the fall of 2020, the federal government also pledged to extend broadband services throughout the country in order to serve cities as well as rural and remote communities (Innovation, Science and Economic Development Canada 2023).

Local governments possess various policy tools and strategies to meet their community's infrastructural requirements. They include land-use and urban planning, licensing and regulation, community-led initiatives, financial incentives and fees, and demand management practices, such as advocacy leadership, civic engagement, and good corporate citizenship (ICLEI 2010, 2). However, alternative policy and social-technical innovations are required if local governments are to pursue the ambitious environmental goals of the kind laid out by the federal government.

As Xiaoling Zhang (2015, 2) explains, regenerative sustainability offers one approach:

[Regenerative sustainability] provides an alternative to seeking to solve individual problems with the objective of causing "less harm" or even "net zero" solutions that minimize or mitigate harmful human activities. Instead, the objective is to engage and to empower people to focus upon integrated, system's approaches for creating and re-creating buildings, neighbourhoods, urban areas and regions through a "net positive" or "regenerative" lens in the expectation that this will increasingly yield synergistic benefits far beyond the current norms.

Regenerative sustainability embraces more than a green building approach that focuses on the technical and physical aspects of the built environment. Green building technologies have been aimed at limiting biophysical harm and being carbon-neutral – a response that first emerged to address the growing awareness of planetary boundaries and the "limits to growth" discourse (2). Biophysical considerations and blue-green infrastructure efforts are included in the regenerative sustainability framework. However, it operates within a different conceptual space because it also advances the notion of achieving net-benefit, or net-positive, synergistic effects from the interactions between humans and their environment (J. Robinson and Cole 2015). Emphasis is placed on the co-evolutionary relationship between humans and the landscapes that they inhabit, which require governing systems that are adaptive, flexible, and reflective (see the conclusion). In such a paradigm, sustainability is recognized as a contested idea, and governance is

viewed as a process-oriented form of public decision making that is both inclusive and collaborative. As John Robinson and Raymond J. Cole cogently point out, it is important to acknowledge that although science has a crucial role to play in sustainability decision making, "the ultimate decision as to what is understood by a sustainable society is a matter of negotiation and choice" (10). British Columbia, for example, decided to build a biosphere centre on Vancouver Island, the Clayoquot Biosphere Trust, with funding from senior governments, foundations, the private sector, and philanthropy. The construction of the centre has been guided by regenerative building principles that emphasize holistic, self-sufficient principles, with a focus on seven performance areas referred to as PETALS: "Place, Water, Energy, Materials, Health and Happiness, Equity, and Beauty" (Clayoquot Biosphere Trust 2022).

In the ever-evolving process of transitioning city governance to local sustainability, an apt description of the governing process involved might be "urban tinkering" (Elmqvist et al. 2018), which draws on biological models of evolution. Thomas Elmqvist and colleagues define "urban tinkering" as follows:

A mode of operation, encompassing policy, planning and management processes, that seeks to transform the use of existing and [the] design of new urban systems in ways that diversify their functions, anticipate new uses and enhance adaptability, to better meet the social, economic and ecological needs of cities under conditions of deep uncertainty about the future. (1549)

Urban tinkering encourages "safe to fail"[1] experimental approaches, innovation, drawing on nature for lessons and solutions, and adaptive management and governance (Elmqvist et al. 2018, 1551). Specifically, it emphasizes a complex systems approach that incorporates social, ecological, and technological considerations. Solutions are integrated and frequently multi-functional, serving a variety of purposes. Social opportunity and broadly diverse forms of engagement are essential components of this approach, requiring that social, policy, and physical space be provided to foster creative and possibly unconventional "tinkering" that can help to break down old path-dependent "decision-making patterns" (1560).

A transition toward sustainability does not demand wholesale demolition of the existing stock of grey infrastructure any more than it requires the jettisoning of all past governing practices. But this infrastructure needs to be incorporated into more holistic understandings of urban systems and approaches in a way that goes far beyond the provisioning of discrete functional services. For that to occur, it is important for policy makers to understand the metabolism of the urban system.

URBAN METABOLISM AND GOVERNANCE

> *The urban metabolism concept ... refers to the "collection of complex socio-technical and socio-ecological processes by which flows of materials, energy, people, and information shape the city, service the needs of its populace, and impact the surrounding hinterland" (Currie and Musango 2016). Cities have been characterised by linear processes where resources and wastes enter and leave the city boundaries respectively. The challenge is to transition from a linear perspective to a networked and cyclical perspective, in which wastes become new inputs, reducing dependence on the hinterland for resources.*
>
> – Musango, Currie, and B. Robinson 2017, 2

Urban regenerative sustainability involves an understanding of urban metabolism. The concept of metabolism – the exchange of matter between an organism and its environment – was adopted in the mid-1960s by Abel Wolman (1965) to analyze the overall flow of materials through a city. Wolman attempted to quantify what he referred to as the metabolism of a city, or its exchange of matter with its environment, by measuring inputs like water, food, and fuel and outputs in the form of waste and pollution. Long the purview of the natural sciences, this concept of urban metabolism has expanded over the years to become a well-developed stream of inquiry of industrial ecology. In this analytical approach, attempts are made to quantify the material stocks and flows of a human-built system, be it an industrial area, city, region, or some other district. Rising concerns associated with climate change have stimulated research on urban metabolic flows to include carbon emissions (Davoudi and Sturzaker 2017).

An urban metabolic system comprises not only a city's physical material flows but also its social metabolism – that is, the need for social systems that "maintain and reproduce their biophysical stocks (like human and livestock population, and built artefacts) for their survival and evolution" (Fraňková, Haas, and Singh 2017, 9). A social system requires the services of nature to sustain itself. The way that a service is provided and used affects the storing and accumulation of stocks (or resources) and their flows throughout the urban system (e.g., the waste that will be used, recycled, or discharged into the soils, water, or air). What was once considered waste is reconceptualized as a valued stock to be reused as a material resource within a circular economic system (see below). As Yulia Kalmykova and Leonardo Rosado (2015, 1) observe, urban metabolism (UM) research is a valuable tool in support of work that advances a circular economy, which is a concept that has gained traction in industry and urban governance throughout the world: "Implementation of a Circular Economy (CE) at the urban level is one of the factors in a sustainable urban metabolism and could decrease the pressure caused by cities – through more efficient use and reuse of resources – while also supporting the economy. Knowledge about the UM also makes it possible to identify opportunities for CE design and for CE progress." Metabolism of Cities (n.d.), a global network of researchers that includes some Canadian cities, describes urban metabolism as an "approach to study the sustainability of cities by quantifying and unpacking material and energy flows." This information is then made available to policy makers. These kinds of studies provide essential data for cities wishing to pursue a circular economy approach. An analysis of material waste flows, for example, was conducted for the City of Guelph and Wellington County as part of their initiative to build a circular smart city (Dillon Consulting, Metabolic B.V., and von Massow 2021).

Governing institutions play a determining role in shaping the urban metabolism. They influence the use, provision, and distribution of resources and services, raising questions of health, well-being, equity, and social justice. As Martin Dijst and colleagues (2018, 196) argue,

> Urban metabolism is about how we use resources. It deals with understanding and measuring flows and stocks. The normative claim in urban metabolism studies is that resources should be used efficiently in both production and consumption. We argue that in governance of UM there should be equal emphasis on equity because both efficiency and equity are prerequisites for social wellbeing.

The equitable distribution of resources throughout a geographic area is an important, but not the only, consideration with respect to environmental and social justice. Dijst and colleagues (2018, 197) caution that when talking about the distribution of material resources, considerations related to social justice and human well-being should be understood as greater than the possession of material goods. They argue that holistic approaches are required – ones that reduce the consumption of material goods while promoting social equality. They stress that siloed approaches can lead to policies that, despite their aim to reduce energy consumption, further marginalize vulnerable populations and reduce their overall well-being. A well-governed urban metabolism is one that is both equitable and efficient.

When striving for this outcome, local governments need to undertake urban metabolic assessments in order to acquire essential baseline and ongoing data about resource use and requirements. This is essential information for the development of key indicators that can be used in collaborative decision-making processes. The standardization of that data allows intra- and intercity comparisons for purposes of benchmarking and progress reporting (Musango, Currie, and B. Robinson 2017, 18). Open-data policies facilitate these processes. Eco-industrial parks, for example, rely on metabolic assessments to quantify the stocks and flows of resources. These eco-industrial parks are commonly shared areas where companies located together on a property share and recycle resources in a symbiotic fashion in order to reduce waste

and pollution and to optimize the use of energy, water, and materials. The objective is to have a closed-loop system as much as possible. In Canada, eco-industrial parks are not as well developed as in other parts of the world, but initiatives based on these principles have taken place at various scales across the country. More recently, concepts such as industrial symbiosis, circular economies, and infrastructural ecology are garnering policy attention.

UTILITIES AND SYNERGISTIC SYSTEMS

> *Infrastructural ecology is a planning paradigm that emulates the closed-loop, sharing logic of natural ecosystems. It suggests that features of our power, water, sanitation, transport, and food systems may be strategically combined, collocated, or otherwise linked for mutual benefit. Such interconnected systems then can cascade (or pass along) waste energy or water and nutrients for another's reuse, arrangements that can reduce pollution and greenhouse gas emissions, while lowering demand for new resource inputs.*
>
> – H. Brown 2018

The holistic, closed-loop (or circular) design of municipal infrastructure requires multi-level governance and shared responsibilities for managing energy, water, waste, transportation, data sharing, and broadband services. Blatchford, Edmonton, is one such neighbourhood under development based on this type of sustainable infrastructure (see Box 12.1).

ENERGY TRANSITIONS

Canada, as a signatory to the international Paris Agreement to combat climate change, has adopted multi-level governing strategies to pursue a low-carbon future. Canada's climate plan (Environment and Climate Change Canada 2022b) has directed hundreds of millions of dollars toward the adoption of electrical systems that produce no carbon emissions, power technologies that are renewable, and other related efforts (see Figure 12.1). Much of this funding is to flow to municipalities in order to support the installation of smart grid and other low-carbon technologies, help communities transition away from coal-fired systems, and reduce energy use. In December 2020, the federal government also raised its carbon taxes to reach $170 per tonne by 2030 (Tasker 2020). The carbon tax is aimed at making fossil fuels expensive in order to encourage the adoption of low-carbon alternatives.

Cities have a major role to play in reducing dependence on fossil fuels. Many local electric utilities, for example, are introducing energy-efficient features into their systems. Energy constitutes one of a municipality's largest expenses and also accounts for a major portion of GHG emissions. As a result, localities across Canada have adopted Community Energy Plans (CEPs). Often, there are two plans: a community-wide energy plan and a corporate energy plan to address city-owned infrastructure. These plans take into account the community's energy use related to land-use policies, transportation systems, building developments, infrastructure, and public educational programs (see Box 12.2).

Electricity generation and transmission fall under the domain of provincial responsibility, with large-scale generators transmitting energy long distances throughout the province. As Mark Winfield

BOX 12.1 Blatchford, Edmonton: A neighbourhood built on sustainable infrastructure

Blatchford, a massive neighbourhood development in Edmonton, Alberta, is designed to incorporate sustainability principles in energy, water, waste, and transportation and will eventually accommodate 30,000 people. Its energy goal is to achieve carbon neutrality using 100 per cent renewable resources powered by a city-owned utility: a District Energy Sharing System (utilizing a geo-exchange field, as well as a sewer heat exchange system). Blue-green infrastructure principles have been applied in its landscape design incorporating urban agriculture. Its water management system features bioswales, rain gardens, cisterns, and stormwater ponds, and water efficient technologies. Built in the centre of the city on a decommissioned airport site, it used recycled materials from the old airplane hangers diverting most of the material from the landfill. The development capitalizes on available public transit and is designed to encourage active transit (City of Edmonton n.d.-d).

12.1 Windmills, Prince Edward Island, 2014

BOX 12.2   Climate Change Toolkit, British Columbia: Energy-use initiatives in municipal Community Energy Plans (CEPs)

Land Use
- urban containment boundaries
- intensification, infill, conversion
- brownfield remediation
- street trees
- new street design
- zoning and development rules
- agriculture and food security

Transportation and Fleets
- low carbon fuels
- fleet management, vehicle "right-sizing"
- bike and pedestrian paths and facilities
- anti-idling campaigns
- asphalt reclamation
- HOV [high-occupancy vehicle] lanes
- traffic signal synchronization
- transit and paratransit

Buildings
- green building and sustainability checklists
- energy audits and retrofits
- solar thermal "ready"
- high efficiency lighting and heating
- xeriscape landscaping; "green" roofs and walls
- building orientation and solar rights

Infrastructure
- water pricing and metering
- waste heat recovery
- stormwater and wastewater management
- solid waste reduction; landfill gas capture
- combined heat and power opportunities
- district energy utility opportunities
- renewable energy opportunities

(Green Communities Committee n.d.)

and colleagues (2021, 38) note, "Except on federal or Indigenous lands, provinces hold ultimate control over municipal governance structures and public and private land-use planning. Provinces are therefore in very strong positions to set the overarching rules under which locally or community-initiated energy and climate change planning and plan implementation takes place." In their study of community energy plans in Ontario, British Columbia, and Nova Scotia, the authors conclude that provinces exert a very strong influence in constraining community energy plans. All three provinces have undertaken initiatives that emphasize "the expansion or renewal of large, centralized electricity-generating resources" (50).

Local hydro utilities (or local distribution companies) have had the responsibility of distributing electricity to homes, businesses, and organizations. In recent years, local utilities have been investigating, experimenting with, and creating programs that conserve energy by increasing efficiency, adopting alternative forms of energy, and reducing energy waste. The Government of British Columbia's (n.d.-a) Climate Action Toolkit, for example, was introduced by a partnership between the Green Communities Committee (which includes representatives from the province and the Union of BC Municipalities) and the Fraser Basin Council. The toolkit was developed to provide advice to BC municipalities, foster collaboration, and share lessons learned (Green Communities Committee n.d.). Canada's largest city, Toronto, has developed a Green Standard (see Box 12.3).

Other Canadian cities have adopted strategies designed to suit their specific requirements. As Christina E. Hoicka and Julia L. MacArthur (2018, 165) note, place-based community energy systems employ various approaches given local characteristics: "The changing geography of generation and demand means that the functions of energy projects such as local demand management, distribution/ system management and supply that coincide with communities require different forms of management, oversight, delivery, availability of labour, and economics of procurement."

For an energy program to achieve social-ecological sustainability, considerations of social equity need to be incorporated into the design. The

BOX 12.3 The Toronto Green Standard

Joel Arthurs (pers. comm., November 12, 2020), supervisor, Energy Management, City of Toronto, outlines the goals and requirements of the city's Green Standard:

The Toronto Green Standard was introduced as a City of Toronto planning environmental initiative for new city-owned and private-sector building developments. The Green Standard was aimed at improving air quality, reducing energy and GHG emissions, diverting waste from landfills, and enhancing ecological functions by integrating landscapes and habitats into construction, among other environmental priorities.

Toronto City Planning first brought the Toronto Green Standard to City Council in 2006 as a voluntary standard for new construction. Over time, aspects of the standard became mandatory and increasingly stringent. By January 2020, energy and GHG emission intensity requirements were set at [levels] above [those] of the Ontario Building code (with an efficiency standard required to exceed the provincial code by a minimum of 15 per cent).

A Development Charge Refund program allows developers to collect a partial refund of development charges for voluntarily exceeding the minimum requirements laid out by the Standard; these amounts are increased each year, since 2018. Some of the requirements of the Green Standard include:

- twenty percent of parking spaces must provide electric vehicle supply equipment (EVSE) and the remaining spaces must be designed for future EVSE installation;
- bicycle parking and shower facilities [are available] in non-residential buildings;
- ... tree canopy [is increased] by planting along public boulevards, street frontages, and throughout surface parking lots at a ratio of one tree for every five parking spaces;
- stormwater [is retained] from all surfaces through infiltration, water harvesting, reuse, and evapotranspiration. This requirement is for runoff generated from a minimum of 5 mm depth of rainfall; and

- light pollution is reduced by requiring all exterior fixtures [to] be Dark Sky compliant.

The City of Toronto also aims to lead by example in achieving its carbon [emission] goals as specified in ... the city's climate action strategy [*TransformTO Net Zero Strategy*, 2021]. Under the strategy, Toronto's GHG reduction targets include a 30 percent reduction by 2020 and a 65 percent reduction by 2030, based on 1990 levels. By 2050, the City is aiming to achieve net-zero. By 2026 all new City-owned buildings and additions of more than 100m^2 must be net-zero energy and emissions. This is also the case for all new buildings, including private construction, by 2030. On October 2, 2019, City Council voted unanimously to declare a climate emergency and accelerate the carbon-reduction initiatives. The Toronto Green Standard is updated every four years.

Note: At the time of writing, it is unclear how new provincial legislation introduced in the fall of 2022 to accelerate housing development will affect these requirements.

Town of Bridgewater, Nova Scotia, for example, has introduced an energy-based poverty-reduction program that recognizes the human toll that comes with the rising cost of providing stable and clean forms of energy (Town of Bridgewater 2023). In 2019, the town was awarded $5 million in the Government of Canada's Smart City Challenge "for its proposal to reduce energy poverty" (Infrastructure Canada 2019b).

Smart Grids

Canadian cities have different social, institutional, economic, and physical constraints that affect how they might best transition to a low-carbon future.

Successful transitions to a low-carbon community not only require innovative technological initiatives but also call for deep and meaningful societal and institutional changes:

> The central challenge in transitions concerns how radical innovations get a footing in niches and then compete with and transform existing regimes. This is often an uphill struggle because niche-innovations are initially more expensive and face social acceptance problems, while existing regimes and incumbents are locked into place: they have set rules and expectations, and they control the infrastructure, which is designed for incumbency rather than novelty. (Victor, Geels, and Sharpe 2019, 17)

The use of transition experiments is widely advocated given such barriers to innovation and the uncertainty about which mix of policies, technologies, and approaches will work best, particularly in countries as vast and disparate as Canada. Experimental transition projects "are explicitly linked to a larger vision of the long-term transformation of energy systems and ... are consciously understood as trials to test the viability of innovations and to explore possibilities for change" (Rosenbloom et al. 2018, 370).

These experiments in various cities encourage the risk taking that is necessary for innovation and offer an opportunity for learning both from successes and from failures, as well as the possibility of scaling up if they prove promising. They can also help to build capacity through the development of partnerships and knowledge sharing across sectors, actors, and innovators. Moreover, place-based transition experiments can engage and educate members of the public – an essential outcome if a low-carbon society is to be realized (371–73). Through joint action and partnerships, successful socio-technological experiments and initiatives can then be diffused into other municipalities.

Many local hydro utilities have adopted smart grid approaches that harness alternative forms of energy appropriate to the climatic and physical attributes of a locality (see Box 12.4).

A smart grid uses information and communications technologies (ICTs) to monitor, control, and optimize energy use, increase energy efficiencies, and reduce outages. Its adaptive design allows it to integrate renewable sources of energy into the system or even to operate as a micro-grid. Known as a social-technical approach, a smart grid is developed with the recognition that user behaviour is an important consideration because it affects energy consumption. Smart grid technologies make it possible

---

BOX 12.4 Local energy distribution systems and smart grid technologies

The following are only a few of the many examples of how local energy distribution systems are evolving to incorporate smart grid technologies and to use renewable resources (see Figure 12.1) in addressing their energy goals:

- The Regional Municipality of York, Ontario, announced the formation of the province's first local electricity market in 2019. This local network can be integrated into the provincial

electricity system and "will allow resources like solar panels, energy storage, and consumers capable of reducing their electricity use to compete to be available during periods of high demand" (Independent Electricity System Operator 2019).

- The City of Prince George, British Columbia, historically known for its forest-based economy, has developed a Downtown Renewable Energy System – a district energy system

that uses "local, renewable, and carbon-neutral" sawmill residuals (i.e., waste from wood) to heat water that is pumped to downtown businesses (City of Prince George n.d.).

- The City of Yellowknife, Northwest Territories, has established a Biomass District Energy System fuelled by wood pellets, with an anticipated reduction in GHG emissions of 829 tonnes a year and significant cost savings (Federation of Canadian Municipalities 2018a, 2018c).

to engage consumers in monitoring and managing their own energy use. Smart metering, for example, provides information about residential energy use, and based on that data, financial incentives can be offered to reduce consumption. Instead of relying solely on large-scale generators to transmit energy to distant cities, provinces can use smart grids not only to introduce alternative forms of energy into the mix but also to conserve energy, to improve cost efficiency, and to ensure the stability of supply. Mark Winfield and Scott Weiler (2018) suggest that in Ontario smart grids have been facilitated by a complicated institutional framework. The regime that emerged in the 1990s after the breakup of Ontario Hydro, an electric utility that had been set up as a Crown corporation, created niches for policy and technological innovations. As Winfield and Weiler note, "The result has been greater policy analytic capacity to deal with dynamic issues, and by implication greater resilience, than might be the case with a single vertically integrated monopoly" (1933).

Water Distribution Systems

Similar to other utilities, local water distribution systems are provincially regulated. Most cities in Canada draw their water from lakes and rivers, although some large regions, such as the Region of Waterloo, rely heavily on groundwater. Despite Canada's reputation for being a water-rich country, its water quality and quantity are threatened by contaminants, floods, drought, and climate change. Although collaborative, watershed-based planning and governance are now taking place in many areas throughout Canada, these boards or agencies may not always have the needed provincial political support.

Within municipalities, utilities distribute water through an infrastructure of pipes and valves. Degraded pipes and aging or poorly managed city infrastructure introduce contaminants, such as lead and other pollutants, into urban water systems and soils. Also, depending on how it is developed and managed, wastewater infrastructure can affect the geology of the watercourses and increase erosion and floods. Wastewater is carried through either combined or single sewers. Combined sanitary and storm sewers are typical in older municipal areas developed in the early twentieth century, with rain, snow, and sewage all being carried to wastewater treatment plants or discharged into lakes, rivers, or the ocean. In single sewers, stormwater is carried through drains and pipes that are separate from those that convey household waste and other wastewater. As André St-Hilaire, Sophie Duchesne, and Alain N. Rousseau (2016, 274) discuss,

- The City of Summerside, Prince Edward Island, owns Summerside Electricity, an electric utility that is generated primarily by the windmills of its Summerside Wind Farm. Almost half of the city's electricity is produced by wind power. This utility "sells, produces, transmits, [and] distributes" electricity to 7,000 residential and commercial customers and also exports electricity to New Brunswick via submarine transmission cables (City of Summerside n.d.).

- Smaller municipalities are also putting innovative energy systems in place. In 2020, the Town of Raymond in southern Alberta announced that it would be achieving net-zero energy in its operations by installing 2,700 solar panels on its municipal buildings (G. Robinson 2020).

In the case of district cooling systems, the heat that is drawn out of the building can be repurposed and used for hot water or space heating. This approach also improves the efficiency of the district cooling infrastructure by returning colder water to the system, which requires less cooling in a closed-loop system.

Energy projects such as those mentioned above can be scaled up. Smart grids may be integrated into a larger smart city plan that incorporates water, heat, power, and transportation service provision (Gass, Echeverría, and Asadollahi 2017).

In urbanized systems, the hydrological cycle is highly conditioned by the significant proportion of impervious areas, and by the installation of drainage systems. Networks of pipes for potable water supply and wastewater collection co-exist in parallel systems. These changes in water routing, combined with the generation of various pollutants from urban activities and land surfaces, govern the water quality of receiving watercourses, but also alter their physical characteristics.

When there are extreme rain events, the stormwater can exceed the capacity of combined sewer systems, and contaminants from sewage can then be introduced directly into the waterways. In response, the City of Vancouver (n.d.) and other parts of British Columbia and Canada have been working toward replacing their combined sewers with separated sewer systems.

A number of Canadian municipalities are introducing stormwater management initiatives using blue-green infrastructure thinking as part of their natural asset management approach. The goal is to reproduce the natural water cycle and to minimize the impact of urbanization on water quality. These outcomes are to be achieved through the construction of infrastructure that improves the quality of stormwater runoff (St-Hilaire, Duchesne, and Rousseau 2016). The City of Okotoks, for example, was nationally recognized in 2018 for its Living Soils Filtration Project, which uses the soils and plants of a 3,600 square metre bioretention bed (or rain garden) to filter the city's stormwater runoff. The use of these natural processes helped to improve water quality while reducing flooding (Federation of Canadian Municipalities 2018c; "Okotoks Receives" 2018). Other efforts of Canadian municipalities include daylighting (i.e., the opening-up of urban streams and watercourses long buried under pavement); the introduction of permeable pavement in homes, businesses, and public areas; the reduction of salt use on roadways in winter; water conservation initiatives and public education programs; grey-water systems; rainwater collection; wastewater treatment; the retention of wastewater to heat buildings using heat pump technology; and the reintroduction of natural plantings and buffer zones.

WASTE AND THE CIRCULAR ECONOMY

> *The circular economy (CE) concept is gaining weight as an alternative to the make-use-dispose paradigm (EC [European Commission] 2011). The CE concept aims at extending the useful life of materials and promotes recycling to maximize material service per resource input while lowering environmental impacts and resource use. Reducing inputs of raw materials to the economy is a main goal of CE strategies.*
>
> – Tisserant et al. 2017, 628–29

Waste management responsibilities in Canada are shared at all levels of government. The Canadian federal government controls the international and interprovincial movement of hazardous waste. It facilitates best practices and provides grants and project funding to effectively manage resources and to reduce waste. In 2019, for example, the federal government first announced that it would ban single-use plastics and set standards to hold companies responsible for the production of plastics. Canadians are estimated to throw away 3 million tonnes of plastic waste each year, only 9 percent of which is recycled, with the rest ending up in landfills or in the environment, polluting freshwater systems and oceans, harming wildlife, and introducing microplastics into drinking water (Environment and Climate Change Canada 2023). In 2020, the government announced a comprehensive plan to move toward zero plastic waste by 2030 and to reduce waste through a circular economy approach. The circular economy model has been widely embraced by businesses and governments around the world. The Ellen MacArthur Foundation (n.d.) helped to popularize the concept and link it to economic opportunities.

The federal government collaborates with the provincial and territorial governments, which are responsible for setting waste policies and regulations and for monitoring municipal and other waste facilities. Municipal governments are responsible for the collection, recycling, composting, and disposal of household waste. The concept of the 3Rs – reduce, reuse, and recycle – is often associated with notions of a circular economy, with recycling frequently employed by governments in aspirational policy documents (see Box 11.5). A principle underpinning the concept of the circular economy is that the understanding of economic growth should be decoupled from the consumption of material goods. Although the notion of the 3Rs has been around for many decades, the rapid consumption of material inputs has continued apace. However, the application of cost accounting to material flows has become quite sophisticated and can offer useful information about how to optimize waste management and material efficiency (Tisserant et al. 2017, 629).

Diversion from the waste stream is a key component in any waste management strategy. Governments are now looking to the private sector to take financial and physical responsibility for the materials that they produce, including post-consumer goods. This approach is referred to as Extended Producer Responsibility (EPR) and can be applied to materials such as packaging, electronics and batteries, hazardous waste, household goods, and pharmaceuticals (Trudeau and Giroux 2020, 5). Traditional mechanisms are still employed, including restrictive bylaws, waste management fees, and public education programs that promote the importance of the 3Rs while providing information about carefully separating waste and composting. Some cities are now also diverting waste in more innovative ways, such as Guelph-Wellington's project to create a circular food economy supported by a data hub and by its associated Circular Opportunity Innovation Launchpad (COIL).

Despite ongoing efforts aimed at reducing, reusing, and recycling (and refusing in the first place), municipalities are still left to contend with large volumes of waste entering their landfills and are challenged to come up with new approaches. Many of them have adopted new technologies such as capturing and reusing landfill gases as fuel, using drones and other ICTs to collect data, and using new materials to control GHG emissions and odours.

A number of municipalities, large and small, have engaged in comprehensive Integrated Waste Management. The Regional District of Kitimat-Stikine in British Columbia, for example, received a Sustainable Communities Award in 2018 from the Federation of Canadian Municipalities (2018c) for its approach to building a new waste management facility. The facility exceeded provincial environmental standards, significantly improved the diversion of waste (including 100 percent of sewage sludge), launched a public education campaign, planted a phytoremediation orchard onsite, and hired locally based contractors (Federation of Canadian Municipalities 2018b, 2018c).

In Canada, municipalities have been learning from the pilot projects and innovations of their counterparts in the Circular Cities and Regions Initiative, a peer-to-peer scheme founded to share best practices in implementing a circular economy approach. This partnership between the National Zero Waste Council, the Federation of Canadian Municipalities, RECYC-QUÉBEC, and the Recycling Council of Alberta provides mentorship and educational support from circular economy educators and practitioners. At the time of writing, twenty-five Canadian municipalities are participants in the initiative (Circular Cities and Regions Initiative 2022). A circular economy approach comes with many challenges, including the costs of adopting new systems. At the municipal level, it is a concept that has yet to evolve beyond waste flows to become a more holistic approach that includes the consideration of urban social metabolism and social justice. But as the above examples show, not only are the tools, technologies, and approaches available, but they can also be successfully implemented when a city possesses the political and societal will and capacity to make use of them.

MULTIMODAL TRANSPORTATION

Conventional notions about the liberal economic advantages obtained with the introduction of the automobile have long been known. In 1905, the first Ford Model C rolled off the assembly line in Walkerville, Ontario (now part of Windsor). The ensuing decades saw the automobile play a defining role in twentieth-century life, enabling the urban middle class to realize dreams of home ownership while fuelling the rapid growth of automobile-dependent suburbs (van Lierop, Maat, and El-Geneidy 2017, 49).

Industry and services sprang up around the automobile, and cities were increasingly planned around their use. To this day, roads are still viewed as a universal service by municipalities, with individual transit riders required to pay fares.

To be sure, material prosperity was enjoyed by a large swath of the population during the twentieth century, many of whom embraced the suburban lifestyle and the physical freedom offered by automobiles. This development was accompanied by serious social and environmental problems that have affected quality of life. Congestion, pollution, increased GHG emissions, inequitable zoning systems, and the loss of biodiversity and arable land are the most visible manifestations of the changes in consumer and policy choices. Some advocate the adoption of technological advances such as electric vehicles to address environmental issues. Despite their growing popularity, electric vehicles do not offer a panacea. They result in lower emissions compared to conventional automobiles, but electric vehicles still require that energy, which often comes in the form of fossil fuels, be produced and processed to provide electricity. Compared to mass transit and active transportation, Alexandre Milovanoff (2020) notes, electric vehicles' "potential to reduce greenhouse gas emissions disappears because of their life cycle emissions and the limited number of people they carry at one time." Moreover, transportation-related environmental issues are not just about emissions, nor are they simply technological or engineering problems to be solved.

Transportation choices shape a city and are a major factor in whether a city is lively and livable, now and into the future. Should scarce urban space be dominated by vehicles – electric, autonomous, or otherwise – or by people and valued physical places? Should the goal be to move cars or people? In short, the municipal policies and practices that have prioritized the automobile, viewed as an important part of the liberal economic paradigm and all that it entails, are not sustainable. Moreover, advocates of alternative forms of transportation, such as a good transit system, suggest that a green-economy approach can generate its own sets of opportunities for commerce and society. Urban decision makers are now encouraging alternative forms of transportation that foster livelier, more equitable, and healthier cities. Planning documents, urban visioning statements, and city halls across the country regularly proclaim the urgent need to encourage people to get out of their cars and either take public transit or engage more in active forms of transportation. Local governments have begun to invest heavily in infrastructure that encourages multi-modal transportation.

Transit-Oriented Development

> *In North America and Europe, both city and regional governments are implementing transit-oriented development (TOD) policies to provide more socially, environmentally, and economically sustainable communities ... One way to reduce the negative effects of urban sprawl is to build denser, mixed-use developments with the aim of reducing reliance on the automobile, by making other modes more accessible and available. Densifying urban areas around existing and new rail stations, and discouraging automobile use, are expected to yield significant benefits for cities, such as increases in the use of sustainable travel modes for certain trips.*
>
> – van Lierop, Maat, and El-Geneidy 2017, 49

Forms of urban rail transit – light rail, street car, subway, and commuter rail – are a common sight along the main streets of Canada's large cities, as well as in the rapidly growing Region of Waterloo (Figure 12.2).

Urban rail transportation has a long history by Canadian standards. In the mid-1800s, with advancements in electric power, the horse-drawn trams that could be seen in the main streets of Toronto and Montreal were replaced by streetcars. Canada's first electric streetcar traversed the Windsor waterfront along Riverside Drive in 1886. Streetcar systems were well established in a number of Canadian cities by the early 1900s. Over time, however, their predominance diminished with the advent of the automotive industry. Nevertheless, in Canada's largest cities – Toronto, Vancouver, and Montreal – streetcars maintained a presence, along with other modes of transportation. In 1978, Edmonton introduced the first light-rail transit system in North America, followed by Calgary and, eventually, other large cities (Sullivan 2015).

Many municipalities have made notable efforts to foster a multi-modal transportation system – that is, one that combines different forms of transport to facilitate efficiency and effectiveness when moving people or goods. The objective is to link different, more sustainable, and equitable modes of transportation. For example, when property in a city's centre is both desirable and expensive, many people are forced to move to less-expensive, peripheral urban areas characterized as transit deserts because mass transit is infrequent or unavailable. In such situations – all too common in Canadian metropolitan areas – hundreds of thousands of people find themselves with long commuting times tacked onto their working day.

The private automobile still accounts for the vast majority of trips taken in Canadian cities. It is a considerable challenge to convince people to forgo the convenience of their cars and to take mass transit or some form of active transportation – particularly in the winter. Through urban planning and the use of fees, it is possible to make the automobile a less convenient and more expensive option. Adding bicycle lanes, introducing traffic-calming measures, lowering speed limits, and limiting parking options can all encourage the adoption of alternatives to the automobile.

To address equity issues and to encourage behaviour changes in people who have their own vehicles, mass transit must be readily available, accessible, easy to navigate, affordable, appealing, reliable, and comfortable. Questions of scale are also important since transit systems can be effective, efficient, and equitable only if they are well integrated. For example, Metrolinx (n.d.), a regional transportation agency created by the Ontario government in 2006 to serve the Greater Toronto and Hamilton Area, is anticipating that it will need to serve over 10 million people by 2041. It has been developing a multi-modal transportation system that includes buses, streetcars, light rail, heavy rail, subways, and active forms of transportation, with the hope that people will move seamlessly between the different modes of transport. This massive, challenging initiative is supported by a

12.2 Light-rail transit, Region of Waterloo, Ontario, 2020 | Evangelos Kattides

multi-level government investment in rapid transit. Metrolinx's (n.d.) long-term regional plan acknowledges the need for this densely populated area to be adaptable and to plan for future uncertainty. Examples include accommodating the introduction of autonomous vehicles and other technologies and mitigating the impact of sudden adverse events caused by climate change or pandemics. Other challenges include problems posed by existing traffic gridlock and conflicting political ambitions about how to address it, financial limitations, and adapting the existing transportation system that was developed at any earlier time with different requirements.

As the COVID-19 pandemic illustrated so graphically, living and mobility patterns can shift quickly, substantially, and dramatically. In the past few decades, plans for population growth have encouraged densification and the provision of transportation systems to reduce commuting times for people travelling into city centres. Such densification leads to the development of high-rise buildings, which require large water mains and large reservoirs to meet standards related to fire flow – or the rate of water supply necessary for manual firefighting. Their development also generates the need to build streets and/or transit systems that can handle large peak movements of people. During the pandemic, many people and employers realized the benefits of working from home.

If this trend continues, a lot of current infrastructure investment might be left "stranded" (W. Kennedy, pers. comm., December 30, 2020). In addition, there are social justice considerations for the densification and gentrification of areas serviced by a convenient fixed-rail system. Historically, areas in the core, which are closest to amenities, services, and jobs, have higher housing costs, with less affordable housing options relegated to the periphery.

Given the rapid development of technology, such as self-driving cars, along with the changing patterns of human mobility and commuting, transportation systems need to be flexible and adaptable. Do rail systems help to fulfill these requirements even though they are costly to build, maintain, operate, and fix in place? To be sure, they can be built along the spine of a community, with a major goal of encouraging urban densification. They can also provide a much greener alternative to the private automobile – that is, if people opt to use transit rather than cars.

Moshe Givoni and Anthony Perl (2020), however, draw attention to the tremendous and growing costs associated with building and maintaining transportation systems and infrastructure that one day might become obsolete. Worth questioning are the well-entrenched assumptions embedded in transportation planning approaches that maximize infrastructure growth to provide optimum physical mobility. In these scenarios, maximum mobility is typically viewed as a societal benefit (82). For example, assumptions about transportation mobility are rooted in an era that was focused on moving goods and people long distances, with the response over time being to build ever more infrastructure in order to reduce congestion (which may, in fact, encourage it). However, conceptions of maximum mobility did not address social equity concerns, resulting in limited transportation options for many people on the peripheries of urban areas, who are required to commute long distances to work.

Motivations may go further than pragmatic attempts to satisfy a public need. Perhaps underpinning the enthusiasm for maximizing transportation and mobility are local aspirations for cities to be perceived as global and cosmopolitan (Givoni and Perl 2020, 82). Noting that society is in a period of "deep uncertainty," Givoni and Perl suggest that it might be wise not to "lock society into mobility trends" that may be inefficient or even damaging (89). Before a city invests in new infrastructure, they recommend consideration of a wider suite of alternatives, offering an approach that relies on "four core design principles: renew, redesign, repurpose, and remove (the 4Rs)" (88). As they explain,

> Considering more diverse options should become a norm in transport infrastructure planning. The implications of broadening infrastructure redevelopment options could enable a major change in the delivery of future mobility and facilitate a reduction in the need for new infrastructure. In addition to considering more options to build and renew, the new approach also calls for developing transport infrastructure that can be more easily (and cheaply) adapted to changing futures and changing mobility needs. (89)

For local decision makers, such cautions are worth keeping in mind as they determine how to invest in sustainable transportation alternatives for cities designed around the automobile. For example, information and communications technologies have made it possible for many to work from home. Over the past two decades, there has been a trend toward home-based office work. This trend was accelerated with the arrival of the COVID-19 pandemic, raising the question of whether workers need to be physically clustered in cities. With many more people working from home, flexible interurban transit systems may one day become more of a priority than commuter rails.

Active Transportation

One important mode of transit is active (or human-powered) transportation, such as walking, cycling, and skateboarding. Active transit is seen to have many benefits in terms of public health and safety, environmental benefits, urban livability, and community well-being. In 2009, the Public Bike System Company, headquartered in Longueuil, Quebec, launched its bike-share system BIXI Bikes in Montreal, the first of its kind in North America. Although it experienced early financial difficulties, the initiative gained popularity and has been emulated and adopted in other parts of North America and the world. It is now well integrated into Montreal's transit system.

Despite the noted attributes of active forms of transportation, one cycling advocate and analyst, Cameron Roberts (2020), laments that their widespread adoption is still akin to trying to peddle into a headwind. Although cycling enthusiasts and proponents have formed effective political coalitions of interest, powerful, entrenched forces still present formidable barriers to the adoption of these more sustainable forms of transportation. Roberts argues that "motorists, car producers, road builders, and others with a vested interest in the continued domination of the private automobile are a powerful political bloc, while professional experts in town planning or traffic engineering tend to privilege cars over alternatives" (1). That said, safer and more convenient forms of infrastructure, such as the dedicated cycling lanes and wider sidewalks that have popped up in cities around the country, are evidence of an expanding cycling and active transportation culture.

Digital Infrastructure and Broadband

Digital infrastructure – by which data, information, and knowledge are carried on the Internet – is as important as the other forms of infrastructure discussed above. The modern city depends on reliable, high-speed Internet services. So-called smart cities rely on high-speed Internet provided by broadband to operate utilities that manage energy, waste, natural and built assets, and transportation, to offer health, education, and social services, and to facilitate industry and commerce. Reliance on Internet services is as acute in rural areas as it is in densely packed metropolitan cities. As with so many other topics covered in this book, the COVID-19 pandemic revealed the important role of an efficient digital infrastructure in maintaining and sustaining all aspects of a functioning municipality and its denizens. The pandemic generated a worldwide movement toward home-based work, highlighting the crucial importance of reliable and high-speed broadband coverage. Broadband refers to a variety of "high-capacity transmission technologies that are used to transmit data, voice, and video across long distances and at high speeds. Common mediums

of transmission include coaxial cables, fiber optic cables, and radio waves" (Fernando 2022).

Demonstrable perils are embedded in highly centralized infrastructure systems, including telecommunications. A widespread Rogers Communications outage as a result of a systems error in the summer of 2022 highlights the dependence of people on functioning digital infrastructure. Rogers is one of three telecommunications companies in Canada that monopolize the market. Millions of people were affected for periods ranging from one to several days when they were left without phone, television, and Internet services; banking, ATM, and debit and credit card services; and government and some health and emergency services.

Provincial and federal governments have invested billions of dollars in broadband and the Internet. In 2020, the federal government announced an addition of $1.75 billion to a Universal Broadband Fund as part of its ongoing Connecting Canadians program. The goal is to address "connectivity" gaps where need is most acute, namely in rural and remote Canada and in areas with only intermittent coverage offered by mobile wireless services (Innovation, Science and Economic Development Canada 2021). Larger regions with more resources have benefited from their denser populations and ICT business growth, with municipal governments teaming up to form partnerships, such as the Toronto-Waterloo Innovation Corridor. In rural southwestern Ontario, the small municipality of Stratford – with a population of about 33,000 in 2021 – has taken advantage of its proximity to this corridor with the strategic decision to invest in its digital infrastructure. Stratford was an early adopter of the concept of a smart city (City of Stratford 2019). In advance of most of its counterparts, Stratford has invested in city-wide Internet and broadband coverage, establishing a high-quality digital infrastructure that is a key element of its economic development strategy (which has enabled it to become a testing site for autonomous vehicles) and a key component in its delivery of municipal services and programs. Other small cities and regions across Canada have also been early ICT adopters. In the maritime province of New Brunswick, for example, the cities of Fredericton and Moncton have earned designations as "intelligent communities," and in 2016 the largely rural province demonstrated leadership with a program to provide widespread cell coverage and access to high-speed Internet (Government of New Brunswick 2016).

CONCLUSION: INFRASTRUCTURE PROVISION IN AN EVOLVING CITY

Government approaches to infrastructure provision have been founded on assumptions of resource abundance and supply-side management. The centralized provision of services is vulnerable to widespread systems and services disruption in the face of unpredictable climate events and a lack of built-in redundancies. The approach is based on an unsustainable economic model. Questions need to be posed about the supply-side versus the demand-side management of resources and services. Canadian governments have not conventionally been oriented toward managing public demand for services. In the twentieth-century, an economy powered by fossil fuels supported the supply of services in dense urban areas. In the twenty-first-century era of climate change and other social-ecological considerations, an integrated systems approach is in order. Both public demand for services and reconfiguring cities to manage this demand are necessary elements of a sustainable strategy. Provincial governments that promote a centralized approach to service provision are working counter to sustainable local initiatives. The Ontario Progressive Conservative government, for example, has imposed an energy regime that relies on the provision of natural gas, while cancelling many planned local, renewable projects.

Contrast the economic and environmental costs of this approach with the outcomes of one that reconceptualizes environmental goods and services as renewable and opens up new economic opportunities. Winfield (2022) notes that distributed energy resources, such as rooftop solar systems and household- and facility-level technologies for energy storage, can offer cost-effective alternatives sufficient to meet additional capacity needs for the next ten years. When environmental goods and services are regarded as renewable, waste is no longer waste but a reusable resource that feeds into a circular economy. Realizing net-benefit, or net-positive, synergistic effects from the interactions between humans and their environment opens

up new possibilities (J. Robinson and Cole 2015), such as the deep decarbonization of cities, which entails decarbonizing the power supply, increasing energy efficiency, and substituting electricity for fossil fuels. "Net negative electric cities" would "sequester more carbon than they emit in total, through provision of electricity with negative carbon intensity" (C. Kennedy et al. 2018, 18). Such possibilities, however, are limited by a lack of political will and imagination.

On a final but, perhaps, most important note, much of this chapter's discussion concerns how to reconceptualize both the physical arrangements of infrastructure and the institutional arrangements needed to achieve a more sustainable outcome. In the coming decades, however, the discussions held in municipal council chambers will also need to be grounded in a more fundamental set of questions about the relationship between the built environment and the social-ecological urban metabolism. When considering modes of public transit like fixed-rail systems, for example, is the goal simply to address how to meet public demand while providing services in a more environmentally friendly, inclusive, and accessible manner? Perhaps some more essential questions need to be asked. As noted at the beginning of this book, municipalities cannot simply add more services to their already daunting stack of responsibilities. It is time for local governments to consider whether they should continue to provide traditional (and often growing) levels of service or whether they should repurpose expenditures to meet different and evolving service needs.

The challenge ahead, therefore, is to consider cities in a holistic manner. Urban decision making for sustainable, resilient cities needs to go beyond providing "smarter" and technologically driven supply-side solutions or focusing on discreet sectors or utilities. Required are unifying frameworks for urban environmental sustainability, such as those that can assess urban metabolism or urban resilience (Bristow and Mohareb 2020, 300). The highly unpredictable cities of the future will require comprehensive data that can inform adaptive, nimble, and responsive forms of governance.

Exploiting the benefits of distributed and adaptable systems is by no means a recently adopted governing strategy. The early Vikings, for example, achieved notable fame for their ability to venture far from Scandinavia to Europe, Africa, and North America while gaining control of kingdoms and valuable trading routes. Why would this be the case? The Vikings came from a rugged and inhospitable land, lived in small scattered settlements, and lacked any form of central government. According to archaeologist Jan Bill (2020), much can be attributed to the versatile design of their lightweight long boats, which could readily navigate difficult river systems, land on beaches, and be carried over land. The Vikings' success depended on their dispersed system of government, coupled with fast, efficient boats that could transport intrepid Viking warriors or material goods (Bill 2020). In North American history, similar benefits were realized by the lightweight birchbark canoes designed by Indigenous people thousands of years ago and later adopted by Voyageurs, who used them up and down their trading routes. Much like the Viking ships and the birchbark canoes that were steered through vast water-based systems, some municipalities are redesigning urban infrastructure to create efficient, distributed systems that will enable adaptation to changing situations. These systems offer flexibility in the context of rapidly escalating global changes. Analogous to the rivers, lakes, and oceans that enabled the rapid and early deployment of small, nimble vessels, a municipality's infrastructure comprises an essential platform on which to navigate toward a sustainable future.

If a complex systems lens is applied to a city as a whole in order to measure its urban metabolism and its material stocks and flows, a very different governing strategy emerges. The instrumental approach to providing distributed, networked services more efficiently will still comprise an important component of a sustainable strategy – but not all of it. Governing efforts need to be directed at reducing public demands for goods and services and at redirecting material and waste flows. Holistic urban design does not affect only the biophysical and built shape of a municipality but also human well-being, which also needs to be fostered if the goal is to achieve a regenerative infrastructure with a net-positive outcome. Consequently, as discussed in the next chapter, attention must be paid to building the overall health of the whole community.

NOTE

1 "Safe to fail" refers to small, localized experiments where there are no great costs to the workers or staff involved if the effort is considered unsuccessful, thereby encouraging new innovations and learning. In local governance, safe to fail is a useful element of institutional learning so that governments can respond to emerging challenges and let go of past practices that are counterproductive.

13 Healthy Cities
Well-Being, Diversity, and Inclusion

INTRODUCTION: HEALTH AND WELL-BEING

> *Imagine for a moment that you're standing at the edge of the river. You see a kid floating by, and that kid is struggling, drowning. Brave soul that you are, you tear off your shoes, dive into the water, and haul that kid to shore. You feel exhilarated. You saved a life. But then, before you're even dry, another kid comes floating by, and you dive in again. Then along comes kid number three, and four, and five. You're calling everyone you know to help you haul kids out of the river. Eventually, hopefully, one of you was wise enough to ask, "who keeps chucking these kids into the river?" and heads upstream to try and find out.*
>
> – Meili and Piggott 2018, 341

Poor health is often a result of social, economic, and environmental factors. This observation surely comes as no surprise. Even so, the dominant policy approach to poor human health is to treat the symptoms of the problem rather than the root causes. This approach is similar to an "end-of-pipe" solution to pollution, where technology is used to try to mitigate the damage that could have been prevented upstream. The vast majority of health-related resources are dedicated to treating illness and disease. This medical model is necessarily a key element of public health care. However, recognizing its value and important role need not come at the cost of addressing the primary

determinants of health. Resources can be distributed in a way that allows for the application of a suite of approaches needed to tackle the complex challenges inherent in ensuring public health, well-being, and safety.

The siloed, disease-based model of health care persists despite the definition of health first set out in the 1948 Constitution of the World Health Organization (n.d.-a): "Health is a state of complete physical, mental and social well-being and not merely the absence of disease or infirmity." As Canadian public health scientist Dennis Raphael (2018, 23) argues, health policy would be more efficacious if it holistically addressed the primary determinants of health, such as "conditions of childhood, income, education, employment security and working conditions, food and housing security, and availability of health and social services." To this list could be added additional social and environmental determinants related to questions of political and social inclusion, social and spatial justice, one's sense of place and belonging, personal safety and security, and the quality of one's social-ecological environment. Social movements are also promoting a social and governing shift in approaches to public health. For example, the global network People's Health Movement includes health activists, civil society organizations, and academics in its efforts to address social, environmental, and economic determinants of health.

People deprived of essential support related to their living and working conditions can experience lifelong and intergenerational health challenges.

Throughout Canadian history, governing institutions have consistently underserved or discriminated against racialized, vulnerable, or marginalized[1] peoples (Arya and Piggott 2018). Given this book's focus on local governance, the term "underserved" is apt. Thomas Piggott and Aaron Orkin (2018, 14) offer the following: "Whereas *vulnerable* or *marginalized* identify the problem with an individual, *under-served* points to a system failure that leaves a group of individuals with an unmet need. *Under-served* also creates an avenue for rectifying this unmet need, by way of bridging the gap between needs and services by creating more appropriate or adequate services."

Over the past century, notable progress has been made in some areas of public health and wellness, markedly reducing rates of morbidity and mortality. Some municipalities have also started to take concrete measures to become more publicly inclusive and welcoming to people with varied social, economic, and cultural backgrounds. Nevertheless, a significant proportion of people in Canadian cities are marginalized politically and socially on a daily basis and have consistently been underserved by governing institutions. Moreover, underserved communities require additional attention and resources to address complex problems. For example, people did not experience the COVID-19 pandemic the same way, with underserved populations being much more severely affected. As communities worked to recover from the many impacts of the pandemic, Jeremy Stone (2020) called for the application of recovery justice, which recognizes that "more than equality is needed." Vulnerable communities needed focused help to begin to recover from the devastating effects of the pandemic. Equal treatment does not lead to equitable outcomes given that different populations need different amounts and types of resources and services.

Social justice is a fundamental component of a sustainable, healthy community. In his work, economist and philosopher Amartya Sen (1985) nicely unpacks the formidable challenges of attempting to find a perfect definition of justice and the institutional arrangements that would achieve it. In its place, he ties the notion of human rights to the capability approach, which has been very influential in the creation of the United Nations Human Development Index as well as other indices and indicators of well-being. Sen looks at the question of human rights in terms of well-being and agency. According to the United Nations Development Programme (2010, 2), "Human development is the expansion of people's freedoms to live long, healthy and creative lives; to advance other goals they have reason to value; and to engage actively in shaping development equitably and sustainably on a shared planet. People are both the beneficiaries and the drivers of human development, as individuals and in groups."

Martha C. Nussbaum (2011, 33), who has further developed the capabilities approach, argues that "when we keep our eyes focused on what people are actually able to do and be, we quickly see that they do not have the ability to participate in political debate, to vote, to run for office, and so forth, if they are inhibited by extreme poverty, lack of education, and ill health – at least they do not have these entitlements securely, or on a basis of equality." The manner in which a society treats its most vulnerable members is an important indicator of the overall health of the polity and society as a whole. Communities are collectively stronger and healthier if the most vulnerable in society are well served, treated with compassion, and regarded with respect.

THE HEALTHY CITIES AND COMMUNITIES MOVEMENT

In 1986, the First International Conference on Health Promotion, organized by the World Health Organization, was held in Ottawa. The conference concluded with the signing of the Ottawa Charter for Health Promotion. It signalled the rising global consensus that public health was inextricably linked to and dependent upon social, economic, and environmental health. Trevor Hancock, a public health officer and the first leader of the Green Party of Canada, was a major player at the conference. Hancock was one of the founders of the Healthy Cities and Communities movement, which emerged from the Ottawa Charter. With Fran Perkins, he created a mandala of public health that has been widely cited and used throughout the world (see Figure 13.1).

Shortly thereafter, the Healthy Cities and Communities approach spread to thousands of cities

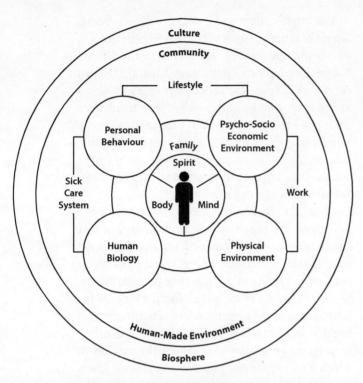

13.1 The mandala of public health: A model of the human ecosystem | Trevor Hancock and Fran Perkins, 1985

throughout the world. It is still a widely promoted concept adopted by municipalities – although its ideals have yet to be fully, or even partially, realized. It is based on principles that address the primary determinants of health, including social justice and equality, individual and community empowerment, and a healthy environment. Over time, the concept has evolved and become more nuanced in the academic and applied literature, aligning with the principles of sustainability discussed in Chapter 1 (e.g., see Langmaid et al. 2020).

Hancock (2009, 2011) notes, however, that after a promising and exciting start, the ideals contained in the Ottawa Charter have largely remained unfulfilled at the federal, provincial, and regional levels of government. He lists a number of reasons why this is the case. Perhaps the predominant challenges are a lack of political will and an inability to coordinate action because of fragmented approaches to governance. Moreover, local governments are further constrained by inadequate local institutional structures

and funding, as well as by limited municipal decision-making capacity. Critically needed, Hancock suggests, are the prioritization of "sustainable and equitable human development, rather than the economy"; "whole of government," multi-sectoral, and collaborative approaches to change; "national and provincial anti-poverty strategies"; and the empowerment of citizens and communities to "create the conditions for healthy living" (Hancock 2009, 2011). These recommendations are echoed by many others in the fields of community health and sustainability both domestically and internationally. The goals of the Healthy Cities and Communities movement align with the United Nations Sustainable Development Goals (SDGs) (United Nations General Assembly 2015).

Despite these acknowledged limitations, during the twenty-five years since the signing of the Ottawa Charter, numerous related healthy community initiatives have taken place at all levels of governance. International efforts include those of many bodies operating under the auspices of the United Nations and the Pan American Health Organization's Healthy Municipalities, Cities and Communities Movement (HMCC), among many others. The Canadian national government provided post-COVID recovery funding to the Canadian Healthy Communities Initiative (Community Foundations of Canada n.d.-a). The Canadian Institute of Planners adopted a Healthy Communities Policy to prevent the spread of infectious diseases and to address the many sustainability concerns that affect human health. Topics range from global climate change to the built environment (Canadian Institute of Planners n.d.). Provincial and local efforts have also taken place across Canada. These efforts, such as building resilient neighbourhoods, are sometimes broad in scope and multifaceted, whereas other undertakings focus on a particular aspect of health determinants, such as poverty alleviation, safety, food security, inclusivity and diversity, community asset mapping, communications and transportation in rural areas, healthy physical activity and wellness, and various areas of biophysical (or environmental) health. Healthy Communities and related efforts, however, lack the requisite national and provincial coordination as well as sufficient legislative and funding support.

THE EMERGENCE OF UNIVERSAL HEALTH CARE AND PUBLIC HEALTH

At the start of the twentieth century, the prevailing discourse focused on scientific management, professionalization, efficiency, and a reductionist approach to tackling societal ills. Proliferating diseases and the search for medical and scientific solutions frequently sidelined preventative public health initiatives. This was also the case when it came to the allocation of the bulk of government funding – a situation that prevails to this day. That said, over the course of the ensuing decades, important advances were achieved in public health. The early urban reform movement stimulated policy changes that would bring some order to very chaotic cities. At that time, urban areas were rife with unsanitary conditions and associated diseases, as well as unsafe living conditions. Subsequently, sanitation and water systems were developed to deal with waterborne diseases such as cholera and typhoid. Other contagious diseases, including polio and measles, continued to exact heavy tolls well into the middle of the twentieth century until high rates of vaccination brought them under control (Public Health Agency of Canada 2008, ch. 2). The adoption of public health measures was accelerated by the toll exacted by the deadly Influenza Pandemic of 1918–19. The virus was disseminated across Canada by soldiers coming home from the First World War. As the old saying reminds us, our collective failure to learn from history has doomed us to repeat the tragedies of the past (see Box 13.1).

In both pandemics, the social determinants of health played a role in morbidity and mortality outcomes, with vulnerable communities most severely affected. Also, during both pandemics, many members of the public evidenced similar behaviours: they were often unwilling to follow government edicts, were confused by inconsistent public messaging, and

were baffled by governments' inability to coordinate a unified response across jurisdictions. However, large numbers of citizens demonstrated a willingness to unite in order to help neighbours and vulnerable community members.

The establishment of the federal Department of Health in 1919, government responses to the Depression in the 1930s, and the growth of the welfare state all emphasized a widespread political recognition that the state had a responsibility to protect the health and welfare of citizens. To that end, the federal government centralized responsibilities for health and social services. However, in the province of Saskatchewan, municipalities came up with some creative approaches to address health concerns during the Depression. Saskatchewan's political culture of the time was informed by populism, a desire for local self-government, and a good dose of practical necessity. For example, in the

---

BOX 13.1 The Influenza Pandemic of 1918–19

Mark Osborne Humphries (2013, 129) offers the following observation of the deadly Influenza Pandemic of 1918–19. It is an observation that could just as readily be applied to the COVID-19 pandemic of 2020–21:

It became clear during the pandemic that disease did not cloister itself in one part of the community; instead, it spread across physical and social barriers. Regardless, the severity of the crisis and the mortality rate were both increased by poverty, overcrowding, and other underlying conditions. In the end, the failure to address these issues before the pandemic – and to thus prevent the crisis from unfolding in the first place – was identified as responsible for the unprecedented loss of life ... The epidemic led to contact across diseased boundaries, and Canadians were thereby familiarized with the plight of those who were often seen as the "other" rather than as legitimate neighbours. This contact united communities in the fight against the disease and at least temporarily weakened boundaries defined by class, ethnicity, and gender.

As with the COVID-19 pandemic, the impact of the virus that swept the world over a century ago was not equally experienced by all segments of the population.

early 1920s, it was difficult for rural Saskatchewan to attract and retain physicians. As a solution, many municipalities established a program whereby the municipalities paid physicians regular salaries for their services. The scheme worked well for both doctors and patients. By 1944, one-third of Saskatchewan's municipalities had doctors on their payrolls, providing a measure of security and predictability for all concerned (Lipset 1971, 250–51). Some urban areas also set up municipally run hospitals and medical care cooperatives (or community clinics).

These early precursors of Canada's Medicare system were populist responses to a world that appeared indifferent to local rural needs. As political sociologist Seymour Martin Lipset (1971, 251–52) once observed, "Repeated challenges and crises forced the western farmers to create many more community institutions (especially cooperatives and economic pressure groups) than are necessary in a more stable area. These groups in turn provided a structural basis for immediate action in critical situations." Also noteworthy are Lipset's observations about the healthy civic culture of the farmers he encountered: "The farmers are interested in their society and its relations to the rest of the world. Winter after winter, when the wheat crop is in, thousands of meetings are held throughout the province by political parties, churches, farmers' educational associations, and cooperatives. There are informal gatherings, also, in which farmers discuss economic and political problems" (11).

The lively local political culture and citizen participation experienced in early-twentieth-century rural Saskatchewan communities offer some useful lessons. For example, they lead one to wonder how governing bodies might have made more effective use of both civic culture and the local knowledge of health practitioners in the COVID-19 pandemic. One group of physicians argues,

The secret to dealing with a wicked problem is to think outside of the box. We need to let go of professional and jurisdictional barriers. We need to move beyond health care's traditional silos. People and communities are affected differently by the pandemic and will have different ideas and strategies for how to best reach their communities with

vaccines. To do that, we have to find ways to trust each other.

A wicked problem will not be solved by one sector and requires the input and efforts of entire communities. People do not exist in, nor do they think they belong to, a single sector, a specific hospital or a single health-care discipline. (Keresteci, Kaplan-Myrth, and Dosani 2021)

Members of the public may be more willing to trust public health information if it comes from their local doctor, community wellness centre, nurse practitioner, or pharmacist rather than from centralized communications that filter down from the federal and provincial governments. Personal contact of this kind was particularly important during the COVID-19 pandemic, with its enormous mental health impacts.

New Public Health and Local Public Health Units

The New Public Health [NPH] is a comprehensive approach to protecting and promoting the health status of the individual and the society with social equity and efficient use of resources. The NPH incorporates a programmatic approach to health services with multiple parallel interventions to reduce the burden of disease and continue reduction in morbidity and mortality, and to improve quality of life, especially for an aging population. The ongoing challenge is to translate research findings into concrete action for the benefit of the population.

– Tulchinsky and Varavikova 2010, 32

The concepts of sustainable development and New Public Health emerged in the late 1980s. They were "reactions to the unintended negative impacts of industrial modernization ... Ultimately, these movements pursue the same goal: the well-being of all humans and a 'holistic human development'" (Weisz and Haas 2016, 560). By the end of the twentieth century, they had become more integrative, broadening in ways that recognized interdependencies between individuals, their communities, and the broader environment. At all levels of government, this New Public Health model focused on the institutional and public administration tools that could be used to foster the coordination of services and social movements and to encourage community participation and collaboration between health and the other community services (Tulchinsky and Varavikova 2010, 26).

Local municipal or regional public health units are charged with pursuing this rather ambitious goal. Public health units are seen as the authority responsible for providing informed, evidence-based advice on how to protect the public health of a population and how to reduce health inequities. These units fall under the jurisdiction of provincial governments, which in turn are responsible for providing health services. Local public health units typically report to a Board of Health or to a Regional Health Authority. The federal government has responsibility for coordinating national planning and actions in areas of shared interest, such as the provision of vaccines during global pandemics (Canadian Public Health Association 2019).

In recent decades, members of civil society and nongovernmental organizations have acquired recognition as important players in health promotion. One progressive example is the Leeds, Grenville, and Lanark District Health Unit, which worked with approximately eighty other community agencies to create the Lanark, Leeds, and Grenville Health Forum in the spring of 2000. Promoted by the medical officer of health, Charles Gardner, the goals of the forum were to evaluate the determinants of health of the population and to develop a plan to strengthen the overall health of the region. After monitoring interventions and assessing their effectiveness, the forum modified plans and approaches. The initiative was deemed promising and worthwhile on a number of fronts. The wide-ranging topics included considerations of individual well-being, health education, access to health care, and poverty-related health issues. Lacking government funding to pay for its planning and coordinating activities, however, the forum could not be sustained (Gardner, Arya, and M.L. McAllister 2005). Public health is an area of local government that demonstrates the striking mismatch between the importance of the policy area and the lack of local control of vital financial resources and political control. The monumental and varied tasks that have fallen on the shoulders of public health units reach into every aspect of local governance.

The NPH movement and the responsibilities of local public health authorities have continued to evolve. The mandates of regional health units vary considerably across the country. Some focus mainly on immediate physical health issues, such as food safety, sanitation, and the prevention of infectious disease, whereas others recognize that public health cannot effectively be promoted without addressing the primary determinants of health and without acknowledging the connections between its ecological and social determinants. Their mandates are part of a wider collaboration with civil society and are informed by evidence-based science and by the collection of reliable social and health data. On Vancouver Island in British Columbia, the Alberni Clayoquot Health Network was formed in 2012 to serve the Alberni Valley, Clayoquot Sound, and Barkley Sound regions. Supported by a grant from the Vancouver Island Health Authority, this network has developed a formal memorandum with the Alberni Clayoquot Regional District. It relies on a networked partnership and takes a community-based approach to health (see Box 13.2).

The broadened role of public health units includes their engagement in health advocacy. In 2016, one instance of this advocacy work led the Government of British Columbia to declare a drug emergency in response to a rapid increase in death rates from drug overdoses – attributed mostly to fentanyl and other powerful synthetic opioids. This pronouncement was followed in 2020 by the City of Vancouver's passage of a motion requesting that the federal government decriminalize the personal possession of illicit drugs. The public health officers at the provincial and municipal levels had provided independent advice and recommendations that advocated decriminalization (e.g., see Henry 2019). Vancouver's motion was the first of its kind passed by a municipality in Canada and was later supported by many large city mayors. However, in this case and others, beyond needing political institutional support, extensive public consultation with those most directly affected is required if such initiatives are to be effective.

BOX 13.2   Alberni Clayoquot Health Network

Mission

To speak with a collective voice on regional and local health issues by facilitating dialogue and understanding amongst citizens and stakeholders. The Network is a community driven mechanism that helps to build partnerships and capacity; share concerns, ideas and resources and create innovative solutions that impact the social determinants of health and work towards sustainable healthy communities.

Guiding Principles

In all that we do, we:

A. Employ a population health approach that focuses on improving the health and well-being of the entire population of the region and across the lifespan.

B. Focus on the social determinants of health and address policies that impact health inequities.

C. Believe that health is a shared responsibility and that collaboration leads to innovation.

D. Are solution oriented & committed to building on community assets, strengths, efficiencies, social capital and reduce duplication.

E. Utilize approaches that build knowledge, health literacy, capacity and citizenship.

F. Acknowledge that local realities, population demographics, socio-economics and health indicators can vary significantly (remote, rural, and urban).

G. Recognize that the Health Network exists within the ha'houlthee (chiefly territories) of the Nuu-chah-nulth First Nations. We strive to find new, better and culturally appropriate ways to collaborate, plan and work together that legitimize traditional knowledge. (Alberni Clayoquot Health Network n.d.)

ECO-HEALTH

> *By unsustainably exploiting nature's resources, human civilisation has flourished but now risks substantial health effects from the degradation of nature's life support systems in the future. Health effects from changes to the environment including climatic change, ocean acidification, land degradation, water scarcity, over-exploitation of fisheries, and biodiversity loss pose serious challenges to the global health gains of the past several decades and are likely to become increasingly dominant during the second half of this century and beyond.*
>
> – Rockefeller Foundation–*Lancet* Commission on Planetary Health (Whitmee et al. 2015, 1973)

As noted above, the concept of eco-health is gaining salience in public health policy. According to David Waltner-Toews (2009, 87), "Ecohealth draws on the latest theories of social-ecological complexity and integrates it with publicly-engaged, policy-relevant science. Ecohealth approaches are participatory, systems-based approaches to understanding and promoting health and wellbeing in the context of social and ecological interactions."

The degradation of nature's life support systems is adversely and inequitably affecting human health. Natural assets and nature-based solutions to environmental degradation benefit human health by mitigating the impacts of climate change and promoting biodiversity while providing green spaces and clean air, water, and soils (Marselle et al. 2019).

Locally managed systems approaches – such as those used in regional integrated watershed governance – are appropriate vehicles for supporting an eco-health approach. As Margot W. Parkes and colleagues (2010, 696) posit, "The watershed construct provides a place-based unit within which to understand, and manage interactions between social systems, ecosystems and health demonstrating characteristics of coupled natural-human systems, ... complex adaptive systems ... and social-ecological systems."

The responsibilities of local governments include water supply, stormwater drainage, flood management, and land-use planning, all of which affect biodiversity and water systems. The bridging of public health considerations with integrated water governance can take place at a scale that allows for interjurisdictional collaboration in a manner that protects public health, vital watersheds, and the ecosystems that depend on them. Such cooperative efforts can also be educational in helping local public officials to recognize that their actions have impacts that reach far beyond their immediate areas of responsibility.

Similarly, Paivi Abernethy (2016) has designed a framework for collaboration between practitioners in health promotion and sustainability governance at the regional scale. Meaningful collaboration, Abernethy argues, first requires the identification of common ground between the two fields, both in terms of values and outcomes. This foundation could then offer a base for collaboration (see Box 13.3).

These kinds of connections between the biophysical environment and human health have been gaining attention beyond the public health community. The global spread of infectious diseases, now increasingly frequent, certainly lends credibility to the eco-health approach. The devastating COVID-19 pandemic was a global moment of punctuated equilibrium with the potential to jolt decision makers into introducing new policy approaches in pursuit of healthy and sustainable communities.

ONE HEALTH AND COVID-19

Rising human and livestock populations, global travel and trade, degraded social-ecological systems, and climate change are all contributing factors to emerging infectious diseases (EIDs). These diseases sometimes infect animals and then evolve into a new human disease – referred to as zoonotic diseases. Canada has been affected by many EIDs, including COVID-19, Severe Acute Respiratory Syndrome (SARS-CoV), Acquired Immune Deficiency Syndrome (AIDS), the H1N1 and H5N1 influenzas, bovine spongiform encephalopathy (or "mad cow disease"), West Nile virus, Lyme disease, and bacterial food diseases.

BOX 13.3 Eco-health collaboration between practitioners in health promotion and sustainability governance at the local and regional levels

Sustainability scientist Paivi Abernethy (2016, 464–65) discusses the benefits of an eco-health collaborative approach that bridges the conceptual silos between practitioners in health promotion and sustainability governance, noting that they have some shared goals:

Both health promotion and sustainability governance involve commitment to supporting local livelihoods and resilient SES [social-ecological systems], in a just and equitable manner, while practising precautionary damage control. Furthermore, both fields favour addressing their respective challenges in a participatory and inclusive manner, which promotes respectful knowledge sharing and mutual learning. Acknowledging the fundamental similarities, in the ideal approaches of respective fields, creates the first foundation to constructive collaboration.

She further argues,

Cross-sectoral engagement, including non-governmental stakeholders, has a potential to enable ... broader and better integrated local monitoring efforts that in turn facilitate more meaningful and efficient decision-making. In addition to the natural scientific understanding of human or ecosystem well-being, mutual understanding of social processes relevant to these issues could be improved by increased cooperation. Public health practitioners could convey their health promotion expertise on awareness creation and community engagement. Environmental sector participants, familiar with collaborative learning and networking ideas in deliberative governance processes, could in turn share their knowledge of conflict resolution and consensus building.

Typically, medical and government responses have focused on surveillance and on vaccine development and distribution (Waltner-Toews 2017). With respect to COVID-19, for example, there was an impressive degree of collaborative global scientific effort to openly share data in order to develop methods to test for and treat the virus and to develop vaccines in less than a year. Vaccines and scientific research with respect to treating EIDs are crucial in a pandemic battle.

Despite such Herculean efforts and accomplishments, however, more holistic strategies are needed in order to limit the development and transmission of EIDs in the first place given their prevalence, seriousness, adaptive capacity, and resilience. An increase in zoonotic diseases is a trend that has been identified by many analysts over recent decades. In 2004, the Wildlife Conservation Society brought global attention to the importance of fostering animal, human, and ecosystem health to prevent such diseases. Since that time, global international organizations have developed the framework One Health, which has given rise to partnership efforts throughout the world. The World Health Organization (n.d.-b) offers the following definition: "One Health is an integrated, unifying approach that aims to sustainably balance and optimize the health of people, animals and ecosystems." Waltner-Toews (2017), however, points out that EIDs are continuing to accelerate and that much more robust systemic efforts must be undertaken to address the ongoing challenges. Linkages need to be strengthened between those practitioners and scholars who see the problem as biomedical or biological and those who see "EIDs as products of social, economic and political forces" (2). Solving wicked problems of this kind requires collaborative efforts with "broad public participation" (8).

The ecosystem approach to health (or eco-health), which recognizes that health outcomes are a result of the interactions of complex social and ecological systems, offers one framework for addressing the root causes of EIDs. Human health, as noted above, is predicated on the social determinants of health, and vulnerable, underserved populations disproportionately experience the devastating impacts of these diseases. Unless more institutional attention and resources are directed at addressing the factors that encourage the development of EIDs, they will continue to accelerate. This situation means that researchers and policy makers need to incorporate social, economic, political, biomedical, and ecological factors into their decision frameworks and models.

If these root causes remain unaddressed, EIDs will keep spreading, along with social inequality, food insecurity, and environmental degradation. These challenges cannot be tackled by top-down, scientific approaches alone. Rather, bottom-up approaches that incorporate public participation, local governance, and local knowledge systems are needed in order to strengthen community-level capacity and to build resilient systems: "Sustainable life-support for humans and other organisms ... includes the entire range of possible ecosystem functions, including provision of water, food, and disease control through biodiversity. Land-use, urban planning, and agriculture are as important to public health outcomes as the institutions normally assigned to deal with health issues" (Arya et al. 2009, 34–35).

In addition, healthy outcomes will not be achieved unless municipalities learn how to address the social determinants of health, such as poverty, housing, safety, education, a sense of place and belonging, social inclusion, and justice. Local institutions can also perform a vital service by providing policy arenas that bridge various communities of interest concerned with health promotion, biophysical sustainability, and social justice. The integration of knowledge brought to the table by members of these diverse groups would make it possible to address broader systemic considerations (Abernethy 2014; Baugh Littlejohns and N. Smith 2014; Raphael 2018).

LOCAL SOCIAL PLANNING AND COMMUNITY SERVICES

At a municipal level, responsibility for addressing many social challenges rests with social planning departments (in the larger cities) or with community-development services, although many issues cut across all departments and local government as a whole. This was certainly not the case in early Canadian history – well before the introduction of social service ministries and departments. In the late 1800s and early

1900s, municipalities (along with churches and some volunteer groups) took responsibility for providing limited charitable services and poorhouses for vulnerable people. People with no financial resources or other supports had few options but to turn to these miserable "houses of refuge," which blamed the poor for their circumstances, effectively punishing people for being in a vulnerable position (a bias that persists today). People in poorhouses were typically controlled by the state and society, stripped of their independence, treated much like inmates, and forced to do menial labour in unhealthy conditions. Subsequent events, such as the Depression and the Second World War, led to the growth of the welfare state, and the federal and provincial governments began to provide social services. These programs came in the form of health and education, income and employment assistance, child and family services, care homes, and social housing.

Over the course of the twentieth century, local governments experienced a decline in authority that was matched by a growth in provincial control over local policy. One of the most prominent examples is education policy, an area that was primarily the purview of local school boards governed by elected trustees. Canada's numerous school boards underwent provincially imposed amalgamations in the 1960s and '70s and again in the 1990s, accompanied by stronger provincial control (Woolstencroft 2002). Public school boards are still elected separately in municipal elections. They retain several administrative responsibilities, such as overseeing the delivery of educational programs and determining financial priorities, including building and maintaining schools. The provincial and territorial governments, however, retain primary responsibility for curriculum development. Sometimes, local school boards develop initiatives to incorporate the lived experiences and contributions of diverse cultural communities into the school curriculum.

The provincial and territorial governments are also constitutionally responsible for social and welfare services. In some jurisdictions, many of these services have been delegated to municipal government, or they are provided through some form of shared responsibility, with the senior government maintaining control

over funding and policy while leaving service delivery in the hands of local governments. Ontario, for example, created the Consolidated Municipal Services Managers Board and the District Social Services Administration Board in the late 1990s. In the process, the responsibility for delivering social services, including social assistance, child care, and social housing, was downloaded from the province to the municipalities.

Governments rely heavily on the volunteer sector and on organizations such as social planning councils for the provision of a wide range of social services, including settlement services for new immigrants and refugees, services for at-risk and vulnerable populations, substance abuse treatment, food security, public safety, work-skills development, cultural services, and the provision of affordable housing and shelters. Typically, local social planning involves the municipal government working with members of the community to address a variety of social needs, community development, and official city planning. In recent years, policy considerations have expanded to include social justice and equity, overt and systemic racism, inclusion, and belonging. Many municipal governments also employ social planners in their departments of social planning or in their departments of community development and planning. Some social planners work outside a department and act as a liaison between community groups and city hall, with their jobs involving "a complex mix of advocacy, education, and negotiation" (Walmsley and Kading 2018b, 202). They also advise local councils on the distribution of community grants to various charitable and nonprofit organizations.

POVERTY AND HOUSING

> We know without question that poverty is the best predictor of poor health outcomes, the early development of chronic illness, increased hospitalization and chance of imprisonment, family breakup, family violence, and school dropout rates that in themselves lead to lower earning prospects. Not acting to address the problem directly borders on the criminal.
>
> – Segal 2019, 170

The eradication of poverty is listed as the first of the United Nations Sustainable Development Goals. To that end, in 2018, the Government of Canada introduced a national poverty-reduction strategy with a target of cutting Canada's poverty rate by 50 percent. The strategy addresses many areas of social and economic well-being, including housing, health, education, early child care, clean water, and skills development, with an estimated $22 billion allotted for the overall initiative (Employment and Social Development Canada 2018, 6). At that time, Canada's official poverty rate was 8.7 percent of the population, with 4.7 percent living in deep income poverty. A significant minority of people reported suffering from chronic homelessness or unmet housing needs (12.7 percent), food insecurity (8.7 percent), and unmet health needs (11.2 percent) (Statistics Canada 2020a). Poverty also leads to social and political exclusion. This can be as a result of financial poverty (e.g., not even having money to afford transportation to recreational or community activities) or of more systemic forces that make it difficult to participate (e.g., feelings of social alienation or a lack of political efficacy) (Oudshoorn 2018, 130).

Local governments are responsible for the shape of poverty in their communities in numerous ways. There is much they can do to alleviate social inequity, such as provide social housing, facilitate the building of rental housing, require that new housing development contain some affordable housing units, address food insecurity, offer differential fares or passes for public transit or community facilities, introduce public health and safety measures, offer free, accessible, safe, green spaces as well as recreational places throughout the city, and support volunteer community efforts. For example, in Saint John, New Brunswick, the network Living SJ (2020) aims to end "generational poverty by removing the education, health and employment barriers for families who live in low-income neighbourhoods."

Municipalities can also foster social inclusion and social justice through collaborative approaches that address the intersectionality of poverty and discrimination related to racism, gender, immigration, ageism, and other factors. According to Carey Doberstein (2016, 820), "Collaborative governance is often

justified, implicitly or explicitly, on the basis of what [management scholar Chris] Huxham (1993) has termed the *collaborative advantage*," namely that these approaches "are created to resolve policy and coordination problems that could not be achieved by an organization or a government department acting alone."

These partnerships do make a difference, but they also need support from senior levels of government. As Christopher Walmsley and Terry Kading (2018b) observe, austerity regimes imposed on local governments foster a climate of restraint in cash-strapped municipalities. Persuading local governments to make expenditures on social initiatives that do not appear to generate revenue, therefore, has proven difficult. Conversely, with the support of higher levels of government, municipalities can operate collaboratively to effectively address social concerns. For example, during the first two decades of the twenty-first century, the Province of Alberta, under the New Democratic government, collaborated with other governments and with public and private organizations to address homelessness. These organizations partnered with seven municipalities – Calgary, Grande Prairie, Lethbridge, Edmonton, Medicine Hat, Red Deer, and the Regional Municipality of Wood Buffalo – in an effort to end homelessness. As a result, between 2008 and 2018, 23,000 homeless people were housed and supported. These approaches are grounded in community-level systems planning and implementation (Homeward Trust Edmonton n.d.).

Affordable housing is an issue that has been attracting more public and policy attention due to soaring housing and rental prices, particularly in larger cities. It is also a policy concern related to questions of homelessness, poverty, employment, and local economic development. Recognizing the importance of this policy area, the federal government introduced a National Housing Strategy in 2017. Homelessness is a "particularly devastating form of poverty" (Oudshoorn 2018, 133). Without a home, it is difficult for a person to achieve a sustainable livelihood, participate in the broader community, or remain healthy.

Local governments can encourage the development of affordable housing in a number of ways, such as controlling rental rates, creating and ensuring the enforcement of tenant-protection bylaws, revising approaches to zoning, providing supportive services, and collaborating with other governments, organizations, and citizens – particularly those who have lived experience. Mixed-zoning areas can be designed to reduce public reliance on cars and to increase community interaction. Residential neighbourhoods can be planned to ensure that schools, stores, and public transportation are within walking distance, along with nearby attractive parks and public meeting places to foster a sense of community.

PUBLIC SAFETY AND POLICING

The primary role of government is to protect its people. At the local level, police services have the assigned role of maintaining law and order.[2] Public safety, however, also involves protecting the peace, health, and safety of members of the public. Protective services in a municipality include fire, emergency, public health, and community services. Protection of public welfare is a collective responsibility that cuts across all departments and reaches into civil society. Ensuring the peace and security of people is not solely the purview of police services, although policing commands a large portion of the municipal budget. One analysis of Canada's largest cities, regions, and provincial capitals with their own police forces found that more than half of these municipalities allocated 15 percent or more of their 2020 operating budget to policing. This figure was even higher in western Canadian cities, where 20 percent or more of the budget is allocated to police services (Ho 2020).

The sizable budget allocated to policing has not alleviated growing societal concerns about inequities in public health and safety, particularly with respect to Black, Indigenous, and other racialized or marginalized people. In recent years, public protests have been galvanized in response to racist behaviour (both systemic and overt) and to police violence toward racialized groups. Protest movements such as Idle No More, Land Back, and Black Lives Matter have been effective in calling governments to account and highlighting social and institutional injustices. Widespread protests have called for the "defunding" of police forces.

Many marginalized or underserved people have documented historic and enduring reasons for mis-trusting governments – and police in particular. Historically, for example, Indigenous people were subjected to forced displacement onto reserves and saw their children taken away to residential schools by the Royal Canadian Mounted Police. For their part, Black Canadians have also been subjected to a long history of institutionalized abuses and have suffered intergenerational, social, and economic disparities and ongoing traumas. Generations of Black Canadians and other ethnic and racialized groups have witnessed the actions of police tasked with enforcing a social order that has been influenced by practices of discrimination and segregation.

Racism and discrimination have also been causal variables in the incarceration of a disproportionate number of racialized Canadians. In 2016, for example, Indigenous people comprised approximately 4 percent of the Canadian population but 25 percent of the federal prison population, the latter figure rising to 48 percent for men in the prairie provinces. This outcome might be attributed to the intersectionality of colonialism, poverty, intergenerational trauma, forced displacement, racism, and a lack of mutual trust (Arya and Piggott 2018; Parent and Parent 2019, 153). In 2017, Black Canadians accounted for 3.5 percent of the national population but 8.6 percent of the federal incarcerated population (Foster 2020). Reports of discrimination are now being acknowledged and validated by public institutions. For instance, the findings of the Ontario Human Rights Commission's (2020) inquiry into racial profiling and discrimination by the Toronto Police Service confirm that "Black people are more likely than others to be arrested, charged, overcharged, struck, shot or killed by Toronto police."

A social justice approach could be used to reframe policing and other institutional norms, rules, procedures, and practices. By realigning responsibilities and resources, they could be distributed to other community services and societal actors. If these steps were enacted, Sir Robert Peel's ninth rule of community policing could be achieved: "The test of police efficiency is the absence of crime and disorder, not the visible evidence of police action in dealing with it" (Reith 1948, 65).

In London, England, in 1829, Sir Robert Peel created the Metropolitan Police, founded on the notion of community policing. Peel's nine rules of policing are still held up as ideals today. His principles emphasize "crime prevention, community trust and engagement, reasonable force is a last resort, impartiality without favour, never above the law, the police are the public and the public are the police, efficiency through crime prevention" (Ottawa Police Service n.d.). Community policing has been described as a collaborative partnership between the police and the community whereby policing is undertaken by consent of society based on a relationship of trust.

As Richard Parent and Catherine Parent (2019, 152) note, police actions must be seen as legitimate if they are to be effective, and such legitimacy is awarded when police are perceived to act with integrity, fairness, and respect:

> When law enforcement occurs with the consent of the general public, it implies that officers have demonstrated a sincere concern and thus are permitted to exercise authority to manage conflicts, maintain social order, and solve problems in the community. In other words, police have earned the legitimacy to conduct policing.

Many members of underserved populations who have had negative interactions with police services, as well as a large constituency of other citizens, however, do not believe that Peel's rules have been upheld according to the principles of social justice. Intense public scrutiny of policing's expanding role (i.e., mission creep) as well as concerns about racism and violence have led to a widespread movement calling for a defunding of the police. This issue has gained considerable salience on the agendas of police services, police boards, and city councils across the country. Police services are now being challenged to develop and implement action plans to address systemic racism within police work and in the communities that police are charged to protect. In various parts of Canada, police representatives have acknowledged and apologized for racists actions, including violence, unwarranted harassment, and street checks of racialized people. Some of the fundamental components of the plans focus on measures to promote anti-racism, equity, and inclusion in policing. Many police services have also held consultations with members of racialized communities, who have shared their lived experiences of racism and inequity. Conversely, the consequences of social inequity, such as homelessness, have also generated a counter-reaction among some public groups that see the answers in electing "law and order" candidates who run for municipal office – candidates who are sympathetic to providing more funding to police.

Other underserved populations, such as those suffering the effects of poor mental health, addictions, or homelessness, who also include racialized people, have been subjected to harmful interventions by police. It is now becoming recognized in practice that it is more helpful and effective if other representatives of community services, such as social and health workers, were involved when intervention is necessary. One multi-stakeholder report on community safety in Toronto recommends that responsibilities and resources in a number of areas be reallocated as follows:

- from the policing of homeless persons to homeless outreach programs, safe consumption sites, and transitions to affordable housing
- from the policing of people with mental health challenges to crisis response programs, safe beds, and other crisis services
- from the policing of youth to the expansion of youth hubs and outreach workers as well as the provision of "peer mediation and alternative conflict-resolution supports" in all secondary schools
- "from criminal justice interventions in gender-based violence to programs that support and assist survivors in navigating safety needs and the implementation of transformative justice programs to prevent future violence"
- "the reassignment of 911 services to an accountable, independent, non-police emergency-response provider tasked with assigning the most appropriate personnel and services to calls and concerns from the public." (Toronto Neighbourhood Centres 2021, 24)

As highlighted by social movements such as Black Lives Matter and Idle No More, overt police brutality has been a major cause of concern. But at the root of the issue is the reality that racialized groups have always been subject to harmful discrimination by Canadian governing and social institutions – despite the fact that Canada is often viewed as one of the most multicultural societies in the world. In the large multicultural cities of Toronto and Vancouver, people of non-European origin collectively form the majority of the population overall and sizable majorities in various city neighbourhoods. Yet these proportions are not reflected in leadership positions in Canada's governing institutions. Racialized people remain underrepresented and underserved by governing institutions, despite their many notable achievements and contributions, which are woven into the fabric of Canada's history, economy, and society.

Forms of discrimination may be overt and deliberate, or they may result from systemic racism or implicit bias, with people being subjected to daily micro-aggressions or invalidations. "Systemic racism occurs when one group's collective bias is backed with legal authority and institutional control. It transforms into a system that gets embedded in every policy, and practice" (Meyer 2020). As Lorne Foster (2020) observes,

> Racism is so deeply enmeshed in the fabric of our society's social order that it often appears both natural and normal ... White Canadians are positioned with a structured advantage that produces unfair gains and unearned rewards while imposing impediments to employment, education, housing and health care for Black people and other Canadians of colour.

These kinds of patterns of institutional behaviour influence all areas of local governance. The health and sustainability of marginalized groups would be strengthened if the principles of social justice were integrated into institutional policy and practice – thereby strengthening the local community as a whole. Some municipalities across the country have established specific offices and positions to address questions of racism, diversity, and inclusion. Examples include the City of Toronto's Confronting Anti-Black Racism unit, tasked with implementing its action plan to address racism; the African Nova Scotian Affairs Integration Office, which forms part of the Halifax Regional Municipality's Diversity and Inclusion Office; the City of Waterloo's team of staff focused on addressing Indigenous initiatives and on anti-racism, accessibility, and equity; the Region of Waterloo's Anti-Racism Advisory Working Group; the City of Montreal's commissioner on racism and systemic discrimination; the City of Calgary's Anti-Racism Action Committee; and the City of Vancouver's wider strategy, which encompasses a number of departments and has included the hiring of anti-racism and cultural-redress planners.

Policing can be pivoted to an ethic of community safety, well-being, and health. Such an ethos can be embedded in all aspects of policing services, with an emphasis on including affected and underserved communities in decision processes by listening to their stories and learning from their experiences. When success in policing is assessed, the adoption of metrics rooted in indicators of individual and community health can also go a long way toward shifting policing culture and behaviour. This change can be facilitated by networking and collaborating with other community services and agencies, including public health, housing, and social services, and by establishing bridging organizations that bring different communities of interest together. One initiative in this direction that has received considerable attention and has been emulated in a number of jurisdictions is the hub model developed by Community Mobilization Prince Albert in Saskatchewan (see Box 13.4).

In 2014, the Waterloo Regional Police Service based its Situation Tables on the hub model (J. Brown and Newberry 2015, 8). The concept has spread to other municipalities in Ontario and elsewhere.

SPATIAL JUSTICE AND A "RIGHT TO THE CITY"

> *The right to the city ... is the right of all inhabitants, present and future, permanent and temporary, to inhabit, use, occupy, produce, govern and enjoy just, inclusive, safe and sustainable cities, villages and human settlements, defined as commons essential to a full and decent life ...*

It envisions the effective fulfillment of all internationally agreed Human Rights and Sustainable Development Goals, while dealing specifically with a dimension of urban problems that classic human rights' standards do not tackle: namely, spatial exclusion, its causes and consequences. At the same time, it provides a territorial approach that can enhance policy pertinence and coherence.

In this regard, it [makes] claims for (i) the social function of the city; (ii) quality public spaces; (iii) sustainable and inclusive rural-urban linkages; (iv) inclusive economies; (v) inclusive citizenship; (vi) enhanced political participation; (vii) non-discrimination; (viii) gender equality; and (ix) cultural diversity.

– UCLG 2019a, 2–3

The universal right to the city, first conceptualized in 1968 by philosopher Henri Lefebvre, has gained salience in political forums around the world, from the global to the local. The concept has been championed by various United Nations initiatives and organizations, such as the *New Urban Agenda* (Conference on Housing and Sustainable Urban Development 2017), UN-Habitat, UNESCO, and the United Nations Sustainable Development Goals.

The politics of planning influence how we choose to organize our lives in a spatial and physical context. Planning, historically, was viewed largely as a scientific, objective process that separated incompatible uses through subdivision and zoning. Planning is not objective; decision makers must make choices between competing values. Decisions about the specific mix of land-use development, public and private spaces, and protected natural areas are informed by political ideology, institutional structures, and the constitution of influential elites; it is far from a scientific, neutral process. Zoning decisions – whereby incompatible land uses are separated into zones, with land parcelled into commercial areas, suburbs, light industrial areas, parks, and so on – carry their own inherent biases. The historic choices of influential actors have collectively contributed to today's city form. That said, the spatial organization of cities is not

---

BOX 13.4   Community Mobilization Prince Albert's hub model

Chad Nilson (2014, 17), a consultant to the University of Saskatchewan's Centre for Forensic Behavioural Science and Justice Studies, describes a collaborative intervention model developed by the City of Prince Albert, Saskatchewan:

In 2011, a group of Prince Albert police officers, educators, social workers, mental health professionals, addictions counsellors and several other human service providers embarked upon a mission to remove the institutional barriers that prevented communication and cooperation among them. Doing so, they believed, would allow for more efficient and effective reductions in risk among individuals with composite needs. To achieve this, the Prince Albert group of professionals ... initiated Saskatchewan's first government-led model of collaborative risk-driven intervention: the *Hub.*

In its simplest form, the Hub in Prince Albert is a form of community mobilization that mobilizes various human service resources around the composite needs of high risk individuals ... Through communication and a specified process of information sharing, professionals around the Hub table collaborate to design an intervention that quickly meets the most pressing and immediate needs of the individual or family. The premise behind such a tactic is that the existing system of isolated support has been inadequate for some individuals and families. Through collaborative intervention, all of an individual's complex needs have the potential of being met – ultimately reducing risk more efficiently and effectively than if that individual were to try and access professional supports one by one.

influenced solely by political actors, institutions, or top-down planning processes. It is a result of complex connections between all the inhabitants of a city and a result of their interactions with social-ecological systems. Cities are organized spatially in response to socio-economic, political, cultural, and biophysical interactions.

SHIFTING SUBURBAN POLITICAL LANDSCAPES

The postwar growth of suburbs, where the majority of Canadians reside, highlights socio-economic stratifications present in the spatial organization of municipalities. A stereotypical depiction of suburbs includes "homogeneous landscapes of gendered domesticity, detached housing, white middle-class nuclear families, and heavy automobile use" (Moos et al. 2015, 64). These patterns of development come with the attendant costs associated with social isolation and environmental impacts (Moos et al. 2015).

In recent decades, however, the concept of *post-suburbia* has emerged to acknowledge the growing diversification of these areas, which are characterized by complex interactions of mixed landscapes and heterogenous populations. As Anthony Perl, Matt Hern, and Jeffrey Kenworthy (2020, 205) observe,

> Long derided for their ubiquitous blandness, homogeneity, and cookie-cutter design features, Canaburbs exhibit unmistakable layers of differentiation from one another and from suburbs elsewhere in the world, which is obvious to anyone who makes the effort to observe them in detail. What constitutes a suburb is contested and shifting, and the edges of where the city ends and the suburbs begin are not hard and fast. Thus, urbanists will have to eschew easy characterizations of suburban attributes and activities and instead come to understand their histories, construction, and development if they are to make sense of Canada's urban future.

By recognizing these changing landscapes, analyses of suburban processes can rise above the simplistic dichotomies of density versus sprawl and periphery versus urban core. An example discussed by Roger Keil (2015, 592) is the evolving Toronto region, where "dynamic post-suburbanizing processes are underway, and where new forms of political constellations are constantly being born." With its many implications for local planning, this reframing has relevance to this study of local governance.

These diversifying, post-suburban places warrant consideration as neighbourhoods and subdivisions with unique sets of dynamics, attributes, and requirements. Viewing these areas as more than planned zones to be managed in a top-down fashion opens up democratic possibilities; they can become recognized as communities where all the residents contribute to the shaping of their local environment. As so persuasively argued by Warren Magnusson (2015, 256), a right to the city requires local self-government. He emphasizes the importance of governance at the level where people live their daily lives while advocating the empowerment of people to govern in their own neighbourhoods, where "everyone is part of the relevant public" (277). For such aspirations to be realized, people need more places to congregate than privately owned and managed shopping malls – with their own implicit and explicit political-spatial boundaries. Given their historical provenance, suburbs have not been spatially designed to encourage public debate or inclusive forms of civic engagement. The democratic airing and sharing of differences, identities, ideas, and cultures require public spaces where people can raise issues, protest, negotiate conflict, and co-create their own sense of place and community. Neighbourhood political associations and other civic bodies can be encouraged by local governments to provide inclusive physical spaces in suburban areas and in locations such as libraries, underused old shopping malls, and parks. Public spaces can also encourage more public interaction through pedestrian-friendly and universal design. Considerable policy creativity is required to facilitate civic engagement in addressing the limitations to community space that are produced by the private ownership of land and by housing pressures.

The inexorable march of private development into areas that were once seen as public commons has encouraged local governments to incentivize developers to turn privately owned land into public spaces such as parks, plazas, and atriums. These privately owned public spaces (POPS) are built by private developers and open for use by the public. Troy Glover (2022) observes that these spaces are not necessarily accessible since their management and design aspects (e.g., gated access) can give the impression of a private space, and members of the public remain unaware that they are public spaces. One way of facilitating access, he suggests, is to have a diverse city-supported POPS committee. Given the limitations of POPS, he argues that their use should supplement the development of "high-quality public space" (Glover 2022).

SOCIO-SPATIAL JUSTICE

Powerful public and private political actors have had a dominant influence on shaping urban socio-spatial patterns. These configurations have also been influenced by the choices that residents make themselves. For example, people who share similar traditions and languages are often drawn together, forming culturally cohesive neighbourhoods. Ethnic enclaves can play an important role in social cohesion. Mohammad Qadeer and Sandeep Kumar

(2006) discuss how elderly people or people who rarely leave home can have companionship with others who speak the same language and share interests, and children can become socialized in their own culture. In such enclaves, communities can work together to have more effective political voices and form social networks to help people (particularly new immigrants) acquire jobs. Moreover, ethnic stores and services, places of worship, culturally appropriate food, and cultural celebrations all reinforce a sense of local community and belonging. All of these elements comprise a healthy, civil society. Moreover, these enclaves can enrich cities as a whole, making varied cultural, political, and economic contributions that enhance innovation and problem solving. That said, there are drawbacks if people do not take part in the wider social, economic, and political affairs of the city (13). This is particularly the case if people are effectively disenfranchised from participating in the wider community due to the intersectionality of factors such as poverty, a lack of education, racism, and spatial inequality. When individuals live in enclaves that are underserved by societal,

---

BOX 13.5   A case of socio-spatial injustice in urban planning: A reflection

Jen Vasic (pers. comm., January 2021), councillor in the City of Waterloo, reflects on socio-spatial injustice in the city:

Waterloo, where I am a city councillor, has an expressway running through its centre forming a ring road, albeit an incomplete one. This urban design feature isn't unique to Waterloo; rather, it was popularized in [the] 1950s [in the] United States to reduce congestion in response to a rapidly increasing number of people buying cars and driving from their suburban homes

into city centres (Semuels 2016). Unfortunately, building these expressways had dire implications for racialized people – Black people especially – who, because of racism, were unable to access the kind of employment that would make homeownership in these neighbourhoods affordable to them. And, even if homeownership there was financially accessible[,] it was a hostile place for racialized people who were seen to be undesirable neighbours and who would, consequently, drive down real estate prices. While this practice looked

somewhat different in Canada [than in the United States], it had similar effects. In many places, expressways separate affluent neighbourhoods from those that are not ... For example, according to recent Canadian census data, around 65% of households in Waterloo with annual incomes at $30,000 or below are concentrated ... on the west side of the expressway [in one neighbourhood of the ward I represent]. This reality is captured by the term racialization of poverty, coined by Grace-Edward Galabuzi, which reflects that economic, and governing institutions, their ability and willingness to participate in those institutions are seriously curtailed.

Global socio-spatial polarization, with cities stratified into rich and poor areas, is now attracting a measure of public attention. Such polarization might be categorized by three types of areas: (1) high-income developments that contain luxury condominiums and housing or gated communities with high-tech security fences, (2) shrinking middle-class neighbourhoods with a mix of housing types, and (3) low-income underserved parts of a city that lack many services and amenities. This polarization is reinforced by feedback loops over time. The adverse impacts of socio-spatial and income polarization and ethno-cultural divides are underscored by recent studies of large Canadian metropolitan cities, such as those undertaken by the Neighbourhood Change Research Partnership (n.d.). Social and political discrimination and racism contribute to socio-spatial polarization and spatial injustice. Louis Guay and Pierre Hamel (2014, 73) define spatial justice as "access to urban public services, facilities, and resources for all residents. When people or neighbourhoods do not have access to some public resources, such as public transport and green spaces, owing to their spatial location, there is a spatial justice problem." The design of social and political territories, as well as physical spaces, and how people interact with them strongly influence a sense of belonging, a civil and just society, and healthy communities (see Box 13.5). A sense of alienation, stimulated by forms of spatial injustice, is often reinforced over generations.

One proposed approach to addressing the problems of chronic housing shortages and social polarization has been mixed-use and inclusionary zoning. Mixed-use zoning, which combines varied uses like shopping, housing, public facilities, and banks within walkable distances, has long been advocated as fostering more dynamic, socially diverse, and lively neighbourhoods. Well-known urban analyst Jane Jacobs first advocated this approach in the early 1960s (Moos et al. 2018, 7). Markus Moos and colleagues (2018) suggest that such efforts are not necessarily affordable without other forms of government support. Housing located in dynamic, lively neighbourhoods with

racialized individuals are disproportionately represented in lower-income areas.

Another outcome of the racialization of poverty is that those who fled to the suburbs – a phenomenon commonly referred to as white flight – also had the money, time, and social capital to accrue even more of those resources, directing much political attention towards them and away from where it was needed most. A reverse trend has been seen in more recent years, ... known as the suburbanization of poverty[,]

which sometimes makes home ownership more affordable in suburban areas than in downtown cores. Still, one thing remains consistent: lower-income neighbourhoods get less political attention than more affluent neighbourhoods. This problem and equity as a solution [are] what led me to run for council in the first place. Healthy and safe communities require the redistribution of municipal resources, including money and time, into culturally informed and community-led health and public safety initiatives.

While enjoying the convenience of driving on the expressway that runs through our city, I remind myself that just as this particular road was never completed as intended, we too can stop creating policies that exclude diverse communities from fully and meaningfully participating in the social, economic, and political lives of their cities and start to become more equitable, and consequently, safer, and healthier.

nearby amenities can also go up in price, making them unaffordable to people with limited incomes. To be inclusive, mixed-use zoning also needs to be accompanied by meaningful affordable housing policies that endure over the long term. The concept of inclusionary zoning has emerged to respond to this need. Inclusionary zoning is an approach taken by cities to ensure that a portion of housing units in a proposed development is provided at affordable rates. Tools that cities have used as incentives for developers include density bonuses, zoning variances, and fee waivers. Although inclusionary zoning as a concept is appealing, it is no panacea for what many see as a housing crisis. Because it is a market-driven approach, only a portion of housing provided in a development is designated as affordable. Inclusionary zoning is unlikely to solve the rapidly accelerating need for affordable housing. It is no substitute for nonmarket affordable housing. There is also the question of how long such units will remain affordable and which mechanisms will remain in place over time to ensure that they continue to be so. One study suggests that inclusionary zoning is "a necessary but not sufficient tool in the affordable housing toolbox" (August and Tolfo 2018, 11).

Throughout Canadian history, many groups have been forcibly displaced from their homes and territories, losing their sense of belonging and community. The brutal legacy of the colonial past, for example, continues to have a destructive impact on First Nations, Métis, and Inuit peoples. The racialized spaces of the colonial system of reserves, where Indigenous people were first sequestered, are connected to the inner-city, underserved areas to which many have migrated in search of employment and housing (Razack 2002, 129). They disproportionately experience poor living conditions and are concentrated in the more dilapidated and neglected sections of cities and towns, a number of which have been subjected to industrial contamination. This form of subjugation, referred to as "environmental racism" by Ingrid Waldron (2021), also applies to other racialized groups. Waldron explains,

Environmental racism refers to racial discrimination through the disproportionate location of environmentally hazardous projects in Indigenous, Black, and other racialized communities. This involves the lack of political power these communities have to fight back against the placement of these industries in their communities; the implementation of policies that allow these harmful projects to be placed in these communities; the slow rates of cleanup of contaminants and pollutants in racialized communities; and the lack of representation of Black, Indigenous, and other racialized communities in mainstream environmental groups and on decision-making boards, commissions, and regulatory bodies.

The historic community of Africville, Nova Scotia, offers an example of environmental racism. Africville was a socially vibrant African Nova Scotian community where generations had lived without the benefit of public services such as water, garbage removal, and sewerage. Over time, the city used the area for a slaughterhouse, a fertilizer plant, and an open-pit dump. Residing near contaminated sites of this kind, African Nova Scotians have long suffered the health effects of hazardous living conditions (Waldron 2021). Residents were displaced in the 1960s, and their valued community was demolished, ostensibly as part of an urban renewal project. In 1997, Africville became a National Historic Site and is now depicted as "a site of pilgrimage for people honouring the struggle against racism" (Government of Canada n.d.). In 2010, on behalf of the city, the mayor of Halifax Regional Municipality apologized for its destruction (Tattrie, Cooper, and Ma 2021).

Other groups that have experienced forms of spatial injustice include new immigrants to Canada, people with religious or ethnic differences, and people facing gender discrimination. A right to the city requires comprehensive policies spanning considerations of service delivery, housing, safety, income equity, transportation, spatial justice, and political participation. Public recognition of these spatial constraints has led to action in parts of the world, including Canada. For example, in 2019, a joint declaration titled "The Right to the City for Women" was signed on Women's Day by the mayors of Mexico City, Montreal, and Barcelona (UCLG 2019b).

ACCESSIBLE CITIES AND UNIVERSAL DESIGN

Over the decades, municipal governments have taken steps to make cities more walkable, age-friendly, and accessible for people with challenges that impede their free movement around their communities. Universal design is now a well-known concept, and cities have incorporated elements of it into urban design and planning. Article 2 of the *Convention on the Rights of Persons with Disabilities* defines universal design as "the design of products, environments, programmes and services to be usable by all people, to the greatest extent possible, without the need for adaptation or specialized design" (United Nations 2006, 4). Canada ratified the convention in 2010. The implications of the definition and its effective application throughout Canada have been inconsistently applied and somewhat narrowly interpreted.

Public washrooms are a case in point. How a city chooses to design and maintain its washrooms sends a message about who is welcome and who can feel safe in these spaces. A tourist visiting a city for the first time may be attracted by scenic marketing brochures, but a more lasting impression may be formed by the availability, cleanliness, and accessibility of public washrooms (see Figure 13.2). Their design can reinforce stereotypes. Homeless people who have no access to a toilet or a place to wash will find it difficult to apply for a job or will feel unwelcome in public areas if they cannot use the services provided by a public washroom. A sense of safety and belonging can be compromised by washroom design. When designed in a heteronormative or binary way, as has conventionally been the case, public washrooms can exclude some individuals on the basis of gender. People who use a wheelchair may find themselves in a long lineup for the one accessible toilet, only to find out that it is not completely accessible. Change tables for babies may be available only in a washroom designated for women. Elderly people may find themselves unable to pull open a heavy washroom door. These are only a few of a multitude of examples of design flaws that exclude people with individual needs from public spaces. Another aspect of inclusive design is local signage, including the use of clear symbols instead of words, maps and trailhead signs for greenspaces, audio indicators on streetlights, and flashing emergency

13.2 Inclusive self-cleaning washroom, Hoffer Park, Elora, Ontario, 2023

lights in buildings for the hearing impaired (C. McAllister 2011, pers. comm., June 18, 2021).

CONCLUSION: INCLUSIVE HEALTHY CITIES

> *What does it mean to be human and alive? And when the myriad peoples of the world answer that question, they do so in the 7,000 different voices of humanity. And those voices and those answers collectively become our overall human repertoire for dealing with all the challenges that will confront us as a species in the coming centuries ... Every culture has something to say, each deserves to be heard.*
>
> – Davis 2018

Healthy, sustainable communities require local strategies to respond effectively to the complex system requirements of modern human settlements. As Wade Davis (2018) has noted, humanity has a varied repertoire of the ways that the world can be perceived and understood. These diverse perspectives and sets of local knowledge can be harnessed to solve problems, whether emerging infectious diseases or climate change, and can help to govern contemporary, multicultural cities.

For this to happen, local governments need to recognize the value of cultural and social diversity and to adopt the policies and practices required to promote a just society and polity. In the process, it is necessary to recognize, redress, and implement approaches that tackle overt and systemic forms of discrimination. Municipalities have instituted some collaborative initiatives, such as the Alberni Clayoquot Health Network and Community Mobilization Prince Albert's hub model, bringing health, social, and protective services to affected communities. The Alberni Clayoquot policy statements embrace many of the sustainability criteria delineated in Box 1.1. The organization also collaborates with the Alberni Community Foundation, drawing on its *Vital Signs* reports (Community Foundations of Canada n.d.-b), and with the Clayoquot Biosphere Trust, offering an interesting example of networked governance. This cooperative network appears to possess many of the characteristics of successful sustainability initiatives discussed in Chapter 1.

Urban and regional planning can ensure a more geographically equitable distribution of services, introduce inclusive, universal urban design approaches, and expand public gathering places, such as community gardens and parks. By implementing such plans, municipalities can foster a widespread sense of belonging, civic responsibility, and local democracy, creating the foundation for a healthier, more productive community. The ways that governments respond to (or ignore) the needs and preferences of Canada's varied society fundamentally shapes the social, institutional, and physical landscapes of cities. The priorities of Canadians are necessarily the priorities of a multicultural society. Failure to recognize and address these priorities undermines democratic processes and the overall health of communities. As is the case with almost all such policy aspirations, both political will and political capacity are required in generous measure. Cities are moulded by influential groups and decision makers whose views are reinforced by systemic, entrenched biases about the nature of the ideal community. Different communities of interest vie to set local decision-making agendas, with the politically and economically powerful frequently prevailing. A socially just community is an equitable, inclusive community, which means, among other things, that individuals have the right and the ability to make choices about those forces that most directly affect them.

The COVID-19 pandemic laid bare the ethical deficits in governing administrations, many driven by liberal-capitalist calculations and increasing social polarization. The collective institutional failure to protect vulnerable members of society resulted in immense human, ecological, and economic costs. As discussed in the next chapter, resilient local economies critically depend on socially just and ecologically healthy communities.

NOTES

1 In this book, the term "marginalized" refers to people who have been socially or politically pushed to the margins (i.e., effectively disenfranchised). The term "vulnerable" refers to people who are at greater risk in terms of health, well-being, and personal safety. The tragedy that has unfolded in long-term care facilities over the years, one exacerbated manyfold by COVID-19, offers a striking example of this vulnerability with regard to the elderly.

2 A municipal police force is typically accountable to a mayor or to either an elected police board or a commission comprised of civilians. In Ontario and Quebec, municipalities without their own police force rely on provincial policing services, and elsewhere in Canada, they contract policing from the Royal Canadian Mounted Police.

14 Diversifying Local Economies
Valuing Community Assets

INTRODUCTION: DEFINING LOCAL PROSPERITY

> *Our interest in building new worlds involves making credible those diverse practices that satisfy needs, regulate consumption, generate surplus, and maintain and expand the commons, so that community economies in which interdependence between people and environments is ethically negotiated can be recognized now and constructed in the future.*
>
> – Gibson-Graham 2008, 623

Prosperity, as an aspiration, has conventionally been associated with the pursuit of a good life and social success through the acquisition of material wealth. However, it is ever more apparent that material economic growth is accompanied by spiralling ecological, societal, and economic costs. This concern is now being addressed by public agendas as policy makers re-evaluate the utility of employing a one-dimensional economic indicator, such as GDP, to measure success. A case in point is the work of the Institute for Competitiveness and Prosperity (ICAP), established to raise public awareness of economic factors affecting Ontario's economic progress. At its inception in 2001, ICAP (2016, 9) used GDP "as a broad proxy for prosperity." Fifteen years later, however, the institute had broadened its measurement of prosperity using the following indicators: Internet access, civic engagement, social networks, education, health, environmental quality, housing, income, jobs, life satisfaction, and safety (ICAP 2016). The institute's final report also concluded that "without decisive action on Climate Change, Ontario will face more severe weather, flooding, and poorer air quality, all of which stand to decrease our economic competitiveness and quality of life" (Steeve and So 2019, 2).

In the context of municipalities, economic prosperity has also been the primary indicator of success and therefore the core objective of local governments. Early economic development strategies focused on "boosting" the local economy by attracting outside capital and enterprises that could expand the local tax base and provide revenues. Today, the limitations of this strategy in terms of diversifying and sustaining local economies are widely acknowledged, encouraging a reconceptualization of local development. For example, a related (but not synonymous) concept is community economic development. Rather than concentrating efforts on luring businesses away from other localities, community economic development emphasizes building on the internal strengths of a community. This place-based approach, adopted by many nonprofit organizations, primarily values the unique social and natural assets of a community. These assets are used to build individual and organizational capacity (Blakely and Milano 2001; Mancini and Mancini 2015).

Social and environmental concerns linked to economic development have also given rise to the concept of sustainable local economic development. As presented by Les Newby (1999, 67), among its core principles are "quality of life (including and linking social, economic and environmental aspects); fairness and equity; participation and partnership; care for the environment/respect for ecological constraints; [and] thought for the future and the precautionary principle." These underlying principles complement other development approaches throughout the world, such as the United Nations Sustainable Development Goals (SDGs), specifically Goal 11: "Make cities and human settlements inclusive, safe, resilient and sustainable" (United Nations General Assembly 2015, 21).

For their part, business organizations are embedded in community life. They play a defining role in the shape of a city and in its political and social dynamics. Small businesses, in particular, have long been considered the backbone of an economy. In 2021, small businesses employed 10.3 million individuals in Canada, comprising 63.8 percent, or almost two-thirds, of the total labour force (Tam, Sood, and Johnston 2022). Many of these private enterprises have acknowledged public concerns about the social and environmental impact of their endeavours. They have responded with strategies to engage in what is sometimes referred to as corporate social responsibility. The "triple bottom line" model was introduced in the 1990s to incorporate considerations of financial, social, and natural capital when making business decisions. Since then, private-sector organizations and associations have created many sets of environmental and social standards of practice. Certified B Corporations, for example, are legally required to consider the impact of their activities on the social and ecological environment. The "B" stands for "Beneficial," based on the premise that these enterprises are to make money while acting as a "force for good" and to "create inclusive, environmentally sustainable prosperity" (Business Development Bank of Canada n.d.).

Analysts who embrace a "deep sustainability" perspective question the utility of attempts to accommodate natural and social capital by relying on models that use conventional economic assumptions. They view them as fundamentally incompatible with the concept of sustainability. In the 1960s and '70s, economist Nicholas Georgescu-Roegen (1977) introduced a new concept that came to be known as ecological economics, which incorporates recognition of the finite limits of the earth's resources and the unsustainability of the global model of economic growth. Herman E. Daly (1996, 31), who helped to develop the field of ecological economics, has observed that the dominant economic model of capitalist growth requires an "increase in matter/energy throughput that sustains the economic activities of production and consumption of commodities." Daly has offered an alternative model known as steady-state economics, defined by William E. Rees (2014, 6n30) as follows:

> An economic steady state implies a more or less constant rate of energy and material throughput, compatible with the regenerative and assimilative capacities of the ecosphere. The steady state is not to be confused with a stagnant state. A steady-state economy can be dynamic, constantly changing with the rise of new and the decline of "sunset" industries. It is an economy dedicated to qualitative improvement in well-being, not merely quantitative growth.

The burgeoning field of ecological economics has branched out into many subfields of inquiry. In certain policy areas, sophisticated ecological-economics models have been employed to assess and to place a value on the services of social-ecological systems. These models can be employed by decision makers when undertaking project calculations based on the implications of various trade-offs between material, social, and biophysical assets.

One normative outcome of ecological-economics thinking is degrowth, which has also emerged in response to concerns about the dominant models of economic growth. The degrowth model seeks to counter the inevitable depletion and inequitable distribution of resources under the dominant models and to avoid the dangers posed by a tightly coupled, interdependent, global economy (see Box 14.1).

The concept of degrowth has achieved a measure of salience in academic and some political circles. The degrowth discourse is frequently associated with relocalization. As Rees (2014, 15) suggests, a steady-state economy "must also reconsider the role of globalization and trade and begin the relocalization of much economic activity at the community and regional levels."

Recent decades have seen the expansion of community-based movements to promote sustainable, equitable local economies and to build community connections. Elements of the aspirations contained in these bottom-up, relocalization models are evocative of ancient gathering places – open public spaces where people congregated to exchange material goods and ideas while advancing political, social, and economic objectives.

Municipal decision makers are now being challenged to go beyond linear economic models of local development and to transition away from the reductionist economic cost-benefit analyses used to determine community priorities. Many local governments are now exploring how to deploy a range of indicators in order to assess community well-being and biophysical sustainability. Along with governments, important players in these efforts consist of a diversity of entrepreneurial social organizations and businesses that contribute to sustainable, creative local economies and communities.

LOCAL ECONOMIC DEVELOPMENT

Local economic development (LED) has always held a predominant place on local agendas as a means of achieving community objectives. Its provenance stretches far back into preindustrial times. In trad-itional societies, goods were exchanged in well-known gathering places between nomadic peoples, tribes, or travellers from dispersed villages. These occasions served as an opportunity not only to exchange goods but also to undertake political and territorial negotiations and to hold celebrations. Perhaps the most well-known gathering place in Western history is the ancient Greek agora, a space for public gatherings, political assembly, and commercial enterprise in the heart of the city-state. One of many examples in Canada is that of The Forks in Winnipeg, Manitoba, located at the junction of the Red and Assiniboine Rivers. It "has been a meeting place for over 6,000 years. Indigenous peoples traded at The Forks, followed by European fur traders, Scottish settlers, railway pioneers and tens of thousands of immigrants" (The Forks n.d.). Today, cities and towns invariably showcase their own versions of the agora, typically in the form of public squares, farmers' markets, city halls, and densely zoned commercial and residential areas. A thriving central business district has often been viewed as an important indicator of a prosperous local economy (see Figure 14.1).

The concept and practice of local development have transformed and expanded since the early days of Canada's industrial development. Throughout its history, Canada's staples-based economy has often been associated with the primary resource industries that have capitalized on the country's huge geography and abundant natural resources. Rex A. Lucas's (1971) classic *Minetown, Milltown, Railtown* depicts community life in the country's single-industry company towns, which were largely controlled by company bosses and managers. Over time, the local community councils in these towns acquired more independent political authority. The economic viability of the resource-based communities remained heavily dependent on a single industry. When the mine or mill closed or when major transportation routes shifted, these communities invariably declined. The need for economic diversification was, and continues to be, most pressing in rural and remote towns and cities. Local economic development, as a field, has often been associated with economically depressed rural communities, but larger cities also rely on commercial development for the provision of revenues.

14.1 Kingston Market and City Hall, Ontario, 2021. The oldest market in Ontario, it was formally established in 1801 and is now considered the centre of trade and commerce. | Brian Jarus

In the 1930s, during the Depression, Canadian municipalities – both large and small – competed with each other to boost their local economies by luring major industries, with their associated revenues and jobs. Also known as "smokestack chasing," this boosterism saw local governments entice industry and other businesses with incentives like grants, land, tax breaks, and promises of infrastructure. This strategy retained considerable sway through much of the twentieth century.

Critiques of these approaches have come from many directions. As discussed above, municipalities' single-minded pursuit of large enterprises in order to attract them to their communities might be viewed as a temporary and partial solution to their difficulties. Moreover, the benefits of these strategies are inequitably distributed. From a local democratic perspective, developers and other business elites have often had ready access to city hall when pursuing their agendas. Other interest groups and citizens that lack the economic assets to bolster their positions have been frequently squeezed out of local decision-making processes. As Louis Guay and Pierre Hamel (2014, 94)

suggest, "The two faces of modernity – market inequality and democratic inequality – are profoundly interrelated." Today, we are witnessing rising social and economic polarization in municipalities. And in the context of ecological degradation and climate change, the protection of environmentally sensitive areas and natural assets continues to be eclipsed by the inexorable quest for economic development opportunities.

In the past few decades, recognition of some of these limitations has led to a broadening of local economic development, both in conceptualization and in practice. Today, typical elements of LED include public-private partnerships, networking, and citizen participation; economic diversification; and considerations related to quality of life. In the absence of a universally shared definition of LED, George Edward Treller (2014, 7) offers some defining characteristics:

- LED is a participatory and inclusive process that involves the participation of a range of stakeholder interests.

- LED is a bottom-up approach that is about local people making local decisions about local issues.
- LED is undertaken for the purpose of fostering some qualitative and/or quantitative improvement in economic well-being.
- LED takes place in a defined territory, most commonly congruent with a political boundary.
- LED encompasses the pursuit or facilitation of some manner of economic stimulation.

The emphasis is on regional networking and horizontal partnerships that can help communities to cooperate and to be competitive. Treller argues that the factors enabling LED include favourable economic circumstances and opportunities, natural assets and environmental sustainability, a thriving civic society and social capital, and transparent and accountable public institutions with the capacity and political will to develop and implement successful economic strategies (14–15).

Many analysts, such as Neil Bradford and Allison Bramwell (2014, 7–8), also stress the importance to urban economies of innovation that is driven by the acquisition and integration of knowledge:

Simply put, competitiveness in the knowledge-based global economy is about far more than land development. Innovation is crucial and rather than a static or natural endowment, it is a social process driven by interactive learning among multiple economic players, each holding different kinds of knowledge and commanding particular skills ... Research institutions such as universities, public laboratories, and knowledge transfer intermediaries are an indispensable foundation for business development and economic innovation.

Numerous communities of interest, both public and private, have also acknowledged problems associated with the conventional approaches to economic development, which have an inequitable social impact and impede urban economic growth (Magdoff and Tokar 2009, 1; Bradford and Bramwell 2014, 3). Municipal documents throughout the country highlight the need to redress such economic inequalities. One initiative of this kind has been developed by the African Nova Scotian community in partnership with the Halifax Regional Municipality and the Halifax Partnership. Halifax's mayor has stated that the

---

BOX 14.2 The African Nova Scotian Community and the Road to Economic Prosperity Action Plan

In Halifax, the Road to Economic Prosperity Action Plan was publicly introduced in January 2021 as a collaborative five-year initiative developed and owned by the African Nova Scotian community with the objectives of encouraging economic development and the community's priorities. The collaborative effort includes the African Nova Scotian community, the Halifax Regional Municipality, and the Halifax Partnership – a public-private economic development organization. The action plan is directed at encouraging the community's growth and prosperity through three strategic priorities:

1. Build Unity and Capacity Among African Nova Scotians
2. Establish Land Ownership, Develop Infrastructure, and Attract Investment
3. Increase Participation in Education, Employment, and Entrepreneurship

(African Nova Scotian Road to Economic Prosperity Advisory Committee 2020, 7)

Halifax's African Nova Scotian Affairs Integration Office, created in 2012, has a mandate to improve municipal service delivery and engagement while fostering employment equity within the Halifax Regional Municipality.

The measurement and evaluation of this plan are based on the African Nova Scotian Prosperity and Well-Being Index (modelled after the Halifax Index) (African Nova Scotian Road to Economic Prosperity Advisory Committee 2020, 23). The Halifax Index, similar to other municipal wellness indices, employs benchmarks that go beyond conventional economic considerations to include community health and well-being and to incorporate environmental sustainability indicators in order to assess economic growth.

initiative aims "to ensure African Nova Scotian residents play a significant role in building a prosperous future for the Halifax region, where everyone can match their ambitions to opportunity" (African Nova Scotian Road to Economic Prosperity Advisory Committee 2020, 5) (see Box 14.2).

MEASURING WELL-BEING AND SOCIAL ASSETS

Throughout history, societal governing arrangements have included systems of exchange and methods of valuation that favour certain types of economic behaviour over others and that privilege certain groups of people over others. When government policies use indicators of success that focus solely on GDP, it comes as no surprise that other community assets are ignored or undervalued. In the latter part of the twentieth century, an alternative model was developed by the country of Bhutan, which introduced the world to Gross National Happiness (GNH). The GNH proved compelling due to its simplicity as a concept and as a critique of the inadequacies of gross national product as a measure of success. It quickly acquired an audience and advocates in various forums throughout the world.

International agencies like the United Nations and governments – from the national level, such as New Zealand and Iceland, to local municipalities – have been looking at how best to factor in considerations of human happiness (or well-being) when determining policy priorities. Well-being indices, including the Canadian Index of Wellbeing (n.d.), have been adopted throughout the world. Canada's index, which assesses whether residents are thriving, employs eight indicators: community vitality, democratic engagement, education, environment, healthy populations, leisure and culture, living standards, and time use. Many local governments and organizations are now investigating new economic models and alternative forms of valuation to foster sustainable community development. Tangible applications of the Canadian Index of Wellbeing can be found in the Community Foundation of Canada's (n.d.) *Vital Signs* reports, which assess well-being in Canadian municipalities. Since 2017, these reports have aimed to align their data sets with the United Nations Sustainable Development Goals. That framework also allows the

organization to assess Canadian data using global indicators, taking an approach that extends beyond the local:

> Vital Signs uses local knowledge to measure the vitality of a community and support action towards improving collective quality of life. Local data gathered through the program is used to support evidence-based, *locally-relevant* solutions to improve the quality of life at the community level. Vital Signs aims to inspire civic engagement, to provide focus for public debate, and to help a range of actors take action and direct resources where they will have the greatest impact. (Community Foundations of Canada n.d.-b)

However, happiness is a highly subjective concept, particularly in a cross-cultural context. To address these limitations, Amartya Sen (1985) has distinguished between happiness as an emotion and happiness as an assessment of one's own quality of life – or well-being (J. Hall and Helliwell 2014). Sen has advanced the understanding of human well-being by introducing the "capability approach," defined in the *Stanford Encyclopedia of Philosophy* as follows:

> The capability approach purports that freedom to achieve well-being is a matter of what people are able to do and to be, and thus the kind of life they are effectively able to lead ... Real freedom in this sense means that one has all the required means necessary to achieve that doing or being if one wishes to. That is, it is not merely the formal freedom to do or be something, but the substantial opportunity to achieve it. In this way, the capability approach changes the focus from means (the resources people have and the public goods they can access) to ends (what they are able to do and be with those resources and goods). This shift in focus is justified because resources and goods alone do not ensure that people are able to convert them into actual doings and beings. Two persons with similar sets of goods and resources may nevertheless be able to achieve very different ends depending on their circumstances. (Robeyns and Byskov 2020, sec. 1.1)

BOX 14.3 Asset-Based Community Development (ABCD)

Asset-Based Community Development, introduced by John P. Kretzmann and John L. McKnight (1993), offers an alternative to an institutional, top-down approach to urban problem solving and service provision. It demonstrates how community development can be fostered by mobilizing community assets such as the following:

- the skills of local residents
- the power of local associations
- the resources of public, private and non-profit institutions
- the physical infrastructure and space in a community
- the economic resources and potential of local places
- the local history and culture of a neighborhood

(Asset-Based Community Development Institute n.d.)

The capability approach also supports freedom of choice and the meaningful participation of people in defining and choosing what is meant by well-being. As a result, it complements deliberative democracy (Pelenc and Ballet 2015). The capability approach has influenced the development of quality-of-life indicators.

The use of quality-of-life indicators, including natural and social assets, is relatively new in municipal policy making. Financial capital and revenue production are essential to local governments when providing goods and services. As a result, many private-sector interests have long benefited from privileged access to city halls across the country given the perception that they are producers, rather than consumers, of revenues. In the late twentieth century, a business management approach to local government (adopted in many parts of the country and elsewhere) promulgated the perception that city residents were best viewed as customers and consumers. The ostensible goal was to improve municipal services to the public through better practices. Such a label, however, contains the implication that a citizen is only a consumer

of services rather than someone who can make an important contribution as a member of the community.

In contrast, community-development nonprofit organizations, such as the well-known Working Centre in Kitchener, Ontario, have demonstrated how to effectively recognize the value of the social assets of all city residents. The Working Centre values as a core principle the contributions of people traditionally underserved and marginalized by dominant institutions (Mancini and Mancini 2015, 8). An asset-based approach to community development was first conceptualized by John P. Kretzmann and John L. McKnight (1993) in their book *Building Communities from the Inside Out: A Path toward Finding and Mobilizing a Community's Assets*. Today, what is now known as Asset-Based Community Development (ABCD) has become widespread (see Box 14.3). This approach emphasizes the unique sets of skills and capacities that can be drawn on for community development (Asset-Based Community Development Institute n.d.).

Valuing people for their assets is no longer confined to the nonprofit, nongovernmental sector. Increasingly, members of the public are now being viewed by local governments as possessing important attributes, or assets, and the ability to make meaningful contributions to their communities. Moreover, pressure is mounting for more inclusive, democratic, local decision-making processes. This is particularly the case as governments consider alternative approaches to addressing the many "wicked" problems that require local, context-dependent solutions.

DEGROWTH

From fast-growing parts of the environmental and environmental justice movements, to community responses to a post-carbon necessity and a climate-challenged world, to an embrace of new domesticity in crafting, a range of movements offer new modes of organization, forms of resistance, and prefigurative models of democratic living, all immersed in re-formed relations with each other and the natural world.

– Schlosberg and Coles 2016, 160

In the context of climate change and concerns about the social-ecological impacts of global economic trade and large-scale economic activity, local economic development has gained renewed widespread attention, albeit reconfigured. The stimulus has come from diverse policy communities, including academic disciplines, social movements, the private sector, and government organizations.

The transdisciplinary field of ecological economics arose to address the shortcomings of the conventional economic growth model. It was first conceptualized to tackle the problems of the limits to material growth posed by planetary boundaries. Later, it was expanded into various streams of thought, incorporating considerations of social justice, well-being, and sustainable livelihoods. For the purposes of this book, ecological economist Robert Constanza (2010) offers a useful definition:

> It's an attempt to look at humans embedded in their ecological life-support system, not separate from the environment. It also has some design elements, in the sense of how do we design a sustainable future. It's not just analysis of the past but applies that analysis to create something new and better ...
>
> The three interrelated goals of ecological economics are sustainable scale, fair distribution, and efficient allocation. All three of these contribute to human well-being and sustainability.

The goals of sustainable scale, fair distribution, and efficient allocation stimulated the development of a stream of thought known as "degrowth" to counter the unsustainable trajectory of the dominant global economic growth model. Martin Weiss and Claudio Cattaneo (2017, 220–21) characterize degrowth as "a radical call for a voluntary and equitable downscaling of the economy towards a sustainable, just, and participatory steady-state society ... Degrowth postulates that indefinite economic growth on a finite planet is impossible; facilitating growth as the overarching aim of socio-economic policy will eventually lead to involuntary economic decline with far-reaching social and political consequences."

The assumption that efficiencies are gained through the global exchange of goods and services and that benefits are accrued through accompanying economies of scale is called into question when social-ecological costs are factored into the calculations. Viewed through an ecological-economics lens, global trade activities may be seen as generating "diseconomies of scale" if enlarging the scale of the activity increases the cost per unit. The link between human-caused greenhouse gas emissions and climate change is a case in point (Tello and González de Molina 2017, 34).

The degrowth movement does not advocate individual deprivation or economic shrinkage but reconceptualizes a vibrant economy and what society and its institutions choose to value and prioritize. Here, emphasis is placed on social well-being over material wealth. The idealized small-scale, craft-based, post-carbon, diversified local economy has been championed by many degrowth advocates. To achieve this objective, local communities have to operate at a desirable spatial scale.

RELOCALIZATION

> *Relocalization is a strategy to build societies based on the local production of food, energy and goods, and the local development of currency, governance and culture. The main goals of relocalization are to increase community energy security, to strengthen local economies, and to improve environmental conditions and social equity. The relocalization strategy developed in response to the environmental, social, political and economic impacts of global over-reliance on cheap energy.*
>
> – Post Carbon Institute 2021

An early large-scale movement in relocalization was the idea of transition towns. In the first decade of the new millennium, concerns about global dependency on fossil fuels gave impetus to the Transition Towns movement. Permaculture instructor Rob Hopkins (2009, 144) began the movement in Totnes, England, in 2006. The initiative spread throughout the United Kingdom and internationally. As it is a social movement, local governments are expected to act only in a supporting role, with the movement operating independently and on its own terms (144). In an effort to wean society from fossil fuels, transition towns focus on strengthening local resilience through relocalization. One of the principal foundations of the movement is permaculture (permanent agriculture), an approach that sustains local food systems and food security using ecologically sound principles. It is viewed as a remedy for the ills associated with the unsustainable agro-industrial complex that dominates global food systems.

One study on the emergence of transition towns in Canada reports mixed "evidence for movement success and impact" depending on the context (Poland et al. 2019, 195). At the time of writing, a number of municipalities across Canada that have been pursuing transition town agendas, whether formally or informally, may no longer be advancing the movement under the transition town banner. However, the study also "indicates that 77% are involved in other community groups (often addressing similar issues)" (195). Many groups across the country with sustainability aspirations now participate in similar initiatives with somewhat different emphases and names (Francis 2016, 144–61).

Other degrowth groups focus on approaches that open up new economic spaces. One example is "sustainable consumption," which recognizes the need to change consumption and production patterns.[1] Strong sustainability approaches, which require a fundamental paradigm shift in societal consumption patterns and forms of economic valuation, prioritize well-being over material consumption. In a strong sustainability environment, members of a community are not viewed primarily as consumers of material goods but as citizens who contribute to and benefit from the strengthening of societal well-being (Lorek and Fuchs 2013, 38).

One example is local artisanal crafters and makers – who are often seen not only as participants in precarious low-wage professions but also as artists who value the autonomy and space needed to sustainably produce and enrich local communities with their creations. In one study, Caroline Kovesi and Leslie Kern (2018) investigate the contributions of artisan vendors in urban markets. These markets – often situated in the heart of a community – serve an important societal, political, and economic purpose in municipalities. Conventional calculations based on market economics do not capture the value of these contributions to community well-being beyond consideration of their contributions to economic development, such as assisting the tourism industry. However, local markets can play a much more important role – one that is often undervalued – as "a place for community, resilience, and social justice" (172).

One examination of the craft vendors in the City of Ottawa's Byward Market reveals that these artists value their ability to be self-employed, to create individual works of art, and to share a sense of community with other vendors. They are in precarious economic positions, however, and are subject to long hours and often unpredictable working conditions. In cities where gentrification is taking place, it can be difficult to sustain a livelihood. Local governments often have an important role in determining the operations of markets that are situated on public lands. They can provide a more supportive environment by ensuring that markets are regulated in a fair, equitable manner and that vendors have a meaningful voice in the functioning of municipally owned markets (Kovesi and Kern 2018).

Post-materialist social movements have coalesced around a collective resistance to what they see as destructive dominant forms of political, economic, and social power. In response to this power, they have introduced alternative economies, including local trading systems and barter exchange, cooperatives and nonprofits, permaculture, sharing, and crafting and makers' movements. These trends are directed at "unplugging from the mega-circulations of global capitalism, and the importance of creating alternative flows that keep materials and making at the personal and community level" (Schlosberg and Coles 2016, 165). Some emerging social configurations of power and collective responses are contributing to a more diverse dynamic in local political economies. Community organizer Joseph Wasylycia-Leis discusses how local festivals can contribute to this dynamic in his study of the Winnipeg Folk Festival and the Harvest Moon Festival in Manitoba (see Box 14.4).

BOX 14.4 Celebrating community: Local music festivals and sustainable relocalization in southern Manitoba

Community organizer Joseph Wasylycia-Leis (pers. comm., November 25, 2022; see also 2016) explains how community-based festivals can foster shared values and identity:

> Sustainable relocalization aims to increase resilience and wellbeing in local communities as a response to interrelated social-ecological threats emerging on a global-scale. This grassroots social and environmental movement requires place-based identity, local social capital, postconsumer values, skills and knowledge for community self-reliance, participation in local alternative economic activities, and ultimately the transformation of culture and human behavior.

> Community-based festivals can foster sense of place, political consciousness, eco-localist values and shared identity, as well as support knowledge, practices and economic innovations associated with local resilience. The Winnipeg Folk Festival and the Harvest Moon Festival, for example, appear capable of fostering shared identity among communities of place and practice, social networks and capital, skills and knowledge, and cultural values. As liminal spaces, these festivals offer opportunities for participants to strengthen social bonds and experience communal forms of living while the event communities may enable public education and social movement action. Opportunities and limitations for contributing to relocalization depend largely on a festival's size, design, organizational mission, and involvement of community stakeholders. These festivals can contribute to community building and a shift towards local sustainability.

Feminist scholar J.K. Gibson-Graham (2008) reframes economies away from those locked into the structural determinism of neoliberal economics and governing institutions. Conventional market models, for example, do not capture 30 to 50 percent of the economic activity that takes place in nonmarket settings and household work (615). Analysts have conceptualized these activities as *diverse economies,* which refers to "transactions (including all the market, alternative market and non-market transactions that circulate goods and services), labor (including wage labor, alternatively compensated labor and unpaid labor) and enterprise (including all the non-capitalist and capitalist enterprises that produce, appropriate and distribute surplus in different ways)" (616). Gibson-Graham's diverse-economies schema offers multiple entry points for community economic innovation that values societal and ecological well-being. Importantly, it points to existing, very real, economic activities that are taking place. Western liberal-democratic decision-making processes are not solely locked into the dictates of neoliberal market economics. Transactions conducted in the informal economy constitute a sizable portion of local economic activity, even if they have not been formally recognized or factored into cost-benefit analyses.

This book offers many examples of municipalities promoting economic development initiatives that require less use of ecological goods and services (or material throughput) while encouraging more sustainable alternatives. The challenge here, as argued by Robert Krueger, Christian Shulz, and David C. Gibbs (2018), is what happens to these alternative economic initiatives when they become institutionalized within an existing set of political-economic structures. They use the example of the sharing economy, which was originally positioned in the context of the degrowth movement, where resource-efficient, equitable alternative economic spaces emerged, often using the Internet as a tool for peer-to-peer sharing. The Internet platform, however, also allowed the sharing economy to be scaled up, enabling large companies to exploit the opportunities of the sharing economy based on "traditional ideas of profit maximization and surplus allocation" (584).

THE SHARING ECONOMY AND THE GIG ECONOMY

> *Our understanding of sharing cities and the sharing paradigm also encompasses alternative visions for cities, which enable the sharing of the city, its spaces, infrastructures, and services without necessarily relying on commercial intermediaries, online technologies, or even the explicit discourse of sharing cities. More often than not, such alternative visions arise outside of existing power structures, in citizens' movements, counter-cultural spaces and protest. But they can be state-led.*
>
> – McLaren and Agyeman 2019, 175

Across Canada and the globe, the urban sharing economy is associated with creative economies and urban experiments. City decision makers are promoting economic development with the establishment of maker spaces, innovation hubs, campuses, and districts where shared spaces are used to facilitate collaborations and to incubate new businesses. Cities are also using these strategies to attract young, educated professionals and to encourage new economic activities. As Tara Vinodrai (2018, 34–35) notes, local governments have not developed an adequate social safety net for workers in these high-risk, precarious forms of employment. Moreover, initiatives designed to establish areas such as innovation districts may also lead to social exclusion and inequalities related to real estate development, housing affordability, and land-use patterns. Members of the millennial generation comprise the primary cohort participating in the new sharing economy, frequently (but not always) powered by Internet-based platforms for sharing spaces, goods, and skills (Vinodrai 2018).

The sharing economy can be implemented across "five categories: 1) for-profit, 2) social enterprise/ cooperative, 3) non-profit, 4) community sharing, and 5) public sector organizations" (Cooper and Timmer 2015, 190). The sharing list is lengthy and associated with many, if not most, aspects of city life, including accommodation (e.g., vacation rentals and co-housing), mobility (e.g., cars, bikes, and scooters), tools (e.g., 3-D printers, equipment, and power and hand tools),

community spaces (e.g., for gardening, cooking, crafting, making, reading, creating, direct marketing, and reusing and repurposing goods), skill sharing, education, civics, small-business seminars, and health promotion.

The sharing economy is aimed at unlocking "the idling capacity found in the untapped social, economic, and environmental value of underutilized assets" (Cooper and Timmer 2015, 7). Globally, it represents billions of dollars of economic activities by both the for-profit and nonprofit sectors. These activities are often introduced at a pace that far outstrips regulatory processes, with governments left scrambling to react to these new economic innovations as they arise.

Some may view the sharing economy as a promising vehicle for minimizing the resource-intensive production of materials by promoting access to goods rather than their ownership (Cooper and Timmer 2015, 7). It can also foster social innovation, economic inclusion, social trust, and community networking. It is a powerful economic force that has been harnessed by a wide range of economic actors, from powerful global corporations to small community groups. For local governments, then, the sharing economy may offer a means to foster healthy, sustainable communities – but it can also undermine them. Sustainability aspirations can be hindered by some negative effects associated with freelance or part-time work, a central characteristic of the sharing economy. One example is the less structured and nontraditional gig economy, which emerged along with the sharing economy. Gig workers are employed to complete short-term jobs (or gigs) for negotiated sums. These jobs are typically mediated through online platforms such as Uber and Lyft, among others (Sung-Hee, Liu, and Ostrovsky 2019).

It is a phenomenon that requires close observation and analysis given that at least one in five workers in Canada is thought to be employed in some sort of gig work (Bierman, Schieman, and Glavin 2019). The gig and sharing economies may signal aspirations for individual freedom, decentralized workplaces, and more sustainable use of materials. However, alternative outcomes may also occur. One study reveals that gig economy workers are considerably more likely than other workers to report feelings of helplessness and powerlessness (Bierman, Schieman, and Glavin 2019).

The activities associated with the digital platforms of the sharing economy also raise questions for local democracy. As Sean Geobey (2018, 105) observes, these platforms are often owned by the private for-profit sector, so there is no democratic participation, and governing institutions can only react to these economic transitions rather than co-evolving with them. A lack of regulatory oversight can encourage innovation and experimentation, but it can also facilitate control by powerful monopolies. It is by no means a given that all transactions of the sharing economy contribute to a more sustainable community. Much depends on context, conceptualization, application, and implementation. This economy is a force to be acknowledged (and possibly harnessed) by local governments, but not all approaches benefit local communities. Sebastian Vith and colleagues (2019, 1024) conclude that different governing arrangements can be associated with four framings of the sharing economy, each with its own outcome: "'societal endangerment,' 'societal enhancement,' 'market disruption,' and 'ecological transition.'" The strategies that local governments choose to pursue clearly have ethical and political implications. Given the potential pitfalls, some analysts suggest that local governments apply a sustainability filter to determine which sharing economy activities to advance (see Box 14.5).

LIMITS TO DEGROWTH?

The dangers posed to social equity, biophysical sustainability, and viable economies by the current material-growth trajectory are clear to even a casual reader of environmental news. The path forward is muddier, however, when contemplating societal and institutional transitions to be achieved through alternative strategies – such as degrowth and relocalization. As Sylvia Lorek and Doris Fuchs (2013, 39) acknowledge, "Much of today's global economy is set up for the provision of mass consumption and the associated necessary inducement of ever-increasing levels of consumption. There is only limited room for enterprises to distinguish themselves or their products on the basis of social and environmental conduct with corresponding price margins." Mark Carney

---

BOX 14.5 Supporting a sustainable sharing economy: Guiding questions for local governments

Rosemary Cooper and Vanessa Timmer (2015, 25) suggest that local governments consider the following questions when determining what elements of the sharing economy to support:

1. **Living within ecological means**
   Does the Sharing Economy activity support absolute reductions in energy and materials flows to live within our ecological means?

2. **Resilience**
   Does the Sharing Economy activity enhance resilience and climate adaptation?

3. **Natural systems**
   Does the Sharing Economy activity protect and restore natural systems?

4. **Equity**
   Does the Sharing Economy activity advance equity and social inclusion and embrace diversity?

5. **Prosperous local economies**
   Does the Sharing Economy activity advance economic vitality and diversity, a level of self-reliance, and decent jobs?

6. **Quality of life**
   Does the Sharing Economy enhance social connectivity and wellbeing for all?

(2020), a former governor of both the Bank of Canada and the Bank of England and a vocal advocate of addressing climate change, also argues that market forces are needed for a just transition to "net zero":

The solutions to the climate crisis are intimately tied to our fiscal, economic, and social wellbeing. We need to leverage these social coalitions that have formed for climate action, but those coalitions won't and shouldn't hold if we don't have a just transition. We can't achieve environmental sustainability if we sacrifice our economy and with it, peoples' livelihoods. Similarly, we won't devise all the necessary solutions or implement them with sufficient speed without market forces.

The degrowth project through relocalization does pose considerable challenges, including considerations of ideology, equity, scale, politics, and economics. Ideological considerations are also associated with degrowth. Suggesting that a first step forward is to identify the "wicked dilemmas" involved in attempting to introduce degrowth strategies through radical change, Kaitlin Kish and Stephen Quilley (2017, 306) note,

> Broadly progressive commentators (left, liberal and green) who are actively considering this prospect of radical systemic change based upon a rejection of economic growth, are at the same time, and in ways not immediately apparent to themselves, tied to the current liberal order precisely because of very explicit, normative commitments to diversity, cosmopolitanism, individualism and (more ambivalently) technical progress.

Liberalism, individualism, and cosmopolitanism, along with their associated normative values, are embedded within the structures of the dominant market-based political, economic, and social systems.

Equity concerns are relevant when contemplating who can afford to participate in efforts to transition toward sustainability. Anyone seriously invested in growing their own food, for example, will readily attest to the amount of individual time and physical energy expended, particularly those engaged in sustainable water harvesting and permaculture. Moreover, given that women traditionally have been responsible for their family's food provisioning, questions of social and gender equity in such a post-materialist scenario inevitably arise (Appavoo 2014). Sustainability projects are often most readily afforded by those who have the capacity and resources to pursue them.

Scale is another consideration with reference to the degrowth movement. Many of the normative assumptions associated with degrowth literature see meaningful, innovative change taking place at the local scale. The community level is where efforts are seen to be most effective at stimulating radical cultural, political, and economic change toward a post-materialist, just society. Within this perspective, Elisabetta Mocca (2020, 80) explains, "A localized economy would then enable the tackling of resource problems by reducing the distance between production and consumption. In so doing, the environmental impact of productive activities would be contained, while enabling the revitalization of local economies." In addition, the economic downscaling would include a participatory "local ecological democracy" – eco-utopian villages – possibly organized spatially around the concept of bioregions (81). Mocca, however, suggests that these conceptualizations are supported more by normative assumptions than by compelling evidence (85). There are many examples of local innovations toward sustainability in Canada and throughout the world. A number are discussed in this book. Missing from the literature, however, are clearly delineated pathways for transforming modern capitalist societies into these localized entities – a conundrum readily brought home when contemplating large, metropolitan agglomerations, as noted above. The digital, highly interconnected, technologically driven, mobile society does not align well with the ideals presented in small, post-growth, eco-utopian scenarios.

People generally tend to think in terms of a particular location when conceiving of an economic activity. Location economics, for example, considers place characteristics to see which economic activities take place in a location and why. This was the case in the time of the ancient agoras or marketplaces, and it remains the case today, as seen in the central business districts and in the locations of huge Amazon distribution centres. However, as Richard Shearmur (2018, 65) discusses, it is worth considering the implications if "economic activity and value-creation are no longer tied to particular locations." This was yet another point driven home by the experience of the COVID-19 pandemic, which clearly demonstrated that a great deal of economic activity could take place through the use of information and communications technologies (ICTs). How would the sustainability aspirations of degrowth and the sharing economy play out in the context of knowledge-related jobs that are not tied to a specific location?

Sustainable consumption will not move beyond the fringes of societal change any time soon if it relies solely on individual voluntary sacrifice or on degrowth activities that depend on the formation of utopian eco-villages. Rather, sustainable consumption requires economic and political spaces – within institutions and society writ large – that make room for diverse and innovative approaches aimed at addressing context-specific challenges. These innovations may include eco-villages, but they can also include a diversity of other economic activities. Change is driven not only by the urgency of ecological thresholds, climate change, and societal inequality but also by social movements, local innovations, and coalition building (Lorek and Fuchs 2013, 40). As some analysts conclude, "There is currently no de-growth regime, in whole or in part, in place. While aspirations towards this might exist among certain actors in localities ... we have no sense of how these ideas, when introduced, become transformed by local and regional economic development politics" (Krueger, Schulz, and Gibbs 2018, 585). Nevertheless, the degrowth discourse has contributed to extensive societal consideration of the possibilities offered by diverse approaches to economic arrangements. It has also stimulated a global conversation about values and how to meaningfully incorporate them into political decision-making processes in the interest of sustainability.

The existence of highly urbanized, interconnected societies does not preclude the presence of the more sustainable possibilities offered by aspects of the degrowth agenda or by sharing and diverse economies. Sustainable alternatives are offered by emerging economic models, including the circular economy (discussed in earlier chapters) and Kate Raworth's (2017) "doughnut economy," which incorporates calculations based on planetary and societal boundaries. Much can be achieved in nudging cities toward sustainability through the adoption of principles and approaches that foster desirable social-ecological systems. Governing systems at all scales (not just the local) have a part to play in such transitions. Importantly, to inspire change, transitions require examples of successes – economic and social innovations that can be emulated and shared with other communities and constituencies.

CONCLUSION: VIBRANT COMMUNITY ECONOMIES

Property and business development has always been a key preoccupation of local governments in their pursuit of the revenues needed to provide local services. Given the impact and influence of such development on local communities, its role in transitions toward sustainability requires serious consideration. Private developers are actively involved in shaping local political agendas and, therefore, are important players when considering questions of governance and the environment.

Using only financial economic indicators to determine success, however, gives these private-sector interests a disproportionate influence and inaccurately portrays how well a community is governed. Moreover, financial capital comprises only one aspect of an economy. More robust indicators are now being used throughout the world to assess well-being. The Community Foundations of Canada's (n.d.-b) Vital Signs data program, for example, recognizes that social and biophysical assets are vital to overall human well-being. That said, the ability to generate financial capital also depends on the robustness of essential social-ecological systems – a reality that governments overlook at our collective peril.

Local economies can benefit from the possibilities offered by aspects of sharing and diverse economies. Degrowth initiatives in the context of stimulating local innovations and experiments offer examples that can be emulated in other jurisdictions, opening up new avenues for addressing complex, wicked, context-dependent challenges. Local efforts to diversify the economy, to sustain valued places, and to strengthen community resilience require creative use of physical and social liminal spaces. The Working Centre in Kitchener, Ontario, and the folk festivals in Winnipeg, Manitoba, offer two examples. Both efforts recognize approaches to community development that are based on human assets.

These spaces are particularly important in the face of regressive dictates by senior governments and the pressing need for the development of affordable housing throughout the country. Community and institutional capacity building are required to effectively tackle these challenges and to support new economic approaches. For that to happen, local decision makers must have the political will, resources, and tools to let go of counterproductive approaches and behaviours that may have been better suited for an earlier era. To transition to governing systems capable of addressing contemporary challenges, local governing bodies need to learn from unexpected events and respond to them adroitly, as well as to dynamic social and ecological systems.

NOTE

1 Related to this notion of sustainable consumption is what David Schlosberg and Romand Coles (2016, 161) refer to as "a new and sustainable materialism – one that is embodied by and embedded in collective institutions of material flows."

15 Learning Communities
Adaptive and Innovative Governance

INTRODUCTION: LOCAL LEARNING SYSTEMS

> *Because many aspects of the behaviour of socio-ecological systems are to some extent unpredictable due to cross-scale interactions, emergent properties and the existence of thresholds, the only realistic way to intervene into them is to follow a process of "adaptive learning." As societies and ecosystems co-evolve, decisions and actions made within society alter ecosystems and vice versa, and the perception of this co-evolutionary process in turn influences future decisions.*
>
> – Singh et al. 2010, 384

Governing systems with the internal capacity to tackle "wicked" problems are those that regularly engage with and learn from a diversity of players while collaboratively working on complex tasks (Innes and Booher 2003, 7). Moreover, local decision makers who engage in reflexive practices are more likely to determine what is working, distinguish successes and failures, and know how to change and adapt systems when necessary. Reflexivity – the ability to be self-critical and to question existing assumptions and practices (Feindt and Weiland 2018) – is considered a key element in governing for sustainability.

In the context of transitioning toward sustainability, some long-standing practices are now coming under scrutiny. Subject to question are the effectiveness of conventional, hierarchical decision-making processes and the limited utility of centralized and standardized approaches applied to unique situations and places. Governments have also been engaged in the counterproductive and dangerous dependence on market-based economic indicators to determine local prosperity and well-being. The pursuit of local democracy has also been undermined with the exclusion from political decision-making processes of many societal groups that have been marginalized and effectively disenfranchised.

Resilient, sustainable systems and organizations have been characterized as "nimble" and adaptable in the context of rapidly changing environments (Innes and Booher 2003, 16). The emerging strategies employed by local governments for their flexibility include new emergency response systems (see Chapter 7), smart energy grids (see Chapter 12), and progressive local health networks that convey vital information to underserved populations during health crises (see Chapter 13).

The shift toward sustainability, however, requires more than the ability of local governments to learn and adapt to dynamic environments. Social learning also needs to take place at different scales within the wider community – among organizations, citizens, and other governments. Together, they comprise collective learning systems for place-based governance. Expanded physical, political, and social spaces for public engagement facilitate these interactions. In turn, inclusive forms of civic participation foster a sense of political efficacy, encourage innovative problem solving, and contribute to the legitimacy of governing institutions (see Chapter 4). Collaborative-governance learning systems are seen as an essential tool in the pursuit of sustainability.

ORGANIZATIONAL LEARNING

Over fifty years ago, philosopher and urban planning professor Donald Schön (1973, 6) pointed out that institutions and society are always undergoing processes of change and transformation. Governments and society, he argued, need to understand and manage these transformations: "We must, in other words, become adept at learning. We must become able not only to transform our institutions, in response to changing situations and requirements; we must invent and develop institutions which are 'learning systems.'"

Many researchers have called for transformative learning on the part of government organizations. They have perceived a gap between the wicked challenges presented today on numerous fronts and the seeming inability of public institutions to effectively deal with them. Governments, it is argued, need to engage in transformative learning processes that will allow them to pivot in response to complex situations, instead of using conventional incremental responses.

Peter A. Hall (1993) wrote a seminal article in the 1990s advancing the idea that policy making can be seen as social learning. Exploring how learning might lead to policy change, he poses a series of questions, including the following:

> How do the ideas behind policy change course? Is the process of social learning relatively incremental, as organization theory might lead us to expect, or marked by upheaval and the kind of "punctuated equilibrium" that often applies more generally to political change? Are bureaucrats the principal actors in social learning, or do politicians and societal organizations also play a role? (277)

In the intervening decades, numerous analysts have employed the metaphorical lens of policy making as social learning. Nihit Goyal and Michael Howlett (2019, 258) portray this notion of policy making as "an activity involving governments' efforts to resolve societal issues ... a kind of teaching experience in which 'students' (policymakers) learn 'lessons' from

their and other governments' experiences with specific policy initiatives." They caution that although the question of policy learning is important, the field of inquiry is far from coherent due to a lack of agreement about what defines learning and what "connects learning to policy output(s)" (268). Given the importance of adaptive learning to manage the wicked, complex problems discussed throughout this book, more attention to the connections between learning and policy outcome is warranted.

Institutional learning from past decisions is frequently viewed as path-dependent due to its reliance on habitual practices and ways of thinking and criticized for leading only to task-oriented incremental changes that do not address the root of problems. This type of learning, as conceptualized by Chris Argyris and Donald Schön (1974), is referred to as single-loop learning, which occurs when the detection and correction of organizational errors permits the organization to focus only on its present policies and current objectives. In contrast, correcting organizational errors by modifying the underlaying norms, policies, and objectives is referred to as double-loop learning, which "consists of inquiry into the learning system by which an organization detects and corrects its errors" (Kappler 1980, 292). Double-loop learning engages organizations in questioning original assumptions and objectives, reframing problems, and creating new policies. These two concepts have been popularly presented in the form of questions: "Are we doing things right?" (single-loop learning) and "Are we doing the right things?" (double-loop learning) (Flood and Romm 2018, 262).

Scholars have also explored triple-loop learning, which requires organizations to reflexively question how they are learning and doing things. Such reflexivity can lead to paradigmatic shifts in the way that they operate and address complex problems. Triple-loop learning involves exploring alternative discourses and recognizing the role played by power relations embedded in social systems. It encourages the inclusion of a plurality of societal perspectives in the learning processes (Flood and Romm 1996, 2018). Such transformative learning processes are not necessarily superior at all times. Moreover, when applied in certain contexts, transformative learning can in fact be destabilizing in undesirable ways (Tosey, Visser, and Saunders 2012). However, the ability of local governments to engage in adaptive and sometimes transformative learning processes is considered an important element of sustainable governance. As a result, reflexivity plays a key role in these learning processes. John S. Dryzek and Jonathan Pickering (2017, 353) define reflexivity as follows:

> In the context of governance generally, reflexivity is the ability of a structure, process, or set of ideas to reconfigure itself in response to reflection on its performance ... Reflexivity emphasizes ... the capacity of individuals and institutions to function as deliberate, self-critical agents of change in social-ecological systems ... [and] the specific implications for institutional change that flow from linkages and feedbacks between human and non-human systems, including the need to monitor the impacts of institutions on ecosystems and vice versa, and to rethink and reshape core values and practices.

Reflexivity might take place in governance when choices are made about which sources of knowledge and participants to include in knowledge production, how institutions are to be structured, where and how decisions are to be made, and the dynamics involved in decision-making processes themselves (see also Dryzek and Pickering 2017). Periodic reviews of government operations and practices, scrutiny of core values, and the inclusion of participants with differing world views through deliberative democratic practices are all steps that can be taken to improve governing performance (359). The capacity of governments to develop innovative solutions to complex problems is related to their ability to engage in reflexive learning and to adapt when new governance challenges emerge. An extensive literature has emerged since Schön (1973) first issued the call for institutions and societies to become participatory learning systems.

PARTICIPATORY LEARNING SYSTEMS

Participatory social learning has been defined as "learning by individuals and groups with different kinds of knowledge, experience, perspectives, values, and capacities, working together to better understand and address sustainability challenges through iterative reflection" (Reed and Abernethy 2018, 43). As discussed in Part 1, local governments or, for that matter, all large bureaucratic organizations are not structured to readily engage in participatory social learning exercises. Barriers to institutional change are found in established patterns of path-dependent behaviours, in the entrenchment of dominant elites and ideas that benefit from the status quo, and in the lack of political will to undertake institutional change.

An important aspect of social or institutional learning related to sustainability is the inclusion of diverse forms of knowledge, ranging from scientific (or expert-driven) knowledge to local (or grassroots) knowledge. The sharing and coproduction of knowledge at various scales is considered essential in tackling wicked problems. Maureen G. Reed and Paivi Abernethy (2018, 41) define knowledge coproduction as "a collaborative process in which academic researchers or other stakeholders work together to disclose and create new knowledge." The use of diverse forms of knowledge, in addition to science-driven information, not only expands our general understanding of problems and possibilities but can also reinforce the legitimacy of the decision-making process and outcome. The approach is particularly valuable when the goal is to sustain valuable social-ecological systems, with the solutions being constructed in a specific context or place:

> This kind of context-dependent coordination capitalizes on the spatial interdependencies among diverse local knowledge-holders, which can be shared and refined within the network of embedded, partially informed agents (an extended peer community of managers). In this view, knowledge represents the accumulated and continuously revised wisdom that comes from shared learning in actual places; as practical knowledge that emerges and grows within a community of practice. (Williams 2018, 293)

The challenges of such a task are not to be underestimated. Diverse world views and values, along with power imbalances, can heighten the difficulties in reaching agreement on the way forward. Skilled facilitators and knowledge translators can help to build bridges between disparate groups and organizations by undertaking initiatives, for example, to convey scientific information in layperson's terms and to facilitate cross-cultural communications. Reed and Abernethy (2018, 53; see also 42) emphasize that "skilled research facilitators for knowledge co-production require a mix of concrete operational skills and leadership abilities that are sensitive to differences in culture and logistical needs and are adept at promoting equity across a diverse set of participants."

Bridging organizations can also facilitate the co-production of the knowledge that is applied to sustainability transitions. Examples include biosphere reserves and community forests (see Chapter 8) as well as organizations whose urban planning, development, or regeneration projects integrate different elements of the social, biophysical, and built aspects of urban infrastructure (Kampelmann, Van Hollebeke, and Vandergert 2016). These organizations can be used to bridge barriers to cooperative problem solving between organizations, such as barriers caused by communications difficulties and by differences between organizations operating at different temporal or spatial scales or in distinct political jurisdictions. Knowledge sharing, collaborative learning, and innovative problem solving between participants and organizations call for skilled facilitators, who perform two important roles: "(a) drawing together place-based, experimental knowledge of practitioners and formalized knowledge of academic researchers (bridging); (b) diffusing and applying knowledge across a network of local sites (outscaling) and between local sites and broader policy or program networks (upscaling)" (Reed and Abernethy 2018, 40).

COLLABORATIVE LEARNING AND INNOVATIVE PROBLEM SOLVING

Sustainability literature frequently emphasizes inclusive forms of collaborative learning and innovation. They are considered essential elements in strategies aimed at addressing complex, wicked challenges that extend beyond one political jurisdictional authority or the problem-solving capacity of any particular discipline or knowledge set. New institutional designs and forms of integrative leadership can support collaborative innovation bringing together public and private actors who possess the diverse experiences, skill sets, competences, and ideas. These varied skills are needed to stimulate learning processes and out-of-the-box thinking, build joint ownership over new and bold solutions, and ensure their implementation and consolidation through iterative rounds of prototyping, testing, and revision (Torfing 2019, 8). One way to achieve this outcome, beyond ensuring that there is the requisite political will in place, is to allow for co-initiated innovation or urban tinkering. Eva Sørensen and Jacob Torfing (2018, 414) suggest that "co-initiation tends to build a strong commitment to, and ownership by, active citizens of the process and outcomes."

With co-initiation, members of the public also bring innovative ideas to the decision-making table rather than just being in a position to respond to government-identified and expert-led policies and projects. Still to be developed in local governance analyses are detailed case studies that demonstrate which collaborative processes are successful and how they influence policy outcomes. Neil Bradford (2016, 659) points out that it is important to investigate how these collaborative-governance, knowledge-sharing processes shape local politics because "ideas play a pivotal role in motivating collective action, channeling policy." Drawing on the theory of discursive institutionalism, he offers "discursive localism" as a framework that can be used to analyze how differing collaborative-governance arrangements that generate ideas and are shared through interactive discourse can set local agendas. Bradford's case studies suggest that by examining the normative and cognitive dimensions of policy discourses (i.e., whether they are integrated, disassociated, or fragmented and divisive), we can learn much about how different policy discourses influence local governance arrangements.

COMMUNITIES OF PRACTICE

Communities of practice are formed by people who engage in a process of collective learning in a shared domain of human endeavor: a tribe learning to survive, a band of artists seeking new forms of expression, a group of engineers working

> *on similar problems, a clique of pupils defining their identity in the school, a network of surgeons exploring novel techniques, a gathering of first-time managers helping each other cope.*
>
> – Wenger-Trayner and Wenger-Trayner 2015

Reed and colleagues (2014, 230) argue that "deliberation, dialogue and systematic learning are now considered attributes of good practice for organizations seeking to advance sustainability." To that end, more attention is paid to the role that communities of practice (COPs) play in sustaining social-ecological systems. In the late 1980s, Jean Lave and Etienne Wenger coined the term "community of practice" to denote a means of informal, voluntary social learning that exhibits the characteristics of a system: "emergent structures, complex relationships, self-organization, dynamic boundaries, ongoing negotiations of identity and cultural meaning, to mention a few" (Wenger 2010, 180). The effectiveness of this learning system is said to be dependent on the strength of its domain (or what defines its identity and what it cares about), the community itself (and the quality of the relationships), and its practice: "Each community develops its practice by sharing and developing the knowledge of practitioners in its domain. Elements of a practice include its repertoire of tools, frameworks, methods, and stories – as well as activities related to learning and innovation" (Snyder and Wenger 2010, 110). COPs might be formed to provide mutual assistance at work or in a community of shared interest, to discuss and develop best practices, to share, co-produce, and steward knowledge, or to create new knowledge while developing new practices and innovations (Edmonton Regional Learning Association 2016).

In the context of local governance, we can distinguish between COPs composed of citizens and COPs composed of local and regional municipal governments and professionals. Local government COPs – concerned with questions of local governance – coalesce around particular domains at different scales and multiple levels of government. For example, United Cities and Local Governments (UCLG), a global umbrella network of local governments and their associations, has different COPs, one being the UCLG Community of Practice on Transparency and Open Government (UCLG 2018) (see Box 15.1).

Civic communities of practice, which also operate in the context of cities, have been described as "coalitions, associations, partnerships, and alliances" that "take responsibility for clusters of issues related

---

BOX 15.1 **The United Cities and Local Governments (UCLG) Community of Practice on Transparency and Open Government**

The UCLG Community of Practice on Transparency and Open Government uses a variety of methods to promote government transparency, participation, and accountability in local governments in order to foster sustainability. Approaches include peer-to-peer learning, networking, and local capacity building.

The Community of Practice aims to contribute to the strengthening of the global network so it can become a benchmark for the defense of open governance and public integrity. In order to achieve this objective, it is necessary to work on: **the development of joint solutions; the promotion of collaboration and exchange of experiences and public policies; the fostering of learning and promotion of social innovation.** The growing need of local and regional governments around the world to connect with their citizens in a renewed way encourages the creation and development of this network to promote more efficient local and regional governments in the provision of public services, [and] to increase citizen participation in public management, [while] preventing and fighting corruption and rebuilding trust in the public sector at [the] local level. (UCLG 2018)

to particular civic domains, such as education, economic development, health, housing, public safety, infrastructure, culture, recreation, and the environment" (Snyder and Wenger 2010, 113). "The city, reimagined as a learning system, consists of the constellation of cross-sector groups that provide stewardship for the whole round of civic domains" (114). These COPs are seen as complementary to place-based communities and can serve the role of "stewarding" various issue areas or civic domains (113). One example is the Alberni Clayoquot Health Network (see Box 13.2).

PLACE-BASED LEARNING

Hierarchical, top-down structures do not easily lend themselves to participatory democracy, which is seen as an element of a healthy civic society and active citizenship. If diverse members of the public see their interests reflected in policies and political processes, decisions taken by local governments are more likely to be perceived as legitimate. Along with legitimacy comes more public acceptance of new initiatives and policies and a greater willingness on the part of the public to participate in decision-making processes. Local officials often illustrate the unwillingness of citizens to engage by pointing to low levels of attendance at the public open houses and information sessions that local governments hold to inform people about the latest urban developments. Citizens who have found their efforts ignored in policy outcomes after participating in advisory councils, however, would not be surprised by the lack of public interest. They might respond that low public attendance reflects the fact that these forums are no more than pro forma, desultory efforts by governments to meet their legal requirements to consult the public. If governments wish to engage in meaningful consultation, the location of these meetings is very important. Going to the places where people live and socialize is much more likely to encourage public participation than expecting them to become informed about, locate, and attend meetings at city hall. That is particularly important when consulting underserved populations whose members may not have the incentive or ability to attend meetings in an institutional setting – a place that might also appear intimidating and unwelcome.

PUBLIC SPACES FOR LEARNING

Knowledge both is an outcome of governance and creates the conditions for it. It contributes to, comes to be embedded in, and helps to construct shared beliefs, discourse, practices, policies, and visions. Thus, the city transformations envisioned by advocates of knowledge co-production cannot be understood as mere exercises in creating and applying knowledge, however broadly sourced across diverse participants; rather, they are exercises in reconfiguring the relationships between and institutional configurations of both how cities think and how they act.

– Muñoz-Erickson, Miller, and Miller 2017, 2

Knowledge is embedded in a set of power arrangements and often seen in political and social arenas as a form of currency to be retained or shared according to certain cost-benefit analyses (Wenger 2010, 190). The establishment of reflective social learning systems requires the expansion of publicly accessible and inclusive spaces where people from diverse backgrounds can come together to learn, share, and co-create knowledge. In the process, it is possible to stimulate an engaging civic culture, a sense of community, and a lively civil discourse. These sharing spaces include public places such as museums, art centres, local festivals, educational facilities, outdoor environmental programs, parks, public gardens, maker spaces, recreation centres, town squares, city halls, and libraries.

Libraries are a good case in point. They have broadened from yesteryear's vital, but hushed, reading sanctuaries into lively community hubs of social learning. Calgary's library, for example, has adopted a mission with the goal of "empowering community by connecting you to ideas and experiences, inspiration, and insight." This mission is founded on inclusion according to the principles "of a just society, chief among them respect, dignity, and equity," curiosity about new ideas and perspectives, and collaboration between individuals and groups (Calgary Public Library n.d.). Libraries are also learning centres that can be used to help address issues of

BOX 15.2 Libraries as social learning centres: The case of the Brodie Street Library

The Brodie Street Library is located in Thunder Bay, Ontario, a northern city that has been the subject of reports of social and institutional violence and racism against First Nations people. Tanya Talaga (2019) has discussed the library's innovative program:

> While reading old issues of the Chronicle-Journal, there was a constant collection of folks who'd wander in from the cold to use the free Wi-Fi service and computers, to get in touch with family in northern Ontario fly-in communities and others that would come to sit and read from the stacks. The library offered safe space in a troubled and grieving city. This has been a collaborative effort led by Indigenous liaison Robyn Medicine, community hub librarian Samantha Martin-Bird and the library's Indigenous advisory board ... The city's libraries have worked hard to address the needs of the community, to stay relevant in this time of crisis ... At the Brodie branch, there are now street outreach nurses from the Thunder Bay district health unit every Friday afternoon ... On Thursday afternoons, there is a walk-in social work service ... Both the public health nurses and the social work service come in to the library's space at no cost to the library – a lesson to city council that a positive difference can be made even without additional funding from higher levels of government. The library has even created a "relationship building and reconciliation action plan," a recommendation of both the truth and reconciliation report and the inquiry into the youth deaths in the city.

social discrimination and racism, offering a place of healing and reconciliation (see Box 15.2).

Similar efforts to diversify offerings and to sustain and value the cultural traditions of Indigenous peoples and other underserved groups have been introduced in public libraries across Canada. For example, during the COVID-19 pandemic, the Thompson-Nicola Regional District Library offered the online workshop Learn Secwepemctsin, one of the Salish languages in the interior of British Columbia (Thompson-Nicola Regional District 2021) (see Figure 15.1).

Public libraries have also broadened their range of offerings, moving beyond books and audio-visual materials to rent out equipment such as skates and 3-D printers. Libraries in Halifax, Kitchener, and Edmonton, for example, have made space for community kitchens to help teach food literacy, such as knowledge about healthy eating habits and local food cultures. Library representative Mary Chevreau notes that food literacy is "just another type of literacy" (cited in C. Thompson 2020).

Emerging public meeting spaces include digital forums provided by local governments and other

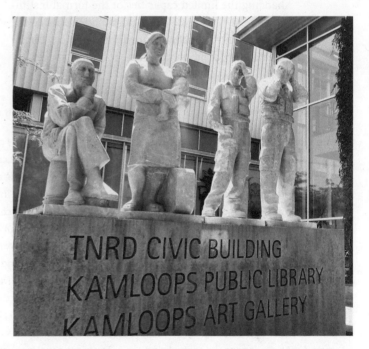

15.1 Thompson-Nicola Regional District Library, Kamloops, British Columbia, 2012

public bodies. Because technocratic and other digitally literate elites can readily capture the systems architecture and proprietary technology, thereby taking control of the information, certain societal groups can be effectively disenfranchised. The development of digital civic infrastructures is one possible response to this emerging concern. The design of these digital platforms, including their content, could involve the participation of diverse members of the public working with experts to co-design the systems (Weise, Coulton, and Chiasson 2017). The participatory ethos advanced when designing a digital civic infrastructure is similar to that of collaborative-governance models.

By expanding physical and virtual inclusive public spaces for social learning, local governing bodies can foster a civil, educated, participatory community that learns about a diversity of perspectives, cultures, and languages. These community-learning hubs can provide supportive arenas for collective governing efforts. In the process, they offer a potential arena for community action toward sustainability, thereby enhancing the limited capacities of the formal institutions of government. Other possibilities outside the realm of intentionally planned public places can be created (or found) in the realm of liminal spaces.

LIMINAL SPACES AND MEETING PLACES

Liminal (i.e., transitional or threshold) spaces are those places between one state of being and another. In ecological terms, this space refers to a place where two distinct ecological landscapes overlap and create a new zone. An example might be the boundary or interface between two distinct ecological communities, such as forests and grasslands.

Liminal spaces can also be identified as physical transitional areas in cities that appear unused, such as an undeveloped lot, back alley, or abandoned property. These areas present opportunities for diverse groups of people to gather and foster a collective sense of place and belonging by using the spaces as community gardens, for outdoor community arts, or as small parks for public meetings (see Figure 15.1). These spaces might also be cultural meeting places, such as folk festivals and fairs, where a sense of community can be strengthened.

In addition, liminal spaces might be cast in political or sociological terms, where silos are broken down between governing structures or between people with different ideologies, world views, or sets of knowledge. As is the case in ecology, where novel ecosystems can emerge when two distinct communities overlap (also known as the edge effect), new political spaces

---

BOX 15.3   **Creating places through liminal spaces: The Working Centre model in Kitchener, Ontario**

The Working Centre was established by Joe Mancini and Stephanie Mancini in 1982 in downtown Kitchener, Ontario. The organization has created an extensive network of community participants to tackle problems of unemployment and poverty. The foundational objectives of the Working Centre are to give people the tools that they need to create their own work and to foster continuous ways of learning and cooperating. Adopting a grassroots model that challenges the centralizing, hierarchical structures of large organizations, the Working Centre has grown horizontally, with many partners, collaborators, and participants introducing new ideas and projects. These projects are organized into six areas: the Job Search Resource Centre, St. John's Kitchen, Community Tools, Access to Technology, Affordable Supportive Housing, and the Waterloo School for Community Development (The Working Centre n.d.). In the words of Mancini and Mancini (2015, 75–76),

> There are countless groups that need access to places where they can organize craft and cultural

societies, spiritual discovery, and productive co-operatives. These all create room for the practice of reciprocal relationships, creating opportunities for co-operation, the lifeblood of the city.

An important part of integrated communities [is] the interconnections between people that help build community. The liminal space of informal and formal supports is a refuge that people use to bump into each other and form reciprocal relationships.

can open up when collaboration takes place between actors and political systems. In socio-political terms, this interaction can lead to disruptions that undermine the existing order, but it can also generate new environments and innovative solutions. As discussed by the founders of the Working Centre, a charitable organization in Kitchener, liminal spaces can be used to advance social justice: "Liminality is about initiating personal and collective development by creating places and spaces where people can re-engage in community, and thereby remember to trust the other, reflecting back the openness they experienced" (Mancini and Mancini 2015, 74) (see Box 15.3).

Policy Niches and Learning

A related concept is policy niches. As Adrian Smith and colleagues (2016, 411) explain, "Niches are constituted by networks of local experimentation, facilitated and co-ordinated by an intermediary infrastructure of shared knowledge, guidance, and resource provision. Influence arises through workable knowledge taken up by an increasing number and variety of actors, which becomes increasingly standardised and institutionalised." Decentralized or distributed systems create opportunities for local or place-specific experimentation in the context of new approaches or inventions. For example, new information communications technologies (ICTs) support smart grid technologies to manage and monitor information and electricity flows (see Chapter 10). Mark Winfield and Scott Weiler (2018, 1931) point out, "The emerging Smart Grid is seen to have the potential to facilitate challenges to existing economic and institutional structures by allowing new entrants, particularly 'behind the meter' (BTM), into energy supply and services markets." Policy niches can be used in any number of areas, some facilitated by ICTs, to introduce supportive initiatives for innovative economic projects, to permit new entrants into the energy management arena, to experiment with new active transit approaches, and the list goes on.

Policy makers can learn from grassroots activists who have introduced innovative ideas and locally appropriate technologies in areas such as renewable energy, agroecology, and eco-housing. These ideas provide opportunities for policy makers to consider how these innovations might be scaled up with government support (A. Smith et al. 2016, 408). Smith and colleagues, however, have cautioned that existing policy regimes can appropriate "promising niche innovations into incumbent regimes with little transformation" (411). Critical niche analysis, they argue, might be used not only to facilitate innovations in products, processes, or services – by means of single- or double-loop learning, as described above – but also to challenge dominant institutional regimes and discourses by mobilizing "transformative action" (412). One way to engage in transformative action is by using liminal spaces, both physical and metaphorical, that allow for the emergence of new policies, practices, and innovations. These spaces provide important niches for governments and organizations attempting to transition toward sustainability. Policy learning via open-data systems and information sharing between governments can also foster sustainable solutions.

CONCLUSION: TRANSFORMATION THROUGH LEARNING

> *To achieve fundamental changes and, ultimately, a qualitatively new state in a society, key system parameters need to be transformed, and actors' decisions and behaviours need to be adapted. Such an endeavour is quite challenging and requires a sound understanding of past and current transition dynamics to base interventions and ongoing change processes on such knowledge. In support of change, several methods, such as policy formulation, decision-making and monitoring to improve societal self-observation, can enhance a social system's potential for sustainable development.*
>
> – Hausknost et al. 2016, 133

Pathways to sustainability call for societal and institutional transformations – "a significant reordering, one that challenges existing structures to produce something fundamentally novel" (Blythe et al. 2018, 1207). In the context of local government, this reordering includes fostering an ability to negotiate fluid, networked, multi-actor, holistic systems of governance operating at many scales. There is a rich literature looking at how organizations might publicly deliberate, innovate, learn, and engage in transitions toward sustainability (Stirling 2014; Hausknost et al. 2016; Abson et al. 2017; Blythe et al. 2018; Burch et al. 2018; Reed and Abernethy 2018; Rosenbloom et al. 2018; Stirling et al. 2018, N.J. Bennett et al. 2019). These sustainability scholars all stress the importance of learning from inclusive, place-based experiments and bottom-up strategies that are ever-evolving to respond to a dynamic environment.

Beyond some general normative principles – social justice, economic sufficiency, and the social-biophysical health of desired systems – the pursuit of sustainability is aspirational. There is no fixed goal post. Different situations require different government and societal responses. Andrew Stirling (2014, 1) suggests that sustainability transformations "entail more plural, emergent and unruly political re-alignments, involving social and technological innovations driven by diversely incommensurable knowledges, challenging incumbent structures, and pursuing contending (even unknown) ends. Indeed, they may owe more to critical practice of other values, virtues, or social qualities than to utilitarian pursuit of ends at all." Informal communities of practice and networks of social learning systems are now being recognized for their role in fostering collaborative, reflective learning that facilitates transitions toward sustainability. They range from local civic COPs like the Working Centre in Kitchener to global COPs like the UCLG Community of Practice on Transparency and Open Government. Local governments can encourage healthy social learning systems by participating in COPs at multiple levels of governance. They can also nurture COPs by opening up and helping to create public inclusive spaces, such as libraries, public squares, recreational areas, and virtual public spaces online.

Periods of disruption that force a new governing approach can also lead to triple-loop learning. Natural disasters as a result of climate change have decimated communities. In the process of rebuilding, new governing approaches and perspectives often emerge. The COVID-19 pandemic disrupted global patterns of social-ecological interactions, revealing many fault lines in entrenched forms of governance. Issues such as social inequality, work patterns, health, global mobility, and supply chain disruptions stimulated worldwide conversations about improved approaches to governance and led to innovative partnerships among policy communities. However, as the intensity of the pandemic diminished, the public desire for change was often supplanted by the desire to get back to the pre-pandemic "normal" way of doing things.

In sum, the transition models exhibit undeniable limitations that can undermine any sustainability aspirations. In terms of governance, the principles of public administration were put in place to ensure clear lines of accountability, transparency, and responsibility, to produce knowledgeable public servants, to ground decisions in valid, expert information, and to foster stability in government. To be sure, for every one of these principles, the converse can and does happen: information becomes hidden or obscure, the buck is passed, powerful elites dominate, and governing bodies become inflexible, rigid, and unable to respond to complex challenges. However, the governing systems advocated in the sustainability literature – the outcomes of which rely on knowledge and decisions co-produced by a network of distributed sources of information and participants – can also lead to obfuscation and a lack of accountability. Due to such a dynamic, the old political science question of who governs becomes ever more elusive. Without transparent lines of accountability, political spaces can open up for the opportunistic few who know how to navigate complex governance arrangements. In addition, many sustainability aspirations, such as low-carbon economies and local food production, require trade-offs that can disproportionately affect society's most vulnerable. As mentioned earlier, too effective a pluralism can paralyze decision-making processes. It is, however, in this very pluralism that the possibility for transformation resides. Opening up political spaces to a diversity of participants also opens up the opportunities to pursue agendas of social justice, environmental sustainability, civic learning, and creative problem solving.

Reflections
Local Governance in Transition

An understanding of contemporary local governance requires knowledge of public institutions – their structures, underpinning theories and ideologies, historical provenances, use of political power, decision-making processes, and administration of the public interest (see Chapters 1–6). This knowledge is essential but not sufficient. Today, students and practitioners of governance who care about the long-term resiliency of communities and the people who live in them need to be informed about other influential forces. Some of these considerations, introduced in Chapter 1 and discussed throughout this book, include complex social-ecological systems, temporal and spatial scale, urban metabolism and resiliency, networking, collaborative decision making, sustainability ethics, diversity, distributed integrated systems, redundancy, eco-health, social justice, adaptive co-learning, and innovation.

The application of a historical and geographical lens reveals the uniqueness of individual Canadian communities situated in a physically huge and politically diverse geographic space. Temporal and spatial variables influence governance and its outcomes, particularly the viability of valued social-ecological systems. Canada has accrued considerable material wealth over its history, capitalizing on its rich endowment of natural resources. In the twentieth century, it was able to establish a welfare state with a national health care system, social services, and a highly developed market economy. But these accomplishments came at a considerable cost, particularly to marginalized communities. The twentieth century was ushered in with notions of scientific management and business-like efficiencies, both of which facilitated rapid urban growth. The mantra that "time is money" became familiar. As the century progressed, urban sprawl and suburban development led to dependence on the vehicle, reshaping cities and rural areas while firmly establishing fossil-fuelled economies throughout the world. By the twenty-first century, early industrialization had given way to fast-paced cities and instantaneous global digital communications. The tentacles of globalization had reached further into national and local economies with the emergence of agro-industry, media conglomerates, energy corporations, and other massive monopolies – further endangering the diversity of local ecosystems, polities, economies, and civil society. Alarms were sounding as economies, governments, and societies became increasingly interlinked, rigid, and fragile. Climate change, environmental degradation, and social injustice are just a few of the entangled "wicked" problems with cascading effects that characterize the policy challenges of the twenty-first century. Cities now require approaches to governance and learning that must be multi-scaled, interdisciplinary, collaborative, and adaptive if they are to maintain resiliency into the future (see Chapter 2).

Governing a territorially large and culturally disparate country such as Canada requires considerable negotiation. Canada has a history of intergovernmental collaboration given its federal composition (see Chapter 3). Local governments, however, are not assigned legislative authority in the Constitution and have limited resources and authority to respond to expanding responsibilities. In various parts of the country, senior governments have demonstrated some alarming, authoritarian tendencies to dismantle local democracy and any progress toward a sustainable future. The gap is widening between the growing responsibilities assigned to local governments and the capacity required to address these responsibilities. Throughout history, many provincial governments have wielded a heavy hammer, striking down local efforts to respond to the social and environmental requirements of their communities – a tendency that has serious implications for sustainability. Ideally, there would be a meaningful "right-sizing" of jurisdictional authority, with some devolution of responsibility and authority to those governing entities most capable of dealing with an issue, as well as a refashioning of the financial base of local government (W. Kennedy, pers. comm., December 30, 2020).

But Canadian local governments are positioned far from this ideal. Good policy making is not simple. Good governance is complex. Reductionist, unilateral, blanket pieces of legislation and policies imposed by senior governments do not achieve sustainable, livable cities. As history tells us, governments that enforce such approaches do not foster a good life for their citizens – now or in the long term. Take the issue of accessible housing. If a provincial government decides to use this problem to advance its own market-oriented agenda by undermining local democracy and destabilizing local governments, will the number of housing units go up more quickly in the short term? Probably. Will this policy approach achieve the ultimate goal of accessible housing and livable cities? Most likely not. Processes for development approval are in place for a reason, as are environmental assessments, protected areas, public consultation, planning studies, and careful design. Indisputably, local decision processes can be made more efficient, effective, and equitable, aligning them with the principles of good public administration. If local governments are given the capacity to make the decisions that directly affect their communities – and if they have the political will to

learn from their mistakes and from each other (see Chapter 15) – they can build more accessible, livable, and sustainable cities.

The growing complexity of decision making is reflected by a shift in the governance literature and in various political jurisdictions away from a focus on the legal-political model of government and intergovernmental relations and toward the more inclusive approach of multi-level governance. These governing arrangements include informal agreements, partnerships, and networking between governments, nongovernmental organizations, the private sector, and the public. Partnerships help to shore up the abilities of municipalities to address complex policy issues that spill over boundaries and to share innovative solutions to challenging problems. They also enable them to have a more effective voice in domestic and international affairs.

Despite a lack of legal and fiscal capacity, municipal governments have tools at their disposal that can help to foster local democracy and public participation, both of which are requisite elements of a sustainable community. Citizens, possessing diverse sets of knowledge, backgrounds, and capabilities, can be engaged to enhance city decision making either as elected representatives or as participants in governance at all stages of the policy cycle – from setting the agenda through to implementation and monitoring. Again, although the reality is far from ideal, public consultations and the encouragement of inclusive participation in local decision making are becoming much more the norm than was the case historically (see Chapters 4 and 5). Public engagement includes deliberative democracy, participatory budgeting processes, and crowd-sourced policy making, which is often facilitated by virtual townhalls, polls, and electronic forms of consultation. Importantly, attention must be paid to ensuring the political engagement of diverse members of society. Low levels of participation in local elections reflect the public's lack of interest in municipal government. Given the threats posed to local democracy and good governance, this is an issue that all municipalities would do well to address.

Local governments also need to reconsider their administrative institutions and policy processes.

Modern bureaucratic systems have been structured not only to deliver services efficiently and effectively but also, ostensibly, to hold public officials accountable for their actions. Top-down rational, technical approaches have proven effective in delivering public services that rely on fairly standardized, uniform tasks, although they still have embedded biases that benefit certain interests over others. These practices are not sufficient when it comes to dealing with climate change, environmental degradation, and the responsibilities for social, health, and other services that have been offloaded by senior governments. Conventional institutional governing practices have set the world on a collision course with ecological boundaries and tipping points. They are not up to the task of governing complex social-ecological systems that require collaborative discussions, social learning, and knowledge co-creation among many diverse communities of interest (see Chapter 6).

Change requires political will. Path-dependent actions and resistance to change are well known to anyone in local government who has attempted to encourage innovations or transitions toward sustainability. The political will to stay the course often trumps the political will for change. But change does happen. Sometimes, it is incremental and staggered, occurring through internal policy diffusion. Other times, it is the result of an exogenous policy shock, such as a natural disaster caused by climate change. The efforts of a political champion, such as a mayor, local activist, or social movement, can be successful in introducing an initiative. Change can also be a result of learning from a successful innovation introduced by another municipality, the private sector, or other actors, including academia. Incentives and grants from senior governments or from philanthropic foundations can also encourage learning and change. This book has offered a number of examples of these developments from across the country.

The necessity of sustaining valued social-ecological systems requires the cooperative efforts of political and administrative actors at all scales of governance. However, adopting intricate governing arrangements can also obscure lines of accountability and transparency and can consume significant human and fiscal resources. A plurality of voices in decision-making processes can also lead to policy paralysis. Conversely, policy approaches that are technical and rational can encourage the formation of technocratic elites who serve only a narrow set of short-term interests. As noted earlier, what is being called for is not the jettisoning of all past governing practices. Rather, as Joop Koppenjan, Philip Marcel Karré, and Katrien Termeer (2019a, 15) suggest, a sort of "smart hybridity" is needed, where existing structures are adjusted to align with local innovations and with the use of informal mechanisms to bridge gaps in multi-scale governance arrangements.

In the context of complexity, diversity, and uncertainty, there is no optimal approach (Head and Alford 2015, 715). Decision and policy processes require discussion and negotiation among disparate interests. As Charles Conteh (2016, 237) argues, a new form of accountability is needed in these complex environments – one that emphasizes principles of "trust, openness and reciprocity rather than mechanical instruments of control." Adhering to these principles requires social accountability (with all parties held mutually accountable), institutional learning and adaptation, public reporting and peer review, deliberative forums, and processes that are consensual and reciprocal. Brian W. Head and John Alford (2015, 722) also call for new leadership models that recognize and make use of a more distributed network of information, interests, and power (see Chapter 7). These kinds of changes will involve some disruption in existing governing systems. Wicked problems are not static but fluid and ever-shifting. They cut across administrative silos, hierarchies, governments, organizations, and communities of interest. In this evolving environment, public managers in local government are going to require the skills of "collaborative capability builders" (Weber and Khademian 2008).

Despite legislative and resource constraints, local governments do have the means and capacity to strengthen their ability to promote and nurture sustainable communities. The local boosterism of earlier years is now being nudged aside by the polycentric, municipal networking that has facilitated collaborative governance efforts in various political arenas, from the local to the global (Bradford and Bramwell 2014, 14). Alternative governing bodies – watershed groups, biosphere reserves, community forests, and climate change organizations – are examples of multi-scale governance initiatives based on sustaining social-ecological systems (see Chapter 8).

These partnerships and networks, supported by influential communities of interest, help to strengthen the political authority of municipalities. Global events extend into the heart of municipalities. Climate change is a case in point. To address the multifaceted aspects of climate change and its cascading effects, cities are collaborating in global municipal forums such as ICLEI – Local Governments for Sustainability and C40 Cities. These and other international organizations are embracing sustainability initiatives such as the United Nations Sustainable Development Goals (SDGs), the Paris Agreement on climate change, the *New Urban Agenda,* and *Right to the City* (see Chapter 9).

Governments can also foster sustainability through the use of information and communications technologies (ICTs). Political communications and their means of transmission – both message and medium – have always been a key consideration in questions of effective governance. This has certainly been the case throughout the political history of Canada, where the availability and accessibility of evidence-based information has long been considered critical to good political decision making. Certainly, it is required when making decisions about how to address the public needs and preferences in a municipality. Reliable data are required for a multitude of local decision-making processes, such as quantifying and managing energy or material flows in the urban metabolism, assessing where and how to build infrastructure, to provide social services, and to support livelihoods, and assessing how to sustain valued biophysical systems. But data are value-laden, with specific variables being chosen by those who have their own sets of biases and constraints. In an era of wicked problems, data have distinct implications for different groups of people who interact with each other and within social-ecological systems at different times and in various places. Information is perceived and interpreted differently by diverse communities of interest. As the old saying goes, "information is power," and it has been wielded in ways that benefit certain groups of people over others. It can be used to set up surveillance systems and to exploit private information, raising concerns about social control and privacy. It can also be employed to enhance democratic discourse in the pursuit of solutions to seemingly intractable problems. There are ample examples of both scenarios. Ideally, government communications and the technologies that support them will be used to build inclusive democratic communities, open-data sharing hubs, social learning communities, and networks of knowledge. Unfortunately, they have also deepened and extended existing inequalities. They are the tools in the hands of those with the capacity and power to wield them (see Chapter 10).

The inexorable incursion of privatization initiatives into what were once public spaces raises serious questions about the loss of public gathering places, a sense of belonging and place, civic engagement, and local democracy. Development-friendly governments operating within short-term electoral cycles pay short shrift to the implications. From a biophysical perspective, the colonization of ecosystems and the spread of development into rural and wilderness areas have led to a loss of species diversity – despite the spectre of collapsing vital ecosystems that have been pushed beyond sustainable thresholds. Development has also spread into what was once arable land. Agro-industrial growth has caused the demise of many family farms and farming communities, adversely affecting local economies. Given these concerns, many local governments across Canada are re-evaluating how they value and manage natural assets because they have recognized that sustaining ecological goods and services is a prerequisite for a healthy economy and society. Local food movements have encouraged governments to establish food councils in order to make policies that support local foodscapes and food security in the form of urban permaculture, community gardens, food forests, and circular food economies. In the quest for sustainable landscapes, many municipalities are exploring how best to support biodiversity and to create sustainable alternatives to grey infrastructure. The degree to which they go from exploring these concerns to developing meaningful, inclusive policy processes and effective implementation depends a great deal on the political will and capacity in individual municipalities, which can vary tremendously (see Chapter 11).

Throughout history, cities have been built on the linear throughput of resources that are then converted into waste. Governments are now challenged to develop circular systems where waste is viewed as a resource. Before these systems can be developed, governments need data that assess and measure a city's metabolism (or the exchange of matter between an organism and its environment). With such information, it is possible to make more efficient use of resources and to design a circular economy that depends on a continuous circular flow of materials. One example is the circular food economy project underway in Guelph-Wellington, Ontario. Closed loops or circular designs are also being introduced in various infrastructure projects throughout the country. Smart grid, distributed, and alternative energy systems are all examples of efforts to reduce cities' global greenhouse gas (GHG) emissions, lower their carbon footprint, and reduce their dependency on fossil fuels. Water management approaches that emulate the natural water cycle might be used to improve water quality. The design and implementation of circular, distributed systems also require public participation and education. Moreover, these policy strategies include the demand-side management of resource use, as opposed to the conventional supply-side management of infrastructure provision. Urban transportation systems across the country are still primarily oriented toward facilitating mobility. That said, governments have begun to invest more heavily in infrastructure that encourages multi-modal transportation in order to expand the use of transit services and the use of active forms of transportation. The provision of broadband has become an essential part of urban infrastructure, not just for social, health and safety, and commercial purposes but also because it facilitates the measurement of systems efficiencies and the reduction of waste.

Metabolic or ecological concepts of the city encompass a holistic framing of planning and design, replacing the reductionist planning and provision of discrete services. For example, rather than simply focusing on developing new and innovative forms of infrastructure to enable mobility, demand can be managed through urban design, public education, and ICTs. The COVID-19 pandemic made it abundantly clear that a vast portion of the population does not need to commute into city centres to be productive workers. Flexible, adaptable systems are more aligned with the requirements of managing human interactions with complex systems.

Cities can aspire to reach beyond the role of limiting ecological damage. The focus can shift to net-positive outcomes in building and design. Regenerative design and development are social-ecological, systems-based concepts that emphasize the importance of local collaboration throughout a project. Such designs build the "regenerative, self-renewing" capabilities of the development in question (J. Robinson and Cole 2015, 4). Advancing the concept further, John Robinson and Raymond J. Cole advocate the adoption of "regenerative sustainability" (6). This approach emphasizes the importance of the decision-making process and recognizes that sustainability is a contested concept and that there is no single correct way to pursue a net-positive environment. Collaboration and negotiation about which social-ecological systems are to be sustained, and how, constitute key elements in any local governing strategy that strives toward sustainability (see Chapter 12).

Healthy communities are also socially just, equitable communities. As the COVID-19 pandemic so brutally drove home, dominant economic and political paradigms and the policies that they inform are not up to the task of redressing deep fissures in Canadian communities characterized by growing economic, social, and political polarization. Because of spatial and other forms of social injustice, large segments of the population have been subjected to underserved and degraded living environments. People residing in these unhealthy areas frequently suffer from poverty, overt and systemic racism, poor outcomes in both morbidity and mortality, limited access to services, a lack of spaces conducive to feelings of personal safety, and societal exclusion. The primary determinants of health – income, education, employment, working and living conditions, food, housing and security, and access to health and social services – all fall under the rubric of local public health and are experienced locally. Yet the vast proportion of health funding is allocated based on a medical model that treats symptoms, not the root causes of poor health. Well over half a century ago, in 1948, the World Health Organization (n.d.-a) called this medical approach into question: "Health is a state of complete physical, mental and social well-being and not merely the absence of disease." Provincial governments maintain control over the health system, seriously underfunding local public health. These short-sighted policies contribute to societal stratification, degraded living environments, poverty, alienation, and an intergenerational loss of community and individual well-being – interlinked problems that can generate health crises that in turn lead to reactive, expensive government expenditures.

New approaches to public health that are more integrative and holistic have emerged. Similar to related efforts, New Public Health (NPH) is a multilevel, multi-sectoral, inclusive, diverse, and collaborative approach that networks with other organizations that affect the health of a community. The Alberni Clayoquot Health Network is one example. A complementary model is eco-health, which promotes health and well-being in the context of social-ecological interactions (Waltner-Toews 2004).

Well-being and health are also related to personal safety and a sense of belonging. Although Canada is a wealthy nation, many people suffer from precarious housing and living conditions, societal and institutional discrimination, racism, and abuse. These underserved members of society also experience harmful interventions by police and other government services. Marginalized people may be unable to participate fully in community life, to enjoy the benefits that it offers, and to experience a sense of belonging, all of which are factors that affect their health and well-being. This spatial injustice might be addressed by the meaningful adoption of the UN-recognized principle of a "right to the city." Local governments can choose from many tools, such as universal city design and policies focused on mobility and accessibility, when engaging in inclusive, collaborative decision making (see Chapter 13).

Conventionally, material wealth has been used as the primary indicator of good and successful governance. A broader set of indicators, one that considers ecological, social, and economic well-being, offers a more meaningful reflection of the health of a community. One example is the Canadian Index of Wellbeing. This understanding of well-being can be further expanded if natural and social assets and capabilities are factored into local decision-making models designed to foster sustainable outcomes. Advocates of degrowth and diverse economies note that a range of alternative economic activities at the local level are not captured by conventional economic metrics. Government recognition of the contributions of natural and social assets and acknowledgment of the benefits of diverse forms of economic activity can generate opportunities for local innovation. Relocalization movements advocate transitions to a post-carbon economy, sustainable consumption, closed-loop design, local food production, local economic development, and smart grid, distributed, and alternative energy systems. Fostering a sense of community through festivals and civic gatherings is an important component of these movements. To a greater or lesser degree, most local governments endorse and promote aspects of these efforts (see Chapter 14).

At the heart of transitions to sustainable communities are local governments that embrace social systems of learning. Good governance and openness to new approaches and ideas are critical to solving social-ecological problems. To achieve this outcome, local decision makers need to participate in reflexive processes that enable them "to function as deliberate, self-critical agents of change in social-ecological systems" (Dryzek and Pickering 2017, 353). Engaging in transformative learning processes can facilitate the kinds of policy innovations and urban experiments needed to address complex, wicked problems. Knowledge sharing among diverse members of the community who possess different types of knowledge and ways of thinking is an important element of the process. In these environments, the function of local administrators may shift from recommending and making decisions based on their own expertise to facilitating the transfer of knowledge between diverse constituencies (Reed and Abernethy 2018). Expert navigation and bridge building are required given the challenges in achieving agreement among participants who hold different world views and opinions about the best way forward. Municipalities can learn from each other by participating in communities of practice that share data, experiences, and public policies.

It is important to include members of the public as a means to stimulate local innovation and a healthy, active, civil society. If people participate in open, inclusive, public processes, they also experience political and personal efficacy and are more likely to view as legitimate the decisions made by government. Communities, not just their institutions, need to become places of social learning. Local governments can create places of community learning and knowledge sharing. Libraries are no longer just about reading but also offer programs and activities that bring communities together. In addition to libraries, the places where people might congregate, share, and co-create include public parks, woodlots, gardens, museums, squares, and recreational areas.

With the encroachment of private development on spaces that were once held in common, local governments need to think creatively about liminal (transitional) spaces, turning them into valued places for sharing and learning. Built spaces, alleys, deserted areas, and unused lots can be repurposed as community places. Liminality can also be used to foster a mutual understanding and sense of community by opening up new political spaces that bring together groups of people who normally would not cross paths in their daily lives.

Adopting new forms of governance and opening up more political spaces are two ways to create new pathways in a community's nervous system. Transitioning to sustainability requires a measure of neuroplasticity in our governing systems so that they can form flexible and adaptive pathways when the old well-trodden ones fail or lead to destructive behaviour. At the core of governing for sustainability is the ability of local governments, organizations, and members of the public to become self-organizing communities of learning.

WICKED OPPORTUNITIES

> *What if we were to accept that the goal of theory is not to extend knowledge by confirming what we already know, that the world is a place of domination and oppression? What if we asked theory instead to help us see openings, to provide a space of freedom and possibility? As a means of getting theory to yield something new.*
>
> – Gibson-Graham 2008, 619

We live in a time of unprecedented uncertainty. Climate change, societal injustice, unsustainable economies, political upheavals, and other existential threats have revealed the limitations of entrenched institutional and policy responses. Tremendous resources can be made available when there is the political will to do so – as illustrated in the cases of the COVID-19 pandemic and the 2008 financial crisis. In large part, however, these resources have yet to be directed in ways that support social-ecologically sustainable communities. But there is a robust literature that offers possible ways forward and many policy innovations that show promise, a number of which have been discussed in this book. In the words of Warren Magnusson (2009, 116),

> The political is in another world, a world of action and human possibility, a world of imagination and desire, a world that articulates what we are striving to be or to remain in the face of another world that is already imposed on us ... What we need (now especially) is the impermissible possibilities of the present – the ones that are out of scale with the particular version of modernity that has become dominant – [the possibilities that] *can* be nurtured, *can* be acted out, and not irrationally.

Uncertainty can be viewed as opportunity. When conventional governing responses are widely perceived to be inadequate, liminal spaces can open up political spaces for experimentation. Crises can bring out the worst and the best in people and their political representatives. Wicked, complex problems dominate many policy agendas today. They require new transdisciplinary approaches, context-specific experiments, and inclusive problem-solving approaches.

The ability of communities to sustain themselves can be adversely affected by major disruptions to daily community life, which might come in the form of natural disasters, major technological innovations, civil unrest and protests, or pandemics. These disruptions threaten stability, undermining the ability of local governments to deliver services and programs. But they also open up political spaces to address problems that were festering well before the disruptions. The COVID-19 pandemic revealed all the fault lines in the global political-economic system, as the most defenceless members of society were overwhelmingly and disproportionately impacted by the deadly disease. It is worth repeating the popular truism that a main indicator of society's overall health and well-being is how well it takes care of its most vulnerable. In Canada, during the pandemic, there were widespread calls for government action to redress policy neglect in areas such as long-term care, public safety, affordable housing, social justice, and environmental degradation. Sustainability scientists are now considering "just transformations to sustainability" in order to tackle entrenched, structural forms of inequality (N.J. Bennett et al. 2019). Long-term sustainability is not possible without attention to social justice.

Ultimately, if cities are to progress toward sustainability, they need to become communities of social learning and practice in order to respond effectively to dynamic environments. Doing so can help cities to build resiliency so that they are in a better position to respond to and recover from shocks that arrive in the form of natural or human-made catastrophes or other adverse events. Resilient communities require local systems of governance that are capable of learning, adapting, collaborating, and making decisions that promote healthy communities – both socially and ecologically. A tall order. Nevertheless, it is the only way forward.

As we move through the twenty-first century, transitions to a just, sustainable future will depend on our societal ability to learn how to embrace new approaches and practices. This book discusses some fairly sophisticated efforts to put into place the political and societal changes that are needed in local governments and communities. Many of these initiatives rely on advanced technological systems operating across temporal and spatial scales and jurisdictional boundaries. None of these changes, however, will be realized without the political will and capacity to ensure the implementation of the enabling structures and policies – ones supported by an ethos that promotes tolerant and inclusive social learning communities. In the words of Canadian scientist, social activist, and peace advocate Ursula M. Franklin,

However fancy our systems of transmitting, collecting, and manipulating knowledge may become, [their] roots are human. It's people – it's their hearts, their hands, and their minds – that together produce the knowledge the world needs for its betterment, and in the end whatever we do has to be caring and respectful of all people in all places. (Franklin and Freeman 2014, 132)

References

Abernethy, P. 2014. "Bridging Theories, Concepts, Organisations, and Collective Knowledge for Health and Sustainability Integration." PhD diss., University of Waterloo. https://uwspace.uwaterloo.ca/handle/10012/8955.

–. 2016. "Bridging Conceptual 'Silos': Bringing Together Health Promotion and Sustainability Governance for Practitioners at the Landscape Scale." *Local Environment* 21 (4): 451–75.

Aboriginal Justice Implementation Commission. 1999. *Report of the Aboriginal Justice Inquiry of Manitoba.* http://www.ajic.mb.ca/reports/final_toc.html.

Abson, D.J., J. Fischer, J. Leventon, J. Newig, T. Schomerus, U. Vilsmaier, H. von Wehrden, P. Abernethy, C.D. Ives, N.W. Jager, and D.J. Lang. 2017. "Leverage Points for Sustainability Transformation." *Ambio* 46 (1): 30–39.

African Nova Scotian Road to Economic Prosperity Advisory Committee. 2020. *Road to Economic Prosperity for African Nova Scotian Communities: Summary Report and Action Plan.* Halifax: African Nova Scotian (ANS) with Halifax Regional Municipality and Halifax Partnership. https://halifaxpartnership.com/sites/default/uploads/ANS-Road-to-Economic-Prosperity-Action-Plan-Report.pdf.

Agriculture and Agri-Food Canada. 2019. *Food Policy for Canada: Everyone at the Table.* https://agriculture.canada.ca/sites/default/files/legacy/pack/pdf/fpc_20190614-en.pdf.

Alberni Clayoquot Health Network. n.d. "How We Work." https://achn.ca/about-achn/how-we-work/.

Albrecht, G.A. 2019. "Solastalgia: The Homesickness You Have at Home." In *Earth Emotions: New Words for a New World*, 27–61. Ithaca, NY: Cornell University Press.

Alcantara, C., and J. Nelles. 2016. *A Quiet Evolution: The Emergence of Indigenous-Local Intergovernmental Partnerships in Canada.* Toronto: University of Toronto Press.

Anderson, E. 2013. *Municipal "Best Practices": Preventing Fraud, Bribery and Corruption.* Vancouver: International Centre for Criminal Law Reform and Criminal Justice Policy. https://icclr.org/wp-content/uploads/2019/06/Municipal-Best-Practices-Preventing-Fraud-Bribery-and-Corruption-FINAL.pdf.

Andrew, C. 1997. "Globalization and Local Action." In *The Politics of the City: A Canadian Perspective,* ed. T.L. Thomas, 139–50. Scarborough, ON: ITP Nelson.

Ansell, C., and J. Torfing. 2015. "Introduction: How Does Collaborative Governance Scale?" *Policy and Politics* 43 (3): 315–29. https://bristoluniversitypressdigital.com/view/journals/pp/43/3/article-p315.xml.

Appavoo, D. 2014. "Recognizing the Role of Gender and Food Security in Type 2 Diabetes Nutrition Education in Rural Southwestern Ontario." PhD diss., University of Waterloo. http://hdl.handle.net/10012/8348.

Argyris, C., and D.A. Schön. 1974. *Theory in Practice: Increasing Professional Effectiveness.* San Francisco: Jossey-Bass.

Armitage, D., F. Berkes, and N. Doubleday, eds. 2007. *Adaptive Co-management: Collaboration, Learning, and Multi-level Governance.* Vancouver: UBC Press.

Armitage, D., A. Charles, and F. Berkes, eds. 2017. *Governing the Coastal Commons: Communities, Resilience and Transformation.* London: Routledge.

Armstrong Strategy Group and Unlock Democracy Canada. 2021. *Ontario 2021: Municipal Democracy Index.* https://assets.website-files.com/5afc355b1a0e8d3a1105b120/6166e42d8de59764697466a0_MDI%202021.pdf.

Artibise, A.F.J., and G.A. Stelter. 1995. "Conservation Planning and Urban Planning: The Canadian Commission of Conservation in Historical Perspective." In *Consuming Canada: Readings in Environmental History,* ed. C. Gaffield and P. Gaffield, 152–69. Toronto: Copp Clark Pitman.

Arya, A.N., J. Howard, S. Isaacs, M.L. McAllister, S. Murphy, D. Rapport, and D. Waltner-Toews. 2009. "Time for an Ecosystem Approach to Public Health? Lessons from Two

Infectious Disease Outbreaks in Canada." *Global Public Health* 4 (1): 31–49.

Arya, A.N., and T. Piggott, eds. 2018. *Under-Served: Health Determinants of Indigenous, Inner-City, and Migrant Populations in Canada.* Toronto: Canadian Scholars.

Assembly of First Nations. n.d. "A Declaration of First Nations." In Government of Alberta, *Walking Together: First Nations, Métis and Inuit Perspectives in Curriculum,* 1. https://www.learnalberta.ca/content/aswt/aboriginal_and_treaty_rights/documents/declaration_first_nations.pdf.

Asset Management BC. n.d. *Asset Management BC Strategic Plan (2018–2021).* https://www.assetmanagementbc.ca/wp-content/uploads/Asset-Management-BC-Strategic-Plan.pdf.

Asset-Based Community Development Institute. n.d. "History." https://resources.depaul.edu/abcd-institute/about/Pages/History.aspx.

Association of Municipalities Ontario. 2022. *AMO Submission on Bill 23, More Homes Built Faster Act, 2022 and Plan.* November 16. https://www.amo.on.ca/sites/default/files/assets/DOCUMENTS/Submissions/SC_HICP-LTR_AP_AMO_Submission_Bill%2023_More_Homes_Built_Faster_Act_20221116.pdf.

August, M., and G. Tolfo. 2018. "Inclusionary Zoning: Six Insights from International Experience." *Plan Canada* 58 (4): 6–11. https://viurrspace.ca/handle/10613/23108.

Bai, X., T. Elmqvist, N. Frantzeskaki, T. McPhearson, D. Simon, D. Maddox, M. Watkins, P. Romero-Lankao, S. Parnell, C. Griffith, and D. Roberts. 2018. "New Integrated Urban Knowledge for the Cities We Want." In *Urban Planet: Knowledge towards Sustainable Cities,* ed. T. Elmqvist, X. Bai, N. Frantzeskaki, C. Griffith, D. Maddox, T. McPhearson, S. Parnell, P. Romero-Lankao, D. Simon, and M. Watkins, 462–82. Cambridge: Cambridge University Press.

Bannerman, S., and A. Orasch. 2020. "Privacy and Smart Cities: A Canadian Survey." *Canadian Journal of Urban Research* 29 (1): 17–38.

Barney, D. 2000. *Prometheus Wired: The Hope for Democracy in the Age of Network Technology.* Chicago: University of Chicago Press.

Baugh Littlejohns, L., and N. Smith. 2014. "Building Bridges between Health Promotion and Social Sustainability: An Analysis of Municipal Policies in Western Canada." *Local Environment* 19 (4): 449–68.

Baumgartner, F.R., C. Breunig, C. Green-Pedersen, B.D. Jones, P.B. Mortensen, M. Nuytemans, and S. Walgrave. 2009. "Punctuated Equilibrium in Comparative Perspective." *American Journal of Political Science* 53 (3): 603–20.

Beattie, S. 2018. "Ford's Council-Slashing Plan Criticized from Coast to Coast." *Toronto Star,* September 3. https://www.thestar.com/news/municipal-elections/ford-s-council-slashing-plan-criticized-from-coast-to-coast/article_dd573c1b-83b0-54df-99ed-ce067214a47d.html.

Beattie, S., and D. Rider. 2018. "With Clarity from Court, Toronto Councillors Turn Attention to 25-Ward Election." *Toronto Star,* September 19. https://www.thestar.com/news/municipal-elections/with-clarity-from-court-toronto-councillors-turn-attention-to-25-ward-election/article_26c8143a-fa2f-535f-8f1b-1cae530dc9de.html.

Bendell, J. 2018. *Deep Adaptation: A Map for Navigating Climate Tragedy.* Ambleside, UK: Institute for Leadership and Sustainability (IFLAS), University of Cumbria. https://insight.cumbria.ac.uk/id/eprint/4166/.

Bennett, E.M., P. Morrison, J.M. Holzer, K.J. Winkler, E.D.G. Fraser, S.J. Green, B.E. Robinson, K. Sherren, J. Botzas-Coluni, and W. Palen. 2021. "Facing the Challenges of Using Place-Based Social-Ecological Research to Support Ecosystem Service Governance at Multiple Scales." *Ecosystems and People* 17 (1): 574–89.

Bennett, N.J., J. Blythe, A.M. Cisneros-Montemayor, G.G. Singh, and U.R. Sumaila. 2019. "Just Transformations to Sustainability." *Sustainability* 11 (14), art. 3881. https://www.mdpi.com/2071-1050/11/14/3881.

Berkes, F. 2009. "Evolution of Co-management: Role of Knowledge Generation, Bridging Organizations and Social Learning." *Journal of Environmental Management* 90 (5): 1692–702.

–. 2017. "Environmental Governance for the Anthropocene? Social-Ecological Systems, Resilience, and Collaborative Learning." *Sustainability* 9 (7), art. 1232. https://www.mdpi.com/2071-1050/9/7/1232.

Bierman, A., S. Schieman, and P. Glavin. 2019. "Workers in the Gig Economy Feel Lonely and Powerless." *The Conversation,* November 20. https://theconversation.com/workers-in-the-gig-economy-feel-lonely-and-powerless-127188?%202021.

Bill, J. 2020. "What Was So Special about Viking Ships?" *TED-Ed,* January 21. https://ed.ted.com/lessons/what-was-so-special-about-viking-ships-jan-bill.

Bingham, R. 2013. "Viola Desmond." *The Canadian Encyclopedia,* January 13. https://www.thecanadianencyclopedia.ca/en/article/viola-desmond.

Bird, K., S.D. Jackson, R.M. McGregor, A.A. Moore, and L.B. Stephenson. 2016. "Sex (and Ethnicity) in the City: Affinity Voting in the 2014 Toronto Mayoral Election." *Canadian Journal of Political Science* 49 (2): 359–83.

Black, E.R. 1975. *Divided Loyalties: Canadian Concepts of Federalism.* Montreal/Kingston: McGill-Queen's University Press.

–. 1982. *Politics and the News: The Political Functions of the Mass Media.* Toronto: Butterworths.

Blackmore, C., ed. 2010. *Social Learning Systems and Communities of Practice*. London: Springer.

Blais, P. 2010. *Perverse Cities: Hidden Subsidies, Wonky Policy, and Urban Sprawl*. Vancouver: UBC Press.

Blakely, E.J., and R.J. Milano. 2001. "Community Economic Development." In *International Encyclopedia of the Social and Behavioral Sciences*, ed. N.J. Smelser and P.B. Baltes, 2346–51. Oxford: Pergamon.

Blank, Y. 2010. "Federalism, Subsidiarity, and the Role of Local Governments in an Age of Global Multilevel Governance." *Fordham Urban Law Journal* 37 (2): 509–58.

Blay-Palmer, A., G. Santini, M. Dubbeling, H. Renting, M. Taguchi, and T. Giordano. 2018. "Validating the City Region Food System Approach: Enacting Inclusive, Transformational City Region Food Systems." *Sustainability* 10 (5), art. 1680. https://www.mdpi.com/2071-1050/10/5/1680.

Bloomfield, E. 1987. "Building Industrial Communities: Berlin and Waterloo to 1915." In *Manufacturing in Kitchener-Waterloo: A Long-Term Perspective*, ed. D.F. Walker, 5–34. Waterloo: Department of Geography, University of Waterloo.

Blythe, J., J. Silver, L. Evans, D. Armitage, N.J. Bennett, M.-L. Moore, T.H. Morrison, and K. Brown. 2018. "The Dark Side of Transformation: Latent Risks in Contemporary Sustainability Discourse." *Antipode* 50 (5): 1206–23.

Bradford, N. 2016. "Ideas and Collaborative Governance: A Discursive Localism Approach." *Urban Affairs Review* 52 (5): 659–84.

–. 2018. *A National Urban Policy for Canada? The Implicit Federal Agenda*. Montreal: Institute for Research on Public Policy. https://irpp.org/wp-content/uploads/2018/11/A-National-Urban-Policy-for-Canada-The-Implicit-Federal-Agenda.pdf.

–. 2020. *Policy in Place: Revisiting Canada's Tri-level Agreements*. Toronto: Institute on Municipal Finance and Governance, Munk School of Global Affairs and Public Policy, University of Toronto. https://tspace.library.utoronto.ca/handle/1807/102474.

Bradford, N., and M. Baldwin. 2018. "New Forms of Civic Leadership." *Municipal World* 128 (10): 19–20, 44.

Bradford, N., and A. Bramwell. 2014. *Governing Urban Economies: Innovation and Inclusion in Canadian City-Regions*. Toronto: University of Toronto Press.

Brandes, O.M., and D.B. Brooks. 2007. *The Soft Water Path in a Nutshell*. Ottawa/Victoria: Friends of the Earth Canada/POLIS Project on Ecological Governance, University of Victoria. https://poliswaterproject.org/polis-research-publication/soft-path-water-nutshell/.

Breux, S., J. Couture, and R. Koop. 2019. "Influences on the Number and Gender of Candidates in Canadian Local Elections." *Canadian Journal of Political Science* 52 (1): 163–81.

Bristow, D.N., and E.A. Mohareb. 2020. "From the Urban Metabolism to the Urban Immune System." *Journal of Industrial Ecology* 24 (2): 300–12.

Brouillet, E. 2011. "Canadian Federalism and the Principle of Subsidiarity: Should We Open Pandora's Box?" *Supreme Court Law Review: Osgoode's Annual Constitutional Cases Conference* 54 (1): 601–32. https://digitalcommons.osgoode.yorku.ca/sclr/vol54/iss1/21/.

Brown, H. 2018. "Infrastructural Ecology: Embedding Resilience in Public Works." *Public Works Management and Policy* 24 (1): 20–32.

Brown, J., and J. Newberry. 2015. *An Evaluation of the Connectivity Situation Tables in Waterloo Region*. Guelph, ON: Taylor Newberry Consulting. https://cfbsjs.usask.ca/documents/research/research_papers/AnEvaluationoftheConnectivitySituationTablesinWaterlooRegion.pdf.

Bulkeley, H., A. Luque-Ayala, C. McFarlane, and G. MacLeod. 2018. "Enhancing Urban Autonomy: Towards a New Political Project for Cities." *Urban Studies* 55 (4): 702–19.

Bullock, R., K. Jastremski, and M.G. Reed. 2017. "Canada's Model Forests 20 Years On: Towards Forest and Community Sustainability?" *Natural Resources Forum* 41 (3): 156–66.

Burch, S., S. Hughes, P. Romero-Lankao, and H. Schroeder. 2018. "Governing Urban Sustainability Transformations: The New Politics of Collaboration and Contestation." In *Urban Planet: Knowledge towards Sustainable Cities*, ed. T. Elmqvist, X. Bai, N. Frantzeskaki, C. Griffith, D. Maddox, T. McPherson, S. Parnell, P. Romero-Lankao, D. Simon, and M. Watkins, 303–26. Cambridge: Cambridge University Press.

Bush, E., B. Bonsal, C. Derksen, G. Flato, J. Fyfe, N. Gillett, B.J.W. Greenan, T.S. James, M. Kirchmeier-Young, L. Mudryk, and X. Zhang. 2022. *Canada's Changing Climate Report in Light of the Latest Global Science Assessment*. Ottawa: Government of Canada. https://changingclimate.ca/site/assets/uploads/sites/2/2022/03/CCCR-2022-Supplement-Final.pdf.

Bush, E., and D.S. Lemmen, eds. 2019. *Canada's Changing Climate Report*. Ottawa: Government of Canada. https://changingclimate.ca/CCCR2019/.

Business Development Bank of Canada. n.d. "3 Steps to Becoming a Certified B Corp." https://www.bdc.ca/en/articles-tools/business-strategy-planning/manage-business/3-steps-to-becoming-certified-b-corp.

C40 Cities. 2018. "One Year after Trump Decision to Withdraw from Paris Agreement, U.S. Cities Carry Climate Action Forward." Press release, June 1. https://www.c40.org/news/one-year-after-trump-decision-to-withdraw-from-paris-agreement-u-s-cities-carry-climate-action-forward/.

–. 2020. "Global Mayors Launch COVID-19 Economic Recovery Task Force." Press release, April 15. https://www.c40.org/news/global-mayors-covid-19-recovery-task-force/.

Calgary Public Library. n.d. "Mission and Vision." Accessed February 5, 2021. https://calgarylibrary.ca/about-the-library/mission-and-vision/.

Canadian Biosphere Reserve Association. n.d. "Frequently Asked Questions." https://www.biospherecanada.ca/faq.

Canadian Environmental Law Association. 2000. "Anti-pesticide By-law Challenged at Supreme Court." Media release, December 6. https://cela.ca/anti-pesticide-by-law-challenged-at-supreme-court/.

Canadian Index of Wellbeing. n.d. "Domains and Indicators." https://uwaterloo.ca/canadian-index-wellbeing/what-we-do/domains-and-indicators.

Canadian Institute of Planners. n.d. "Healthy Communities." https://www.cip-icu.ca/Issues/Healthy-Communities.

Canadian Mortgage and Housing Corporation (CMHC). 2017. "Canadians Get Affordable Housing Help." Press release, November 22. https://www.newswire.ca/news-releases/canadians-get-affordable-housing-help-659377843.html.

Canadian Museum for Human Rights. 2018. "One Woman's Resistance: Viola Desmond's Story." January 29. https://humanrights.ca/story/one-womans-resistance.

Canadian Press. 2023. "A Timeline of Key Events in Ontario's Greenbelt Controversy." *CBC News*, September 21, updated October 10. https://www.cbc.ca/news/canada/toronto/ont-greenbelt-timeline-1.6974715.

Canadian Public Health Association. 2019. "Public Health in the Context of Health System Renewal in Canada." May 21. https://www.cpha.ca/public-health-context-health-system-renewal-canada.

Carey, G., A. Kay, and A. Nevile. 2019. "Institutional Legacies and 'Sticky Layers': What Happens in Cases of Transformative Policy Change?" *Administration and Society* 51 (3): 491–509.

Cargnello, D.P., and M. Flumian. 2017. "Canadian Governance in Transition: Multilevel Governance in the Digital Era." *Canadian Public Administration* 60 (4): 605–26. https://onlinelibrary.wiley.com/doi/full/10.1111/capa.12230.

Carlisle, K., and R.L. Gruby. 2019. "Polycentric Systems of Governance: A Theoretical Model for the Commons." *Policy Studies Journal* 47 (4): 921–46.

Carney, M. 2020. "Reith Lectures 2020 – How We Get What We Value." *BBC Radio 4*, December 2–23. https://www.bbc.co.uk/programmes/articles/43GjCh72bxWVSqSB84ZDJw0/reith-lectures-2020-how-we-get-what-we-value.

Carvalho, G. 2018. *Climate Finance for Canadian Cities: Is Debt Financing a Viable Alternative?* Toronto: Institute on Municipal Finance and Governance, Munk School of Global Affairs and Public Policy, University of Toronto. https://tspace.library.utoronto.ca/handle/1807/82766.

Casier, L. 2019. "How Can Public Procurement in Canada's Trade Agreements Contribute to Sustainable Development?" International Institute for Sustainable Development, April 4. https://www.iisd.org/blog/sustainable-public-procurement-trade.

Cassidy, F., and R.L. Bish. 1989. *Indian Government: Its Meaning in Practice*. Lantzville, BC/Halifax: Oolichan Books/Institute for Research on Public Policy.

Castán Broto, V., G. Trencher, E. Iwaszuk, and L. Westman. 2019. "Transformative Capacity and Local Action for Urban Sustainability." *Ambio* 48 (5): 449–62.

Castells, M. 2016. "A Sociology of Power: My Intellectual Journey." *Annual Review of Sociology* 42 (1): 1–19.

Chapin, F.S., P.A. Matson, and P.M. Vitousek. 2011. *Principles of Terrestrial Ecosystem Ecology*. 2nd ed. New York: Springer.

Chicago Climate Charter. n.d. "North American Climate Summit." https://northamericanclimatesummit.splashthat.com/.

Chronéer, D., A. Ståhlbröst, and A. Habibipour. 2019. "Urban Living Labs: Towards an Integrated Understanding of Their Key Components." *Technology Innovation Management Review* 9 (3): 50–62. http://www.diva-portal.org/smash/get/diva2:1302420/FULLTEXT01.pdf.

Churchman, C. West. 1967. "Wicked Problems." *Management Science* 13 (4): B141–42.

Circular Cities and Regions Initiative. 2022. "Peer-to-Peer (P2P) Network." https://canadiancircularcities.ca/p2p-network/Pages/default.aspx.

Cisco. n.d. "What Is a Smart City?" https://www.cisco.com/c/en/us/solutions/industries/smart-connected-communities/what-is-a-smart-city.html.

Cities for Climate. 2015. "Paris City Hall Declaration: A Decisive Contribution to COP21." Presented at the Climate Summit for Local Leaders, Paris, France, December 4. https://www.uclg.org/sites/default/files/climate_summit_final_declaration.pdf.

Cities-IPCC. 2018. "Tackling the Challenges of Mitigation and Adaptation." Paper presented at the Cities and Climate Change Science Conference, Edmonton, March 5–7. https://citiesipcc.org/beyond/campaign/.

City of Boisbriand. n.d. "Commissions et comités." https://www.ville.boisbriand.qc.ca/vie-democratique/commissions-et-comites.

City of Edmonton. n.d.-a. "Change for Climate – Edmonton Declaration." https://www.edmonton.ca/city_government/environmental_stewardship/change-for-climate-edmonton-declaration.

–. n.d.-b. "Edmonton's Global Conservation Commitments and Partnerships." https://www.edmonton.ca/city_government/environmental_stewardship/edmontons-global-conservation-commitments.

–. n.d.-c. "Integrated Infrastructure Services." https://www.edmonton.ca/city_government/city_organization/integrated-infrastructure-services.

–. n.d.-d. "Welcome to Blatchford." Accessed December 3, 2020. https://www.edmonton.ca/projects_plans/blatchford.aspx.

City of Guelph and Wellington County. 2019. *Creating Canada's First Circular Food Economy.* https://guelph.ca/wp-content/uploads/Creating-Canadas-First-Circular-Food-Economy.pdf.

–. 2022. *Our Circular Future.* https://pub-guelph.escribemeetings.com/filestream.ashx?DocumentId=22317.

–. n.d. "Guelph-Wellington Civic Data Utility Project." https://datahub.foodfuture.ca/pages/data-utility-overview.

City of Kingston. 2010. *Sustainable Kingston Plan.* https://www.sustainablekingston.com/sustainable-kingston-plan.

City of Kitchener. 2019. *Kitchener, Changing for Good: Our Corporate Climate Action Plan for Sustainability.* https://www.kitchener.ca/en/resourcesGeneral/Documents/DSD_Kitcheners_Corporate_Climate_Action_Plan.pdf.

–. 2021. "2020 Sustainability Report." https://www.kitchener.ca/en/strategic-plans-and-projects/sustainability-report.aspx.

–. n.d. "Strategic Plan for the Environment." https://www.kitchener.ca/en/strategic-plans-and-projects/strategic-plan-for-the-environment.aspx.

City of Montreal. 2020. "Montréal Climate Plan: Objective Carbon-Neutral by 2050." December 15. https://montreal.ca/en/articles/montreal-climate-plan-objective-carbon-neutral-2050-7613.

–. 2022. *The Montreal Pledge.* https://portail-m4s.s3.montreal.ca/pdf/vdm_montreal-pledge_2022.pdf.

–. n.d.-a. "Direction générale adjointe – Qualité de vie." https://montreal.ca/en/departments/direction-generale-adjointe-qualite-de-vie.

–. n.d.-b. "Laboratoire de l'innovation urbaine de Montréal." https://montreal.ca/en/departments/laboratoire-de-linnovation-urbaine-de-montreal.

City of Prince Albert. n.d. "Boards and Committees." https://www.citypa.ca/en/city-hall/boards-and-committees.aspx.

City of Prince George. n.d. "Downtown Renewable Energy System." https://www.princegeorge.ca/community-culture/environment-sustainability/downtown-renewable-energy-system.

City of Saint John. 2022. "City of Saint John Service Alignment." https://www.saintjohn.ca/sites/default/files/2022-03/Service%20Alignment%20-%20English%20%281%29.pdf.

City of St. John's. n.d. "Engage! St. Johns." https://www.engagestjohns.ca/.

City of Stratford. 2019. "Intelligent Community." https://www.stratford.ca/en/do-business/intelligentcommunity.aspx.

–. n.d. "Advisory Committees and Local Boards." https://www.stratford.ca/en/inside-city-hall/advisorycommittees.aspx.

City of Summerside. n.d. "Electricity." https://www.summerside.ca/residents/electricity.

City of Toronto. 2019. *Toronto's First Resilience Strategy.* https://www.toronto.ca/ext/digital_comm/pdfs/resilience-office/toronto-resilience-strategy.pdf.

–. 2021. *TransformTO Net Zero Strategy.* https://www.toronto.ca/services-payments/water-environment/environmentally-friendly-city-initiatives/transformto/.

–. n.d. "Property Tax, Water & Solid Waste Relief Programs." https://www.toronto.ca/services-payments/property-taxes-utilities/property-tax/property-tax-rebates-and-relief-programs/property-tax-and-utility-relief-program/.

City of Vancouver. 2018. *Vancouver: A City for All People, Women's Equity Strategy 2018–2028.* https://vancouver.ca/people-programs/womens-equity-strategy.aspx.

–. n.d. "Separating Sewage from Rainwater." https://vancouver.ca/home-property-development/separating-sewage-from-rainwater.aspx.

CivicAction. n.d. "About Us." https://civicaction.ca/about-us/.

Clapp, J. 2012. *Food.* London: Polity.

Clayoquot Biosphere Trust. 2022. "Living Building Challenge." October 5. https://clayoquotbiosphere.org/initiatives/blog/2022-10-03/living-building-challenge.

–. n.d. "An Ecosystem of Possibility." https://clayoquotbiosphere.org/.

Climate Emergency Declaration Organization. 2023. "Climate Emergency Declarations in 2,346 Jurisdictions and Local Governments Cover 1 Billion Citizens." September 8. https://climateemergencydeclaration.org/climate-emergency-declarations-cover-15-million-citizens/.

ClimateActionWR. n.d. "Who Are We?" https://climateactionwr.ca/.

Colverson, S., and O. Perera. 2011. *Sustainable Development: Is There a Role for Public-Private Partnerships? A Summary of an IISD Preliminary Investigation.* Winnipeg: International Institute for Sustainable Development. https://www.iisd.org/publications/report/sustainable-development-there-role-public-private-partnerships-summary-iisd.

Community Foundations of Canada. n.d.-a. "Canada Healthy Communities Initiative." https://communityfoundations.ca/initiatives/canada-healthy-communities-initiative/.

–. n.d.-b. "Vital Signs." https://communityfoundations.ca/initiatives/vital-signs/.

Conservation Ontario. n.d.-a. "About Conservation Ontario." https://conservationontario.ca/about-us/conservation-ontario.

–. n.d.-b. "Integrated Watershed Management." https://conservationontario.ca/policy-priorities/integrated-watershed-management.

Constanza, R. 2010. "What Is Ecological Economics?" *Yale Insights,* May 11. https://insights.som.yale.edu/insights/what-is-ecological-economics.

Conteh, C. 2016. "Rethinking Accountability in Complex and Horizontal Network Delivery Systems." *Canadian Public Administration* 59 (2): 224–44.

Cooper, R. and V. Timmer. 2015. *Local Governments and the Sharing Economy.* Vancouver: One Earth. http://www.localgovsharingecon.com/uploads/2/1/3/3/21333498/localgovsharingecon_report_full_oct2015.pdf.

Coyne, A. 2017. "Bewitched and Bewildered by the Liberals' National Housing Strategy." *National Post,* November 24. https://nationalpost.com/opinion/andrew-coyne-bewitched-and-bewildered-by-the-liberals-national-housing-strategy.

Crawford, K.G. 1954. *Canadian Municipal Government.* Toronto: University of Toronto Press.

Critchley, B. 2017. "Ottawa Becomes First Municipality in Canada to Issue Green Bonds." *Financial Post,* November 3. https://financialpost.com/news/fp-street/ottawa-becomes-first-municipality-in-canada-to-issue-green-bonds.

Crombie, D.H., B. Hall, A. Eggleton, D. Miller, and J. Sewell. 2022. "'Strong Mayors' Act Undemocratic." *Toronto Star,* August 16. https://www.pressreader.com/canada/toronto-star/20220816/281745568173095.

Cunningham, H. 2012. "Gated Ecologies and Possible Urban Worlds." In *The Natural City: Re-envisioning the Built Environment,* ed. I. Leman Stefanovic and S.B. Scharper, 149–59. Toronto: University of Toronto Press.

Curato, N., D.M. Farrell, B. Geissel, K. Grönlund, P. Mockler, J.-B. Pilet, A. Renwick, J. Rose, M. Setälä, and J. Suiter. 2021. "Introduction." In *Deliberative Mini-publics: Core Design Features,* 1–16. Bristol, UK: Bristol University Press.

Currie, P.K., and J.K. Musango. 2017. "African Urbanization: Assimilating Urban Metabolism into Sustainability Discourse and Practice." *Journal of Industrial Ecology* 21 (5): 1262–76.

Dahl, R.A. 1961. *Who Governs? Democracy and Power in an American City.* New Haven, CT: Yale University Press.

Dale, A., W.T. Dushenko, and P. Robinson. 2012. *Urban Sustainability: Reconnecting Space and Place.* Toronto: University of Toronto Press.

Daly, H.E. 1996. *Beyond Growth: The Economics of Sustainable Development.* Boston: Beacon.

Davis, W. 2009. *The Wayfinders: Why Ancient Wisdom Matters in the Modern World.* Toronto: House of Anansi.

–. 2018. "Wade Davis: Light at the Edge of the World." *CBC Radio,* November 26. https://www.cbc.ca/radio/ideas/wade-davis-light-at-the-edge-of-the-world-1.4499962.

Davoudi, S., and J. Sturzaker. 2017. "Urban Form, Policy Packaging and Sustainable Urban Metabolism." *Resources, Conservation and Recycling* 120: 55–64.

DeMarco, J. 2001. "Overview of the Hudson Decision." Paper presented at the Federation of Canadian Municipalities' Big City Mayors' Caucus, Winnipeg, October 21.

Department of Finance Canada. 2017. "Government's Plan to Build a Strong Middle Class Receives Royal Assent." News release, June 22. https://www.canada.ca/en/department-finance/news/2017/06/government_s_plantobuildastrong middleclassreceivesroyalassent.html.

–. 2019. *Investing in the Middle Class: Budget 2019.* https://www.budget.canada.ca/2019/docs/plan/toc-tdm-en.html.

Diefenbach, T. 2019. "Why Michels' 'Iron Law of Oligarchy' Is Not an Iron Law – and How Democratic Organisations Can Stay 'Oligarchy-Free.'" *Organization Studies* 40 (4): 545–62.

Dijst, M., E. Worrell, L. Böcker, P. Brunner, S. Davoudi, S. Geertman, R. Harmsen, M. Helbich, A.A.M. Holtslag, M.-P. Kwan, B. Lenz, G. Lyons, P.L. Mokhtarian, P. Newman, A. Perrels, A.P. Ribeiro, J. Rosales Carreón, G. Thomson, D. Urge-Vorsatz, and M. Zeyringer. 2018. "Exploring Urban Metabolism – Towards an Interdisciplinary Perspective." *Resources, Conservation and Recycling* 132: 190–203. https://www.sciencedirect.com/science/article/pii/S0921344917302926.

Dillon Consulting, Metabolic B.V., and M. von Massow. 2021. *Our Food Future: Food and Food Waste Flow Study: Work Package 1.* Guelph: City of Guelph and County of Wellington. https://guelph.ca/wp-content/uploads/Food-and-Food-Waste-Flow-Study-Report-WP1.pdf.

Doberstein, B., J. Fitzgibbons, and C. Mitchell. 2019. "Protect, Accommodate, Retreat or Avoid (PARA): Canadian Community Options for Flood Disaster Risk Reduction and Flood Resilience." *Natural Hazards* 98: 31–50.

Doberstein, C. 2013. "Metagovernance of Urban Governance Networks in Canada: In Pursuit of Legitimacy and Accountability." *Canadian Public Administration* 56 (4): 584–609. https://www.researchgate.net/publication/259547918_Metagovernance_of_urban_governance_networks_in_Canada_In_pursuit_of_legitimacy_and_accountability.

–. 2016. "Designing Collaborative Governance Decision-Making in Search of a 'Collaborative Advantage.'" *Public Management Review* 18 (6): 819–41.

Docquir, P.F., and M.L. Stasi. 2020. "The Decline of Media Diversity – and How We Can Save It." Centre for International Governance Innovation, January 21. https://www.cigionline.org/articles/decline-media-diversity-and-how-we-can-save-it/.

Dryzek, J.S. 2005. *The Politics of the Earth: Environmental Discourses.* Oxford: Oxford University Press.

–. 2014. "Institutions for the Anthropocene: Governance in a Changing Earth System." *British Journal of Political Science* 46 (4): 937–56.

Dryzek, J.S., and J. Pickering. 2017. "Deliberation as a Catalyst for Reflexive Environmental Governance." *Ecological Economics* 131: 353–60.

Dunlap, R.E. 2016. "Foreword II." In *Social Ecology: Society-Nature Relations across Time and Space,* ed. H. Haberl, M. Fischer-Kowalski, F. Krausmann, and V. Winiwarter, ix–xiv. Cham, Switzerland: Springer.

Easton, D. 1953. *The Political System: An Inquiry into the State of Political Science.* New York: Alfred A. Knopf.

–. 1965. *A Systems Analysis of Political Life.* New York: John Wiley and Sons.

Edmonton Regional Learning Association. 2016. "What Is a Community of Practice?" https://www.communityofpractice.ca/background/what-is-a-community-of-practice/.

Eidelman, G. 2018. "Gabriel Eidelman on the Opportunities for a New Toronto City Council." Accessed January 22, 2019. https://publicpolicy.utoronto.ca/gabriel-eidelman-on-the-opportunities-for-a-new-toronto-city-council/.

Ekstrom, J.A., and O.R. Young. 2009. "Evaluating Functional Fit between a Set of Institutions and an Ecosystem." *Ecology and Society* 14 (2), art. 16. https://ecologyandsociety.org/vol14/iss2/art16/.

Ellen MacArthur Foundation. n.d. "The Butterfly Diagram: Visualising the Circular Economy." https://ellenmacarthurfoundation.org/circular-economy-diagram.

Elmqvist, T., J. Siri, E. Andersson, P. Anderson, X. Bai, P.K. Das, T. Gatere, A. Gonzalez, J. Goodness, S.N. Handel, E. Hermansson Török, J. Kavonic, J. Kronenberg, E. Lindgren, D. Maddox, R. Maher, C. Mbow, T. McPhearson, J. Mulligan, G. Nordenson, M. Spires, U. Stenkula, K. Takeuchi, and C. Vogel. 2018. "Urban Tinkering." *Sustainability Science* 13 (6): 1549–64. https://link.springer.com/article/10.1007/s11625-018-0611-0.

Employment and Social Development Canada. 2018. *Opportunity for All: Canada's First Poverty Reduction Strategy.* https://www.canada.ca/en/employment-social-development/programs/poverty-reduction/reports/strategy.html.

Endangered Language Alliance Toronto. n.d. "Toronto's Languages." https://elalliance.com/toronto-languages/.

Environment and Climate Change Canada. 2022a. "Canada's National Adaptation Strategy Will Protect Communities and Build a Strong Economy." News release, November 24. https://www.canada.ca/en/environment-climate-change/news/2022/11/canadas-national-adaptation-strategy-will-protect-communities-and-build-a-strong-economy.html.

Environment and Climate Change Canada. 2022b. *2030 Emissions Reduction Plan – Canada's Next Steps for Clean Air and a Strong Economy.* https://www.canada.ca/en/environment-climate-change/news/2022/03/2030-emissions-reduction-plan--canadas-next-steps-for-clean-air-and-a-strong-economy.html.

–. 2023. "Plastic Waste and Pollution Reduction." https://www.canada.ca/en/environment-climate-change/services/managing-reducing-waste/reduce-plastic-waste.html.

Environmental Sustainability Research Centre. n.d. "Niagara Adapts." https://brocku.ca/esrc/niagara-adapts/.

European Commission. 2011. *Communication from the Commission to the European Parliament, the Council, the European Economic and Social Committee and the Committee of the Regions Roadmap to a Resource Efficient Europe.* COM(2011)571. Brussels: European Commission. [Cited in Tisserant et al. 2017.]

Evans, B., M. Joas, S. Sundback, and K. Theobald. 2006. "Governing Local Sustainability." *Journal of Environmental Planning and Management* 49 (6): 849–67.

Federation of Canadian Municipalities. 2018a. "Case Study: Switch to Biomass Cuts Costs and GHG Emissions in Yellowknife." https://greenmunicipalfund.ca/case-studies/case-study-switch-biomass-cuts-costs-and-ghg-emissions-yellowknife.

–. 2018b. "Community-Backed Waste Project Supports Terrace, BC, Economy." https://fcm.ca/en/resources/gmf/case-study-community-backed-waste-project-supports-terrace-bc-economy.

–. 2018c. "Sustainable Communities Awards 2018: Honouring Innovative Environmental Initiatives in Canadian Municipalities." News release, February 1. https://fcm.ca/en/news-media/news-release/gmf/sustainable-communities-awards-2018.

–. 2019. *A Year of Bold Investments: Green Municipal Fund, 2018–2019 Annual Report.* https://fcm.ca/en/news-media/gmf/investments-fcm-green-municipal-fund.

–. 2021. "Municipalities Welcome Key Step toward a Community-Rooted Recovery." News release, March 25. https://

fcm.ca/en/news-media/news-release/municipalities
-welcome-key-step-toward-community-rooted-recovery.

–. n.d.-a. "About FCM." https://fcm.ca/en/about-fcm.

–. n.d.-b. "Global Covenant of Mayors in Canada." https://
fcm.ca/en/programs/partners-climate-protection/global
-covenant-mayors-in-canada.

Feindt, P.H., and S. Weiland. 2018. "Reflexive Governance:
Exploring the Concept and Assessing Its Critical Potential
for Sustainable Development: Introduction to the Special
Issue." *Journal of Environmental Policy and Planning* 20 (6):
661–74.

Fernando, J. 2022. "What Is Broadband High-Speed Internet,
and How Does It Work?" *Investopedia*, December 31. https://
www.investopedia.com/terms/b/broadband.asp.

Fischer, F. 2004. "Professional Expertise in a Deliberative
Democracy." *Good Society* 13 (1): 21–27.

–. 2006. "Participatory Governance as Deliberative Empowerment: The Cultural Politics of Discursive Space." *American
Review of Public Administration* 36 (1): 19–40.

Fisher, R. 2020. "The Subtle Ways That 'Clicktivism' Shapes the
World." *BBC Future*, September 15. https://www.bbc.com/
future/article/20200915-the-subtle-ways-that-clicktivism
-shapes-the-world.

Fischer-Kowalski, M., and K.-H. Erb. 2016. "Core Concepts
and Heuristics." In *Social Ecology: Society-Nature Relations
across Time and Space*, ed. H. Haberl, M. Fischer-Kowalski,
F. Krausmann, and V. Winiwarter, 29–62. Cham, Switzerland:
Springer.

Flood, R.L., and N.R.A. Romm. 1996. "Plurality Revisited:
Diversity Management and Triple Loop Learning." *Systems
Practice* 9 (6): 587–603.

–. 2018. "A Systemic Approach to Processes of Power in Learning Organizations: Part I – Literature, Theory, and Methodol-
ogy of Triple Loop Learning." *Learning Organization* 25 (4):
260–72.

Flynn, A., and Z. Spicer. 2017. *Re-imagining Community
Councils in Canadian Local Government.* Toronto: Institute
on Municipal Finance and Governance, Munk School of
Global Affairs and Public Policy, University of Toronto.
https://tspace.library.utoronto.ca/handle/1807/80452.

Food and Agriculture Organization of the United Nations.
2008. *An Introduction to the Basic Concepts of Food Security.*
http://www.fao.org/3/a-al936e.pdf.

Food Secure Canada. 2013. "What Is Food Sovereignty." August
14. https://foodsecurecanada.org/2013/08/14/what-is-food
-sovereignty/.

–. 2019. "A Food Policy for Canada, 'Everyone at the Table' –
An Important First Step." Press release, June 17. https://
www2.foodsecurecanada.org/pressrelease-national-food
-policy-launch.

–. n.d. "What We Do." https://www2.foodsecurecanada.org/
who-we-are/what-we-do.

Forkey, N.S. 2012. *Canadians and the Natural Environment
to the Twenty-First Century.* Toronto: University of Toronto
Press.

The Forks. n.d. "The Forks." https://www.theforks.com/about/
the-forks.

Foster, L. 2020. "What Is the Black Canadian Experience?"
Toronto Star, February 26. https://www.thestar.com/opinion/
contributors/what-is-the-black-canadian-experience/
article_a00969ab-f2f8-5e9a-8bb5-81ec68fdb534.html.

Found, A. 2021. *Development Charges and Housing Affordability: A False Dichotomy?* Toronto: Institute on Municipal
Finance and Governance, Munk School of Global Affairs
and Public Policy, University of Toronto. https://tspace.
library.utoronto.ca/handle/1807/108068.

Francis, G. 2016. *Striving for Environmental Sustainability
in a Complex World: Canadian Experiences.* Vancouver: UBC
Press.

Franklin, U.M. 2006. *The Ursula Franklin Reader: Pacifism as
a Map.* Toronto: Between the Lines.

Franklin, U.M., with S.J. Freeman. 2014. *Ursula Franklin
Speaks: Thoughts and Afterthoughts, 1986–2012.* Montreal/
Kingston: McGill-Queen's University Press.

Fraňková, E., W. Haas, and S.J. Singh. 2017. "Introduction:
Key Concepts, Debates and Approaches in Analysing the
Sustainability of Agri-food Systems." In *Socio-metabolic
Perspectives on the Sustainability of Local Food Systems:
Insights for Science, Policy and Practice*, ed. E. Fraňková, W.
Haas, and S.J. Singh, 1–24. Cham, Switzerland: Springer.

Frantzeskaki, N., A. Dumitru, J. Wittmayer, F. Avelino, and
M.-L. Moore. 2018. "To Transform Cities, Support Civil
Society." In *Urban Planet: Knowledge towards Sustainable
Cities*, ed. T. Elmqvist, X. Bai, N. Frantzeskaki, C. Griffith,
D. Maddox, T. McPhearson, S. Parnell, P. Romero-Lankao,
D. Simon, and M. Watkins, 281–302. Cambridge: Cam-
bridge University Press.

Franzke, C.L.E., A. Ciullo, E.A. Gilmore, D.M. Matias, N.
Nagabhatla, A. Orlov, S.K. Paterson, J. Scheffran, and J.
Sillmann. 2022. "Perspectives on Tipping Points in Integrated
Models of the Natural and Human Earth System: Cascading
Effects and Telecoupling." *Environmental Research Letters*
17: 015004. [Cited in Singh et al. 2022.]

Friendly, A. 2016. *Participatory Budgeting: The Practice and
the Potential.* Toronto: Institute on Municipal Finance and
Governance, Munk School of Global Affairs and Public
Policy, University of Toronto. https://tspace.library.utoronto.
ca/handle/1807/82707.

Gabrys, J. 2010. "Telepathically Urban." In *Circulation and
the City: Essays on Urban Culture*, ed. A. Boutros and W.

Straw, 48–63. Montreal/Kingston: McGill-Queen's University Press.

Galley, A. 2015. *Community Benefits Agreements*. Toronto: Mowat Centre, School of Public Policy and Governance, University of Toronto. https://mowatcentre.munkschool. utoronto.ca/wp-content/uploads/publications/110_community_benefits_agreements.pdf.

Gardner, C., A.N. Arya, and M.L. McAllister. 2005. "Can a Health Unit Take Action on the Determinants of Health?" *Canadian Journal of Public Health* 96 (5): 374–79.

Gass, P., D. Echeverría, and A. Asadollahi. 2017. *Cities and Smart Grids in Canada*. Winnipeg: International Institute for Sustainable Development.

Gastem v. Ristigouche. 2018. *Gastem Inc. v. Municipalité de Ristigouche-Partie-Sud-Est,* 2018 QCCS 779. https://www.canlii.org/fr/qc/qccs/doc/2018/2018qccs779/2018qccs779.html?autocompleteStr=gaste&autocompletePos=3.

Gelderblom, D. 2018. "The Limits to Bridging Social Capital: Power, Social Context and the Theory of Robert Putnam." *Sociological Review* 66 (6): 1309–24.

Geobey, S. 2018. "Planning for the Sharing Economy." In *The Millennial City: Trends, Implications, and Prospects for Urban Planning and Policy,* ed. M. Moos, D. Pfeiffer, and T. Vinodrai, 93–106. New York: Routledge.

George, B., M. Baekgaard, A. Decramer, M. Audenaert, and S. Goeminne. 2018. "Institutional Isomorphism, Negativity Bias and Performance Information Use by Politicians: A Survey Experiment." *Public Administration* 98 (1): 14–28. https://onlinelibrary.wiley.com/doi/full/10.1111/padm.12390.

George, C., and M.G. Reed. 2017. "Operationalising Just Sustainability: Towards a Model for Place-Based Governance." *Local Environment* 22 (9): 1105–23.

Georgescu-Roegen, N. 1977. "The Steady State and Ecological Salvation: A Thermodynamic Analysis." *BioScience* 27 (4): 266–70.

Gerecke, K. 1977. "The History of Canadian City Planning." In *The Second City Book: Studies of Urban and Suburban Canada,* ed. J. Lorimer and E. Ross, 150–61. Toronto: Lorimer.

Gibbins, R. 2000. "Federalism in a Digital World." *Canadian Journal of Political Science* 33 (4): 667–89.

Gibson, C.C., E. Ostrom, and T.K. Ahn. 2000. "The Concept of Scale and the Human Dimensions of Global Change: A Survey." *Ecological Economics* 32 (2): 217–39.

Gibson, R.B. 2013. "Avoiding Sustainability Trade-Offs in Environmental Assessment." *Impact Assessment and Project Appraisal* 31 (1): 2–12. https://www.tandfonline.com/doi/epdf/10.1080/14615517.2013.764633?needAccess=true&role=button.

–. 2017. *Sustainability Assessment: Applications and Opportunities*. London: Routledge.

Gibson, R.B., and S. Hassan. 2005. *Sustainability Assessment: Criteria and Processes*. London/Sterling, VA: Earthscan.

Gibson-Graham, J.K. 2008. "Diverse Economies: Performative Practices for 'Other Worlds.'" *Progress in Human Geography* 32 (5): 613–32.

Giddens, A. 1984. *The Constitution of Society: Outline of the Theory of Structuration*. Cambridge: Polity.

Gillis, R.P., and T.R. Roach. 1986. "The American Influence on Conservation in Canada: 1899–1911." *Journal of Forest History* 30 (4): 160–74.

Givoni, M., and A. Perl. 2020. "Rethinking Transport Infrastructure Planning to Extend Its Value over Time." *Journal of Planning Education and Research* 40 (1): 82–91. https://journals.sagepub.com/doi/epub/10.1177/0739456X17741196.

Global Affairs Canada. 2021. "International Trade Agreements and Local Government: A Guide for Canadian Municipalities." http://www.international.gc.ca/trade-agreements-accords-commerciaux/ressources/fcm/complete-guide-complet.aspx?lang=eng.

Global Covenant of Mayors for Climate and Energy. n.d. "Our Initiatives." https://www.globalcovenantofmayors.org/our-initiatives/.

Glover, T. 2022. "Accessibility Key to Making Privately Owned Public Spaces Successful." *Waterloo Region Record,* September 13. https://www.therecord.com/opinion/accessibility-key-to-making-privately-owned-public-spaces-successful/article_987c3f73-4675-5931-9782-8f44f8364fd9.html.

Good, K.R. 2019. "Municipalities Deserve More Autonomy and Respect." *Policy Options,* November 29. https://policyoptions.irpp.org/magazines/november-2019/municipalities-deserve-more-autonomy-and-respect/.

Goodman, N., and Z. Spicer. 2019. "Administering Elections in a Digital Age: Online Voting in Ontario Municipalities." *Canadian Public Administration* 62 (3): 369–92.

Government of Alberta. n.d. "Municipal Sustainability Initiative." https://www.alberta.ca/municipal-sustainability-initiative.

Government of British Columbia. n.d.-a. "About the BC Climate Action Toolkit." https://toolkit.bc.ca/about/.

–. n.d.-b. "BC Climate Action Charter." https://toolkit.bc.ca/learn/climate-action-charter/.

–. n.d.-c. "BC Infrastructure Benefits." https://www2.gov.bc.ca/gov/content/governments/organizational-structure/ministries-organizations/crown-corporations/bc-infrastructure-benefits.

Government of Canada. 2023. "Open Government across Canada." https://open.canada.ca/en/maps/open-data-canada.

–. n.d. "Africville National Historic Site of Canada." https://www.pc.gc.ca/apps/dfhd/page_nhs_eng.aspx?id=1763.

Government of New Brunswick. 2016. "New Brunswick Leads Canada in Providing High-Speed Internet Access." News release, May 8. https://www2.gnb.ca/content/gnb/en/news/news_release.2016.05.0372.html.

Government of Northwest Territories. 2022. *Northwest Teritories Official Languages Act: Have Your Say.* https://haveyoursay.nwt-tno.ca/30527/widgets/124206/documents/80992.

Government of Nunavut. n.d. "Official Languages." https://www.gov.nu.ca/culture-and-heritage/information/official-languages.

Goyal, N., and M. Howlett. 2019. "Framework or Metaphor? Analysing the Status of Policy Learning in the Policy Sciences." *Journal of Asian Public Policy* 12 (3): 257–73.

Graham, K. 2018. "Leading Canada's Cities? A Study of Urban Mayors." PhD diss., University of Western Ontario. https://ir.lib.uwo.ca/etd/5745/.

Graham, K.A.H., and S.D. Phillips with A.M. Maslove. 1998. *Urban Governance in Canada: Representation, Resources and Restructuring.* Toronto: Harcourt Brace.

Graney, E. 2019. "Fort McMurray Lessons Loom Large as High Level Wildfire Burns." *Edmonton Journal,* May 21. https://edmontonjournal.com/news/local-news/fort-mac-lessons-loom-large-as-high-level-wildfire-burns.

Great Lakes and St. Lawrence Cities Initiative. 2017. "Great Lakes & St. Lawrence Cities Initiative Mayors Mobilize over Great Lakes Restoration and Climate Change." Greater Niagara Chamber of Commerce, June 15. https://gncc.ca/great-lakes-st-lawrence-cities-initiative-mayors-mobilize-great-lakes-restoration-climate-change/.

–. 2018. "Canadian and US Mayors Reject Rhetoric, Stand United for Shared Economic Prosperity: Mayors Pledge to Protect Urban Natural Spaces, Contribute to National Target." Tay Township, June 14. https://www.tay.ca/news/canadian-and-us-mayors-reject-rhetoric-stand-united-for-shared-economic-prosperity/.

–. n.d. "About the Great Lakes and St. Lawrence Cities Initiative." https://glslcities.org/about/.

Green Communities Committee. n.d. "Energy Planning: Planning for Energy Use." Accessed November 12, 2020. http://www.toolkit.bc.ca/Plan-Do/Energy-Planning.

Gregory, D. 1984. "Space, Time, and Politics in Social Theory: An Interview with Anthony Giddens." *Environment and Planning D: Society and Space* 2 (2): 123–32.

Grodzins, M., and D.J. Elazar. 1984. *The American System: A New View of Government in the United States.* New Brunswick, NJ: Transaction Books.

Groulx, M., M.C. Brisbois, C.J. Lemieux, A. Winegardner, and L. Fishback. 2017. "A Role for Nature-Based Citizen Science in Promoting Individual and Collective Climate Change Action? A Systematic Review of Learning Outcomes." *Science Communication* 39 (1): 45–76.

Guay, L., and P. Hamel. 2014. *Cities and Urban Sociology.* Don Mills, ON: Oxford University Press.

Gunderson, L.H., and C.S. Holling. 2002. *Panarchy: Understanding Transformations in Human and Natural Systems.* Washington, DC: Island Press.

Guyadeen, D., J. Thistlethwaite, and D. Henstra. 2018. "Evaluating the Quality of Municipal Climate Change Plans in Canada." *Climatic Change* 152 (1): 121–43.

Haberl, H., K.-H. Erb, M. Fischer-Kowalski, R. Groβ, F. Krausmann, C. Plutzar, M. Schmid, and V. Winiwarter. 2016a. "Introduction." In *Social Ecology: Society-Nature Relations across Time and Space,* ed. H. Haberl, M. Fischer-Kowalski, F. Krausmann, and V. Winiwarter, xli–lxii. Cham, Switzerland: Springer.

Haberl, H., M. Fischer-Kowalski, F. Krausmann, and V. Winiwarter, eds. 2016b. *Social Ecology: Society-Nature Relations across Time and Space.* Cham, Switzerland: Springer.

Hachard, T. 2022. *A Seat at the Table: Municipalities and Intergovernmental Relations in Canada.* Toronto: Institute on Municipal Finance and Governance, Munk School of Global Affairs and Public Policy, University of Toronto. https://tspace.library.utoronto.ca/handle/1807/111338.

Hall, J., and J.F. Helliwell. 2014. *Happiness and Human Development.* United Nations Development Programme. https://hdr.undp.org/system/files/documents/happinessandhdpdf.pdf.

Hall, N., J.L. Grant, and M.A. Habib. 2017. "Planners' Perceptions of Why Canadian Communities Have Too Many Plans." *Planning Practice and Research* 32 (3): 243–58. https://www.researchgate.net/publication/312864303_Planners'_Perceptions_of_Why_Canadian_Communities_Have_Too_Many_Plans.

Hall, P.A. 1993. "Policy Paradigms, Social Learning, and the State: The Case of Economic Policymaking in Britain." *Comparative Politics* 25 (3): 275–96. https://scholar.harvard.edu/files/hall/files/hall1993_paradigms.pdf.

Hancock, T. 2009. *Act Locally: Community-Based Population Health Promotion: A Report for the Senate Sub-committee on Population Health.* https://sencanada.ca/content/sen/Committee/402/popu/rep/appendixBjun09-e.pdf.

–. 2011. "Health Promotion in Canada: 25 Years of Unfulfilled Promise." *Health Promotion International* 26 (Suppl. 2): ii263–67. https://academic.oup.com/heapro/article/26/suppl_2/ii263/579220.

–. 2016. "Innovations in Policy and Practice: A Work in Progress." *Canadian Journal of Public Health* 107 (3): e220–21. https://www.ncbi.nlm.nih.gov/pmc/articles/PMC6972335/.

Hardin, G. 1968. "The Tragedy of the Commons." *Science,* December 13, 1243–48.

Harris, C. 2008. *The Reluctant Land: Society, Space, and Environment in Canada before Confederation.* Vancouver: UBC Press.

Harvey, D. 1989. *The Condition of Postmodernity: An Enquiry into the Origins of Cultural Change.* Cambridge, MA: Blackwell.

–. 2003. "The Right to the City." *International Journal of Urban and Regional Research* 27 (4): 939–41.

Haudenosaunee Confederacy. n.d. "Historical Life as a Haudenosaunee." http://www.haudenosauneeconfederacy.com/culture.html.

Hausknost, D., V. Gaube, W. Haas, B. Smetschka, J. Lutz, S.J. Singh, and M. Schmid. 2016. "'Society Can't Move So Much as a Chair!' – Systems, Structures and Actors in Social Ecology." In *Social Ecology: Society-Nature Relations across Time and Space,* ed. H. Haberl, M. Fischer-Kowalski, F. Krausmann, and V. Winiwarter, 125–47. Cham, Switzerland: Springer.

Hayes, D., and A. Dobson. 2008. "A Politics of Crisis: Low-Energy Cosmopolitanism." *Open Democracy,* October 26. https://www.opendemocracy.net/en/a-politics-of-crisis-low-energy-cosmopolitanism/.

Head, B.W., and J. Alford. 2015. "Wicked Problems: Implications for Public Policy and Management." *Administration and Society* 47 (6): 711–39.

Healey, P. 2018. "Creating Public Value through Caring for Place." *Policy and Politics* 46 (1): 65–79.

Hecker, S., R. Bonney, M. Haklay, F. Hölker, H. Hofer, C. Goebel, M. Gold, Z. Makuch, M. Ponti, A. Richter, L. Robinson, J.R. Iglesias, R. Owen, T. Peltola, A. Sforzi, J. Shirk, J. Vogel, K. Vohland, T. Witt, and A. Bonn. 2018. "Innovation in Citizen Science – Perspectives on Science-Policy Advances." *Citizen Science: Theory and Practice* 3 (1), art. 4. https://theoryandpractice.citizenscienceassociation.org/articles/10.5334/cstp.114.

Henry, B. 2019. *Stopping the Harm: Decriminalization of People Who Use Drugs in BC.* Victoria: Office of the British Columbia Provincial Health Officer, Ministry of Health. https://www2.gov.bc.ca/assets/gov/health/about-bc-s-health-care-system/office-of-the-provincial-health-officer/reports-publications/special-reports/stopping-the-harm-report.pdf.

Henstra, D., and G. McBean. 2004. *The Role of Government in Services for Natural Disaster Mitigation.* Toronto: Institute for Catastrophic Loss Reduction. https://www.iclr.org/wp-content/uploads/PDFS/the_role_of_government_in_services_for_natural_disaster_mitigatmit.pdf.

Henstra, D., and J. Thistlethwaite. 2017. *Climate Change, Floods, and Municipal Risk Sharing in Canada.* Toronto: Institute on Municipal Finance and Governance, Munk School of Global Affairs and Public Policy, University of Toronto. https://tspace.library.utoronto.ca/handle/1807/81204.

Hepburn, B. 2022. "How to Stop Developers from Profiting from Greenbelt Controversy." *Toronto Star,* November 30. https://www.thestar.com/opinion/star-columnists/how-to-stop-developers-from-profiting-from-greenbelt-controversy/article_c439d6a6-c676-5183-892c-f8c948760027.html.

Ho, S. 2020. "Defund the Police? This Is How Much Canadian Cities Spend." *CTV News,* July 10. https://www.ctvnews.ca/canada/defund-the-police-this-is-how-much-canadian-cities-spend-1.5018506?cache=kyifhaaa.

Hogan, J., M. Howlett, and M. Murphy. 2022. "Re-thinking the Coronavirus Pandemic as a Policy Punctuation: COVID-19 as a Path-Clearing Policy Accelerator." *Policy and Society* 41 (1): 40–52. https://academic.oup.com/policyandsociety/article/41/1/40/6503294.

Hoicka, C.E., and J.L. MacArthur. 2018. "From Tip to Toes: Mapping Community Energy Models in Canada and New Zealand." *Energy Policy* 121: 162–74.

Holden, M.E.G. 2011. "Public Participation and Local Sustainability: Questioning a Common Agenda in Urban Governance." *International Journal of Urban and Regional Research* 35 (2): 312–29.

Homeward Trust Edmonton. n.d. "About Homelessness." Accessed February 4, 2021. https://homewardtrust.ca/ending-homelessness/about-homelessness/.

Hooykaas, A. 2012. "Enduring Gardens: Woven by Friends into the Fabric of the Urban Community." PhD diss., University of Waterloo. https://uwspace.uwaterloo.ca/handle/10012/7154.

–. 2021. "Stewarding Places through Geography in Higher Education." *Journal of Geography* 120 (3): 108–16.

Hopkins, R. 2009. *The Transition Handbook: From Oil Dependency to Local Resilience.* White River Junction, VT: Chelsea Green.

Horak, M. 2012. "Conclusion: Understanding Multilevel Governance in Canada's Cities." In *Sites of Governance: Multilevel Governance and Policy Making in Canada's Biggest Cities,* ed. M. Horak and R. Young, 339–70. Montreal/Kingston: McGill-Queen's University Press.

Howlett, M., and A. Migone. 2011. "Charles Lindblom Is Alive and Well and Living in Punctuated Equilibrium Land." *Policy and Society* 30 (1): 53–62. https://www.tandfonline.com/doi/full/10.1016/j.polsoc.2010.12.006.

Humphries, M.O. 2013. *The Last Plague: Spanish Influenza and the Politics of Public Health in Canada.* Toronto: University of Toronto Press.

Huxham, C. 1993. "Collaborative Capability: An Intra-organizational Perspective on Collaborative Advantage." *Public Money and Management* 13 (3): 21–28.

ICLEI – Local Governments for Sustainability. 2008. *The Durban Commitment: Local Government for Biodiversity.* https://subnationaladvocacyfornature.org/resource/the-durban-commitment-local-governments-for-biodiversity/.

–. 2010. *Cities and Biodiversity Case Study Series: Canadian Best Practices in Local Biodiversity Management.* https://icleicanada.org/project/cities-and-biodiversity-case-study-series/.

–. 2015. *ICLEI Corporate Report 2014.* https://e-lib.iclei.org/wp-content/uploads/2015/07/Corporate-Report-2014.pdf.

–. 2019. "What Is a Resilient City?" https://resilientcities2019.iclei.org/.

–. n.d.-a. "About Us." https://iclei.org/about_iclei_2/.

–. n.d.-b. "ICLEI Corporate Report 2018–2019." https://japan.iclei.org/en/publication/iclei-corporate-report-2018-2019/.

–. n.d.-c. "Our Activities." https://iclei.org/featured_activities/.

–. n.d.-d. "Who We Are." http://www.icleicanada.org/about.

Independent Electricity System Operator. 2019. "IESO Demonstration Project to Test Ontario's First Local Electricity Market." *Canadian Mining and Energy,* September 5. https://www.miningandenergy.ca/energyinsider/article/ieso_demonstration_project_to_test_ontarios_first_local_electricity_market/.

Indigenous Corporate Training Inc. 2015. "What Are Urban Reserves?" March 27. https://www.ictinc.ca/blog/what-are-urban-reserves.

Infrastructure Canada. 2019a. "The Federal Gas Tax Fund." July 8. https://www.infrastructure.gc.ca/plan/gtf-fte-b2019-nat-eng.html.

–. 2019b. "The Government of Canada Announces Winners of the Smart Cities Challenge." News release, May 14. https://www.canada.ca/en/office-infrastructure/news/2019/05/the-government-of-canada-announces-winners-of-the-smart-cities-challenge.html.

–. 2019c. "Government of Canada Launches a New Project to Improve Data for Canadian Cities." News release, July 26. https://www.canada.ca/en/office-infrastructure/news/2019/07/government-of-canada-launches-a-new-project-to-improve-data-for-canadian-cities.html.

–. 2019d. "Nunavut Communities, Nunavut." April 25. https://www.infrastructure.gc.ca/cities-villes/videos/nunavut-eng.html.

–. 2023. "Investing in Canada Infrastructure Program." September 19. https://www.infrastructure.gc.ca/plan/icp-pic-INFC-eng.html.

–. n.d. "Smart Cities Challenge." https://www.infrastructure.gc.ca/cities-villes/index-eng.html.

Ink-Stained Wretches. n.d. "In the News." https://www.ink-stainedwretches.org/in-the-news.html.

Innes, J.E., and D.E. Booher. 2003. *The Impact of Collaborative Planning on Governance Capacity.* Berkeley: Institute of Urban and Regional Development, University of California, Berkeley. https://www.econstor.eu/bitstream/10419/23606/1/WP-2003-03.pdf.

Innis, H.A. 1951. *The Bias of Communication.* Toronto: University of Toronto Press.

Innovation, Science and Economic Development Canada. 2021. "Universal Broadband Fund and Telesat Low Earth Orbit Capacity Agreement." https://www.canada.ca/en/innovation-science-economic-development/news/2020/11/universal-broadband-fund-and-telesat-low-earth-orbit-capacity-agreement.html.

–. 2023. "High Speed Internet for All Canadians." https://ised-isde.canada.ca/site/high-speed-internet-canada/en.

Institute for Competitiveness and Prosperity (ICAP). 2016. *Looking beyond GDP: Measuring Prosperity in Ontario.* https://www.researchgate.net/publication/332869367_Looking_beyond_GDP_Measuring_prosperity_in_Ontario.

Intergovernmental Affairs Canada. 2022. "Provinces and Territories." https://www.canada.ca/en/intergovernmental-affairs/services/provinces-territories.html.

Intergovernmental Panel on Climate Change (IPCC). 2018. *Global Warming of 1.5 °C.* Ed. V. Masson-Delmotte, P. Zhai, H.O. Pörtner, D. Roberts, J. Skea, P.R. Shukla, A. Pirani, W. Moufouma-Okia, C. Péan, R. Pidcock, S. Connors, J.B.R. Matthews, Y. Chen, X. Zhou, M.I. Gomis, E. Lonnoy, T. Maycock, M. Tignor, and T. Waterfield. Cambridge: Cambridge University Press. https://www.ipcc.ch/sr15/download/#full.

International Joint Commission. n.d. "Role of the IJC." https://www.ijc.org/en/who/role.

Isin, E.F. 1992. *Cities without Citizens.* Montreal: Black Rose Books.

Jacobs, J. 1985. *Cities and the Wealth of Nations: Principles of Economic Life.* New York: Vintage Books.

–. 2005. *Dark Age Ahead.* Toronto: Random House Canada.

Johns, C., A. Thorn, and D. VanNijnatten. 2018. "Environmental Regime Effectiveness and the North American Great Lakes Water Quality Agreement." *International Environmental Agreements: Politics, Law and Economics* 18 (3): 315–33.

Johnson, M.T.J., and J. Munshi-South. 2017. "Evolution of Life in Urban Environments." *Science,* November 3. https://www.science.org/doi/10.1126/science.aam8327.

Jones, R.P., and N. Brockband. 2022. "Who Are the GTA Developers Set to Benefit from Ford Government's

Greenbelt Land Swap?" *CBC News,* November 11. https://www.cbc.ca/news/canada/toronto/gta-developers-own-greenbelt-land-swap-1.6648273.

Kalinowski, T. 2017. "Housing Plan Won't Help Middle Class, Experts Say." *Toronto Star,* November 22. https://www.thestar.com/news/gta/housing-plan-won-t-help-middle-class-experts-say/article_890f07da-f8c5-5234-af23-5ef93d622510.html.

Kalmykova, Y., and L. Rosado. 2015. "Urban Metabolism as Framework for Circular Economy Design for Cities." In *Proceedings of the World Economic Forum 2015.* http://publications.lib.chalmers.se/records/fulltext/232085/local_232085.pdf.

Kalvapalle, R. 2018. "Most Torontonians, Ontarians, Canadians Oppose Ford's Use of Notwithstanding Clause: Ipsos Poll." *Global News,* September 19. https://globalnews.ca/news/4463552/doug-ford-notwithstanding-clause-toronto-poll/.

Kampelmann, S., S. Van Hollebeke, and P. Vandergert. 2016. "Stuck in the Middle with You: The Role of Bridging Organisations in Urban Regeneration." *Ecological Economics* 129: 82–93.

Kappler, E. 1980. "Book Reviews: Chris Argyris and Donald A. Schön: Organizational Learning. A Theory of Action Perspective 1978, Reading, Mass.: Addison-Wesley." *Organization Studies* 1 (3): 292–93.

Katz, B. 2017a. "The Complex Interplay of Cities, Corporations and Climate." Brookings Institution, December 8. https://www.brookings.edu/articles/the-complex-interplay-of-cities-corporations-and-climate/.

–. 2017b. "Envisioning the New Localism: Local Governments Have the Real Power to Create Change." *PM Magazine,* December 27. https://icma.org/articles/pm-magazine/envisioning-new-localism.

Katz, S., and D. Roussopoulos. 2017. "At the Crossroads of Cultures: The Distinct Politics and Development of Montréal." In *The Rise of Cities,* ed. D. Roussopoulos, 35–92. Montreal: Black Rose Books.

Keil, R. 2015. "Towers in the Park, Bungalows in the Garden: Peripheral Densities, Metropolitan Scales and the Political Cultures of Post-Suburbia." *Built Environment (1978–)* 41 (4): 579–96.

Kelly, P.M., and W.N. Adger. 2000. "Theory and Practice in Assessing Vulnerability to Climate Change and Facilitating Adaptation." *Climatic Change* 47 (4): 325–52.

Kemp, B., and M. Jiménez. 2013. *State of Local Democracy Assessment Framework.* Stockholm, Sweden: International Institute for Democracy and Electoral Assistance. https://www.idea.int/sites/default/files/publications/state-of-local-democracy-assessment-framework.pdf.

Kennedy, C., I.D. Stewart, M.I. Westphal, A. Facchini, and R. Mele. 2018. "Keeping Global Climate Change within 1.5 °C through Net Negative Electric Cities." *Current Opinion in Environmental Sustainability* 30: 18–25.

Kent, M. 2018. "Canadian Teen Tells UN 'Warrior Up' to Protect Water." *CBC News,* March 22. https://www.cbc.ca/news/canada/autumn-peltier-un-water-activist-united-nations-1.4584871.

Keresteci, M., N. Kaplan-Myrth, and N. Dosani. 2021. "An Effective Vaccination Effort Requires the Efforts of Many Communities." *Toronto Star,* January 25. https://www.thestar.com/opinion/contributors/an-effective-vaccination-effort-requires-the-efforts-of-many-communities/article_5cb8c5f3-26ef-5b61-a1e8-936156e0ec81.html.

Khan, Y. 2011. "It's Not Just Food: Sustainable Food Security for Immigrants: Barriers and Opportunities." MSc thesis, University of Waterloo. https://uwspace.uwaterloo.ca/handle/10012/5698.

Kimber, S. 2019. "Councillor Lindell Smith: Proud Of? Not Is. Will Be Proud ..." *Halifax Examiner,* February 24. https://www.halifaxexaminer.ca/government/city-hall/councillor-lindell-smith-proud-of-not-is-will-be-proud/.

Kish, K., and S. Quilley. 2017. "Wicked Dilemmas of Scale and Complexity in the Politics of Degrowth." *Ecological Economics* 142: 306–17.

Kitchen, H., and E. Slack. 2016. *New Tax Sources for Canada's Largest Cities: What Are the Options?* Toronto: Institute on Municipal Finance and Governance, Munk School of Global Affairs and Public Policy, University of Toronto. https://tspace.library.utoronto.ca/handle/1807/82858.

Kitchen, H., E. Slack, and T. Hachard. 2019. *Property Taxes in Canada: Current Issues and Future Prospects.* Toronto: Institute on Municipal Finance and Governance, Munk School of Global Affairs and Public Policy, University of Toronto. https://tspace.library.utoronto.ca/handle/1807/98034.

Kitchin, R. 2019. "Reframing, Reimagining and Remaking Smart Cities." In *Creating Smart Cities,* ed. C. Coletta, L. Evans, L. Heaphy, and R. Kitchin, 219–30. London: Routledge.

Knaus, C. 2018. "Public Engagement Conundrum: Canadian's Views on Municipal Public Consultations." *Municipal World,* December. https://www.municipalworld.com/feature-story/public-engagement-conundrum/.

Kneuer, M. 2016. "E-democracy: A New Challenge for Measuring Democracy." *International Political Science Review* 37 (5): 666–78. https://www.researchgate.net/publication/310733789_E-democracy_A_new_challenge_for_measuring_democracy.

Kooiman, J., and M. Bavinck. 2013. "Theorizing Governability – The Interactive Governance Perspective." In *Governability of Fisheries and Aquaculture: Theory and Applications,* ed.

M. Bavinck, R. Chuenpagdee, S. Jentoft, and J. Kooiman, 9–30. Dordrecht, Netherlands: Springer.

Koop, R., and J. Kraemer. 2016. "Wards, At-Large Systems and the Focus of Representation in Canadian Cities." *Canadian Journal of Political Science* 49 (3): 433–48.

Koppenjan, J., P.M. Karré, and K. Termeer. 2019a. "New Governance Arrangements: Towards Hybrid and Smarter Government?" In *Smart Hybridity: Potentials and Challenges of New Governance Arrangements,* ed. J. Koppenjan, P.M. Karré, and K. Termeer, 11–28. The Hague: Eleven International.

–, eds. 2019b. *Smart Hybridity: Potentials and Challenges of New Governance Arrangements.* The Hague: Eleven International.

Kovesi, C., and L. Kern. 2018. "'I Choose to Be Here': Tensions between Autonomy and Precarity in Craft Market Vendors' Work." *City and Community* 17 (1): 170–86.

Kretzmann, J.P., and J.L. McKnight. 1993. *Building Communities from the Inside Out: A Path toward Finding and Mobilizing a Community's Assets.* Evanston, IL: Asset-Based Community Development Institute, Institute for Policy Research, Northwestern University.

Krueger, R., C. Schulz, and D.C. Gibbs. 2018. "Institutionalizing Alternative Economic Spaces? An Interpretivist Perspective on Diverse Economies." *Progress in Human Geography* 42 (4): 569–89.

Kunstler, J.H. 2009. *The Long Emergency: Surviving the End of Oil, Climate Change, and Other Converging Catastrophes of the Twenty-First Century.* New York: Grove.

Kymlicka, W., and K. Walker, eds. 2012. *Rooted Cosmopolitanism: Canada and the World.* Vancouver: UBC Press.

Lachman, R. 2020. "Sidewalk Labs' City-of-the-Future in Toronto Was a Stress Test We Needed." *Policy Options,* May 28. https://policyoptions.irpp.org/magazines/may-2020/sidewalk-labs-city-of-the-future-in-toronto-was-a-stress-test-we-needed/.

Laforest, R. 2011. *Voluntary Sector Organizations and the State: Building New Relations.* Vancouver: UBC Press.

Laforge, J.M.L., and C.Z. Levkoe. 2018. "Seeding Agroecology through New Farmer Training in Canada: Knowledge, Practice, and Relational Identities." *Local Environment* 23 (10): 991–1007.

Langmaid, G., R. Patrick, J. Kingsley, and J. Lawson. 2020. "Applying the Mandala of Health in the Anthropocene." *Health Promotion Journal of Australia* 32 (Suppl. 2): 8–21.

Larson, B. 2011. *Metaphors for Environmental Sustainability: Redefining Our Relationship with Nature.* New Haven, CT: Yale University Press.

Leman Stefanovic, I. 2000. *Safeguarding Our Common Future: Rethinking Sustainable Development.* Albany: State University of New York Press.

–. 2012. "In Search of the Natural City." In *The Natural City: Re-envisioning the Built Environment,* ed. I. Leman Stefanovic and S.B. Scharper, 11–35. Toronto: University of Toronto Press.

Leman Stefanovic, I., and S.B. Scharper. 2012. "Introduction: Cultivating the Terrain." In *The Natural City: Re-envisioning the Built Environment,* ed. I. Leman Stefanovic and S.B. Scharper, 3–8. Toronto: University of Toronto Press.

Leo, C. 1995. "The State in the City: A Political Economy Perspective on Growth and Decay." In *Canadian Metropolitics: Governing Our Cities,* ed. J. Lightbody, 27–50. Toronto: Copp Clark.

–. 2006. "Deep Federalism: Respecting Community Difference in National Policy." *Canadian Journal of Political Science* 39 (3): 481–506.

Lightbody, J. 2006. *City Politics, Canada.* Toronto: University of Toronto Press.

Lightbody, J., and L. Kline. 2016. "Dispositional Immobility: An Analysis of Non-decisions as Public Policy in Alberta's City-Regions." *Social Sciences* 5 (4), art. 54. https://www.mdpi.com/2076-0760/5/4/54.

Lipset, S.M. 1971. *Agrarian Socialism: The Cooperative Commonwealth Federation in Saskatchewan: A Study in Political Sociology.* Berkeley: University of California Press.

Living SJ. 2020. "Who We Are." https://livingsj.ca/who-we-are.

Longo, J. 2017. "The Evolution of Citizen and Stakeholder Engagement in Canada, from Spicer to #Hashtags." *Canadian Public Administration* 60 (4): 517–37. https://onlinelibrary.wiley.com/doi/full/10.1111/capa.12229.

Lorek, S., and D. Fuchs. 2013. "Strong Sustainable Consumption Governance – Precondition for a Degrowth Path?" *Journal of Cleaner Production* 38: 36–43.

Lorimer, J. 1972. *A Citizen's Guide to City Politics.* Toronto: Lorimer.

Loucks, L., F. Berkes, D. Armitage, and A. Charles. 2017. "Emergence of Community Science as a Transformative Process in Port Mouton Bay, Canada." In *Governing the Coastal Commons: Communities, Resilience and Transformation,* ed. D. Armitage, A. Charles, and F. Berkes, 43–59. London: Routledge.

Louv, R. 2008. *Last Child in the Woods: Saving Our Children from Nature-Deficit Disorder.* Chapel Hill, NC: Algonquin Books of Chapel Hill.

Low Carbon Cities Canada (LC3). n.d. "Accelerating Urban Climate Solutions across Canada." https://lc3.ca/#overview.

Lowrie, M. 2022. "Big Cities Have a Major Role to Play in Protecting Biodiversity, Experts Say." *CBC News,* December 11. https://www.cbc.ca/news/canada/montreal/big-cities-have-a-major-role-to-play-in-protecting-biodiversity-cop15-1.6682087.

Lucas, J. 2013. *Hidden in Plain View: Local Agencies, Boards, and Commissions in Canada.* Toronto: Institute on Municipal Finance and Governance, Munk School of Global Affairs and Public Policy, University of Toronto. https://tspace.library.utoronto.ca/handle/1807/82711.

–. 2016. *Fields of Authority: Special Purpose Governance in Ontario, 1815–2015.* Toronto: University of Toronto Press.

Lucas, R.A. 1971. *Minetown, Milltown, Railtown: Life in Canadian Communities of Single Industry.* Toronto: University of Toronto Press.

MacDowell, L.S. 2012. *An Environmental History of Canada.* Vancouver: UBC Press.

MacKendrick, N. 2014. "Foodscape." *Contexts* 13 (3): 16–18. https://journals.sagepub.com/doi/full/10.1177/1536504214545754.

Magdoff, F., and B. Tokar. 2009. "Agriculture and Food in Crisis: An Overview." *Monthly Review* 61 (3): 1–16.

Magnusson, W. 1996. *The Search for Political Space: Globalization, Social Movements, and the Urban Political Experience.* Toronto: University of Toronto Press.

–. 2009. "Scaling Government to Politics." In *Leviathan Undone? Towards a Political Economy of Scale,* ed. R. Keil and R. Mahon, 105–20. Vancouver: UBC Press.

–. 2015. *Local Self-Government and the Right of the City.* Montreal/Kingston: McGill-Queen's University Press.

Mancini, J., and S. Mancini. 2015. *Transition to Common Work: Building Community at the Working Centre.* Waterloo, ON: Wilfrid Laurier University Press.

Manor, J., M. Robinson, and G. White. 1999. "Civil Society and Governance: A Concept Paper." Ontario Institute for Studies in Education, University of Toronto, August 26. https://cide.oise.utoronto.ca/civil_society/resources/Manor%20Robinson%20and%20White%20Concept%20Paper.pdf.

Markey, S. 2011. *A Primer on New Regionalism.* Canadian Regional Development: A Critical Review of Theory, Practice, and Potentials, May. http://cdnregdev.rural resilience.ca/wp-content/uploads/2014/12/NR_Primer-WP-CRD4.pdf.

Markvart, T. 2015. "Planning for Social Change Towards Sustainability? Investigating Local Government Strategic Sustainability Planning in Canada." PhD diss., University of Waterloo. https://uwspace.uwaterloo.ca/handle/10012/9225.

Marselle, M., J. Stadler, H. Korn, K. Irvine, and A. Bonn, eds. 2019. *Biodiversity and Health in the Face of Climate Change.* Cham, Switzerland: Springer.

Marshall, A. 2017. "Alphabet Is Trying to Reinvent the City, Starting with Toronto." *Wired,* October 19. https://www.wired.com/story/google-sidewalk-labs-toronto-quayside/.

Martorell, H., and P. Andrée. 2019. "The Commoning of Food Governance in Canada: Pathways Towards a National Food Policy?" In *Routledge Handbook of Food as a Commons,* ed. J. Vivero-Pol, T. Ferrando, O. De Schutter, and U. Mattei, 266–80. London: Routledge.

Maslow, A.H. 1966. *The Psychology of Science: A Reconnaissance.* New York: Harper and Row.

Mayer, A., A. Schaffartzik, F. Krausmann, and N. Eisenmenger. 2016. "More Than the Sum of Its Parts: Patterns in Global Material Flows." In *Social Ecology: Society-Nature Relations across Time and Space,* ed. H. Haberl, M. Fischer-Kowalski, F. Krausmann, and V. Winiwarter, 217–33. Cham, Switzerland: Springer.

McAllister, C. 2011. "Where Have All the Children Gone? Community, Nature and the Child Friendly City." PhD diss., University of Waterloo. https://uwspace.uwaterloo.ca/handle/10012/5835.

McAllister, M.L. 2004. *Governing Ourselves? The Politics of Canadian Communities.* Vancouver: UBC Press.

McCready, H.W., ed. 1929. *Lord Durham's Mission to Canada: An Abridgement of Lord Durham: A Biography of John George Lambton, First Earl of Durham, by Chester New.* Reprint, Toronto: McClelland and Stewart, 1963.

McEachern, C. 2005. "Time's Grip along the Athabasca, 1920s and 1930s." In *History, Literature, and the Writing of the Canadian Prairies,* ed. R.A. Wardhaugh and A.C. Calder, 259–85. Winnipeg: University of Manitoba Press.

McGregor, R.M., A.A. Moore, and L.B. Stephenson. 2016. "Political Attitudes and Behaviour in a Non-partisan Environment: Toronto 2014." *Canadian Journal of Political Science* 49 (2): 311–33.

McKinney, B. 2022. "Welcome to the Great Lakes and St. Lawrence Cities Initiative: A Message from the New Chair of the Cities Initiative." Great Lakes and St. Lawrence Cities Initiative. Accessed November 7, 2022. https://glslcities.org/.

McLaren, D., and J. Agyeman. 2019. "Smart for a Reason: Sustainability and Social Inclusion in a Smart City." In *Creating Smart Cities,* ed. C. Coletta, L. Evans, L. Heaphy, and R. Kitchin, 169–81. London: Routledge.

McLuhan, M., Q. Fiore, and J. Agel. 1967. *The Medium Is the Massage: An Inventory of Effects.* New York: Bantam Books.

McPhearson, T., S.T.A. Pickett, N.B. Grimm, J. Niemelä, M. Alberti, T. Elmqvist, C. Weber, D. Haase, J. Breuste, and S. Qureshi. 2016. "Advancing Urban Ecology toward a Science of Cities." *BioScience* 66 (3): 198–212.

Meadows, D.H., and D. Wright. 2008. *Thinking in Systems: A Primer.* White River Junction, VT: Chelsea Green.

Meili, R., and T. Piggott. 2018. "Thinking Upstream: A Vision for a Healthy Society." In *Under-Served: Health Determinants of Indigenous, Inner-City, and Migrant Populations in*

Canada, ed. A.N. Arya and T. Piggott, 341–51. Toronto: Canadian Scholars.

Metabolism of Cities. n.d. "Our Story." https://metabolismof cities.org/about/our-story/.

Metrolinx. n.d. "About the 2041 Regional Transportation Plan." http://www.metrolinx.com/en/regionalplanning/rtp/.

Meuleman, L. 2018. *Metagovernance for Sustainability: A Framework for Implementing the Sustainable Development Goals.* Abingdon, UK: Routledge.

Meyer, S. 2020. "Systemic Racism and Unconscious Bias in Local Government." *Municipal World,* December. https://www.municipalworld.com/feature-story/systemic-racism -unconscious-bias-local-government/.

Millennium Ecosystem Assessment. 2003. *Ecosystems and Human Well-Being: A Framework for Assessment.* Washington, DC: Island Press. http://pdf.wri.org/ecosystems_ human_wellbeing.pdf.

–. 2005. *Ecosystems and Human Well-Being: Biodiversity Synthesis.* Washington, DC: World Resources Institute. https://www.millenniumassessment.org/documents/ document.354.aspx.pdf.

Milovanoff, A. 2020. "The Myth of Electric Cars: Why We Also Need to Focus on Buses and Trains." *The Conversation,* October 21. https://theconversation.com/the-myth-of -electric-cars-why-we-also-need-to-focus-on-buses-and -trains-147827.

Minnes, S., S.-P. Breen, S. Markey, and K. Vodden. 2018. "Pragmatism versus Potential: New Regionalism and Rural Drinking Water Management." *Journal of Rural and Community Development* 13 (12): 76–99.

Mitchell, R.E. 2006. "Green Politics or Environmental Blues? Analyzing Ecological Democracy." *Public Understanding of Science* 15 (4): 459–80. https://d-nb.info/1186497386/34.

Mocca, E. 2020. "The Local Dimension in the Degrowth Literature: A Critical Discussion." *Journal of Political Ideologies* 25 (1): 78–93.

Moore, A.A. 2017. *The Potential and Consequences of Municipal Electoral Reform.* Toronto: Institute on Municipal Finance and Governance, Munk School of Global Affairs and Public Policy, University of Toronto. https://tspace.library.utoronto. ca/handle/1807/78793.

Moore, A.W., L. King, A. Dale, and R. Newell. 2018. "Toward an Integrative Framework for Local Development Path Analysis." *Ecology and Society* 23 (2), art. 13. https://www. ecologyandsociety.org/vol23/iss2/art13/.

Moos, M., A. Kramer, M. Williamson, P. Mendez, L. McGuire, E. Wyly, and R. Walter-Joseph. 2015. "More Continuity Than Change? Re-evaluating the Contemporary Socioeconomic and Housing Characteristics of Suburbs." *Canadian Journal of Urban Research* 24 (2): 64–90.

Moos, M., T. Vinodrai, N. Revington, and M. Seasons. 2018. "Planning for Mixed Use: Affordable for Whom?" *Journal of the American Planning Association* 84 (1): 7–20.

Morrison, D. 2020. "Reflections and Realities: Expressions of Food Sovereignty in the Fourth World." In *Indigenous Food Systems: Concepts, Cases, and Conversations,* ed. P. Settee and S. Shukla, 17–38. Toronto: Canadian Scholars.

Morrison, T.H., W.N. Adger, K. Brown, M.C. Lemos, D. Huitema, J. Phelps, L. Evans, P. Cohen, A.M. Song, R. Turner, T. Quinn, and T.P. Hughes. 2019. "The Black Box of Power in Polycentric Environmental Governance." *Global Environmental Change* 57, art. 101934. https://www.sciencedirect. com/science/article/pii/S0959378019302729.

Mosco, V. 1989. *The Pay-Per Society: Computers and Communication in the Information Age: Essays in Critical Theory and Public Policy.* Norwood, NJ: Ablex.

–. 2019. *The Smart City in a Digital World.* Bingley, UK: Emerald.

Moscrop, D.R.H., and M.E. Warren. 2016. "When Is Deliberation Democratic?" *Journal of Public Deliberation* 12 (2), art. 4. https://delibdemjournal.org/article/528/galley/4535/ view/.

Mosonyi, S., and D. Baker. 2016. "Bylaw Battles: Explaining Municipal-Provincial and Municipal-Federal Win-Rates." *Canadian Journal of Urban Research* 25 (2): 11–22.

Moss, C., and C. Benty. 2020. *The Joy of Governing: Your How-To Guide to Optimal Governance.* Whitehorse: Association of Yukon Communities. https://cdnsm5-hosted.civiclive. com/UserFiles/Servers/Server_3242987/File/The%20 Joy%20of%20Governing.pdf.

Municipal District of Lesser Slave River No. 124. 2018. "Tricouncil: Finding Strength in Unity." Accessed July 17, 2018. http://www.mdlsr.ca/index.php/your-md/shortcode/ tri-council.

Muñoz-Erickson, T., C. Miller, and T. Miller. 2017. "How Cities Think: Knowledge Co-production for Urban Sustainability and Resilience." *Forests* 8 (6), art. 203. https://data.fs.usda. gov/research/pubs/iitf/ja_iitf_2017_Munoz001.pdf.

Murphy, M.D. 2016. *Landscape Architecture Theory: An Ecological Approach.* Washington, DC: Island Press.

Musango, J.K., P. Currie, and B. Robinson. 2017. *Urban Metabolism or Resource Efficient Cities: From Theory to Implementation.* Paris: UN Environment. https://resourceefficientcities. org/wp-content/uploads/2017/09/Urban-Metabolism-for -Resource-Efficient-Cities.pdf.

Natural Resources Canada. 2017. "Water." https://www.nrcan. gc.ca/maps-tools-publications/tools/geodetic-reference -systems/water/16888.

Neighbourhood Change Research Partnership. n.d. http:// neighbourhoodchange.ca/.

Nelson, C., C.Z. Levkoe, and R. Kakegamic. 2018. "The Need for Contextual, Place-Based Food Policies: Lessons from Northwestern Ontario." *Canadian Food Studies* 5 (3): 266–72. https://canadianfoodstudies.uwaterloo.ca/index.php/cfs/article/view/327.

Newby, L. 1999. "Sustainable Local Economic Development: A New Agenda for Action?" *Local Environment* 4 (1): 67–72.

Nikitas, A., S. Tsigdinos, C. Karolemeas, E. Kourmpa, and E. Bakogiannis. 2021. "Cycling in the Era of COVID-19: Lessons Learnt and Best Practice Policy Recommendations for a More Bike-Centric Future." *Sustainability* 13 (9), art. 4620. https://www.mdpi.com/2071-1050/13/9/4620.

Nikkel, L., M. Maguire, M. Gooch, D. Bucknell, D. Laplain, B. Dent, P. Whitehead, and A. Felfel. 2019. *The Avoidable Crisis of Food Waste: The Roadmap.* Toronto: Second Harvest and Value Chain Management International. https://www.secondharvest.ca/getmedia/73121ee2-5693-40ec-b6cc-dba6ac9c6756/The-Avoidable-Crisis-of-Food-Waste-Roadmap.pdf.

Nilson, C. 2014. *Risk-Driven Collaborative Intervention: A Preliminary Impact Assessment of Community Mobilization Prince Albert's Hub Model.* Saskatoon: Centre for Forensic Behavioural Science and Justice Studies, University of Saskatchewan. https://cfbsjs.usask.ca/documents/research/research_papers/RiskDrivenCollaborativeIntervention.pdf.

Nussbaum, M.C. 2011. "Capabilities, Entitlements, Rights: Supplementation and Critique." *Journal of Human Development and Capabilities* 12 (1): 23–37.

Ogilvie, M. 2020. "Sexism and the City." *Toronto Star,* March 8. https://www.pressreader.com/canada/toronto-star/20200308/281496458340634.

"Okotoks Receives National Recognition for Environmental Stormwater Management." 2018. *Gateway Gazette,* February 12. https://gatewaygazette.ca/okotoks-receives-national-recognition-environmental-stormwater-management/.

O'Neill, S.J., and S. Cairns. 2017. *Defining and Scoping Municipal Natural Assets.* Victoria, BC: Municipal Natural Assets Initiative. https://mnai.ca/media/2018/02/finaldesignedsept18mnai.pdf.

–. 2018. *Towards a Collaborative Strategy for Municipal Natural Asset Management: Private Lands.* Victoria, BC: Municipal Natural Assets Initiative. https://mnai.ca/media/2021/10/reportmnaifeb7.pdf.

Ontario Human Rights Commission. 2020. "New OHRC Report Confirms Black People Disproportionately Arrested, Charged, Subjected to Use of Force by Toronto Police." Press release, August 10. https://www.ohrc.on.ca/en/news_centre/new-ohrc-report-confirms-black-people-disproportionately-arrested-charged-subjected-use-force.

Osborne, S.P. 2006. "The New Public Governance?" *Public Management Review* 8 (3): 377–87.

Ostrom, E. 1990. *Governing the Commons: The Evolution of Institutions for Collective Action.* Cambridge: Cambridge University Press.

–. 2010. "Beyond Markets and States: Polycentric Governance of Complex Economic Systems." *American Economic Review* 100 (3): 641–72.

Ostrom, V., C.M. Tiebout, and R. Warren. 1961. "The Organization of Government in Metropolitan Areas: A Theoretical Inquiry." *American Political Science Review* 55 (4): 831–42.

Ottawa Police Service. n.d. "Our History: Sir Robert Peel's Principles of Law Enforcement 1829." Accessed February 2, 2021. https://www.ottawapolice.ca/en/about-us/our-history.aspx.

Oudshoorn, A. 2018. "Poverty, Homelessness, and Ill Health." In *Under-Served: Health Determinants of Indigenous, Inner-City, and Migrant Populations in Canada,* ed. A.N. Arya and T. Piggott, 129–40. Toronto: Canadian Scholars.

Padró, R., I.M.C. Cattaneo, J. Caravaca, and E. Tello. 2017. "Does Your Landscape Mirror What You Eat? A Long-Term Socio-metabolic Analysis of a Local Food System in Vallès County (Spain, 1860–1956–1999)." In *Socio-metabolic Perspectives on the Sustainability of Local Food Systems: Insights for Science, Policy and Practice,* ed. E. Fraňková, W. Haas, and S.J. Singh, 133–64. Cham, Switzerland: Springer.

Page, J. 2018. "Small Quebec Village, Sued for Trying to Protect Its Drinking Water, Wins Legal Battle." *CBC News,* February 28. https://www.cbc.ca/news/canada/montreal/small-quebec-village-sued-for-trying-to-protect-its-drinking-water-wins-legal-battle-1.4555774.

Pagliaro, J. 2020. "More Civility, More Diversity, Stronger Mandate." *Toronto Star,* October 25. https://www.pressreader.com/canada/toronto-star/20201025/281573768190435.

Parent, R., and C. Parent. 2019. "Diversity and Policing in Canada." In *Policing and Minority Communities: Contemporary Issues and Global Perspectives,* ed. J.F. Albrecht, G.D. Heyer, and P. Stanislas, 145–61. Cham, Switzerland: Springer.

Parkes, M.W., K.E. Morrison, M.J. Bunch, L.K. Hallström, R.C. Neudoerffer, H.D. Venema, and D. Waltner-Toews. 2010. "Towards Integrated Governance for Water, Health and Social-Ecological Systems: The Watershed Governance Prism." *Global Environmental Change* 20 (4): 693–704.

Partelow, S., A. Schlüter, D. Armitage, M. Bavinck, K. Carlisle, R.L. Gruby, A.-K. Hornidge, M. Le Tissier, J.B. Pittman, A.M. Song, L.P. Sousa, N. Văidianu, and K. Van Assche. 2020. "Environmental Governance Theories: A Review and Application to Coastal Systems." *Ecology and Society* 25 (4), art. 19. https://www.ecologyandsociety.org/vol25/iss4/art19/.

Partners for Climate Protection. 2021. "Membership." https://www.pcp-ppc.ca/membership.

Pelenc, J., and J. Ballet. 2015. "Strong Sustainability, Critical Natural Capital and the Capability Approach." *Ecological Economics* 112: 36–44.

Pender, T. 2020. "'The Banana' Busts Rules and Spending Limits for Public Art in Waterloo." *Waterloo Region Record,* July 22. https://www.therecord.com/news/waterloo-region/the-banana-busts-rules-and-spending-limits-for-public-art-in-waterloo/article_c7f0f348-28d7-558c-a068-52d9c93527c9.html.

Perl, A., M. Hern, and J. Kenworthy. 2020. *Big Moves: Global Agendas, Local Aspirations, and Urban Mobility in Canada.* Montreal/Kingston: McGill-Queen's University Press.

Peters, B.G. 1996. *The Future of Governing: Four Emerging Models.* Lawrence: University Press of Kansas.

Piggott, T., and A. Orkin. 2018. "Deconstructing the Concept of Special Populations for Health Care, Research, and Policy." In *Under-Served: Health Determinants of Indigenous, Inner-City, and Migrant Populations in Canada,* ed. A.N. Arya and T. Piggott, 12–22. Toronto: Canadian Scholars.

Plummer, R., J. Baird, A. Dzyundzyak, D. Armitage, Ö. Bodin, and L. Schultz. 2017. "Is Adaptive Co-management Delivering? Examining Relationships between Collaboration, Learning and Outcomes in UNESCO Biosphere Reserves." *Ecological Economics* 140: 79–88.

Plutzar, C., K.-H. Erb, V. Gaube, H. Haberl, and F. Krausmann. 2016. "Of Birds and Bees: Biodiversity and the Colonization of Ecosystems." In *Social Ecology: Society-Nature Relations across Time and Space,* ed. H. Haberl, M. Fischer-Kowalski, F. Krausmann, and V. Winiwarter, 375–88. Cham, Switzerland: Springer.

Poland, B., C. Buse, P. Antze, R. Haluza-Delay, C. Ling, L. Newman, A.-A. Parent, C. Teelucksingh, R. Cohen, R. Hasdell, K. Hayes, S. Massot, and M. Zook. 2019. "The Emergence of the Transition Movement in Canada: Success and Impact through the Eyes of Initiative Leaders." *Local Environment* 24 (3): 180–200.

Pollution Probe. n.d.-a. "About Us." https://www.ecohubmap.com/company/NGO/pollution-probe/83q4m5s2kqrvvumz.

–. n.d.-b. "Home." https://www.pollutionprobe.org/.

Post Carbon Institute. 2021. "Relocalize." https://www.postcarbon.org/Relocalize/.

Press, J. 2017. "Liberals Propose Billions for Affordable Housing, Including Individual Benefits." *National Post,* November 22. https://nationalpost.com/pmn/news-pmn/canada-news-pmn/liberals-look-to-ease-affordability-concerns-with-release-of-housing-strategy.

PROOF (Research to Identify Policy Options to Reduce Food Insecurity). "New Data on Household Food Insecurity in 2022." May 2. https://proof.utoronto.ca/2023/new-data-on-household-food-insecurity-in-2022/.

PSD Citywide. n.d. "Open Cities Index: North America's Most Open Cities." https://www.psdcitywide.com/whitepapers/open-cities-index/.

Public Health Agency of Canada. 2008. *The Chief Public Health Officer's Report on the State of Public Health in Canada 2008: Addressing Health Inequalities.* https://www.canada.ca/en/public-health/corporate/publications/chief-public-health-officer-reports-state-public-health-canada/report-on-state-public-health-canada-2008.html.

Public Sector Digest. 2019. "Canada's Top 20 Most Open Cities Announced – Edmonton Ranks First for Fourth Time" [Attachment #1]. https://www.durham.ca/en/regional-government/resources/Documents/Council/CIP/CIP-2019/CIP-12202019Revised.pdf.

–. n.d. "North America's Top 20 Most Open Cities – 2020." https://www.psdcitywide.com/whitepapers/open-cities-index/.

Pulselli, R.M., and E. Tiezzi. 2009. *City out of Chaos: Urban Self-Organization and Sustainability.* Southampton, UK: WIT Press.

Putnam, R.D. 2020. "Social Capital Primer." http://robertdputnam.com/Bowling-Alone/Social-Capital-Primer/.

Qadeer, M., and S. Kumar. 2006. "Ethnic Enclaves and Social Cohesion." *Canadian Journal of Urban Research* 15 (2): 1–17.

Quilley, S. 2013. "De-growth Is Not a Liberal Agenda: Relocalisation and the Limits to Low Energy Cosmopolitanism." *Environmental Values* 22 (2): 261–85. https://www.researchgate.net/publication/260161341_De-Growth_Is_Not_a_Liberal_Agenda_Relocalisation_and_the_Limits_to_Low_Energy_Cosmopolitanism.

–. 2017. "Navigating the Anthropocene: Environmental Politics and Complexity in an Era of Limits." In *Handbook on Growth and Sustainability,* ed. P.A. Victor and B. Dolter, 439–70. Cheltenham, UK: Edward Elgar.

Raco, M., and J. Flint. 2001. "Communities, Places and Institutional Relations: Assessing the Role of Area-Based Community Representation in Local Governance." *Political Geography* 20 (5): 585–612.

Raghavan, S., and A.N. Farzan. 2021. "Piracy Fears Mount as Ships Take Long Way around Africa to Avoid Blocked Suez Canal." *Washington Post,* 26 March. https://www.washingtonpost.com/world/suez-canal-ship-blockage-ever-given/2021/03/26/357f8ae8-8da8-11eb-a33e-da28941cb9ac_story.html.

Raphael, D. 2018. "The Social Determinants of Health of Under-Served Populations in Canada." In *Under-Served:*

Health Determinants of Indigenous, Inner-City, and Migrant Populations in Canada, ed. A.N. Arya and T. Piggott, 23–44. Toronto: Canadian Scholars.

Raworth, K. 2017. "What on Earth Is the Doughnut?" https://www.kateraworth.com/doughnut/.

Razack, S. 2002. "Gendered Racialized Violence and Spatialized Justice: The Murder of Pamela George." In *Race, Space, and the Law: Unmapping a White Settler Society,* ed. S. Razack, 121–58. Toronto: Between the Lines.

Reed, M.G., and P. Abernethy. 2018. "Facilitating Co-production of Transdisciplinary Knowledge for Sustainability: Working with Canadian Biosphere Reserve Practitioners." *Society and Natural Resources* 31 (1): 39–56.

Reed, M.G., H. Godmaire, P. Abernethy, and M.-A. Guertin. 2014. "Building a Community of Practice for Sustainability: Strengthening Learning and Collective Action of Canadian Biosphere Reserves through a National Partnership." *Journal of Environmental Management* 145: 230–39.

Rees, W.E. 2014. *Avoiding Collapse: An Agenda for Sustainable Degrowth and Relocalizing the Economy.* Vancouver: Canadian Centre for Policy Alternatives, BC Office. https://policyalternatives.ca/sites/default/files/uploads/publications/BC%20Office/2014/06/ccpa-bc_AvoidingCollapse_Rees.pdf.

Reith, Charles. 1948. *A Short History of the British Police.* Oxford: Oxford University Press.

Ridding, L.E., J.W. Redhead, T.H. Oliver, R. Schmucki, J. Mcginlay, A.R. Graves, J. Morris, R.B. Bradbury, H. King, and J.M. Bullock. 2018. "The Importance of Landscape Characteristics for the Delivery of Cultural Ecosystem Services." *Journal of Environmental Management* 206: 1145–54.

Rittel, H.W.J., and M.M. Webber. 1972. *Dilemmas in a General Theory of Planning.* Berkeley: Institute of Urban and Regional Development, University of California.

Roberts, C. 2020. "Into a Headwind: Canadian Cycle Commuting and the Growth of Sustainable Practices in Hostile Political Contexts." *Energy Research and Social Science* 70, art. 101679. https://www.sciencedirect.com/science/article/abs/pii/S2214629620302541.

Robeyns, I., and M.F. Byskov. 2020. "The Capability Approach." *Stanford Encyclopedia of Philosophy,* December 10. https://plato.stanford.edu/entries/capability-approach/.

Robinson, G. 2020. "Town of Raymond Earns 2020 Sustainable Development Award from FCM." Newsletter, September 14. http://raymond.ca/town-of-raymond-earns-energy-award-from-fcm/.

Robinson, J., and R.J. Cole. 2015. "Theoretical Underpinnings of Regenerative Sustainability." *Building Research and Information* 43 (2): 1–11. https://www.researchgate.net/publication/269998640_Theoretical_underpinnings_of_regenerative_sustainability.

Rocher, F., and M. Smith. 2002. *Federalism and Health Care: The Impact of Political-Institutional Dynamics on the Canadian Health Care System.* Ottawa: Commission on the Future of Health Care in Canada. https://qspace.library.queensu.ca/server/api/core/bitstreams/54064b8f-0a77-49ec-b8ce-3d91681bb1cd/content.

Rockefeller Foundation. n.d. *100 Resilient Cities.* https://www.rockefellerfoundation.org/report/100-resilient-cities/.

Romero-Lankao, P., N. Frantzeskaki, and C. Griffith. 2018. "Sustainability Transformation Emerging from Better Governance." In *Urban Planet: Knowledge towards Sustainable Cities,* ed. T. Elmqvist, X. Bai, N. Frantzeskaki, C. Griffith, D. Maddox, T. McPhearson, S. Parnell, P. Romero-Lankao, D. Simon, and M. Watkins, 263–80. Cambridge: Cambridge University Press.

Romero-Lankao, P., O. Wilhelmi, and M. Chester. 2018. "Live with Risk While Reducing Vulnerability." In *Urban Planet: Knowledge towards Sustainable Cities,* ed. T. Elmqvist, X. Bai, N. Frantzeskaki, C. Griffith, D. Maddox, T. McPhearson, S. Parnell, P. Romero-Lankao, D. Simon, and M. Watkins, 92–112. Cambridge: Cambridge University Press.

Rosenbloom, D., J. Meadowcroft, S. Sheppard, S. Burch, and S. Williams. 2018. "Transition Experiments: Opening Up Low-Carbon Transition Pathways for Canada through Innovation and Learning." *Canadian Public Policy* 44 (4): 368–83.

Rutty, C., and S.C. Sullivan. 2010. *This Is Public Health: A Canadian History.* Ottawa: Canadian Public Health Association. https://www.cpha.ca/sites/default/files/assets/history/book/history-book-print_all_e.pdf.

Ryser, L., G. Halseth, S. Markey, and A. Young. 2023. "Tensions between Municipal Reform and Outdated Fiscal Levers in Rural British Columbia." *Canadian Geographies* 67 (1): 150–64.

Salzman, J., and J.B. Ruhl. 2010. "Climate Change, Dead Zones, and Massive Problems in the Administrative State: A Guide for Whittling Away." *California Law Review* 98: 59–120. https://scholarship.law.duke.edu/faculty_scholarship/2133/.

Sancton, A. 2011. *Canadian Local Government: An Urban Perspective.* Don Mills, ON: Oxford University Press.

Sassen, S. 2016. "The Global City: Enabling Economic Intermediation and Bearing Its Costs." *City and Community* 15 (2): 97–108. https://www.researchgate.net/publication/304370767_The_Global_City_Enabling_Economic_Intermediation_and_Bearing_Its_Costs_THE_GLOBAL_CITY.

Sayers, A., and J. Lucas. 2017. *Policy Responsiveness and Political Accountability in City Politics.* Calgary: School of Public Policy, University of Calgary. https://www.policyschool.ca/wp-content/uploads/2017/03/Policy-Responsiveness-Sayers-Lucas.pdf.

Schlosberg, D., and R. Coles. 2016. "The New Environmentalism of Everyday Life: Sustainability, Material Flows and Movements." *Contemporary Political Theory* 15 (2): 160–81. https://link.springer.com/article/10.1057/cpt.2015.34.

Schön, D.A. 1973. "Government as a Learning System." Reprinted in *Social Learning Systems and Communities of Practice,* ed. C. Blackmore, 5–16. London: Springer, 2010.

Science Direct. n.d. "Precautionary Principle." https://www.sciencedirect.com/topics/earth-and-planetary-sciences/precautionary-principle.

Scott, M. 1995. "Educating the Reflective Legal Practitioner." *Clinical Law Review* 2 (1): 231–50.

–. 2019. "'We Know the Recipe' to Reach an Ambitious Climate Goal, Plante Tells UN Summit." *Montreal Gazette,* September 23.

Second Harvest. 2019. "Second Harvest and Value Chain Management International Release the Avoidable Crisis of Food Waste Report." *Cision,* January 17. https://www.newswire.ca/news-releases/second-harvest-and-value-chain-management-international-release-the-avoidable-crisis-of-food-waste-report-878246034.html.

Security and Sustainability Guide. n.d. "C40 Cities Climate Leadership Group." https://securesustain.org/abstract/c40-cities-climate-leadership-group/.

Segal, H. 2019. *Bootstraps Need Boots: One Tory's Lonely Fight to End Poverty in Canada.* Vancouver: UBC Press.

Semuels, A. 2016. "The Role of Highways in American Poverty: They Seemed Like Such a Good Idea in the 1950s." *The Atlantic,* March 18. https://www.theatlantic.com/business/archive/2016/03/role-of-highways-in-american-poverty/474282/.

Sen, A. 1985. "Well-Being, Agency and Freedom: The Dewey Lectures 1984." *Journal of Philosophy* 82 (4): 169–221.

Setzer, J., and M. Nachmany. 2018. "National Governance: The State's Role in Steering Polycentric Action." In *Governing Climate Change: Polycentricity in Action?,* ed. A. Jordan, S. Huitema, H. van Asselt, and J. Forster, 47–62. Cambridge: Cambridge University Press.

Sewell, J. 1972. *Up against City Hall.* Toronto: Lorimer.

Shearmur, R. 2018. "The Millennial Urban Space Economy: Dissolving Workplaces and the De-localization of Economic Value-Creation." In *The Millennial City: Trends, Implications, and Prospects for Urban Planning and Policy,* ed. M. Moos, D. Pfeiffer, and T. Vinodrai, 65–80. Abingdon, UK: Routledge.

Simon Fraser University. 2021. "SFU's Renewable Cities to Establish $21.7 M Metro Vancouver Low Carbon Cities Canada Innovation Centre." *SFU News,* January 12. https://www.sfu.ca/sfunews/stories/2021/01/sfu-s-renewable-cities-to-establish--21-7-m-metro-vancouve.html.

Singh, S.J., H. Haberl, M.R. Chertow, M. Mirtl, and M. Schmid. 2013. *Long Term Socio-ecological Research: Studies in Society-Nature Interactions across Spatial and Temporal Scales.* Dordrecht, Netherlands: Springer.

Singh, S.J., H. Haberl, V. Gaube, C.M. Grünbühel, P. Lisivieveci, J. Lutz, R. Matthews, M. Mirtl, A. Vadineanu, and M. Wildenberg. 2010. "Conceptualising Long-Term Socio-ecological Research (LTSER): Integrating the Social Dimension." In *Long-Term Ecological Research: Between Theory and Application,* ed. F. Müller, C. Baessler, H. Schubert, and S. Klotz, 377–98. Dordrecht, Netherlands: Springer.

Singh, S.J., T. Huang, N. Nagabhatla, P.J. Schweizer, M. Eckelman, J. Verschuur, and R. Soman. 2022. "Socio-metabolic Risk and Tipping Points on Islands." *Environmental Research Letters* 17 (6). https://doi.org/10.1088/1748-9326/ac6f6c.

Singh, S.J., S. Talwar, and M. Shenoy. 2021. "Why Socio-metabolic Studies Are Central to Ecological Economics." *Ecology, Economy and Society – The INSEE Journal* 4 (2): 21–43. https://ecoinsee.org/journal/ojs/index.php/ees/article/view/461.

Sisk, T.D. 2001. *Democracy at the Local Level: International IDEA Handbook on Participation, Representation, Conflict Management, and Governance.* Stockholm, Sweden: International Institute for Democracy and Electoral Assistance. https://www.idea.int/publications/catalogue/democracy-local-level.

Smit, B., and J. Wandel. 2006. "Adaptation, Adaptive Capacity and Vulnerability." *Global Environmental Change* 16 (3): 282–92.

Smith, A., T. Hargreaves, S. Hielscher, M. Martiskainen, and G. Seyfang. 2016. "Making the Most of Community Energies: Three Perspectives on Grassroots Innovation." *Environment and Planning A* 48 (2): 407–32. https://journals.sagepub.com/doi/epub/10.1177/0308518X15597908.

Smith, A., and Z. Spicer. 2018. "The Local Autonomy of Canada's Largest Cities." *Urban Affairs Review* 54 (5): 931–61.

Smith, L. n.d. "District 8 – Peninsula North." https://lindellsmithhfx.ca/.

Smith, P.J. 1987. "The Ideological Origins of Canadian Confederation." *Canadian Journal of Political Science* 20 (1): 3–29.

–. 2017. "Vancouver's Politics: City-Region Governance in Canada's Pacific Metropolis." In *The Rise of Cities,* ed. D. Roussopoulos, 151–98. Montreal: Black Rose Books.

Snyder, W.M., and E. Wenger. 2010. "Our World as a Learning System: A Communities of Practice Approach." In *Social Learning Systems and Communities of Practice*, ed. C. Blackmore, 107–24. London: Springer.

Sørensen, E., and J. Torfing. 2018. "Co-initiation of Collaborative Innovation in Urban Spaces." *Urban Affairs Review* 54 (2): 388–418.

–. 2021. "Accountable Government through Collaborative Governance?" *Administrative Sciences* 11 (4), art. 127. https://www.mdpi.com/2076-3387/11/4/127.

Spicer, Z. 2015. *Cooperation and Capacity: Inter-municipal Agreements in Canada*. Toronto: Institute on Municipal Finance and Governance, Munk School of Global Affairs and Public Policy, University of Toronto. https://tspace.library.utoronto.ca/handle/1807/81247.

–. 2016. "A Patchwork of Participation: Stewardship, Delegation and the Search for Community Representation in Post-amalgamation Ontario." *Canadian Journal of Political Science* 49 (1): 129–50.

–. 2022a. *Digital Dilemmas: Technology, Governance, and Canadian Municipalities*. Toronto: Institute on Municipal Finance and Governance, Munk School of Global Affairs and Public Policy, University of Toronto. https://tspace.library.utoronto.ca/handle/1807/124429.

–. 2022b. *Organizing Canadian Local Government*. Calgary: School of Public Policy, University of Calgary. https://www.policyschool.ca/wp-content/uploads/2022/05/AM.OrgCdnLocGovt.Spicer.pdf.

Spraytech v. Hudson. 2001. *114957 Canada Ltée (Spraytech, Société d'arrosage) v. Hudson (Town)*, 2001 SCC 40. https://scc-csc.lexum.com/scc-csc/scc-csc/en/item/1878/index.do.

St-Hilaire, A., S. Duchesne, and A.N. Rousseau. 2016. "Floods and Water Quality in Canada: A Review of the Interactions with Urbanization, Agriculture and Forestry." *Canadian Water Resources Journal* 41 (1–2): 273–87.

Statistics Canada. 1951. *Census of Canada*. https://publications.gc.ca/site/eng/9.836019/publication.html.

–. 2017. "Toronto, City [Census Subdivision], Ontario and Canada [Country]." Table. In *Census Profile, 2016 Census*. https://www12.statcan.gc.ca/census-recensement/2016/dp-pd/prof/details/page.cfm?Lang=E&Geo1=CSD&Geo2=PR&Code2=01&SearchType=Begins&SearchPR=01&TABID=1&B1=All&type=0&Code1=3520005&SearchText=toronto.

–. 2020a. "Canada's Official Poverty Dashboard: Snapshot, February 2020." https://www150.statcan.gc.ca/n1/pub/11-627-m/11-627-m2020019-eng.htm.

–. 2020b. "Household Food Insecurity, 2017/2018." https://www150.statcan.gc.ca/n1/pub/82-625-x/2020001/article/00001-eng.htm.

–. 2022a. "Census Profile, 2021 Census of Population." https://www12.statcan.gc.ca/census-recensement/2021/dp-pd/prof/index.cfm?Lang=E.

–. 2022b. "While English and French Are Still the Main Languages Spoken in Canada, the Country's Linguistic Diversity Continues to Grow." *The Daily*, August 17. https://www150.statcan.gc.ca/n1/daily-quotidien/220817/dq220817a-eng.htm.

Steeve, J., and D. So. 2019. *Prosperity Scorecard 2019*. Toronto: Institute for Competitiveness and Prosperity.

Stevenson, Garth. 2006. "Federalism in Canada," February 7. Updated by Julie Smyth, Andrew McIntosh, last edited April 21, 2023. https://www.thecanadianencyclopedia.ca/en/article/federalism.

Stirling, A. 2014. *Emancipating Transformations: From Controlling "the Transition" to Culturing Plural Radical Progress*. Brighton, UK: STEPS Centre. https://steps-centre.org/wp-content/uploads/Transformations.pdf.

Stirling, A., I. Scoones, D. Abrol, J. Atela, L. Charli-Joseph, H. Eakin, A. Ely, P. Olsson, L. Pereira, R. Priya, P. van Zwanenberg, and L. Yang. 2018. "Transformations to Sustainability: Combining Structural, Systemic and Enabling Approaches." *Current Opinion in Environmental Sustainability* 42: 65–75.

Stone, J. 2020. "Recovery Justice: More Than 'Equality' Is Needed." Community Economic Development, Simon Fraser University, June 4. https://www.sfu.ca/ced/news/stories-research/recovery-justice-and-the-economic-recovery.html.

Stoney, C., and K.A.H. Graham. 2009. "Federal-Municipal Relations in Canada: The Changing Organizational Landscape." *Canadian Public Administration* 52 (3): 371–94.

Stout, M., D. Collins, S.L. Stadler, R. Soans, E. Sanborn, and R.J. Summers. 2018. "'Celebrated, Not Just Endured': Rethinking Winter Cities." *Geography Compass* 12 (8): e12379.

Stuart, J., P. Collins, M. Alger, and G. Whitelaw. 2016. "Embracing Sustainability: The Incorporation of Sustainability Principles in Municipal Planning and Policy in Four Mid-sized Municipalities in Ontario, Canada." *Local Environment* 21 (2): 219–40. https://www.tandfonline.com/doi/full/10.1080/13549839.2014.936844.

Sullivan, B.E. 2015. "Streetcars." *The Canadian Encyclopedia*, March 4. https://www.thecanadianencyclopedia.ca/en/article/streetcars.

Sung-Hee, J., H. Liu, and Y. Ostrovsky. 2019. *Measuring the Gig Economy in Canada Using Administrative Data*. Ottawa: Analytical Studies Branch, Statistics Canada.

Tainter, J.A. 2011. "Energy, Complexity, and Sustainability: A Historical Perspective." *Environmental Innovation and Societal Transitions* 1 (1): 89–95.

Talaga, T. 2019. "The Library Steps Up in Thunder Bay." *Toronto Star,* March 26. https://www.thestar.com/politics/political-opinion/the-library-steps-up-in-thunder-bay/article_89682e62-266a-589c-96b3-95b3e33f8f68.html.

Tam, S., S. Sood, and C. Johnston. 2022. "Analysis on Small Businesses in Canada, First Quarter of 2022." Statistics Canada, March 3. https://www150.statcan.gc.ca/n1/pub/11-621-m/11-621-m2022004-eng.htm.

Tasker, J.P. 2020. "Ottawa to Hike Federal Carbon Tax to $170 a Tonne by 2030." *CBC News,* December 11. https://www.cbc.ca/news/politics/carbon-tax-hike-new-climate-plan-1.5837709.

Tassonyi, A., and K. Kitchen. 2021. *Addressing the Fairness of Municipal User Fee Policy.* Toronto: Institute on Municipal Finance and Governance, Munk School of Global Affairs and Public Policy, University of Toronto. https://tspace.library.utoronto.ca/handle/1807/106601.

Tattrie, J., C. Cooper, and C. Ma. 2021. "Africville." *The Canadian Encyclopedia,* January 20. https://www.thecanadianencyclopedia.ca/en/article/africville.

Taylor, F.W. 1915. *The Principles of Scientific Management.* New York/London: Harper and Brothers.

Taylor, Z. 2016. *Good Governance at the Local Level: Meaning and Measurement.* Toronto: Institute on Municipal Finance and Governance, Munk School of Global Affairs and Public Policy, University of Toronto. https://tspace.library.utoronto.ca/handle/1807/81210.

–. 2019. *Shaping the Metropolis: Institutions and Urbanization in the United States and Canada.* Montreal/Kingston: McGill-Queen's University Press.

Tello, E., and M. González de Molina. 2017. "Methodological Challenges and General Criteria for Assessing and Designing Local Sustainable Agri-food Systems: A Socio-ecological Approach at Landscape Level." In *Socio-metabolic Perspectives on the Sustainability of Local Food Systems: Insights for Science, Policy and Practice,* ed. E. Fraňková, W. Haas, and S.J. Singh, 27–67. Cham, Switzerland: Springer.

Thompson, C. 2020. "New Kitchener Library Will Be First in Region to Feature Community Kitchen." *Waterloo Region Record,* November 18. https://www.therecord.com/news/waterloo-region/new-kitchener-library-will-be-first-in-region-to-feature-community-kitchen/article_aff2d687-c193-59cd-b12a-f898aa6506ee.html.

Thompson, D., G. Flanagan, D. Gibson, L. Sinclair, and A. Thompson. 2014. *Funding a Better Future: Progressive Revenue Sources for Canada's Cities and Towns.* Ottawa: Canadian Union of Public Employees. https://cupe.ca/sites/cupe/files/funding_a_better_future_0.pdf.

Thompson, E.P. 1967. "Time, Work-Discipline, and Industrial Capitalism." *Past and Present* (38): 56–97. https://www.sv.uio.no/sai/english/research/projects/anthropos-and-the-material/Intranet/economic-practices/reading-group/texts/thompson-time-work-discipline-and-industrial-capitalism.pdf.

Thompson-Nicola Regional District. 2021. "Learn Secwepemctsin from the Comfort of Your Own Home at Your Own Pace." Press release, October 21. https://www.tnrd.ca/learn-secwepemctsin-from-the-comfort-of-your-own-home-at-your-own-pace/.

Tiezzi, E. 1984. *Tempi Storici, Tempi Biologici.* Milan: Garzanti. Translated as *The End of Time.* Southampton, UK: WIT Press, 2003.

Tindal, C.R., S.N. Tindal, K. Stewart, and P.J. Smith. 2013. *Local Government in Canada.* 8th ed. Toronto: Nelson Education.

–. 2017. *Local Government in Canada.* 9th ed. Toronto: Nelson Education.

Tisserant, A., S. Pauliuk, S. Merciai, J. Schmidt, J. Fry, R. Wood, and A. Tukker. 2017. "Solid Waste and the Circular Economy: A Global Analysis of Waste Treatment and Waste Footprints." *Journal of Industrial Ecology* 21 (3): 628–40.

Tollefson, C. 2012. "A Precautionary Tale: Trials and Tribulations of the Precautionary Principle." Paper presented at "A Symposium on Environment in the Courtroom: Key Environmental Concepts and the Unique Nature of Environmental Damage," University of Calgary, March 23–24. https://cirl.ca/sites/default/files/teams/1/2012%20Symposium/ENG_A%20Precautionary%20Tale%20-%20Trials%20and%20Tribulations%20of%20the%20Precautionary%20Principle_Tollefson.pdf.

Tönnies, F. 1887. *Community and Civil Society.* Reprint, Cambridge: Cambridge University Press, 2001.

Torfing, J. 2019. "Collaborative Innovation in the Public Sector: The Argument." *Public Management Review* 21 (1): 1–11.

Toronto and Region Conservation Authority. n.d. "Don Mouth Naturalization and Port Lands Flood Protection Project." https://trca.ca/conservation/infrastructure-projects/don-mouth-naturalization-port-lands-flood-protection-project/.

Toronto Community Benefits Network. n.d. "About Community Benefits." https://www.communitybenefits.ca/info_centre.

Toronto Neighbourhood Centres. 2021. *Rethinking Community Safety: A Step Forward for Toronto.* https://ccla.org/wp-content/uploads/2021/07/Rethinking-Community-Safety-A-Step-Forward-For-Toronto-Full-Report-12.pdf.

Toronto Public Health. 2018. *Toronto Food Strategy: 2018 Report.* https://www.toronto.ca/legdocs/mmis/2018/hl/bgrd/backgroundfile-118079.pdf.

Tosey, P., M. Visser, and M. Saunders. 2012. "The Origins and Conceptualizations of Triple-Loop Learning: A Critical Review." *Management Learning* 43 (3): 291–307.

Tosun, J., and M. Howlett. 2021. "Managing Slow Onset Events Related to Climate Change: The Role of Public Bureaucracy." *Current Opinion in Environmental Sustainability* 50: 43–53. https://www.sciencedirect.com/science/article/pii/S18773 43521000233.

Town of Bridgewater. 2023. "Welcome to Energize Bridgewater." https://www.bridgewater.ca/town-services/energize -bridgewater.

Treller, G.E. 2014. *Building Community Prosperity through Local Economic Development: An Introduction to LED Principles and Practices.* Ottawa: Federation of Canadian Municipalities. https://data.fcm.ca/documents/tools/International/ Building_Community_Prosperity_Through_Local_Economic _Development_EN.pdf.

Trudeau, M., and L. Giroux. 2020. *Solid Waste Management in Canadian Municipalities: A Snapshot.* Ottawa: Federation of Canadian Municipalities. https://data.fcm.ca/documents/ reports/GMF/2020/solid-waste-management-in-canadian -municipalities.pdf.

Truth and Reconciliation Commission of Canada. 2015. *Final Report of the Truth and Reconciliation Commission of Canada.* Vol. 1, *Summary: Honouring the Truth, Reconciling for The Future.* Toronto: Lorimer.

–. 2016. *A Knock on the Door: The Essential History of Residential Schools from the Truth and Reconciliation Commission of Canada.* Edited and Abridged. Winnipeg: University of Manitoba Press.

–. n.d. https://students.indigenous.link/site-sponsors/trc.

Tulchinsky, T.H., and E.A. Varavikova. 2010. "What Is the 'New Public Health'?" *Public Health Reviews* 32 (1): 25–53.

UN-Habitat. United Nations Human Settlement Program. 2002. "The Global Campaign on Urban Governance" Concept Paper, 2nd ed., March.

UN-Habitat. n.d. "Cities and Migration." https://unhabitat. org/gccm-cities-and-migration.

Union of BC Municipalities. 2015. *Truth and Reconciliation at the Local Level.* Richmond/Victoria: Union of BC Municipalities.

United Cities and Local Governments (UCLG). 2012. *Global Charter-Agenda for Human Rights in the City.* https://uclg -cisdp.org/sites/default/files/documents/files/2021-06/ CISDP%20Carta-Agenda_ENG_0.pdf.

–. 2015. "Barcelona Greeted the 1st Retreat for UCLG Secretariats, Committees and Key Partners." February 15. https:// uclg-aspac.org/barcelona-greeted-the-1st-retreat-for-uclg -secretariats-committees-and-key-partners/.

–. 2016. *Co-creating the Urban Future: The Agenda of Metropolises, Cities and Territories.* https://www.uclg.org/sites/ default/files/gold_iv_executive_sumary.pdf.

–. 2018. "About the Community." https://opengov.uclg.org/ en/community-practice.

–. 2019a. *Right to the City.* UCLG Congress, World Summit of Local and Regional Cities, Durban. https://www.uclg. org/sites/default/files/righ_to_the_city_policypaper.pdf.

–. 2019b. "The Right to the City for Women: Open Letter by the Mayors of Mexico City, Montreal and Barcelona on International Women's Day." https://uclg-cisdp.org/en/news/ latest-news/right-city-women-open-letter-mayors-mexico -city-montreal-and-barcelona.

–. 2021a. "The Global Agenda of Local and Regional Governments." https://www.old.uclg.org/en/agenda.

–. 2021b. "Who We Are." https://www.uclg.org/en/organisation/ about.

United Nations. 2006. *Convention on the Rights of Persons with Disabilities.* https://www.un.org/disabilities/documents/ convention/convoptprot-e.pdf.

–. 2021. "Secretary-General's Statement on the Conclusion of the UN Climate Change Conference COP26." November 13. https://www.un.org/sg/en/content/sg/statement/2021-11 -13/secretary-generals-statement-the-conclusion-of-the -un-climate-change-conference-cop26.

–. 2022. "Secretary-General's Press Encounter at COP27." November 17. https://www.un.org/sg/en/content/sg/press -encounter/2022-11-17/secretary-generals-press-encounter -cop27.

United Nations Conference on Environment and Development. 1992. *Agenda 21.* https://sustainabledevelopment. un.org/outcomedocuments/agenda21.

United Nations Conference on Housing and Sustainable Urban Development. 2017. *New Urban Agenda.* https:// habitat3.org/wp-content/uploads/NUA-English.pdf.

United Nations Development Programme. 2010. *The Real Wealth of Nations: Pathways to Human Development.* https:// hdr.undp.org/content/human-development-report-2010.

United Nations Educational, Scientific and Cultural Organization (UNESCO). n.d.-a. "Biosphere Reserves in Europe and North America." https://en.unesco.org/biosphere/ eu-na.

–. n.d.-b. "What Are Biosphere Reserves?" https://en.unesco. org/biosphere/about.

–. n.d.-c. "World Network of Biosphere Reserves." https://en. unesco.org/biosphere/wnbr.

United Nations Framework Convention on Climate Change Secretariat. n.d. "The Paris Agreement." https://unfccc.int/ process-and-meetings/the-paris-agreement/the-paris -agreement.

United Nations General Assembly. 2015. *Transforming Our World: The 2030 Agenda for Sustainable Development.* UN doc. A/RES/70/1. https://www.un.org/en/development/desa/

population/migration/generalassembly/docs/global compact/A_RES_70_1_E.pdf.

Valverde, M. 2018. "Ford's Attack on Toronto Is an Attack on Urban Diversity." *Toronto Star*, July 31. https://www.thestar.com/opinion/contributors/ford-s-attack-on-toronto-is-an-attack-on-urban-diversity/article_2d1a93e8-49c2-505d-8ef0-e5e2e9509dc7.html.

Valverde, M., and A.A. Moore. 2018. "The Performance of Transparency in Public-Private Infrastructure Project Governance: The Politics of Documentary Practices." *Urban Studies* 56 (4): 689–704.

van Lierop, D., K. Maat, and A. El-Geneidy. 2017. "Talking TOD: Learning about Transit-Oriented Development in the United States, Canada, and the Netherlands." *Journal of Urbanism* 10 (1): 49–62.

van Zeben, J.A.W. 2014. "Subsidiarity in European Environmental Law: A Competence Allocation Approach." *Harvard Environmental Law Review* 38: 415–64. https://papers.ssrn.com/sol3/papers.cfm?abstract_id=2791617.

Victor, D.G., F.W. Geels, and S. Sharpe. 2019. *Accelerating the Low Carbon Transition: The Case for Stronger, More Targeted and Coordinated International Action*. Washington, DC: Brookings Institution. https://www.brookings.edu/wp-content/uploads/2019/12/Coordinatedactionreport.pdf.

Village Media. n.d. https://www.villagemedia.ca/.

Villella, S. 2020. "Eye-Catching Primate Sculpture Unveiled Outside New Condo at Former Brick Brewery." *CTV News*, July 16. https://kitchener.ctvnews.ca/eye-catching-primate-sculpture-unveiled-outside-new-condo-at-former-brick-brewery-1.5023642.

Vinodrai, T. 2018. "Planning for 'Cool': Millennials and the Innovation Economy of Cities." In *The Millennial City: Trends, Implications, and Prospects for Urban Planning and Policy*, ed. M. Moos, D. Pfeiffer, and T. Vinodrai, 27–38. Abingdon, UK: Routledge.

Vinokur-Kaplan, D. 2018. "New Public Governance, Social Services, and the Potential of Co-located Nonprofit Centers for Improved Collaborations." *Nonprofit Policy Forum* 8 (4): 445–64. https://www.degruyter.com/document/doi/10.1515/npf-2017-0040/html.

Vischer, R.K. 2001. "Subsidiarity as a Principle of Governance: Beyond Devolution." *Indiana Law Review* 35 (1): 103–42.

Vith, S., A. Oberg, M.A. Höllerer, and R.E. Meyer. 2019. "Envisioning the 'Sharing City': Governance Strategies for the Sharing Economy." *Journal of Business Ethics* 159 (4): 1023–46. https://link.springer.com/article/10.1007/s10551-019-04242-4.

Vogel, B., D. Henstra, and G. McBean. 2018. "Sub-national Government Efforts to Activate and Motivate Local Climate Change Adaptation: Nova Scotia, Canada." *Environment, Development and Sustainability* 22 (2): 1633–53.

Waldron, I. 2021. "Addressing Environmental Racism in Black Communities in Canada." Broadbent Institute. https://www.broadbentinstitute.ca/addressing_environmental_racism_in_black_communities_in_canada.

Walker, B.H., and D. Salt. 2006. *Resilience Thinking: Sustaining Ecosystems and People in a Changing World*. Washington, DC: Island Press.

Walker, C., S. Mason, and D. Bednar. 2018. "Sustainable Development and Environmental Injustice in Rural Ontario, Canada: Cases of Wind Energy and Biosolid Processing." *Journal of Rural and Community Development* 13 (2): 110–29. https://journals.brandonu.ca/jrcd/article/view/1506.

Walmsley, C., and T. Kading, eds. 2018a. *Small Cities, Big Issues: Reconceiving Community in a Neoliberal Era*. Edmonton: Athabasca University Press.

–. 2018b. "Social Planning and the Dynamics of Small-City Government." In *Small Cities, Big Issues: Reconceiving Community in a Neoliberal Era*, ed. T. Kading and C. Walmsley, 193–212. Edmonton: Athabasca University Press.

Waltner-Toews, D. 2004. *Ecosystem Sustainability and Health: A Practical Approach*. Cambridge: Cambridge University Press.

–. 2009. "Food, Global Environmental Change and Health: Ecohealth to the Rescue?" *McGill Journal of Medicine* 12 (1): 85–89. https://www.ncbi.nlm.nih.gov/pmc/articles/PMC2687922/pdf/mjm12_1p85.pdf.

–. 2017. "Zoonoses, One Health and Complexity: Wicked Problems and Constructive Conflict." *Philosophical Transactions of the Royal Society B: Biological Sciences* 372 (1725): 1–9. https://www.ncbi.nlm.nih.gov/pmc/articles/PMC5468696/.

Wang, J., and E. Banzhaf. 2018. "Towards a Better Understanding of Green Infrastructure: A Critical Review." *Ecological Indicators* 85: 758–72.

Wasylycia-Leis, J. 2016. "Celebrating Community: Local Music Festivals and Sustainable Relocalization in Southern Manitoba." MES thesis, University of Waterloo.

Weber, E.P., and A.M. Khademian. 2008. "Wicked Problems, Knowledge Challenges, and Collaborative Capacity Builders in Network Settings." *Public Administration Review* 68 (2): 334–49.

Weise, S., P. Coulton, and M. Chiasson. 2017. "Designing in between Local Government and the Public: Using Institutional Analysis in Interventions on Civic Infrastructures." *Computer Supported Cooperative Work* 26 (4–6): 927–58.

Weiss, M., and C. Cattaneo. 2017. "Degrowth – Taking Stock and Reviewing an Emerging Academic Paradigm." *Ecological Economics* 137: 220–30.

Weisz, U., and W. Haas. 2016. "Health through Socioecological Lenses: A Case for Sustainable Hospitals." In *Social Ecology: Society-Nature Relations across Time and Space*, ed. H. Haberl, M. Fischer-Kowalski, F. Krausmann, and V. Winiwarter, 559–76. Cham, Switzerland: Springer.

Welsh, M. 2019. "Government, Academic Leaders Sign 'Flood Resilient Toronto Charter' to Reduce Threat of Extreme Rainfall." *Toronto Star*, June 3. https://www.thestar.com/news/investigations/government-academic-leaders-sign-flood-resilient-toronto-charter-to-reduce-threat-of-extreme-rainfall/article_01edf850-7588-5621-b17e-06e351deb2de.html.

Wenger, E. 2010. "Communities of Practice and Social Learning Systems: The Career of a Concept." In *Social Learning Systems and Communities of Practice*, ed. C. Blackmore, 179–98. London: Springer.

Wenger-Trayner, E., and B. Wenger-Trayner. 2015. "Introduction to Communities of Practice: A Brief Overview of the Concept and Its Uses." https://wenger-trayner.com/introduction-to-communities-of-practice/.

"'When You're Black, You're at Greater Risk of Everything That Sucks': Foodshare's Paul Taylor on the Links between Race and Food Insecurity." 2020. *Toronto Life*, June 10. https://torontolife.com/food/when-youre-black-youre-at-greater-risk-of-everything-that-sucks-foodshares-paul-taylor-on-the-links-between-race-and-food-insecurity/.

Whitmee, S., A. Haines, C. Beyrer, F. Boltz, A.G. Capon, B.F. de Souza Dias, A. Ezeh, H. Frumkin, P. Gong, P. Head, R. Horton, G.M. Mace, R. Marten, S.S. Myers, S. Nishtar, S.A. Osofsky, S.K. Pattanayak, M.J. Pongsiri, C. Romanelli, A. Soucat, J. Vega, and D. Yach. 2015. "Safeguarding Human Health in the Anthropocene Epoch: Report of the Rockefeller Foundation–*Lancet* Commission on Planetary Health." *The Lancet* 386 (10007): 1973–2028. https://www.thelancet.com/journals/lancet/article/PIIS0140-6736(15)60901-1/fulltext.

Williams, D.R. 2018. "Spacing Conservation Practice: Place-Making, Social Learning, and Adaptive Landscape Governance in Natural Resource Management." In *The SAGE Handbook of Nature*, ed. T. Marsden, 285–303. Thousand Oaks, CA: SAGE.

Wilson, W. 1887. "The Study of Administration." *Political Science Quarterly* 2 (2): 197–222. https://www.jstor.org/stable/2139277.

Winfield, M. 2022. "Ontario's Deepening Hydro Mess." *Policy Options*, August 8. https://policyoptions.irpp.org/magazines/august-2022/ontario-deepening-hydro-mess/.

Winfield, M., S. Harbinson, S. Morrissey Wyse, and C. Kaiser. 2021. "Enabling Community Energy Planning? Polycentricity, Governance Frameworks, and Community Energy Planning in Canada." *Canadian Planning and Policy* 2021 (2): 35–54. https://ojs.library.queensu.ca/index.php/cpp/article/view/14405.

Winfield, M., and S. Weiler. 2018. "Institutional Diversity, Policy Niches, and Smart Grids: A Review of the Evolution of Smart Grid Policy and Practice in Ontario, Canada." *Renewable and Sustainable Energy Reviews* 82 (Part 2): 1931–38.

Wittmer, H., and H. Gundimeda. 2012. *The Economics of Ecosystems and Biodiversity in Local and Regional Policy and Management*. London: Earthscan.

Wolfram, M. 2016. "Conceptualizing Urban Transformative Capacity: A Framework for Research and Policy." *Cities* 51: 121–30.

Wolman, A. 1965. "The Metabolism of Cities." *Scientific American* 213: 179–90.

Woolstencroft, P. 2002. "Education Policies: Challenges and Controversies." In *Urban Policy Issues: Canadian Perspectives*, ed. E.P. Fowler and D. Siegal, 276–94. Don Mills, ON: Oxford University Press.

The Working Centre. n.d. "About Us." https://www.theworkingcentre.org/about-us/82.

World Bank. 2023. "Forced Displacement: Refugees, Internally Displaced and Host Communities." July 5. https://www.worldbank.org/en/topic/forced-displacement.

World Commission on Environment and Development. 1987. *Our Common Future*. https://www.are.admin.ch/are/en/home/media/publications/sustainable-development/brundtland-report.html.

World Health Organization. n.d.-a. "Constitution." https://www.who.int/about/governance/constitution.

–. n.d.-b. "One Health." https://www.who.int/health-topics/one-health#tab=tab_1.

Worte, C. 2017. "Integrated Watershed Management and Ontario's Conservation Authorities." *International Journal of Water Resources Development* 33 (3): 360–74.

Wright, G. 2019. "Integrative Democracy: Mary Parker Follett's Integration and Deliberative Democracy." *Journal of Public Deliberation* 15 (1), art. 4. https://delibdemjournal.org/article/id/587/.

Wulf, A. 2015. *The Invention of Nature: Alexander von Humboldt's New World*. New York: Alfred A. Knopf.

Zeemering, E.S. 2018. "Sustainability Management, Strategy and Reform in Local Government." *Public Management Review* 20 (1): 136–53.

Zhang, X. 2015. "Regenerative Sustainability for the Built Environment – From Vision to Reality: An Introductory Chapter." *Journal of Cleaner Production* 109: 1–10.

Index

Note: "(f)" after a page number indicates a figure; "(b)" after a page number indicates a box; and "(t)" after a page number indicates a table. In subentries, ABCs stands for agencies, boards, and commissions; ICTs, for information and communications technologies; IPCC, for the United Nations Intergovernmental Panel on Climate Change; and UCLG, for United Cities and Local Governments.

Arthurs, Joel, 173(b)
Assembly of First Nations, 30
Asset-Based Community Development (ABCD), 212, 212(b)
Association of Municipalities Ontario, 50
autonomy, municipal: in British Columbia, 49; court cases determining, 52–53; multi-level/polycentric governance and, 26, 54, 91, 121–22

B Corporation certification, 25, 207
Baldwin, Robert, 33
Barney, Darin, 58
Baumgartner, Frank R., and colleagues, 95
Berkes, Fikret, 26, 111, 114
Berlin (Ontario), 33. *See also* Kitchener
bicycles: lanes for, 16, 179; paths/trails for, 73, 172(b); sharing of, 180–81, 216
Bill, Jan, 183
biodiversity, 7, 95, 106, 116, 122, 126, 152, 154–56, 234; of biosphere reserves, 114–15; eco-health and, 190, 192; Edmonton office of, 156; foodscape planning and, 160, 164, 165; importance of scale/context to, 154, 155(b); Montreal conference on, 130, 154; procurement policy and, 86; threats to, 18, 154–55, 164; water management and, 191
biosphere reserves (BRs), 114–15, 120; Charlevoix, 115, 115(f); Clayoquot Sound, 115, 168. *See also* bridging organizations (ecological)
Bird, Karen, and colleagues, 62
Black, Edwin R., 42, 44
Black Canadians: discrimination/racism against, 33, 35(b), 142, 162, 195–97; and environmental racism, 202; food insecurity of, 162; police interactions with, 142, 195–97; and socio-spatial injustice, 200(b). *See also* Halifax: African Nova Scotian community in
Black Lives Matter, 139, 196–97
Blais, Pamela, 88
Blank, Yishai, 53
Blatchford (sustainable Edmonton neighbourhood), 170, 171(b)
Blay-Palmer, Alison, and colleagues, 160
blue-green infrastructure: and foodscapes, 148, 164, 165; and natural assets, 156; neighbourhood built using, 171(b); and regenerative sustainability, 148, 167, 168; and storm-water management, 148, 176
Boisbriand (Quebec): ABCs in, 65(b)
"bonding" and "bridging" networks (social capital), 77
Boundary Waters Treaty (Canada-US), 37(b), 120
Bradford, Neil, 46, 54(b), 224; and Michelle Baldwin, 26, 105; and Allison Bramwell, 210

Bridgewater (Nova Scotia): energy poverty reduction initiative in, 142(b), 173
bridging organizations (ecological), 108, 114–17, 121, 224, 234; and biosphere reserves, 114–15; and citizen/community-based science, 116–17; and model forests, 115–16. *See also* biosphere reserves; place-based governance
bridging organizations (for police/community services): hub model as, 197, 198(b)
British Columbia: biosphere reserve and centre in, 115, 168; collaborative infrastructure provision in, 108; collaborative sustainability planning in, 39, 172; community benefits agreements in, 104; community energy plans in, 171–72, 172(b); community public health in, 189, 190(b), 204, 226; Indigenous relations in, 112–13, 113(f), 227; local asset management in, 103, 156; municipal autonomy in, 49; municipal parties in, 59, 60(b); opioid crisis in, 60(b), 189; sustainable waste management in, 177. *See also* Prince George; Vancouver
British Columbia Climate Action Toolkit, 39, 171, 172, 172(b)
British North America Act. *See* Constitution Act (1867)
broadband Internet service. *See* Internet: broadband
Brock University (St. Catharines, Ontario), 97
Brodie Street Library (Thunder Bay, Ontario), 227(b)
Brouillet, Eugénie, 45, 52, 53
Brown, Hillary, 170
Brundtland Commission, 52, 68, 69; *Our Common Future*, 17, 125
Bulkeley, Harriet, and colleagues, 26, 46, 54, 130
Bullock, Ryan, Kathryn Jastremski, and Maureen G. Reed, 116
Burch, Sarah, and colleagues, 21
bureaucracy, municipal, 6, 61, 79, 80–89, 99, 135, 151; as change-resistant, 70, 94–95, 223; hierarchical/top-down structure of, 11–12, 19, 80, 81, 84, 89, 93, 97, 101, 102–3, 106, 109, 221, 233. *See also* hierarchical/top-down decision-making; multi-scale governance: at city halls; public administration; silos, administrative

Cabot, John, 32
Calgary: anti-racism action committee in, 197; homelessness initiatives in, 194; libraries as social learning centres in, 227; light-rail transit in, 179
Canada: evolution of settlement/governance in, 29–41; Indigenous governance in, 30–32, 54, 111–13; map of provincial boundaries/capitals in, xiv; map showing population of major cities/population density in, xv; and politics of place, 110–11, 111(t); as shaped by fur trade/railway, 13–14, 29, 33, 42, 208. *See also* federal government; federalism; Indigenous peoples; place-based approaches, to multi-scale governance

Printed and bound in Canada

Set in Myriad and Devanagari by Artegraphica Design Co. Ltd.

Unless otherwise indicated, interior photographs are courtesy of the author.

Copyeditor: Robert Lewis

Proofreader: Judith Earnshaw

Indexer: Cheryl Lemmens

Cartographer: Eric Leinberger

Cover designer: John van der Woude